Philip S. Foner

—

The Spanish-Cuban-American War and the Birth of American Imperialism 1895-1902

—

VOLUME I: 1895–1898

Monthly Review Press
New York and London

Copyright © 1972 by PHILIP S. FONER
All Rights Reserved

Library of Congress Catalog Card Number: 79-187595

First Printing

MANUFACTURED IN THE UNITED STATES OF AMERICA

ISBN: 978-0-85345-266-9

The Spanish-Cuban-American War and
the Birth of American Imperialism

VOLUME I: 1895–1898

By Philip S. Foner

History of the Labor Movement in the United States (4 vols.)
The Life and Writings of Frederick Douglass (4 vols.)
A History of Cuba and Its Relations with the United States (2 vols.)
The Complete Writings of Thomas Paine (2 vols.)
Business and Slavery: The New York Merchants and the Irrepressible Conflict
W. E. B. Du Bois Speaks: Speeches and Addresses, 1890-1963 (2 vols.)
The Fur and Leather Workers Union
Jack London: American Rebel
Mark Twain: Social Critic
The Jews in American History: 1654-1865
The Case of Joe Hill
The Letters of Joe Hill
The Bolshevik Revolution: Its Impact on American Radicals, Liberals, and Labor
The Autobiographies of the Haymarket Martyrs
Helen Keller: Her Socialist Years
The Black Panthers Speak
The Voice of Black America: Major Speeches by Negroes in the United States, 1797-1970
American Labor and the Indochina War: The Growth of Union Opposition
The Basic Writings of Thomas Jefferson
The Selected Writings of George Washington
The Selected Writings of Abraham Lincoln
The Selected Writings of Franklin D. Roosevelt

Contents

	Preface	vii
	Introduction	xv
I.	The Second War for Independence Begins	1
II.	Cuban Revolutionary Strategy	14
III.	The War in Oriente and Preparations for the Western Invasion	35
IV.	The Invasion of the West	52
V.	Weyler Versus Maceo	73
VI.	The People, the Economy, and the Revolution	98
VII.	The Military and Political Scene in 1897 and Early 1898	119
VIII.	Latin America and the Cuban Revolution	151
IX.	The American People and Cuban Independence	163
X.	Cleveland Stands Against the Cuban Revolution	177
XI.	McKinley Prepares to Crush the Cuban Revolution	208
XII.	The Road to War	230
XIII.	Imperial Intervention	254
XIV.	Why the United States Went to War	281
	Reference Notes	311

SEE VOLUME II FOR INDEX

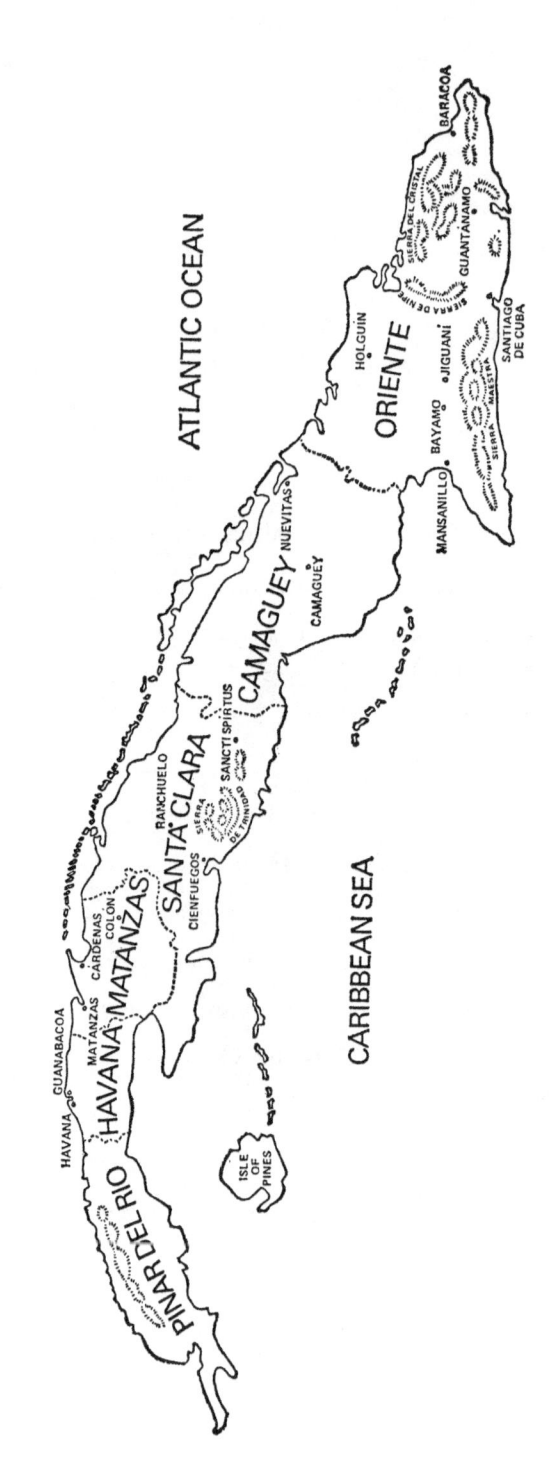

Preface

ALTHOUGH THE EMERGENCE of the United States as a full-fledged imperialist power had been under way since the end of the Civil War, it is generally acknowledged that the real birth of American imperialism began when this country went to war with Spain in 1898, ostensibly in order to end Spanish misrule in Cuba. By the end of the short war, the United States had already annexed Hawaii and was well on the way to annexing Puerto Rico, Guam, and the Philippine Islands, and to imposing a semi-colonial status on Cuba.

These developments are familiar enough to all students of American history. What has been lacking, however, in all accounts of the events which led to the war which ushered in American imperialism, has been the developments within Cuba which preceded American intervention. Writing as recently as 1965 in his book, *America's Road to Empire: The War with Spain and Overseas Expansion* (New York, 1965, p. 117), H. Wayne Morgan notes: "The Cuban rebellion of 1895-1898 has had no adequate historian, leaving many critical questions unanswered." Two years earlier, in his *William McKinley and His America* (Syracuse, New York, p. 566), Professor Morgan had written: "Unfortunately there is no history of the Cuban rebellion in print. . . ." Both observations are correct only if they apply to the English language. For, as the reader will discover, there is a vast body of literature in Spanish by contemporary Cubans and by Cuban historians—as well as by Spaniards—dealing in detail with the Cuban War for Independence. What is truly unfortunate is that nearly all historians in the United States are completely unaware of the existence of this significant historical literature, and that nearly all works dealing with the "Spanish-American War," a name which in itself reflects ignorance of and contempt for the Cubans and their struggle for independence,* do not refer to a single Cuban source and rarely mention the Cubans at all except in derogatory terms. Many leading historians write as if there was not even a war in Cuba before the United States intervened. As recently as 1963, a standard text in United States history (John D. Hicks, et al., *The American Nation*, 4th edition, Boston, 1963, p. 276) stated: "It is an exaggeration to speak of the disorders in Cuba that broke out in 1895 as a revolution . . . Maximo Gomez . . . was utterly unable to maintain a government, or even to keep an army in the field."

In the hope of remedying the shocking state of affairs in historiography illustrated by the above statement, I have dealt at length with the revolutionary armed struggle in Cuba prior to the intervention of the United States. I am confident that no reader will be able to escape the conclusion that the Cuban *mambises,* white and black, were among the outstanding guerrilla fighters of history, that the commanders, especially Máximo Gómez, Antonio Maceo, and Calixto García, were truly great military strategists, and that several of the Cuban military campaigns, especially the fabulous invasion of the West, rank high in the annals of military history.

In describing the emergence of American imperialism during and after the war with Spain, I have discussed developments occurring in the Philippines, but I have concentrated on events in Cuba and Cuban-American relations. The Philippine tragedy has been related in great detail, most recently in Leon Wolff's *Little Brown Brother* (New York, 1960), Tedoro A. Agoreillo, *Muldos: The Crisis of the Republic* (Quezon City, Philippines, 1960), Bonifacio C. Salamanca's *The Filipino Reaction to American Rule, 1901-1913* (The Shoe String Press, 1968), Henry F. Graff's *American Imperialism and the Philippine Insurrection* (Boston, 1969), and William J. Pomeroy's *American Neo-Colonialism: Its Emergence in the Philippines and Asia* (New York, 1970). But only

---

* Professor Samuel Flagg Bemis deserves credit for changing the name of the war from "Spanish-American War" to "Spanish-Cuban-American War" in the 1959 edition of his *Short History of American Diplomacy,* and for acknowledging the contributions of Cuban historians in causing this change. The correct name is "Spanish-Cuban-American War" (*La Guerra Hispano-Cubano-Americana*).

I have at times used the name Spanish-American War in this volume, but only to distinguish it from the war which was already under way when the United States intervened. But the correct name for the military events in Cuba from 1895 to August, 1898 is Spanish-Cuban-American War.

one study has appeared in the last few decades dealing with the United States and Cuba in 1902: David F. Healy's *The United States in Cuba, 1898-1902* (Madison, Wisconsin, 1963). This work, moreover, suffers from the failure on the author's part to consult any sources in Cuba and thus it inadequately covers these years so crucial for the establishment of American imperialism.

The presentation of Cuban-American relations from the time of the war with Spain in 1902 is significant when one realizes that American neo-colonialism in the island under which American domination was masked by a form of independence subject to U.S. intervention and control, became the model for all of Latin America and even for the Philippines. While it is true that American imperialism was associated in the period following the war with Spain with the outright seizure and annexation of colonies, more and more, as the years passed, the Cuban model of neo-colonialism became the characteristic feature of American imperialism. Hence it is of major importance in any analysis of the birth of American imperialism, that the evolution of the Cuban model be fully and clearly understood.

The second part of this volume concentrates on the Spanish-Cuban-American War, the Occupation of Cuba by the United States, the imposition of the Platt Amendment upon Cuba as a condition for ending the Occupation, and the establishment of the Republic of Cuba in 1902. It tells both a joyful and tragic story: joyful in the sense that finally after more than four centuries, Spain's absolute rule over Cuba was ended, and tragic in the sense that the independence of Cuba for which many Cubans had sacrificed their lives turned out to be a pseudo-independence with the island dominated politically and economically by a foreign power, the United States. How Spanish rule was finally overthrown and how the full fruits of victory were snatched from the Cubans is an integral part of the birth of American imperialism.

I am aware that there are those who will criticize the use of the word "Birth" in the title of this work. These scholars will object to the connotation that something basically new occurred during and after the war with Spain. They argue that it also implied that the United States stumbled unexpectedly upon the stage of the world imperialist rivalry at the end of the nineteenth century. In 1912 John Bassett Moore, who was Assistant Secretary of State under James G. Blaine, ridiculed the idea that the expansion that followed the war with Spain was "an entirely new thing in our history, and involved questions which we had never before been obliged to consider." He went on: "It is true that the expansion of 1898 involved, so far as concerns the Philippine Islands, the taking of a step geographically in advance of any that had been taken before; but so far as concerns the acquisition of new territory we were merely following a habit which had characterized our entire national existence." (*Four Phases of American Development, Federalism, Democracy, Imperialism, Expansion* (Baltimore, 1912, pp. 147-48).)

No serious student can assert that American imperialism emerged overnight. Americans have been engaged in expansion for over three hundred years. The seizure of the lands of native Indian and Mexican residents, the appropriation of half of Mexico itself is a familiar story. So, too, is the fact that even in the early years of the Republic, when Americans were preoccupied with continental expansion, they were gaining trade concessions, enclaves and even monopolies in several continents with the active assistance of the United States Navy and Marines. The expansionism of William Henry Seward and James G. Blaine forged a link to the imperialism of William McKinley and Theodore Roosevelt. Yet it is still true that American industry and finance was not really driven to seek foreign markets for surplus products and areas for the investment of excess capital until the last decade of the nineteenth century. This, in turn, produced a fundamental change in the attitude of American economic groups.* "Nothing is more significant of the changed attitude toward the country's foreign trade, manifested by the American manufacturer today as compared with a few years ago," said the financial journal, *Broadstreet's*, on January 29, 1898, "than the almost single devotion which

---

* In his doctoral dissertation, "Anti-Imperialism in the United States, 1865-1895," Harvard University, 1947, Donald Marquand Dozer points out that "rising imperialist spirit," in an effective sense, did not materialize until 1895, and that expansionist projects prior to that year, were successfully resisted, even by many of the same economic forces which were later to become leading proponents of imperialism. Dr. Dozer notes, too, that the word "imperialism" was rarely used in the publications and debates opposing territorial expansion prior to the 1890's, even though he himself uses it in the title of his study. He does so because the opposition to expansionism between 1865 and 1895 "clearly foreshadowed the campaign of 1898-1900 against the annexation of Cuba, Porto Rico, the Hawaiian Islands, and the Philippine Islands." (p. 149). In short, though the roots of imperialism go back before the 1890's, this decade marked the significant transition in its emergence.

he pays to the possible export trade extension." Meanwhile, the budding imperialist circles in the United States became increasingly concerned as they saw the hoped-for-markets passing into the full possession of foreign rivals. With the war with Spain, the developing forces of American imperialism came to a head. The "Birth" was thus the product of a long period of gestation. But as Robert L. Beisner points out in his study of the Anti-Imperialist movement: ". . . it would be foolish to dismiss the years of the Spanish-American War, the Philippine insurrection, and the anti-imperialist movement as an aberration, a meaningless sport in the evolution of American history. It was during this period that Americans first committed themselves to a major role in the international politics of the Far East, first found themselves policing the affairs of the Caribbean, and first fought men of a different color in an Asian guerrilla war." (*Twelve Against Empire: The Anti-Imperialists 1898-1900*, New York, 1968, p. xv.)

In the introductory chapter I have briefly summarized the history of Cuba and of Cuban-American relations prior to the outbreak of the Second War for Independence in 1895. Those who wish to know more of this story are urged to turn to my volumes, *History of Cuba and its Relations with the United States*, volume I (New York, 1962) and volume II (New York, 1963).

I have received most generous help in writing this book. I wish to acknowledge my indebtedness of facilities placed at my disposal by the Archivo Nacional, Havana, the Library of the City Historian of Havana, the National Archives, Washington, D. C., the Chicago Historical Society, the Cincinnati Historical Society, the Connecticut State Library, the Library of Congress, the Newberry Library, Chicago, the New York Public Library, the Rutherford B. Hayes Memorial Library, Fremont, Ohio, the South Carolina Historical Society, the Tamiment Institute Library of New York University, University of California, Berkeley, Library, University of Chicago Library, Columbia University Library, Cornell University Library, Duke University Library, Harvard University Library, University of Florida Library, University of Michigan Library, John M. Olin Research Library of Cornell University, Ohio State University Library, University of South Carolina Library, St. Louis University Library, University of Texas Library, University of Virginia Library, University of Wisconsin Library, and Yale University Library.

I wish to thank Professor Sergio Aguirre of the Department of History of the University of Havana, Dr. Julio Le Riverend, Director, Academy of Sciences, Institute of History, Cuba, Capitán Anibal Escalante Beaton, Enrique H. Morena Plá, and Blas Roca for the opportunity to discuss, either in person or through correspondence, certain historical problems relating to Cuban history during the period covered by this volume. The late Dr. Julio Girona of Havana was extremely helpful in obtaining important documents, articles and books from libraries in Cuba. My wife, Roslyn Held Foner, was of tremendous assistance in translating sources from the Spanish.

PHILIP S. FONER

Lincoln University, Pennsylvania

The Spanish-Cuban-American War and
the Birth of American Imperialism

VOLUME I: 1895-1898

Introduction

DURING THE YEARS 1810-1825 Spain's colonies in the New World revolted and achieved independence. Only Cuba and Puerto Rico remained of what was once the great Spanish empire of the West Indies, Central and South America. Of these two, Cuba was by far the more important to Spain. Following the destruction of the sugar economy of St. Domingue (later to become Haiti), Cuba gradually emerged as the world's largest producer of sugar. By 1838 it was the prize of Spain's reduced Overseas Empire. Its contribution to the Spanish treasury alone made it an important possession for the perpetually bankrupt Spanish monarchy.

As the sugar economy expanded, slaves poured into Cuba from Africa. Between 1762 and 1838 about 391,024 Negroes were brought to the island, and despite the acceptance by Spain in 1817 of a British-inspired agreement to end the slave trade, the flow of slaves from Africa not only continued but increased. Slaves were imported illegally in greater numbers after 1817 than even when the trade was legal.

Cuban white society was mainly made up of Creoles, born in the New World, and Peninsulares who were born in Spain. The political affairs of the island was dominated by the Peninsulares who occupied nearly all of the positions in the colonial bureaucracy. The Peninsulares also dominated the commercial life of the island. The Creoles, on the other hand, were principally landowners—cattle raisers and tobacco, coffee and sugar planters—and the professional people.

An inevitable conflict developed between these two white groups and increased in intensity in the nineteenth century. While the Peninsulares were fanatically pro-Spain, as might be expected from the political and economic advantages Spanish policies afforded them, the Creoles resented the restrictions imposed upon their political aspirations and on their freedom to trade under Spanish mercantilist policies. While Cuba was emerging as the world's largest producer of sugar, the colony was still functioning under Spain's backward and chaotic colonial policies, and a leading characteristic of the island's political life was the notorious corruption of the Spanish officials. Inevitably, the ideas of the Creoles ran counter to Spanish colonial policy. Furthermore, as they came into contact through travel with conditions in other countries, particularly those in nearby United States, the Creoles increasingly resented the corrupt, inefficient and frequently repressive Spanish colonial rule in Cuba.

Some Creoles believed that only through independence could Cuba achieve a modern political and economic form of society. Even during the Latin-American independence struggles, there were Cubans who favored joining the revolutions against Spain and ridding the island of domination by the mother country. In 1825, to assist these revolutionists, Mexico and Venezuela planned an expedition to Cuba to assist them in their independence struggle. But the United States, fearing an independent Cuba would lead to the end of slavery with repercussions in the Southern states, let it be known that it would block any move to liberate Cuba from Spain. Another factor influencing this decision was the belief of the American government that in due time under the operation of the law of political economy, Cuba would fall into the lap of her North American neighbor. The United States was not only becoming a major market for Cuban sugar, but, despite Spanish restrictions, an important source of its manufactured goods. Hence, as John Quincy Adams put it, in time as long as Cuba remained part of Spain, it would, like a ripe apple, fall into the lap of the United States.

Independence movements arose and fell after the 1820's in Cuba. The struggle for liberation from Spain was retarded by the simple fact that the Negro population grew enormously with the rise of the sugar economy. In 1842, the official census reported a population of 1,007,624 inhabitants: 448,291 white, 152,838 free colored, and 436,495 Negro slaves. The danger of slave insurrection increased with the growth of the Black population, and Cuban planters increasingly looked upon the Spanish government, and particularly the Spanish military power on the island, as the major safeguard against rebellious slaves.

To be sure, the value of Spanish protection of person and property in a slave society clashed with the restrictions imposed upon the island by Spanish imperial policies. The Cuban planters demanded the right to buy goods from countries other than Spain and to sell in a market larger than that offered by the mother country. But as long as slavery was the key to Cuba's prosperity and protection against the slaves was embodied in Spanish power, the Creoles swallowed their distaste for the repressive features of Spanish rule and turned a deaf ear to appeals for liberation of the island from the mother country.

However, both Peninsulares and Creoles were opposed to any attempts from Spain, egged on by England, to alter or abolish slavery, the key to the prosperity of Cuba. Consequently it is not surprising that when Spain appeared to be veering towards supporting abolition of slavery, thus seemingly abandoning its role as protector of white Cubans against blacks, schemes of annexation to the United States, where slavery flourished, emerged. But as the fears that Spain would interfere with slavery subsided, annexationist sentiment in Cuba lost its main appeal. Annexationism continued, but the main initiative now came from the predominantly pro-slavery groups in the United States who saw in the annexation of Cuba a vast area for the expansion of the Cotton Kingdom and the acquisition of increased political power in the national government. In the end, Spain's refusal to sell the island to the United States and the opposition of anti-slavery expansionist forces in the North either to purchase or capture of Cuba through filibustering expeditions, doomed the annexationist movement in the United States. With the outbreak of the Civil War in 1861, annexation, for the time being, was dead.

In 1865, Spain, suffering from internal dissension, political and economic difficulties and fearing the rise of independence movements in Cuba, adopted a policy of conciliation towards its colonial possession. A royal decree of November 25, 1865, established a Colonial Reform Commission to discuss proposals for reforms in the island. Despite conservative opposition in Madrid, the Spanish colonies in the Antilles elected twenty commissioners, sixteen of whom came from Cuba, and the remaining four from Puerto Rico.

The election of commissioners in Cuba and the debates in Madrid created a wave of excitement in the island and fostered the hope that at last the long-awaited reform of Cuban political and economic life was on the way. The complete failure of the Reform Commission led to bitter protests in the island, but Spain paid no attention. Indeed, in early 1867, the Spanish government, without consulting the colonies, imposed a new tax on the island ranging from 6 per cent to 12 per cent on real estate, incomes, and all types of business. The new tax, moreover, was on top of the enormous customs duties against which the Cubans had continuously complained. Coming at a time of economic depression in the island, the new tax stimulated a tremendous increase in political discontent and brought to a focus long-standing grievances. This was particularly true in the Eastern or Oriente section of the island where the smaller planters felt the burden of Spanish repression most sharply. Meeting in Masonic Lodges and other political clubs, the rebellious forces planned a revolutionary uprising to liberate the island from Spain.

The revolutionary upheaval came in October, 1868 with the flaming "Grito de Yara" (Cry of Yara), and initiated the first War for Independence which lasted ten years.

The *mambises,* as the rebel forces of white and Negro Cubans were called, ill-armed and half-starving, many armed only with machetes, roamed over the mountains and plains of Oriente, and steadily proved that the belief that the revolt could be easily crushed was an illusion. The Cuban struggle for independence was seriously hampered by a failure to confront squarely the problem of the role of the Negroes and of slavery, by strife and petty jealousies among their leaders, a chronic shortage of supplies and ammunition, the reluctance of the troops of one area to fight in another region, and the inability to win major support for the revolution among the wealthy sugar planters in the West (Occidente) who stood firm with Spain. It was further hampered by the fact that while Spain was able to obtain the most modern rifles from the United States, the attempts of the rebels to win recognition from the North American democracy so as to be able to purchase arms and supplies, were unsuccessful. The United States still hoped that Spain would offer to sell the island, and even when several Latin American countries proposed that Spain be pressured to grant the Cubans independence with compensation to be provided by these countries and the United States, Hamilton Fish, Secretary of State, bluntly rejected the proposal.

Despite these tremendous handicaps, the rebels were able to defy the Spaniards for ten years. The Cubans had a number of outstanding leaders, especially Máximo Gómez, the Dominican leader of the Cuban Liberating Army, and Antonio Maceo, the Negro independence fighter, who proved to be the most successful and most determined military leader during the war. Gómez, a genius at guerrilla warfare, made the Cubans masters of this technique of fighting. Maceo, a free Negro, whose entire family joined the revolution from the beginning, repeatedly defeated the Spaniards in engagements, and rose rapidly to be Brigadier-General of the Liberating Army, and Chief of the Second Division of the First Corps. Although he was compelled to combat racist opposition, the "Bronze Titan," as Maceo was called, continued to fight the Spaniards with undiminished zeal, inspire his men and lead the rebel forces through the difficult and bitter struggle against Spain. Maceo won renown throughout Cuba because he refused to sign the Pact of Zanjoń ending the war in 1878. His "Protest of Baraguá" was a great manifesto of opposition to surrender without achievement of the main goals of the revolution—independence and abolition of slavery— and it made his name a household word in Cuba and gained him international renown.

In reality the Treaty of Zanjoń was nothing but a truce. The first War for Independence had opened an abyss between the Spanish metropolis and its Cuban colony that could never again be closed. Revolutionary activity did not cease after 1878, and it received an added impetus with the abolition of slavery in Cuba. As long as the rich sugar planters of the West depended upon Spain for protection against their slaves, they had clung to their alliance with the mother country. But after slavery was abolished in 1880, the Spanish alliance lost its attraction. The economic advantages of independence, especially free and unlimited trade with the United States, held more attractions.

In the revolutionary movement leading the Second War for Independence in 1895 one among many stands out: José Martí, "the Apostle," a great poet and writer and a genius at political organization. The Spaniards had feared this youth as an embryo revolutionary, and he had been exiled to the Isle of Pines, thence to Spain, and forbidden to return to Cuba—ever! During the first War for Independence, Martí had been jailed and, for seven months, chained in leg irons, he had been forced to work in a stone quarry. In 1880, Martí evaded the Spanish authorities and sailed to New York. There, and in other American cities, he established Cuban revolutionary groups. He also made trips to Jamaica and Latin-American countries to rouse the Cuban emigrés to revolutionary action.

On January 5, 1892, Martí established *El Partido Revolucionario Cubano* (The Cuban Revolutionary Party). In the *Bases* of the Party, Martí set forth the ideas which he had been developing for ten years as the best way to realize Cuba's independence. After asserting that the Party was organized "in order to obtain, with the united forces of all men of good will, the absolute independence of the island of Cuba, and to foment and aid that of Puerto Rico," the *Bases* declared that the new movement did not have for its object "the indefinite prolongation of a war in Cuba," but rather the launching of "a generous and brief war, undertaken to insure the peace and the labor of the inhabitants of the island," and through "a war of republican spirit and method," to achieve the establishment of "a nation capable of assuring the lasting good fortune of her children and of fulfilling in the historical life of the Continent the difficult duties which her geographical situation assigns her." The *Bases* then spoke of establishing democratic processes, of freeing the island from dependence upon the outside world as much as possible, and of substituting "for the economic confusion from which it is dying a system of public fiscal administration which shall immediately open the country to the diverse activities of its inhabitants." Article eight of the *Bases* enumerated the following concrete objectives of the Party:

> (1) to unite in a continuous and common effort the action of all Cubans resident abroad; (2) to encourage sincere relations among the political and historical elements from within and outside the island, which can contribute to the rapid winning of the war and to the greater force and efficacy of the institutions afterwards to be founded; (3) to disseminate in Cuba the knowledge of the spirit and the methods of the Revolution, and to gather together the inhabitants of the island in a movement favorable to their victory, by means which will not place Cuban lives in unnecessary jeopardy; (4) to collect funds for the realization of its program, at the same time opening up continuous, numerous sources of money for the war; (5) to establish discreetly, with friendly peoples, relations which tend to accelerate, with the least possible blood and sacrifice, the end of the war and the foundation of the new Republic which is indispensable to the balance of power of the Americas.

As set forth in the Statutes, also drawn up by Martí, the Party itself was to be composed of clubs which included as members both Cubans and sympathizers who would agree to pay the dues assessed. Each club had a president who was a member of a Council of Presidents. These councils were the intermediaries between the individuals and the national headquarters. The head of the Party in the United States, with offices in New York, was a Delegate, and associated with him was a national Treasurer. Both were to be elected annually by the clubs.

The new revolutionary movement initiated by the Cuban Revolutionary Party was thus not the personal property of any individual or group of individuals. It was based on the organizations of Cuban exiles and would function democratically.

In organizing the Cuban Revolutionary Party, Martí had brought together "as many elements of all kinds as could be recruited." This had been no easy accomplishment. Thousands of the Cuban exiles had been sharply divided between rival factions, and differed drastically about the nature of the revolution and the republic to follow. It was Martí's great contribution that he was able to build unity among so many conflicting interests. He accomplished this, moreover, without yielding to the prejudices of certain elements in the alliance. He refused to yield to those who insisted that he place the Negro in a subordinate position in the revolutionary movement. He likewise rejected the demand of wealthy exiles that the Socialist working class leaders be eliminated from the movement.

To spread the propaganda of the Cuban Revolutionary Party, Martí sought to found a newspaper in New York. On March 4, 1892, *Patria* (Fatherland) was launched, the expenses of the first issue being met by the tobacco workers. Although it did not declare itself to be the organ of the Revolutionary Party, *Patria*, in its first issue, published in full on page 1 the *Bases* "which this newspaper respects and upholds." *Patria*, edited by Sotero Figueroa, a Puerto Rican Negro, was to conduct continuous, unrelenting propaganda for the Party, and was generally recognized as its official organ.

The Revolutionary Party did not consider itself established until the majority of the emigrant clubs had accepted it. By the end of March, 1892, all of the clubs had ratified the *Bases* and Statutes, and on April 8, the clubs of the South, New York, and Philadelphia elected Martí as Delegate and Benjamín Guerra as Treasurer. Two days later, on the tenth, the Cuban Revolutionary Party and its network of representatives and local member councils were formally proclaimed in all the clubs in Key West, Tampa, New York, and other émigré centers.

Thus by April, 1892, the first stage of Martí's work was complete. The Cuban Revolutionary Party was an established organization; groups associated with the Party were active in all the centers of emigration, and through *Patria* its message was reaching thousands—in Cuba as well as outside the island.

It was now time to call in the military and co-ordinate the invading forces and the revolutionary movement in Cuba.

Contrary to previous procedures in the Cuban revolutionary movement, Martí had left the military leaders completely out of his plans until a strong revolutionary organization was formed. Once this was achieved, Martí turned to Máximo Gómez, the man with whom he had split in 1884 because he believed him to be guilty of dictatorial conduct.* He knew that Gómez was the man who by experience and influence was most suited to head the military phase of the liberation struggle. Still, before offering Gómez the post of military chief, Martí polled the exile centers to determine if they favored the step. By mid-August, 1892, the result of the referendum was in. Martí was authorized to offer Gómez the post. This he did in person, on a visit to Gómez in Santo Domingo, September, 1892, inviting him "without fear of refusal, to undertake this new task although I have no other remuneration to offer you than the pleasure of sacrifice and the probable ingratitude of man." Like Martí, the old General put past differences aside. "From this moment you can count on my services," he told the Delegate.

Gómez was impressed by Martí's achievements in organizing and building the Cuban Revolutionary Party. "The triumph of the Cuban Revolution," he wrote in his *Diary,* "is a matter of concord and unification, and, in my opinion, the work that Martí has done up to now is quite consistent, for he is gradually obtaining the unification of the discordant elements." He referred to Martí as "an intelligent and persevering man, and a real defender of the liberty of his country."

On January 3, 1893, General Máximo Gómez was formally appointed military chief of all the men in arms. But many Cubans won-

---

* Martí's dispute with Gómez occurred over what he regarded as the Dominican's tendency to handle the revolutionary movement as though it was his "exclusive property." Following an incident in New York in 1884, Martí sent Gómez a letter announcing that he was withdrawing from the revolutionary movement. He returned after Gómez assured him that he planned no personal dictatorship for the Republic of Cuba.

dered if Antonio Maceo was being left out. Actually, Martí had every intention of enlisting Maceo's services, and shortly after leaving Gómez, he had made a special point of visiting Maceo's mother in Kingston, Jamaica. Mariana Grajales, then 85 years of age, deeply stirred Martí with her stories of the Ten Years' War in which she had lost a husband and so many of her sons. In a letter to Maceo, Martí informed him of the visit and observed that Mariana Grajales was "one of the women who have most moved my heart." Martí could not have chosen a more effective way of approaching Maceo.

On February 1, 1893, Martí offered Maceo a leading place in the new liberation movement, and promised to furnish and deliver the necessary war supplies. Although he was pleased at the idea of no longer having to acquire these materials himself, Maceo hesitated. He had settled in Costa Rica, where he had established a colony—primarily of Cubans with experience in farming—which had turned out to be a great success. A successful plantation owner now, it may have been that Maceo was reluctant to sacrifice his new career. But this is hardly likely, for he had always been ready at a moment's notice to answer a call to fight for Cuba's independence. More likely, his recent experience in Cuba had made him wary of any revolutionary plan known to many people.*

But Martí did not rest until Maceo was recruited for the cause. He visited Maceo in Costa Rica in June, 1893, spending a week with the Negro revolutionary and his family. Like Gómez, Maceo was impressed by Martí's achievements and he finally agreed to join. Before he left, Martí again promised the needed resources and advised Maceo to settle his affairs and get his men ready. The order to move would come from General Gómez.

With Máximo Gómez, Antonio Maceo, Serafín Sánchez, and other military veterans of 1868 residing abroad recruited and given responsibility for arranging military plans, Martí took the next step to solidify the revolutionary movement. One of the great defects of previous revolutionary planning was the attempt to organize the effort entirely from the outside, without effective co-ordination with the revolutionary groups

---

* In 1890 Maceo had organized groups for revolutionary action in Cuba; had himself returned to the island, and set plans for a rebellion. But the news of Maceo's revolutionary plans was leaked to the Spanish, and the conspiracy ended in failure.

inside Cuba; or, as in the case of the movement led by Maceo in 1890, insufficient contact between the revolutionary forces within Cuba and those on the outside. In organizing the Cuban Revolutionary Party, Martí definitely had this problem in mind, and he took steps to remedy the defect. Thus, after the military chiefs residing abroad were recruited, contact was made with the local chieftains in Cuba. Local military leaders were designated for each province and district of the island: General Guillermo Moncada in Santiago de Cuba, General Bartolomé Masó in Manzanillo, General Julio Sanguily in Havana, Pedro E. Betancourt in Matanzas, Manuel García Ponce in Havana, and General Francisco Carrillo in Las Villas.

At the same time, steps were taken to co-ordinate the activities of the invading army with the inhabitants of the island upon whom they would have to depend. Juan Gualberto Gómez was appointed by Martí, with the approval of the Revolutionary Party, as the political co-ordinator within the island. His duty was to select leaders for each local district on the basis of their revolutionary experience and ability, in order to take advantage of the peculiar circumstances which might prevail in the local areas. As the chief civil co-ordinator of the island, Juan Gualberto Gómez was to be responsible for the development of a system of municipal sub-delegates whose duties were to superintend the local propaganda and organization. These local sub-delegates were also to see to the preparation of the men of arms in their localities, supplying them with clothes, shelter, horses, and other necessities, with the advice and approval of the military commanders. In addition, local civil sub-delegates had the duty of applying in their respective localities the following instructions of Martí relayed through Juan Gualberto Gómez:

> Arm the decided, convince the undecided, supply information to all good Cubans, so that none will be ignorant of events. See that each one has munitions and indispensables for the initial moment. For those who are not able to acquire these, you are authorized to recruit funds and employ the measures which occur to your imagination and judgment as necessary to that end.
> The work must be local and cautious in each locality, while general in all the island: in order that the thread of the conspiracy may not be attacked unexpectedly.

Thus José Martí demonstrated again and again that he could supply the organizational qualities so painfully lacking in the previous efforts.

Under his leadership, the Cuban Revolutionary Party became the tightly-knit, efficient "brain" of the revolution. Until this "brain" was created, "the history of Cuban revolutionary separatism . . . had always been an interminable series of more or less glorious failures." With the creation of the Cuban Revolutionary Party as the supreme co-ordinating body, under Martí's direction, the revolution became possible for the first time since the end of the Ten Years' War.

But no matter how effectively it was organized, the Revolutionary Party needed funds to function and to acquire the military stores for the initial expeditions. Martí worked untiringly to raise contributions, visiting Philadelphia, Chicago, Key West, and Tampa. The response of the tobacco workers was consistent. At Martí's suggestion, they agreed to contribute one day's earnings each week—varying from 25 cents to $2.50 per man. In *Patria* of July 2, 1892, Martí paid tribute to the workers of Ocala, Florida, for their regular weekly contribution:

> When all the years spent in hope and despair by the Cuban émigrés are considered; when the constant and unending sacrifice of the exiles is remembered; when the constant pain of existence has taught the real value of money earned with one's own hands; when one knows that every cent taken from them is one less pleasure for their children, less medicine for the ill, less food on the family table—one cannot but read with profound respect the following words in a letter from Ocala: "From this date on we will contribute from our humble wages the insignificant sum of 25 cents a week for the revolution for the independence of our fatherland, Cuba."

In one of his best known poems, Martí wrote:

> With the poor of the earth
> I wish to cast my lot. . . .

As his work in preparing the Cuban revolution went forward, he turned more and more to the humble masses for aid. The wealthy Cubans were cold to appeals for financial contributions, whereas the working people were always ready to give more than was required of them. This came as no surprise to Martí. "Truth," he observed, "is better revealed to the poor and those who suffer." Throughout the history of Cuba's struggle for independence, he noted, it had been "the humble, the barefooted, the helpless" who have given their all for the cause. "The Cuban workers in the north, those heroes of misery, were, in the first war [1868-1878], a constant and effective support."

It was to the self-sacrificing working people of Tampa, Key West, and Ocala that Martí entrusted the fate of the revolutionary movement. "They are the best and most sacred among us," he declared. Describing with pride a meeting of exiled Cuban workers, he asserted: "This is the working people, *the backbone of our coalition*: the shoulder-belt embroidered by a woman's hand in which the sword of Cuba is kept sheathed, the arsenal of redemption where men build and forgive and foresee and love."

By March, 1893, Martí had succeeded in raising organizational expenses and providing a fund of $12,000. Then in April, 1893, an unauthorized insurrection, under the leadership of Manuel and Ricardo Sartorius, broke out in Holguín. With only 30 men involved, the Sartorius revolt was doomed to sudden failure. The inevitable debacle caused the whole revolutionary movement to lose face by demonstrating that the rebels had failed again. Enthusiasm for the Cuban Revolutionary Party, even though it was not involved in the frustrated uprising, waned, and contributions began to dwindle.

On the heels of this set-back came new unfavorable developments for the Revolutionary Party. In May, 1893, an extremely serious economic crisis hit the United States, and by the fall, thousands of shops and factories shut down while thousands more worked part time only. The tobacco industry of the South was so adversely affected that most firms closed their factories. Deprived of a means of livelihood, the Cuban tobacco workers found it impossible to keep up their regular contributions to the Revolutionary Party. Since the tobacco workers of Key West and Tampa had heretofore been "an inexhaustible source of funds for the Revolution," these unfavorable developments did not bode well for the liberation struggle.

In the winter of 1893-94, the tobacco factories of the Key reopened. But now a new crisis emerged. Taking advantage of the business depression, the employers cut wages to the bone. Eight hundred Cuban workers answered by calling a strike. Immediately Spanish agents in Key West approached the employers and offered to assist them to break the strike through the importation of strikebreakers from Cuba. They pointed out that not only would the strikebreakers meet the employers' need in this particular struggle, but they would saturate the labor market and "save the future . . . from importunities on the part of labor."

The Spanish strategy is understandable. The strongest units of the Cuban Revolutionary Party were centered in Key West. (Sixty-one clubs existed in the Key; 15 in Tampa.) A defeat of the strike "would definitely weaken the Party fabric," and deprive it of its most important source of funds.

The employers took up the Spanish proposition, even though as émigrés themselves it might have been expected they would have been somewhat embarrassed to unite with the Spaniards. But their class interests were paramount. A committee of employers went to Havana, conferred with the Captain General, published advertisements, and with the aid of the Spanish authorities, arranged for strikebreakers. In December, 1893, "the first group of Spanish replacements of the Cuban workers left Havana for Key West." When the strikebreakers arrived in Key West, they were met by a picket line of Cuban workers. But the police, armed with revolvers, escorted the strikebreakers to their temporary quarters; and several of the pickets were arrested. A delegation of city officials, headed by the Mayor, welcomed the strikebreakers to Key West.

The strikers sent an appeal to Martí for assistance. He was then in Tampa and made plans to leave for Key West. Meanwhile, he summoned Horatio S. Rubens, a young New York lawyer, to join him. Rubens persuaded Martí to return to New York and help the strikers from that city. He himself went to Key West and gathered information on the importation of the strikebreakers. Because they had been hired before they left Havana, he claimed that the law outlawing contract labor (passed by Congress in 1885) had been violated. Rubens succeeded in having the strikers who were in prison released, and armed with testimony and evidence of various kinds, he carried his case to the Treasury Department in Washington, whose officials had supervision over the Bureau of Immigration. A committee of Key West public officials also went to the capital to defend their action in behalf of the employers, especially the Seidenberg Cigar Co. The Treasury Department decided in favor of prosecuting the charges made by Rubens. Eventually warrants for deportation were issued for about 100 Spaniards, and after more delays over legal technicalities, the "imported

Spaniards were returned to Cuba." With the aid of the Cuban Revolutionary Party, the strikers won a complete victory.

The fact that the Cuban employers had been so eager to co-operate with the Spanish authorities in breaking the strike proved how little they could be relied upon in the struggle for independence. As never before, Martí realized that the revolution had to base itself on the Cuban masses. He pointed out, moreover, that the anti-labor alliance of employers and public officials in Key West proved that "since Cubans had no security in the land of liberty, they ought more than ever to create a free land for themselves."

With the strike over, the tobacco workers revived their weekly contributions to the patriot cause. The clubs throughout the country added their donations to the war funds. The Cuban Revolutionary Party had emerged from the setbacks and crises of 1893-94 with its forces intact and its morale unbroken.

It was time to begin the revolution.

The conclusion that the time had come to start the revolution for the independence of Cuba was greatly influenced by the growing fear that emerging imperialist forces in the United States would succeed in annexing the island before the revolution could liberate it from Spain. Martí had watched with growing apprehension the diplomacy of Secretary of State James G. Blaine. As Uruguay's Consul in the United States, he saw at first hand how Blaine used the Pan American Conference in 1889-1890 to fasten the leadership of the United States upon the Western Hemisphere. He saw, too, in that in Blaine's grand design all of the Caribbean, all of Central and South America would some day fall to the United States. Cuba was the key to this grand vision because of its strategic location in the Caribbean and its potentiality as a source of trade and investment. "That rich island," Blaine wrote on December 1, 1881, "the key to the Gulf of Mexico, and the field for our most extended trade in the Western Hemisphere, is, though in the hands of Spain, a part of the American commercial system. . . . If ever ceasing to be Spanish, Cuba must necessarily become American and not fall under any other European domination." Under this scheme of things, there was no room for an independent Cuba.

Martí noticed with alarm the movement to annex Hawaii, viewing it as establishing a pattern for Cuba. In fact, to Blaine there was a close connection between Hawaii and Cuba. "Hawaii, although much farther from the California coast than is Cuba from the Floridian peninsula," he wrote in 1881, "holds in the western sea much the same position as Cuba in the Atlantic. It is the key to the maritime dominion of the Pacific States as Cuba is the key to the Gulf trade." There was another connection between Hawaii and Cuba. In 1890, 99 per cent of Hawaiian exports consisted of sugar for the American mainland. In that year Congress admitted other foreign sugars (as well as Hawaii's) duty-free; but the Louisiana planters persuaded Congress to give United States growers a bounty of two cents a pound. Hawaii's single-crop economy, controlled by white—mainly American-descended-planters, who had displaced the native Hawaiians from their land, was severely wounded. At the same time, native Hawaiians were becoming more and more dissatisfied with a constitution they had been forced to accept, under which control of the government was in the hands of white foreigners, while property qualifications disfranchised most native citizens. Hawaiian discontent spread after 1891, when Queen Liliuokalania, a "strong and resolute opponent" of white rule, became head of the government. In 1893 the white businessmen, aided by the American minister to Hawaii, John L. Stevens, who had secured for them the protection of American troops, landed from a cruiser, rose up in rebellion. Stevens immediately recognized the provisional government set up by the rebels, who lost no time in dispatching a five-man commission to Washington to negotiate a treaty of annexation. This treaty, sent to the Senate by the retiring President Benjamin Harrison, who favored it, was held up by Democratic opposition, and was still under discussion when Grover Cleveland became President. Cleveland rejected the treaty of annexation.

Although the United States effort to annex Hawaii in 1893 failed, Martí was aware that expansionists both in Hawaii and in the United States were merely waiting for the opportunity to put across annexation. Once Hawaii was annexed, how long would it be before Cuba followed? Like Hawaii, its single-crop economy was becoming more and more linked to the United States, and once Hawaii became part of the American Union there were bound to be pro-annexationist forces in Cuba who would clamor for the benefits of organic union with the North American colossus to prevent discrimination against Cuban sugar.

Then there was Samoa. Martí observed how Blaine publicly paid lip service to the principles of territorial integrity and independence for the Samoans while maneuvering to obtain definite privileges for the United States in Samoa. He saw, too, how in the Berlin Conference of 1889, the United States, Germany and England combined to place Samoa under tripartite control which resulted in the disappearance of Samoan independence. Directly or indirectly the treaty powers influenced the economic and political life on the islands. Would not the same fate await Cuba if it achieved its independence through military intervention on the part of the United States? In 1912 John Basset Moore pointed out that "the significance of the Samoan incident lies . . . in the disposition shown by the United States long before the acquisition of the Philippines, to go to any length in asserting a claim to take part in the determination of the fate of a group of islands, thousands of miles away. . . ." To Martí, watching these developments at the time they occurred, the Samoan incident signified that the United States would go to even greater lengths to determine the fate of the island only ninety miles away, and determine it not in the interest of the Cuban people but in that of American imperialism.

Martí was aware that there was in Cuba a small but economically powerful group which favored annexation to the United States and others who supported calling upon the North American Republic to send troops to Cuba to aid the revolutionists. This Martí unalterably opposed. "I don't want the principle established of putting our fortunes into a body where, because of its influence as a major country, the United States is to exercise the principal part," he wrote to his friend Gonzalo de Quesada. The participation of the United States in Cuba's struggle for independence was fraught with danger: "Once the United States is in Cuba, who will get her out?" The only road for Cuba to follow was to win independence on her own and hold firmly to her sovereignty during and after the revolution. This was the only way to achieve "the reality of independence."

While Martí was in the United States during the early 1890's he saw clearly how the nation was entering fully into the path of imperialism. He read and heard repeated calls for foreign markets for surplus production and capital especially during the business depression that began in 1893. He was particularly disturbed by the fact that many of the American expansionists pointed to Cuba as the ideal area for economic expansion.

INTRODUCTION   xxxi

"Cuba offers a most inviting field for American enterprise," wrote an economic adviser to big business. In an article entitled "Business Opportunities in Cuba" which aroused widespread attention in business circles, Eduardo J. Chibás wrote:

> The wonderful natural resources of the island of Cuba offer an opening for the profitable investment of capital and for the extension of trade. . . . In 1887 the total of exports and imports of Cuba reached $127,784,000 which was 17 percent larger than the foreign commerce of Mexico for the same period, and more than twice as great as the foreign commerce of the five Central American republics combined. In South America, the foreign commerce of Cuba is excelled in extent only by that of Brazil and Argentina. It exceeds that of Chile and of Uruguay and also the aggregate of the six republics of Colombia, Venezuela, Bolivia, Peru, Ecuador and Paraguay. . . . Surely, in all the wealth of Cuba's resources there is some inducement for a more widespread interest in the Cuban trade than has yet been manifested by the enterprising business men of the United States.

Beginning in 1890, Captain Alfred Mahan started his campaign for a navy adequate to support and justify "a vigorous foreign policy." Mahan argued that "whether they will or no, Americans must begin to look outward." An expanding foreign trade was vital to national prosperity. The growing production of the country necessitated control of foreign markets which, in turn made necessary a powerful navy, a strong merchant marine and secure bases and coaling stations from which they could operate. Strategically as well as tradewise, the Caribbean area was crucial; indeed, nothing less than American supremacy in the Caribbean would suffice.

The emphasis on Caribbean bases naturally focused attention on Cuba. Not only would acquisition of the island offer the United States a strong naval station, but it would provide a market for surplus production and an area for the investment of capital. "There are extensive mines in Cuba now lying idle for want of capital," one newspaper commented, "and if the island were annexed to the United States, this field of production would be fully developed." "Cuba" declared the Detroit *Free Press* on May 16, 1891, "would make one of the finest states in the Union, and if American wealth, enterprise and genius once invaded the superb island, it would become a veritable hive of industry in addition to being one of the most fertile gardens of the world. There is a strong party growing up in the island in favor of reciprocity with and annexation to the United States. We should act at once to make this possible." In an article entitled, "Why We Need Cuba," in *Forum Magazine* for July, 1891, General Thomas Jordan called for the "political incorporation" of Cuba into the United States to strengthen this country's military system and to provide a market for surplus production and capital. "All considerations urge us to this acquisition, without regard to European opinion or antagonism." In November, 1891, *Munsey's Magazine* vigorously urged "the extinction of Spain's sovereignty in Cuba by a reasonable financial reimbursement" on the ground that the island was essential for the defenses of the United States and would serve admirably as an outlet for American surplus production. It said flatly: "It may be stated as almost certain that Cuba will be ours before long."

From 1892 onward, the cry that "Cuba will be ours before long" increased in intensity in the expansionist press. In 1895, the *American Magazine of Civics* featured a symposium on the topic, "Ought We to Annex Cuba?" "It makes the water come to my mouth when I think of the state of Cuba as one in our family," wrote Frederick R. Coudert, a leading Wall Street figure. Another spokesman for Wall Street wrote: "Canada will come in time; Mexico will follow Texas and California, and drop into her niche under the stars and stripes, when we are ready. But *we want Cuba now."*

Martí watched the aggressiveness of emerging American imperialism with increasing apprehension. He saw it beginning to spread throughout the Americas and he felt certain that the economic expansionism of the United States would soon engulf Cuba. He noted the growing cult of sea power, and observed with concern how the expansionist forces were building up a strong navy and urging the acquisition of naval bases and coaling stations in the Caribbean. He heard the increasingly bold demands for the annexation of Cuba from the military men and the politicians, and while many businessmen were still passive about the idea of acquiring the island, he knew that important Wall Street groups were backing the demand.

Martí knew, too, that the demand for annexation would meet with a favorable response from wealthy elements in Cuba:

INTRODUCTION   xxxiii

There have always been Cubans, cautious men, proud enough to abominate Spanish domination, but timid enough not to expose their well-being in combating it. This class of men, helped by those who wished to enjoy the benefits of liberty without paying for them with their precious blood, vehemently favor the annexa- tion of Cuba to the United States. All the timid ones; all the irresolute, all those attached to wealth, have marked temptations to support this solution which they believe will cost them little. Thus they appease their conscience as patriots and their fear of being real patriots.

The economic depression in Cuba in 1894 which followed the depression of 1893 in the United States increased the strength of the annexationists in the island. In 1894, the Wilson-Gorman Tariff adopted by the U.S. Congress placed a 40 percent duty on raw sugar, thus removing the advantages which the Cuban producer had enjoyed over other foreign sugars in the American market. He was now confronted with serious competition from heavily subsidized European beet sugar at a time when the world market was glutted. The average price of sugar in New York in 1894 was approximately $3\frac{1}{4}$ cents a pound, the lowest on record.

To add to Cuba's woes, Spain retaliated against the Wilson-Gorman Tariff by returning to the system of discriminatory duties against American imports into Cuba, a system which had been temporarily rescinded after the McKinley Tariff of 1890. With the monopolistic position of the Spanish peninsula merchants re-established, the cost of living soared in Cuba. In January, 1895, an agreement was reached placing American goods on an equality with other foreign products, but by then most of the damage had been done.

The serious economic conditions that engulfed Cuba in the winter of 1894-95 stimulated widespread discussions in the island. One group insisted that annexation to the United States was the only solution for Cuba's difficulties. Spanish laws restricted trade unnecessarily, and Spain, concerned lest closer economic relations between the island and the United States would wean Cuba away from the mother coun- try, would never fully relax its feudal-like grasp on the Cuban econ- omy. One Cuban writer asked: "How much of the Cuban sugar is consumed by Spain?" He estimated that Spain used perhaps 300,000 tons, which left close to 500,000 tons of unsaleable sugar. "Would England buy any? No, she had colonies to supply her needs. Will

France? Less. Germany?—Even less. Italy? Do not even think about it." Only the United States could supply the market and unless closer relations were formed with the North American Republic, there would be no one to buy Cuban sugar.

By the end of 1894, Martí had concluded that it was essential, in order to achieve the independence of Cuba, to thwart the designs and ambitions of the imperialist forces in the United States and their Cuban allies. "We must act," he told his close friend, Gonzalo de Quesada, early in 1895. "Cuba must be free from Spain and the United States." In May, 1895, after the outbreak of the war for independence, he explained why it had been necessary to act. "The Cuban war," Martí wrote, "has broken out in America in time to prevent . . . the annexation of Cuba to the United States."

CHAPTER I
The Second War for Independence Begins

DURING THE YEAR 1894, Martí worked more untiringly than ever at bringing the struggle for Cuban independence to a focus. Month after month, he redoubled his efforts to produce the necessary funds and to tie all the Cubans in the United States together. His most trying problems, however, were, on the one hand, to keep the over-zealous members of the Revolutionary Party quiet while the "finishing touches were being applied" to the carefully guarded details by which the revolution would begin, and, on the other, to act before the Spanish officials could provoke an uprising, force the rebels to declare themselves prematurely, and nip the new movement in the bud. It was necessary, as Martí put it, to "fall on the Island before the Government could fall on the Revolution." [1]

On December 12, 1893, Martí had given the order to the rebels in Cuba to be ready for action by the end of February, 1894. This date passed and the invasion was still not ready. Gómez, as the military commander, would not give his approval. He was not satisfied with the conditions in the province of Camagüey, where support for the revolution was slight and reluctant.

The long delay continued. Martí was waiting for an order from Gómez, but the old general was still preoccupied with the situation in Camagüey province, where the sugar mill owners pleaded for time to finish their harvesting and grinding. They promised money for the invasion if their plea was heeded. But Gómez, who had little respect for moneyed and propertied groups, finally tired of the game, and ordered the movement to be put in motion. In coming to this decision, Gómez said: "This situation will not change; the rich people will never enter the Revolution. We must force the situation—precipitate the events." [2] On September 30, 1894, he wrote to Maceo: "After the 15th of November at the latest, we must all be prepared to move immediately. None the less, if you are completely ready, this letter, which may very well be my last one from here, constitutes the order to move which you desire." [3]

Maceo, although recovering from a bullet wound inflicted by Spanish agents in Costa Rica who had been sent to assassinate him, was overjoyed and impatient to move. Martí, of course, shared his joy. "How can I paint my happiness," the Delegate wrote to Maceo after learning of Gómez's decision, "which is only clouded by the news that you are still not well." [4]

Satisfied with the preparations, Martí organized the Fernandina plan. This plan called for the embarkation of an expeditionary force from Fernandina, Florida. Three yachts, the *Amadis, Lagonda,* and *Baracoa,* were chosen because their speed was superior to the boats used by the Spaniards. Ostensibly the destination was to be Central America, with stops as follows: at a certain point in Florida to take on board Carlos Roloff and Serafín Sánchez with 800 men; in Costa Rica for Maceo, Flor Crombet, and 200 men; and in Santo Domingo for Máximo Gómez's group. All members of this force would go as agricultural workers with suitable tools, which actually would be implements of war. When at sea, of course, the announced destination would be changed from Central America to Cuba. If the captains and the crews of the vessels objected, they were to be confined until the end of the voyage.

By late December, 1894, everything was prepared for the simultaneous embarkation of the three expeditions. In Cuba, the revolutionary leaders were informed of the impending action, although Martí did not reveal the details of the expeditions, and they were ordered to prepare to support and protect the invasion. On December 25, Martí informed Maceo of the imminent departure of the ship designated for his group.

Then the revolutionary leaders suffered an enormous catastrophe. López de Queralta, a member of the expedition belonging to the group of Serafín Sánchez, carefully revealed the plan to one of the captains who, in turn passed the information on to the shipowners. In short order, a Spanish official heard of the plan, protested to Washington, and on January 14, 1895, the federal government detained the three yachts and confiscated the materials of war.

It was a terrible blow. Nearly three years of work and some $58,000 had been lost. But what Martí feared even more was the loss of prestige and confidence in the revolutionary leaders.

Yet the catastrophe had exactly the opposite effect. The scope of the ill-fated Fernandina expeditions, as it was now revealed, startled the revolutionists in Cuba and the exiles in the United States. Who would have thought it possible that Martí could have organized such a detailed undertaking with the limited resources at his command, and carried it out (until the last fatal moment) with such efficiency and secrecy? Enthusiasm for Martí's leadership grew in Cuba and abroad. "Those who had hitherto thought him a poet and a dreamer," recalls Horatio Rubens, "now were more impressed by the magnitude and promise of his plan than its temporary frustration."[5]

All this was heartening to Martí, who had become very despondent when he first heard of the debacle. Heartening, too, was the reaction of the military leaders to the news of the failure of the Fernandina plan. General Gómez informed Martí that he was ready to embark for Cuba by whatever means possible whenever the opportunity presented itself. Maceo reacted in a like manner, as did Serafín Sánchez and the other military chieftains.

The effort to launch the revolution continued without delay. The Revolutionary Party immediately undertook another fund-raising campaign. Martí called upon Key West and Tampa for funds, and $5,573 was raised by the tobacco workers. To this was added 2,000 pesos General Gómez borrowed from President Heureaux of Santo Domingo.

On January 29, 1895, Martí, General Mayía Rodríguez, representing the Commander-in-Chief, Máximo Gómez, and General Enrique Collazo, representing the organization of revolutionists in the island, signed the order for the war to begin. The order promised that "immediate aid of valuable material already acquired" would be sent, and that military forces in Cuba could count on continued and untiring help from abroad.

Juan Gualberto Gómez in Cuba then received the responsibility of setting a date for the uprising, subject to the final approval of a military committee composed of the principal military chieftains abroad. Two basic criteria were adopted to guide the fixing of the date: first, no less than four provinces must be ready for and favorable to the revolution; second, one province besides that of Oriente must be prepared for the landing of military officers from the outside.

After consultation with local leaders, Juan Gualberto Gómez decided that these two conditions were satisfied. The date of February 24, 1895, was agreed upon.

The insurrection began in Cuba on the scheduled day. On February 24, 1895, the *grito* or "cry" was sounded at Baire, a village about 50 miles from Santiago de Cuba. Unfortunately, on that same day, the uprising in the West was defeated by the Spanish authorities. Having learned of the plans for the insurrection, they captured General Julio Sanguily and Don José María Aguirre de Valdés, the supreme and assistant chieftains of the whole Western department, as they were leaving the city of Havana to lead the uprising in the West. Without leadership, the revolution collapsed in the Western provinces on the very day it was supposed to begin. Thus one of the two basic requirements for the beginning of the revolution—that no less than four provinces must be ready for and favorable to the revolution—was not fulfilled.

When the *Grito de Baire* was sounded, the supreme military figures had not yet appeared in Cuba. Máximo Gómez was still in Santo Domingo and Antonio Maceo in Costa Rica. It was imperative that they leave for Cuba as soon as possible. On February 27, Gómez wrote to Maceo: "The smoke of gunfire is visible in Cuba, and the blood of our comrades is being shed on its soil. We have no other choice but to leave from wherever and however we can." Maceo agreed. "I do not think we can afford to wait any longer," he wrote. "We are running a great danger. Once in Cuba, we can depend on the machete to open the breach." [6]

Martí was in Santo Domingo working out the details of the invasion with Gómez when the news of the revolt reached him. At once, he wrote to all the revolutionary clubs and to *Patria* outlining the true character of the war:

> Let the tenor of our words be, especially in public matters, not the useless clamor of fierce vengeance, which does not enter our hearts, but the honest weariness of an oppressed people who hope, through their emancipation from a government convicted of uselessness and malevolence, for a government of their own which is

capable and worthy. Let them see in us constructive Americanism and not empty bitterness. This is our war; this is the Republic we are creating.[7]

This theme was developed in the Manifesto of Montecristi (Santo Domingo), written by Martí and signed by the Delegate and Gómez, March 25, 1895. This historic document, entitled *El Partido Revolucionario Cubano a Cuba* (The Cuban Revolutionary Party of Cuba), opened:

> The revolution for independence, initiated at Yara after a glorious and bloody preparatory process, has now entered a new period of warfare in Cuba, by virtue of the orders issued and the resolutions adopted in Cuba and abroad by the Cuban Revolutionary Party, and as a result of the well balanced association in it of all the elements dedicated to the eradication of the evils and to the emancipation of our country, for the good of America and of the World; and the chosen representatives of the revolution—which as of today is ratified—fully recognize and abide by their duty—without usurping the tone and the declarations that pertain only to the majesty of the duly constituted Republic—of re-stating before the Country, which is not to be stained in blood without reason or without a fair expectation of victory, the precise aims, born of sound judgment and alien to the thirst for revenge, with which this inextinguishable war has been prepared and which will carry it to its logical victory, and which today leads into combat, assembled in a wise and soul-stirring democracy, all the elements that make up Cuban society.

Martí then outlined five points relative to the policy of the war: (1) that the war of independence would be a civilized one; (2) that the participation of the Negro people was necessary for victory, and that the charge that "the Negro race is a threat" was "wickedly made by the beneficiaries of the Spanish regime for the purpose of spreading fear of the revolution";* (3) that non-combatant Spaniards would

---

* Martí pointed out that the "fear of the Negro" was a danger to be overcome in all of Latin America and not only in Cuba. In his essay, "Our America," January, 1891, he warned that "the hour is fast approaching" when the United States "might go so far as to lay hands on us." One of the weapons the expansionists of North America would use to conquer Latin America would be to stir up racial hatred of the Negro. In the same essay Martí emphasized the equal rights of all men, regardless of color—a theme constant throughout his writings: "Whoever foments and propagates antagonism and hate between races, sins against humanity." (José Martí, *Obras Completas*, La Habana, 1946, vol. II, p. 113.)

never be the object of revenge, persecution, or extortion; (4) that private rural wealth which did not intentionally hamper the revolution would be respected, and (5) that the revolution would introduce a new economic life in Cuba.

What kind of a country would Cuba be, after the Revolution? Martí answered:

> A free country with employment available to all and located at the crossroads of the rich and industrial world, will replace, unhindered and with advantage, after a War inspired in the purest abnegation and carried on accordingly, the abashed country, where well-being can be obtained only in exchange for complicity, explicit or implied, with the tyranny of hungry foreigners who bleed and corrupt.[8]

Anxious to bring together in the revolutionary movement "as many elements of all kinds as could be recruited," Martí refrained from spelling out specifically in the Manifesto the full nature of the republic that would follow a triumph over Spain. But he did emphasize that it would be a country in which economic opportunities would exist for all, and not only for the privileged few.*

On March 25, the same day the Manifesto of Montecristi was issued, Antonio Maceo bid farewell to his wife. The Negro leader was bitter because Martí had removed him from command of the expedition

---

* Although he did not write a single book on the subject, Martí did deal in many of his writings with different aspects of the republic that would follow victory over Spain. In general, he believed that the country should be organized on democratic foundations with equal rights for all, regardless of color. Poverty and the concentration of economic power in the hands of the few would be avoided through the social organization of diversified agriculture. It would be a country which would do business with every nation in the world, but free from economic domination by any one of them. Education would be free and available to all, for "an educated country will always be strong and free." "A country where only a few men are wealthy is not rich," Martí wrote. "A country where everyone has a portion is." If everyone had a share in its wealth, the country would maintain "a balance in social questions." Not only would poverty be avoided but also violent class struggles and labor disputes such as he had witnessed in the United States.

The above is only a brief presentation of Martí's views about the nature of the Cuban republic. For a more detailed study, see Antonio Martínez Bello, *Ideas Económicas y Sociales de Martí*, La Habana, 1940, though the author tends to exaggerate Martí's inclination to socialism; Jorge Mañach, *El Pensamiento Político y Social de Martí*, La Habana, 1941; and J. I. Jiménez-Grullón, *La Filosofía de José Martí*, Universidad Central de Las Villas, 1960.

from Costa Rica, placing it entirely in the hands of Flor Crombet, who had said he could organize the expedition with the $2,000 available while Maceo had insisted on a larger sum. In requesting his full co-operation, Martí appealed to Maceo's love of country. "Cuba is at war, General," he wrote. "When that is said, the picture is changed." Martí's plea was effective. Swallowing his wounded pride, Maceo agreed to go along in a subordinate post. "The Nation above all," he explained to his wife. "Forward then for the sake of the native land, and for it, the glory of sacrificing everything." [9]

Crombet, Maceo, his brother José, and 20 other rebels left Costa Rica on the *Adirondack*, an American craft, ostensibly bound for New York. The Spanish Consul in Costa Rica was not fooled, however, and at his warning, the *Adirondack* was kept under a close watch by Spanish cruisers. One the night of March 29, the captain of the *Adirondack*, frightened by possible reprisals, broke his promise to land the insurgents in Cuba, and deposited them instead at Fortune Island in the archipelago of the Bahamas. Here they finally prevailed upon the American Vice-Consul Farrington to rent them his schooner, the *Honor*, and with three sailors as a crew, the 23 rebels sailed for Cuba on the afternoon of March 30. The following day, the schooner was hit by a bad storm, but the seasick rebels recovered sufficiently, on seeing the beacons of Duaba and Baracoa, to break out the weapons and ready the cargo for landing. The schooner was wrecked on the beach near the town of Baracoa. But the first expedition had succeeded in reaching Cuba. The rebels were greeted with joy by the farmers in the area, and the word spread immediately: *"Maceo is here! Viva Cuba Libre!"* [10]

Maceo knew that the presence of the rebels would soon be known to the Spaniards, and that they would be pursued by strong enemy forces. To avoid encirclement and destruction while trying to join the other rebel forces, Maceo led the expeditionaries through the mountains and forests toward the district of Guantánamo. Living on berries and drinking water from streams, the small group of rebels made their way up and down the hills, through tangled undergrowth and dense woods. During a skirmish with Spanish soldiers, General Flor Crombet was killed. Maceo then split the rebels into groups, and, with five followers, moved ahead.

Soon there were left only three of the six, and eight days later, after extreme hardships, these *insurrectos* stumbled into the camp of Brigadier

Jesús Rabí. Of the original 23 invaders who had left Duaba 20 days before, only 13 were still alive, and most of these were prisoners of Spain.

On the very night that Maceo reached the rebel camp, at the point of exhaustion, he issued a general order to the forces of Oriente announcing that General Maceo had arrived and had assumed command of the entire province. The following day he ordered all rebel officers "to hang every emissary of the Spanish government, Peninsular or Cuban, whatever may be his rank, who presents himself in our camps with propositions of peace. This order must be carried out without hesitation of any kind or without attention to any contrary indications. Our motto is to triumph or to die." [11]

That same day, April 21, Maceo issued a proclamation to the people of Cuba urging all Cubans to rise in arms. The response to this call to arms was most gratifying. On April 30, Maceo wrote to his wife:

> I have 6,000 men, well-armed, and with much artillery. . . . By the 15th of the coming month, I will have 12,000 armed men, and much territory conquered. . . .
> Three days ago José [Maceo] told me of the arrival of Gómez, Martí, Borrero, Guerra and two others on the beaches between Guantánamo and Baracoa.[12]

On April 1, 1895, Gómez, Martí, Brigadier Francisco Borrero, Colonel Angel Guerra, César Salas, and Marcos del Rosario, left Montecristi, Santo Domingo, bound for Cuba. (Borrero, Guerra, and Salas were Cubans; Marcos del Rosario was a Dominican Negro.) Although many Cubans in the island and outside felt that he should remain abroad organizing reinforcements for the revolution among the exiles, Martí had decided to go to Cuba with Gómez. His decision was motivated, in part, by the charge of certain critics that he was a mere man of words and that he was afraid to go into battle himself. More important, he felt that a country would not accept "without scorn and indifference" being served "by one who preached the need of dying without beginning by risking his own life." He was convinced, too, that his presence was just as "useful" in Cuba as it was abroad.

All this Martí set down in a letter to Dr. Federico Henríquez y Carvajal of Santo Domingo on the eve of his departure for Cuba. He wrote that he would abide by whatever was deemed necessary to achieve victory. If commanded to stay in the war, he would stay, and if to leave those who were dying, he would "have the courage for that too." "Wherever my first duty lies, in Cuba or outside Cuba, there will I be. ... I called up the war; my responsibility begins rather than ends with it. For me, the country will never be triumph, but agony and duty. ... I shall arouse the world. But my one desire would be to stand beside the last tree, the last fighter, and die in silence. For me, the hour has come."[13]

Gómez, Martí, and their four companions arrived in Inagua with a supply of weapons on April 2, where they found the schooner they had contracted for waiting. But the captain and crew deserted, and the rebels were left stranded. Fortunately, a German freighter, the *Nordstrand*, carrying fruit on the way to Cap Haitien, stopped at Inagua. With the aid of the Haitian Consul and the payment of $1,000, they were able to get the captain to agree to take them as passengers and to put them off at sea in a small boat as he passed Cuba on the return voyage.

On April 10, after a voyage to Cape Haitien and back, the fruit ship sailed from Inagua. By the late afternoon, the rebels could see the peaks of the mountains of Cuba. In the evening, the *Nordstrand* stopped three miles off the coast. The night was dark and stormy, and the captain hesitated to send the six men out into the fury of the wind and sea. But Gómez commanded: "To land." Martí tells the rest in the diary he kept:

> They lower the boat. Raining hard as we push off. Set course wrong. Conflicting and confused opinion in boat. Another downpour. Rudder lost. We get on course. I take forward oar. Salas rows steadily. Paquito Barrero and the General help in the stern. We strap on our revolvers. Steer toward clearing. Moon comes up red behind a cloud. We land on a rock beach, La Playita. I last to leave boat, bailing out. Jump ashore. Great joy.[14]

The place where they set foot on Cuban soil was at the foot of Cajobabo. Gómez kissed the earth.

On February 24, 1895, the *grito* of the Cuban people had been raised at Baire. On March 29, Antonio Maceo and a band of his followers from Costa Rica had landed in eastern Cuba. On April 11, Máximo Gómez, accompanied by José Martí, made his landing. The chief veterans of 1868 and the ideological leader and moving spirit of the revolution were at last in Cuba.

No previous insurrectionary efforts had attained such magnitude in scope or such thorough integration in the planning stages as had the Revolution of 1895. The years of preparation, of frustrations and setbacks were over. The revolution was a fact, and the vision of a *Cuba Libre* could now become a reality.

During the days following the landing at Playitas, Martí felt that his life was reaching its fulfillment. On April 16, he was informed that Gómez as chief of staff, supported unanimously by the other officers, had named him Major General of the Liberating Army. "With an embrace," Martí rejoiced, "they brought my life up to the level of their veterans' glory." On May 2, at the request of its editors, Martí wrote an article for the New York *Herald* defining the purpose of the war in Cuba: "Cuba wishes to be free in order that here Man may fully realize his destiny, that everyone may work here, and that her hidden riches may be sold in the natural markets of America. . . . The Cubans ask no more of the world than the recognition of and respect for their sacrifices." [15]

At La Mejorana, near Santiago de Cuba, on May 4, Martí, Gómez and Maceo met to decide on the strategy to be followed in the war. Among the topics discussed was the question of civil versus military control of the revolution. Martí expressed himself strongly in favor of superiority for the civil over the military authority, and proposed calling a convention of all the civil and military leaders to form a civil government and to elect its officials. As on previous occasions, he maintained that complete military control would be a very bad precedent for a post-war independent republic. The war might end, he feared, with Spain expelled from the island but with a Cuban military dictatorship in control.

This time Gómez sided mainly with Martí. But Maceo took a strong stand for a military *Junta* until victory had been achieved. He felt that the weakness, dissension, petty rivalries and incompetence of the civil government during the Ten Years' War had interfered with the prosecution of the revolution and had ultimately contributed to the collapse of the rebellion. He argued that, in order to avoid this error in the new revolution, the war should be conducted under the control of a small group of the highest military leaders.

The question of civil versus military control of the war was not fully decided. But evidently Martí's viewpoint was more or less adopted, for agreement was reached among the three men that Gómez was to be commander-in-chief of the army, Maceo, military chief of Oriente, and Martí, supreme leader of the revolution abroad and in non-military matters.

On May 18, Martí wrote from Dos Ríos to Manuel Mercado, his friend in Mexico. The letter opened: "I am now, every day, in danger of giving my life for my country." [16] The letter was never finished On May 19, the Spaniards attacked. Though ordered by Gómez to remain with the rear-guard, Martí rode forth to his first encounter with the Spaniards. As he rode through a pass, Spanish soldiers in ambush shot him down. His companion, Angel de la Guardia, tried to rescue his body, but he failed. Gómez's attempts to retake Martí's body was equally futile. The Spaniards carried it away to Santiago de Cuba, where on May 27, 1895, José Martí was buried.

"He died," wrote Charles A. Dana of the New York *Sun,* a friend and admirer of Martí, "as such a man might wish to die, battling for liberty and democracy."

Máximo Gómez paid eloquent tribute to Martí:

> He knew how to seek in book and newspaper the best and brightest facts, putting them before the Cuban workers in the shops in order to instruct them particularly to love things about the Fatherland, so that the Cuban worker should find himself at home with the new society which was to come, in this way creating the Republic by the people and for the people. He preached that the school would be the panacea which would cure all the evils that were the consequence of a former life of exceptionally crude backwardness of privilege and obscurantism. Even as a child, he set himself against the power usurping the rights of his country, and for this he paid by having to wear a brace on his food, since tyranny took special care to extinguish in Cuba every lamp which like "Plácido" could give out the slightest spark of light.* To sum up, Martí was always proud, a rebel against all tyranny and usurpation.[17]

José Martí was a rare combination of man of ideas and man of action. "Ideas were for him weapons in the fight for a better world,

---

* Gabriel de la Concepción Valdés, known as "Plácido," was a free Negro poet in Cuba, executed during the suppression of the slave conspiracy of 1844

in which freedom for Cuba was the first step," one student has correctly observed. He was a man of many talents: a lawyer, a poet, a master of the most exquisite Spanish prose, a great orator, a teacher in many universities in Latin America of language, literature and philosophy, a distinguished journalist, a diplomat, and the organizer of every detail of the Cuban revolution. His writings made him so admired and respected throughout Spanish-speaking America that Argentina, Uruguay and Paraguay made him their consular representative in the United States.

Martí's writings, collected and edited by Gonzalo de Quesada y Miranda, fill 70 volumes. Even this edition is incomplete since there still remains uncollected material scattered in South American newspapers. But in these 70 volumes there is abundant evidence of Martí's broad culture and his remarkable talents as a political thinker and organizer. It is indeed unfortunate that the bulk of these writings are still not available in English. The only collection of Martí's writings in English is *The America of José Martí*, published in New York in 1953. This contains selections from his series of studies of North American life, but does not include his important articles about social and economic conditions in the United States nor those in which Martí expressed his views on the relations of the United States with Latin America, including Cuban-American relations. There are also some selections from Martí's writings about Cuba and the diary of his last days. The translation of the rest of Martí's writings into English is long overdue.

Martí died at the early age of 42. But the example of his unswerving loyalty to the cause of Cuban independence and freedom continued to inspire the insurgents and helped carry them through the bitter and bloody struggles. "The Invading Hymn," written on November 15, 1895, by Enrique Loynaz del Castillo opened with the lines:

> The adored memory of Martí
> Presents Honor to our lives.[18]

Martí's ideas served as guides for future generations of Cuban patriots. As one Cuban scholar and revolutionary wrote in 1953 on the 100th anniversary of Martí's birth: "He was the guide of his time; he was also the forerunner of our own." [19]

On a pine board in the camp at Dos Ríos were the pages of Martí's last letter which, though never completed, set forth what "The Apostle" of free Cuba believed were the tasks then facing the Revolution. It was indispensable, Martí emphasized, to liberate Cuba from Spain. At the same time, it was necessary to take steps to prevent the United States from substituting its own domination of Cuba for that of Spain's, and thus facilitate its domination over all of Latin America.

> It is my duty—inasmuch as I realize it and have the spirit to fulfill it—to prevent, by the independence of Cuba, the United States from spreading over the West Indies and falling, with that added weight, upon other lands of our America. All I have done up to now, and shall do hereafter, is to that end. . . . I have lived inside the monster and know its insides—and my weapon is only the slingshot of David.[20]

A free and independent Cuba, Martí pointed out, must not serve as an auxiliary for the penetration of United States imperialism into Latin America. Those who led the Cuban people in their fight for freedom from Spain, and those who would build the structure of free Cuba after that struggle was won, had the responsibility of creating a nation that would be truly sovereign, of safeguarding Cuba's independence from economic domination by Wall Street and political domination by the United States State Department, and of thereby preventing Cuba from being used by the United States as a bridgehead for the conquest of the West Indies and Latin America.

CHAPTER II
Cuban Revolutionary Strategy

ON FEBRUARY 24, 1895, when the *Grito de Baire* was sounded, beginning Cuba's second and final war for independence from Spain, and for several weeks thereafter, the Spanish Government in Madrid and in Havana was not greatly alarmed by the revolt. After the uprising in the West was defeated by the Spanish authorities,* the prevailing opinion was that the movement would be stopped without too much difficulty.[1]

The official attitude changed abruptly when Madrid received the news that the leaders of the 1868-1878 revolution, Antonio Maceo and Máximo Gómez, were preparing to land in Cuba. Martínez Campos, the Spanish hero of the Ten Years' War, was questioned about the latest Cuban revolt. He answered it gravely, "I attribute great importance to the fact that chieftain Maceo is embarking for Cuba, because I know the prestige he enjoys and the military skill he exhibited in the previous campaign." [2] The government in Madrid shared this concern; it immediately instituted determined measures to meet the situation. Even before Maceo and his twenty-two companions had landed in Cuba on March 31, an announcement was issued by Spain stating: "General Martínez Campos is ready to leave for Cuba to take charge of that command. . . .† On April 2 a battalion of marine infantry will

---

* The original conception of the Revolution called for a simultaneous and general uprising throughout the island. But an unforeseen development resulted in the almost complete failure of the revolt in the West. Having learned of the plans for the insurrection, the Spanish authorities arrested General Julio Sanguily and Don José María Aguirre de Valdés, the supreme and assistant chieftains of the whole Western department, as they were leaving the city of Havana to lead the uprising in the West.

† Martínez Campos supplanted Governor-General Callejas.

depart from the Great Antilles and by April 8 forces up to six thousand men will depart."³ In New York the *World* greeted the announcement with the observation: "When Spain sends its great general Martínez Campos to put down the uprising in Cuba, it means that the trouble is serious."⁴

By the middle of April Spain had followed up the appointment of Martínez Campos to take command in Cuba with the declaration of martial law in the eastern provinces and with continued requests by Prime Minister Canovas del Castillo for additional troops and credits. Spain's strategy in sending Martínez Campos to Havana with unlimited powers and with the promise of full support from his home government was based on the belief that the man who had succeeded in ending the Ten Years' War would convince the *insurrectos* that it was hopeless to continue the struggle.* This optimistic outlook was strengthened late in May when José Martí's untimely death in battle near Dos Ríos led the Spaniards to believe that the Revolution would now collapse. That Martí's death was a staggering blow goes without saying. Martí exercised an ideological influence over the Cuban insurgents that none of his successors could hope to have.† Nevertheless, the contrary to what Spain had expected actually happened. Instead of the Revolution breaking apart in the absence of the great spokesman for *Cuba Libre*, the memory of Martí's personality, his revolutionary ideas, and his many sacrifices on behalf of Cuba, stimulated the struggle to free the

---

* According to Ana Betancourt, who watched the political scene in Madrid for her nephew Gonzalo de Quesada, Martínez Campos had been chosen to pacify the rebels largely because he was "the idol of the free Negroes, who believe, in their ignorance, that they owe their freedom to him." (Ana Betancourt to Gonzalo de Quesada, Madrid, February 6, 1895, *Archivo de Gonzalo de Quesada, Epistolario I, II,* edited by Gonzalo de Quezada y Miranda, Havana, 1948, vol. I, p. 44. Hereinafter cited as *Archivo Quesada.*)

The reference was to the fact that Martínez Campos, as Prime Minister, had presented a project to the Spanish Cortes in November, 1879 for the abolition of slavery in Cuba. For the limitations of this proposal, see Philip S. Foner, *History of Cuba and its Relations with the United States,* vol. II, New York, 1963, pp. 292-93.

† Perhaps the clearest recognition of Martí's special role in the Revolution is the fact that when he died, the Cuban revolutionaries replaced him with three men: Salvador Cisneros Betancourt as provisional president of the Cuban Republic, Enrique José Varona as editor of *Patria,* and Tomás Estrada Palma as Delegate of the Cuban Revolutionary Party However, neither of these three men wielded the influence in Cuban revolutionary circles that Martí had had.

island from Spanish domination. "The Apostle of Cuban independence" became the symbol of the Revolution, and his memory invigorated the revolutionary drive of the people. On July 8, 1895, de Truffin, the Russian Consul in Havana, reported: ". . . in spite of the tireless efforts, of the famed commander [Martínez Campos] and reinforcements brought in from the metropolis (30,000 men), *the uprising is still spreading*. Another 10,000 men are due to arrive from Spain soon; it is asserted that the Marshal had asked for another 25,000 men in September."[5]

Thus Spain's early belief that the rebellion would speedily be crushed proved to be an illusion. Yet, according to all standard works by military analysts, the prospects for the insurgents did not appear bright. The Spanish army already in the island was superior in number, equipment, training, and in almost every essential of warfare. Moreover, a steady stream of reinforcements could be dispatched to Cuba, and the insurgents had no navy to prevent their reaching the scene of conflict. Spanish internal affairs, though still corrupt, were, under the leadership of Prime Minister Cánovas, on a sounder economic basis than they had been during the Ten Years' War. Moreover, the leading parties in Spain afforded the government unqualified cooperation in the suppression of the rebellion—at least in its early stages.* Spain was thus free to devote all her resources to the suppression of the new uprising, and to dispatch troops in almost unlimited numbers in support of the war, drawing her army from a population of 16 million, while Cuba, on the other hand, had to draw her military forces from a native population of 1,600,000.[6]

At the beginning of the war, the forces of Spain in Cuba numbered about eighty thousand: twenty thousand of them were regular Spanish troops and sixty thousand were Spanish and Cuban Volunteers. By December, 1895, 98,412 regular troops had been sent to the island, and the number of Volunteers increased to 63,000 men. Thereafter these forces were steadily augmented by fresh troops from the Peninsula, so that by the end of 1897 there were 240,000 regulars and 60,000 irregulars in the island.[7]

---

* Although Praxedes M. Sagasta, leader of the Liberal Party, favored reforms in Cuba, he also supported military suppression of the rebellion. As one historian has pointed out: "Spanish opinion as a whole was still for repression. . . ." (William C. Atkinson, *A History of Spain and Portugal*, London, 1960, p. 310.)

There were never more than 54,000 people under arms for the insurgents during any time during the war. (The total given for those who served at one time during the entire war was 53,774.[8]) But in the early months of the conflict, the number engaged in fighting was much smaller. It was not until the western provinces were invaded late in 1895 and new recruits from that area added, that the Revolutionary Army attained its maximum strength. For the greater part of the war, the effective combatant force amounted to about 30,000 in number.*

The Spanish army not only greatly exceeded the total strength of the *insurrectos,* but was vastly superior in supplies of weapons and implements of war. From the time of the Ten Years' War, possession of firearms by private individuals in Cuba had been prohibited; arms found in possession of the common people were confiscated. This practically eliminated private arms as an important source for the rebels except as they had been hidden. Hence, but for such arms and supplies as could be captured from the enemy or were turned in by deserters from the Spanish troops, all arms and the all-important ammunition for the revolutionists had to come from outside the country, and primarily from the United States. With the Spanish navy in complete control of Cuban waters, the arrival of supply boats was perilous and uncertain. In addition, the government of the United States, while permitting Spain to buy freely all the munitions she needed, repeatedly prevented expeditions from leaving its shores, the primary base for support of the revolutionists.

A number of expeditions managed to evade the U.S. authorities and avoid the blockade, but despite thousands of dollars sent from Cuba and many thousands collected in the United States, Europe and Latin America, only a few of them arrived, bringing substantial assistance.†

---

* 33,930 Cuban soldiers received payments when the army was disbanded.

† In his *La guerra de independencia de Cuba, 1895-1898,* Miguel Angel Varona Guerrero lists the arrival of thirty-four expeditions and enumerates their contents and personnel. (La Habana, 1946, vol. III, pp. 1306-63.) The report of the U.S. Secretary of the Treasury reveals that between June 11, 1895 and November 30, 1897, sixty expeditions were attempted. Twenty-eight of these expeditions were frustrated through the efforts of the Treasury Department; five were prevented by the Navy Department; four were interrupted by the Spanish Naval patrol; two were wrecked; one driven back to port by storm; one succeeded through the protection of the British, and the fate of another was unknown. Nine vessels were involved in these attempts; five proceeded by steamships of considerable

The three most important expeditions were the Roloff-Sánchez expedition which successfully landed in Cuba on July 24, 1895 with 150 men and 150,000 rounds of ammunition; the Mariano Torres expedition which brought guns to the Cuban army about the same time; and the Francisco Sánchez Hechavarría expedition which brought 100 rifles and 6,000 rounds of ammunition in August, 1895. Despite storms at sea and the vigilance of authorities on shore, these expeditions succeeded. But there were more failures than successes. As one student points out, "There were expeditions planned in Florida that never materialized, there were those planned that were halted upon embarcation, and there were a few that were successful." [9] Some of the expeditions reaching the island contained materials either ruined or unusable. On December 6, 1896, General Calixto García, the veteran of the Ten Years' War, wrote from Bayamo to Tomás Estrada Palma, who had replaced Martí as the Delegate of the Cuban Revolutionary Party in the United States:

> . . . our urgent needs are as follows: cannon bullets, caliber 12, and explosive bullets. But I warn you that those previously received of caliber 12, are of very bad quality, and kindly try to see that they do not cheat you by selling useless and old munitions. . . . Send us much quinine and good vaccine, but better than the stock we have which is completely useless. . . . You will easily see how urgent it is that we receive as soon as possible quinine and vaccines, but I repeat—good vaccine." [10]*

---

size; twelve went on tug boats and one pilot boat, each less than one hundred tons, and two of the five expeditions went aboard the American-owned *Laurada*. (*House Document* 326, 55th Congress, 2nd Session.)

The tug *Dauntless* from Florida made more landings on Cuban soil than any other ship in the years 1895-1898. (*See* Richard V. Rickenbach, "Filibustering with the *Dauntless*," *Florida Historical Quarterly*, vol. XXVIII, April, 1950, pp. 231-53.)

* The letters of Cuban leaders in the field are filled with pleas for arms. Rafael María Portuondo wrote to Gonzalo de Quesada on June 11, 1895, requesting 15,000 rifles and commenting: "I fear that if this is delayed we will be serious weakened." (Cuba Libre, June 11, 1895, *Archivo Quesada*, vol. II, pp. 154-57.) In October, General Carlos Roloff, recently appointed Minister of War in the Cuban provisional government, wrote from Limpios de Taguasco in Santa Clara province complaining of Spain's overwhelming superiority in arms and beseeching Quesada to see to it that arms were shipped to Cuba as soon as possible. (Roloff to Quesada, October 24, 1895, *Archivo Quesada*, vol. II, p. 195.) Antonio Maceo urgently requested that he be sent "one thousand precision arms, preferably the Remington calibre 43, with corresponding ammunition, using one

The rebels had no uniforms, meager rations, little ammunition, and their individual equipment was varied while the Spaniards had the great advantage of standardization of weapons, artillery, and ample supply of ammunition. The great diversity in types and ages of weapons was a constant source of concern for the rebel leaders since they often found themselves with arms of one sort and ammunition of another. Cuban fighters preferred the modern Mauser rifles used by the Spaniards, not only because of their superior range and velocity, but also because they could make use of the ammunition which they often managed to capture from the enemy.* Each Spanish rifleman carried from one hundred to one hundred fifty rounds of ammunition while his Cuban counterpart might have four or five rounds or none at all. Guns were harder to replace than men, and the *insurrectos* put special emphasis on weapons maintenance.[11]

Cuban artillery weapons were not plentiful and the ammunition for them even less so. One obtains an idea of how scarce cannons were among the rebels from the account of Bernabé Boza, chief of Generalísimo Máximo Gómez's staff, of an incident which occurred on November 12, 1895. "Commander Juan Agustín Sánchez reached the encampment [in Camagüey near Las Villas] with a cannon of the period of Christopher Columbus, which was buried no one knows where and found by no one knows whom."[12] Although rusted and without powder or balls, the cannon created a sensation, for it was the only piece of artillery in Gómez's army. It was cleaned, given the name "Trifulca," dragged along by the rebels, and became the darling of Captain Sierra who obtained "powder, wick, projectile, [and] a

---

of the fruit ships of the Banes line." (Maceo to Estrada Palma, Mina de Camasan, Holguín, Sept. 22, 1895, *Antonio Maceo, Documentos para su vida*, Havana, 1945, pp. 123-25.)

* Corrupt Spanish officials also contributed arms and ammunition to Cuban revolutionaries. Elias H. Cheney, United States Consul at Matanzas, reported: "Spain is herself through the treachery of her officials furnishing arms in quiet to the insurgents. There is lying at this moment in this city, a consignment of 500 guns ostensibly designed for the 'Guardia Civil.' Actually about 200 of the guns have been taken out and distributed in lots of about a dozen among trusted Cubans." Later, Chaney reported from Havana that "a regular system of 'underground railroad' . . . exists by means of which information is conveyed and arms and ammunition are placed where they presumably will 'do the most good.'" (Elias P. Chaney to Edwin F. Uhl, July 23, August 31, 1894, U.S. Consular Despatches, Matanzas, National Archives, Washington, D.C. Hereinafter cited as National Archives.)

tremendous brush." "Trifulca" was actually fired at a Spanish fort. On the second firing, the cannon blew up, "and with this," notes Boza wryly in his diary, "was finished the artillery of the Fourth Army Corps." [13]

The only plentiful and standard weapon universally carried by the *insurrectos* was a heavy knife two feet long called the *machete*. It was an implement with which the peasants, Negro and white, who formed the major portion of the rebel army,[14] were familiar and well supplied, since it was commonly used for cutting sugar cane and hacking paths through the tropic vegetation. In battle it was an effective weapon, and a Spanish soldier could quickly lose an arm from a single blow. One contemporary wrote:

> There is a peculiar wild shrill cry the Cubans give that announces a machete charge—a "rebel yell" sure enough, fierce and prolonged—and it means going in at the high speed of horses, for "war to the knife," and there is no doubt and no wonder that the Spaniards are alarmed always by that battle-cry. There has been more hand-to-hand fighting in Cuba than in any war of modern times.

The terrible hand-to-hand combat resulting from the skillful use of the *machete* often enabled rebels, unaided by other arms, to terrorize Spanish troops equipped with artillery and rifles.[15]

"The summer is extremely hot and the royal troops are forced to fight not only against the insurgents but also against the yellow fever which plays havoc with the men. . . ." [16] In this observation, the Russian Consul in Havana put his finger on an important factor to be considered in comparing the opposing armies. The native Cubans were more or less inured to the climate and the diseases, while the new recruits from Spain were highly vulnerable to both. According to official Cuban figures, 3,437 *insurrectos* died of disease; this was fewer than the 5,180 who died of wounds or were killed in battle. In contrast it was estimated that ten of the Spanish conscripts died of disease to every one killed in battle. Small wonder that when Gómez was asked who were his best generals, he replied, "June, July and August." These were the months when yellow fever was rife. This does not mean that the Cuban forces were not hard hit by illness and epidemics, for large numbers were incapacitated for various periods. "We are losing more soldiers as a consequence of the smallpox than in the battlefield," Calixto García reported in December, 1896. Nevertheless, the Cuban cases were not as serious as the Spaniards' and recuperation was much faster.[17]

The rebels' lesser degree of susceptibility to the diseases of Cuba only partially reduced the vast disparity between the Spanish and Cuban forces in numbers and supplies. It is amazing that in an island 730 miles long and an average of 50 miles wide, the Cuban revolutionists, tremendously outnumbered and poorly equipped, were able so effectively to battle the vastly superior Spanish army for over three years without aid from a single foreign power. The story of how this was accomplished is one of the great epics of modern military history.

The military strategy of the Cuban Revolution was formulated by the aged Máximo Gómez, Commander-in-Chief of the Liberating Army. It was the old Dominican's* belief that the basic reasons for the failure of the Ten Years' War were: (1) the fact that the Revolution was confined to the eastern part of the island; and (2) that not enough damage had been inflicted on the Cuban economy to force the wealthy classes to put pressure on the Spaniards to seek peace and to deprive Spain of the revenues with which to continue the war. In 1895 Gómez resolved not to repeat these mistakes. He was determined to extend the struggle throughout Cuba, even to the very extreme western coast, and was determined that the island should be made useless to the Spaniards by destroying every possible source of revenue. Gómez was convinced that the best and possibly the only way for the rebels to win the war was to make it economically disastrous for the Spaniards. A scorched-earth policy would make the whole island a great economic liability for Spain. This would work great hardships on the Cubans, but it was the price they would have to pay for independence. "The chains of Cuba have been forged by her own richness," Gómez argued, "and it is precisely this which I propose to do away with soon." [18] The chief object was the sugar industry which constituted approximately seventy-five percent of Cuban wealth and was the main source of the Spanish Government's revenue from the island. As Gómez noted: "Sugar cannot be allowed because to work means peace, and in Cuba we must not permit working."[19]†

---
* Gómez was born in the town of Baní, Santo Domingo.
† A by-product would be the recruiting of the unemployed into the rebel ranks.

As Gómez pointed out later in the war, this scorched-earth policy was "considered when planning my campaign long before landing in Cuba." [20] He did not wait long before putting it into effect. On July 1, 1895, Gómez strictly prohibited the transport of industrial, agricultural, and animal products to towns and garrisons occupied by Spanish troops.* His circular added: "The sugar plantations will stop their labors, and whoever shall attempt to grind the crops, notwithstanding this order, will have their cane burned and their buildings demolished. The person who, disobeying this order, will try to profit from the present situation of affairs, will show by his conduct little respect for the rights of the Revolution of redemption, and therefore, shall be considered an enemy, and treated as a traitor, in case of his capture." [21]

Nevertheless, throughout the country preparations were made for the grinding of the crop, and on November 6, 1895, Gómez issued a new order which opened: "Animated by the spirit of unchangeable resolution in defense of the Revolution to redeem this colonial people, crushed and despised by Spain, and in accordance with what was set forth in the circular of July 1, I have come to the following decision:

"Article 1. That all plantations shall be totally destroyed, their cane and outbuildings burned and railroad connections destroyed.

"Article 2. All laborers who shall aid the sugar factories—these sources of supplies that we must deprive the enemy of—shall be considered as traitors to their country.

"Article 3. All who are caught in the act, or whose violation of Article 2 shall be proven, shall be shot. Let all chiefs of operation of the Liberating Army comply with this order, determined to unfurl triumphantly, even on ruin and ashes, the flag of the Republic of Cuba." [22]

Both decrees—July 1 and November 6—Gómez informed Estrada Palma "have the same objective: the total paralyzation of all labor in Cuba." [23]

Less than a week after November 6, Gómez issued an open letter to the Cuban people explaining the reasons which had made necessary

---

* Industrial products included leather, timber and wood products; agricultural products included tobacco, coffee, wax, honey. Animal products were, of course, cattle.

"those extreme measures." "After so many years of supplications, humiliations, contumely, banishment and death, when this people of its own will has arisen, there remains no other solution but to triumph, it matters not what means are employed to accomplish it. The people cannot hesitate between the wealth of Spain and the liberty of Cuba. . . ." For those who objected to their properties being destroyed, Gómez had these words: "The Cuban Republic in course of time will help you in reconstruction. But now we must destroy." [24]

Although Gómez's chief objective was to make the economic losses for Spain so great that she would give up the island to stop the drain on her economy, his strategy was also influenced by a motive other than military. Gómez had only contempt for the wealthy Cubans who were quite content to accept Spain's despotic rule as long as their profits continued—profits wrung from exploitation of the Cuban masses. In one of his most moving letters, Gómez wrote:

> When I arrived in this land and saw the plight of the poor workers, I felt wounded with sadness. There was this poor wretch working beside magnificent grandeur; beside all that beautiful richness was so much misery and so much low morality. When I saw the wife and children of the poor worker covered with rags and living in a battered hut, I was touched with the enormity of the contrast. When I asked for the school and was told that there had never been one,* and when I entered innumerable towns and saw no culture, no morality, no clean people, no acceptable living accommodations and was received by the mayor and the priest, then I felt indignant and profoundly disposed against the elevated classes of the country. And in an instant I exclaimed to myself, "Blessed be the torch!" [25]

In Gómez's eyes, then, the war in Cuba was not a conventional conflict nor even solely a guerrilla war, but a revolutionary war. In it, the political, social, economic and psychological factors were as significant as the military ones. This did not mean that Gómez advocated a policy of indiscriminate destruction. In the first of his proclamations and orders, the circular of April 28, 1895, Gómez announced: "All proper-

---

* Such education as existed then in Cuba was largely confined to the leading cities. In 1899, 63.9 percent of the total population could neither read nor write, and most of those who could were in the cities or were former planters. (Cuban Census Office, *Report of the Census of Cuba, 1899*, Washington, D.C., 1900, p. 148.)

ties will be respected whose owners respect us. Only those whose owners aid the enemy or who show hostility to the Revolution will be destroyed, and only after complete proof has been obtained and after repeated warnings have been issued."[26] This policy he adhered to strictly, repeatedly pointing out that "we understand that the Revolution will never feel it necessary, in order to triumph, to be cruel and bloodthirsty."[27]

Gómez was not completely insensible to the lasting damage his policies might inflict on the Cuban economy. He tried to introduce a new plan for the relief of owners of sugar plantations which was intended to result in the saving of several million dollars worth of property that would otherwise go to ruin. Permits were issued to planters who asked for them, which would allow them to plow, and in fact, perform almost any work necessary to the preservation of their properties. This plan, however, was advanced only to lessen the effects of his policies and as a means of hastening the rapid utilization of lands and equipment once the war was over. The grinding of sugar cane remained prohibited as was any sort of production which might accrue to the revenues of Spain.[28]

This policy caused considerable dissension among the civil and military revolutionary figures, and even the latter were not in agreement on the problem. Some were of the opinion that valuable properties should be subject to a type of "protection" fee which owners would pay in order to keep their properties from being damaged. Others enlarged upon this with the idea that sugar mill operators should be allowed to grind cane and produce their product in exchange for considerable regular contributions.

The radical prohibition of sugar production ordered by Commander-in-Chief Máximo Gómez, in order to destroy the resources of the enemy, first met with opposition from Antonio Maceo, second-in-command. Maceo believed that the Revolution would be better served if the planters were allowed to grind sugar cane in return for the payment of certain fixed and regular contributions to the rebel cause. In addition, they must not aid the enemy nor hamper the progress of the rebellion. On the other hand, if the sugar producers did not make such agreements, their machinery and other resources should be ruthlessly destroyed. Maceo was also worried that the effects of Gómez's intransigent policy outside of Cuba would jeopardize Cuban hopes for the recognition of belligerency and would convert foreign owners of property in Cuba from friends into enemies of the Revolution.* At the least, he felt, the prohibition against grinding should be applied only to those who refused or failed to pay a war tax or who disobeyed revolutionary orders.[29]

Soon after assuming command in Oriente, General Maceo made a number of such agreements with the sugar-cane growers and mill operators. These agreements facilitated the acquisition of funds by the revolutionary delegation in New York and provided some implements of war.[30] Viewing this as a success, the mobile governing council in Cuba left the door open for individual chiefs of the Liberating Army and the Delegates in the United States to make their own agreements with sugar producers on the same terms as set forth by Maceo. This, of course, was precisely what Gómez wished to avoid, and he insisted that while there was no liberty in the island and Cuba had to suffer the Spanish yoke, no one had the right to add to Spain's capacity to maintain its tyranny. Despite his strong dislike of them, Gómez did honor the contracts made by Maceo and others. "I am giving orders," he wrote to Estrada Palma, "to respect its [a sugar mill's] interest in grinding in view of the transaction completed by you to the effect of no less than $20,000." But then he showed his extreme dislike of the whole policy by stating critically, "I value highly the Cuban blood that is being shed because of sugar, and if the amount is not adjusted soon, the torch will adjust it all." [31]

Gómez's objection forced the government in arms to examine the problem in detail. The examination produced the following analysis: first, that if the production of sugar crops was permitted, even though Spain benefited, the revolutionists could obtain much needed funds through fees and taxes. On the other hand, if cane grinding was not

---

* Maceo, however, did not allow Estrada Palma to persuade him to go easy with the properties of men who might prove helpful to the revolutionary cause because of their "influence with members of the Congress and with prominent people [in the United States]." The Negro General informed the Delegate that it was necessary to treat each case equally and avoid favoritism which would only prejudice the revolutionary cause. It was only necessary to know if a planter had paid his full tax, "so that if he has not, fire can be applied to his property with a minimum of delay." (Estrada Palma to Antonio Maceo, Sept. 12, 1895, in *Antonio Maceo; documentos para su vida*, La Habana, 1945, p. 146; Antonio Maceo to Estrada Palma, Sept. 22, 1895, Archivo Nacional, Havana, Cuba. Hereinafter referred to as Archivo Nacional.)

allowed, both sides in the war would suffer but with greater harm to the *insurrectos* since the Spaniards had larger sources of financing at their disposal. The civil government then elected to permit sugar grinding for those mill operators who made fiscal arrangements with the Revolution and who fulfilled their obligations on contributions. Conversely, those who did not contribute could not grind. Moreover, the cane fields and mills of all who showed sympathy for Spain and who fortified their properties were to be burned and the owners declared enemies of the Revolution.[32]

This policy was, of course, a serious blow to the general strategy of Gómez who, as we have seen, envisaged the kind of war whereby economic losses for Spain would be so great that she would give up the island to stop the drain on her own resources. Indeed, Gómez relentlessly followed his policy of indiscriminate prohibition of all sugar production where he was in control of the region. As he informed the Delegation in New York, he was "impeding the production of sugar and destroying plantations without entering into transactions of any kind, since on the contrary, even though they pay us interest, they prejudice us too much, and the triumph of the Revolution so far has been terrible and inexorable."[33] But the conflict of policies created a state of confusion which weakened the revolutionary struggle until, as we shall see, exceptions to the rule on the prohibition of grinding became fewer, and the views of other military leaders and government representatives became more closely aligned with those of Máximo Gómez.

In his dispatch of October 18, 1895, de Truffin, the Russian Consul in Havana, noted the differences in rebel ranks over whether or not to allow the planters to grind sugar. He then shrewdly noted: "The very fact that such an important question as harvesting depends on the will of the insurgents gives a sufficiently clear idea of the scale and strength of the uprising."[34]

The organization of the Revolutionary Army was quite complicated on paper. Insurrectionary plans from the beginning envisaged army units extending from one end of the island to the other with two main departments, one for the West and one for the East. The two departments were to have corps, divisions, brigades, regiments, and so forth. Departmental commanders were selected for each of the two areas with Máximo Gómez as Supreme Commander for the whole. The original conception called for a simultaneous and general uprising throughout the island. But this was frustrated by the almost complete failure of the revolt in the West, which nullified a real western department until the invasion of the West was launched. Until then, only small uncoordinated units offered any resistance in the three western departments. These groups were formed haphazardly by revolutionary adherents within the particular areas where they lived, and each operated locally, with only a nuisance value effect. In any event their numbers were few and their effectiveness slight until organized invading units overran the West.[35]

The army occupying the East was given the title of "The Liberating Army." (The army that invaded the West was called "The Invading Army.") Each corps of the Liberating Army was divided into divisions, there never being less than two in any one corps. The divisions were composed of two or more brigades, and these of two or more regiments. If the units were infantry, the subdivisions were called battalions and companies, and if cavalry, they were designated as squadrons and troops. The number of military units from division on down fluctuated according to conditions. Probably the maximum numbers ever attained were respectively fourteen divisions, thirty-six brigades, eighty-two regiments and an undeterminate number of lower units. In addition to these regular gradations, there were some special character, including *escoltas,* or bodyguard troops for upper-level headquarters, more or less independent zonal guerrilla forces, and some expeditionary regiments.

Service forces, that is military branches designed to supply and service units, hardly existed in the usual sense. Theoretically there were branches of military sanitation, but practically speaking, sanitation was the responsibility of each individual soldier. There were some doctors in the field, but their number was very low. In the eastern provinces and especially in the mountains of Oriente, field hospitals were regularly maintained in fixed positions which could be relatively safe because of the terrain. In the West the hospitals were more mobile, being moved constantly from one swamp or forest area to another and hidden with great care.[36] While no engineering corps existed as such, officers were designated as engineers with individual units to take care of their problems. The same applied to artillery, that is, such as was available. Some foreigners and Cubans were given hasty training as artillery officers in the United States and conveyed to Cuba with various expeditions.*

One of the special military units of the Liberating Army was called the *Vigilancia de Costas*. Its function was to advise the military chieftains of the arrival of expeditions of men and arms from the exterior; to impede the disembarkation of the enemy; to prevent the departure of unauthorized persons, and to hinder the exportation of commercial articles.[37]

The scheme of organization presented above would be completely misleading as a clue to the nature of the war. For the Cuban military did not operate as corps, divisions, brigades, etc. in actual battle except on rare occasions. The whole organization was designed so that it would be highly flexible. Rather large forces could be concentrated in integrated units at very short notice, and this was done when it was advantageous. Most of the time, however, units as small as troops and companies operated individually, generally in their own local areas where both officers and men had always lived and were well known.[38] Ordinarily a squadron consisted of two troops, with a maximum strength of one hundred armed men. Such a force was permitted to muster unarmed men designated as *impedimenta*, including servants for officers, camp followers and roustabouts to do all the menial tasks and relieve the armed soldiers from all but actual fighting. These unarmed men quite often took up the arms of the slain and wounded to fill gaps in the fighting contingent, and thereby really constituted a sort of reserve force. The officers of a squadron or a full company of infantry were: a major, a captain, two lieutenants, an *alférez* (second lieutenant), four sergeants, and eight corporals, the number of officers and non-commissioned officers being large in proportion to the number of enlisted men.[39]

The Cuban military structure was designed for quick dispersal and rapid reunion. (It is significant in this connection to note that the ratio of the cavalry units to those of the infantry was thirty regiments of cavalry to fifty-six of the infantry, and this did not include the mounted body guard units attached to the general headquarters of each of the six corps and fourteen divisions.[40]) Under the type of war fought

---

* Frederick Funston came over from the United States to become chief of Cuban artillery. See Frederick Funston, *Memories of Two Wars*, New York, 1914.

by the *insurrectos*, the small unit described above was the real backbone of the army. A general of a brigade or division could promptly mobilize a considerable number of local forces and travel with as many as need be. Yet generals more often than not were accompanied by small commands partly because in the absence of a commissary department, and the impossibility (at least in the western provinces) or organizing one, there was difficulty in feeding a large body of men. A small force could live comfortably on the country, roping a steer or digging up potatoes, as it went along, while the concentration of large forces invariably brought hunger in an island ravaged by a war of destruction.

Cuban military strategy, as developed by Gómez, was based on the realization that the huge disparity between the sizes of the two opponents made the thought of any decisive campaigns to defeat the enemy impossible. The war had to be won by making it economically impossible for Spain to continue the struggle.[41] In carrying out this plan, Gómez placed his forces continually on the offensive while forcing the enemy to remain on the defensive. This was done, first, by forcing the Spaniards to disperse their forces widely throughout the island,* and secondly, by concentrating all attacks against the economy of the island rather than against the military forces of the enemy. Consequently, the great majority of Cuban action against the enemy occurred where and when Spanish forces were defending properties, towns, communication and transportation facilities, and all points having to do with the island's economy. Gómez instructed the Cubans to cut all railroad and telegraph lines, to destroy Spanish forces as opportunity offered, and to attack any small Spanish outposts. Usually the enemy was not fought in the field except when a fight was unavoidable, or when the *insurrectos* wished to capture arms and supplies, or when the Spanish were outnumbered. Of course, the shortages of ammunition also played a part in this policy, and when attacking Spanish positions, Cubans were instructed to capture as many arms as possible.[42]

Cuban strategy required that the *insurrectos* themselves never oc-

---

* De Truffin, the Russian Consul in Havana, made a special point of this aspect of Cuban strategy in one of his dispatches: "Numerous detachments are scattered all over the provinces and this has forced the [Spanish] Commander-in-Chief to maintain considerable number of troops wherever there is some townlet, hamlet or strategic points that needs defending. . . ." (De Truffin to the Russian Ambassador to Madrid, Oct. 14, 1896, *International Affairs*, Moscow, March, 1964, p. 123.)

cupy a town or fixed position where they could be a target for superior enemy forces. The strategy did not call for the rebels to occupy towns permanently. Rather the aim was to route the Spanish garrisons when the rebels had superior numbers, to capture supplies and ammunition, and then to burn the town in order to deprive the Spaniards of bases. It was the regular policy of the insurrectionary forces to see that women and children were given opportunity to leave towns which were attacked.

Thus the rebel strategy envisaged no fixed battle lines, no large campaigns, and no great concentrations which the Spanish army could overwhelm. (Only one large campaign was launched by the rebels during the entire war. This was the invasion of the West which lasted from October, 1895 to January, 1896.) Instead, rebels infiltrated areas strongly occupied by Spaniards; they assembled, struck, and then dispersed to re-form later and repeat the process. Replying to Spanish criticism that "Cuban generals don't put up a fight," Gómez remarked, "This means they don't put up a fight on the Spanish-chosen territory. They put up a fight when they want to, and they refuse to enter a combat which would favor the enemy." [43] Commenting on this, the New York *Tribune* pointed out that the Cuban rebels "act just as the wily 'Swamp Fox' Marion did in South Carolina when he baffled and humiliated and utterly wore out an overwhelming force of Britain's picked troops." [44]*

While the Cuban army operated in seemingly independent units, there was actually close cooperation and interdependence among the component parts. When attacks were planned on particularly strong positions, diversionary actions drew the attention of the Spaniards elsewhere. Threatened or trapped revolutionary units were able to escape by repeated multiple attacks from other units upon the rear and flanks of the Spanish attackers. Close co-ordination was made possible by the effective intelligence system maintained by the revolutionists, which kept them completely advised of the movement of their enemies. Their intelligence system owed its success to the fact that large numbers of

---

* Francis Marion, the "Swamp Fox," was the great guerrilla fighter of the American Revolution. He operated successfully in South Carolina with small militia units against vastly superior British forces, striking only when the odds were in his favor and vanishing when they were not.

the country people sympathized with and aided the *mambises*.* Grover Flint, the American journalist and artist who spent four months with the Liberating Army in 1896, wrote in his book, *Marching with Gómez*, "No man is so poor that he cannot cheerfully give food for the army. This proves also the truth of the saying here that the Spaniard owns only the ground he stands on. *The news of every movement of the Spaniard is quickly reported*."[45]† He also made it clear that good conduct toward the people rewarded the *insurrectos* with good intelligence, protection and cooperation.

Blending into the population, the *insurrectos* were impossible to isolate. Occasionally caught off-guard, the fleet-footed rebels were able to vanish in a matter of minutes. They scattered in the fields and could not be distinguished from the peasants around them. Of course, it was easier to identify the cavalry but they too were quartered by friendly peasants.

A Spanish military expert offered a fairly accurate, though prejudiced, account of the *mambises* in action:

> They ride incessantly here and there, and when their horses are tired, they seize any they come across. They frequently rest during the day, and march at night, in as light order as possible, carrying only a hammock, a piece of oilcloth, cartridges, machete

---

* During the first and second Wars for Independence in Cuba, the Cuban guerrilla fighters were commonly called *mambises*. The word originated in Santo Domingo. Juan Ethninius Mamby, a Negro Spanish officer, joined the Dominicans who were fighting against Spain for independence in 1846. The Spanish troops called the Dominican guerrilla fighters, "the men of Mamby." Then the word "mambies" was applied to all in Santo Domingo who fought against Spain. When the Ten Years' War broke out in Cuba, Spanish soldiers were sent to the island from Santo Domingo to help put down the revolution, and they called the Cuban revolutionary fighters "mambises." The word was taken over by the Cuban revolutionists. ("Los Mambises," *Bohemia*, June 4, 1965, p. 102.)

† Flint worked so hard taking notes and drawing pictures of the *mambises* that even Gómez, who was usually indifferent to foreign correspondents, was impressed, and seated the American at his table. On May 20, 1896, Flint was named *Comandante Honorario* (Honorary Commander) by General Lacret.

Flint's work contains one of the best first-hand accounts of Cuban tactics. Gerardo Castellanos, the Cuban historian, praises Flint not only for "the spirit of justice which he has shown for our liberators," but for his illustrations "which no journalist, native or foreign, has equalled." (José Manuel Pérez Cabrera, *Historiografía de Cuba*, México, 1962, pp. 291-92.) In an excellent contemporary review of Flint's book, Elbert G. Hastings called it "the only detailed account of the insurgents' life and doings that has been published." ("With Gomez in the Cuban Skirmishes," *National Magazine*, vol. VIII, May, 1898, p. 151.)

and rifle. They live by marauding. The country people feed them, and help them so far as they can, and where these insurgents don't find sympathy, the machete, the torch and the rope are good arguments. In the woods they find good shelter, places for storage and for hospitals.

They are divided in groups, more or less numerous, to which they give the pompous names of regiments and brigades, and they never accept a fight unless their number is far superior to that of our troops. They place themselves in ambush, selecting narrow passages in the woods, fords and lagoons. They always run after firing, and if pursued, they leave a small body charged with firing on their pursuers, while the main body advances rapidly and then stops, and by circling around, get to the rear of our troops and harass them. When they go a long distance, they divide into small parties, make the journey at night in the woods, and then several groups assemble, until necessity compels them to part again, and meet anew on a preconcerted spot. Their infantry is always in loose order, hiding among the bushes, and always protected by the cavalry. At times a group separates from the main body, the mission being to attract the attention of the government troops, while the main body charges "al machete." Such are the insurgents of Cuba, and their ways of fighting.[46]

What the Spanish expert was saying was that the Cuban rebels were superb guerrilla fighters! After all, it is doubtful if any people at that time knew more about guerrilla fighting than did the *mambises,* for many of them were graduates of ten years of education in this type of warfare in Cuba's first war of independence. Their three greatest leaders, Máximo Gómez, Antonio Maceo, and Calixto García, were also graduates of this school, having participated actively in the Ten Years' War.

In addition to good leadership, the *mambises* had strong motivation. They understood why they were fighting and what they were fighting for. Night after night, the rebels would discuss the aims of the war as set forth in some article or editorial in one of the five papers the revolutionists published: *El Cubano Libre* (Oriente); *Boletín de Guerra* (Camagüey); *La República* and *La Sanidad* (Las Villas), and *La Independencia* (Manzanillo). The printing shop of *El Cubano Libre,* published at the direction of Antonio Maceo, was visited by an American reporter. He wrote in the National Magazine:

It must be extremely embarrassing [for the Spaniards] to receive with regularity a newspaper well edited, with twelve wide columns of news matter and editorial paragraphs full of unrestrained acrimony for Spain, and printed on territory which Spain still claims for her own subjugation!

Time and time again the Spaniards have sent troops out in the vicinity on the fields where this paper was supposed to be printed, and equally as many times they have returned to their point of starting with ranks decimated, and without having silenced the most powerful voice on the Cuban fields—the voice that comes from the mountains of Cayo del Rey. . . .

The newspaper is circulated gratis in the ranks of the insurgent army. It has become an institution which does much to elevate the spirit of the *soldados de la manigua* ("soldiers of the long grass"), the Cuban insurgents. It is teaching the women, the children and the illiterate to read, who have not had the chance under the schoolless reign of Spain.[47]

Armed rebel teams wandered through the countryside distributing copies of the insurgent papers to the peasants. They entered a village at dusk, when the peasants had finished work and had time to listen, and they spent hours reading from the articles and editorials in the papers.

Thus, though materially inferior to the Spanish forces, the rebels had good leadership and motivation—and these often counted for more than materiel in the kind of unorthodox conflict waged in Cuba.

General Martínez Campos, the Spanish commander, was also a graduate of the Ten Years' War, and having been successful in ending that struggle, believed that by using the same strategy he had employed in 1878, he could speedily triumph over the rebels in 1895. Martínez Campos' strategy was: (1) to distribute sufficient force at various points over the island to suppress the spread of the rebellion; (2) to concentrate troops west of Oriente to wall in the *insurrectos* effectually, and confine them to a limited field of action, meanwhile preventing destruction of property in this area; and (3) to push the rebels into a corner of Oriente, crush the penned-up Cubans by sheer weight of numbers, and end the war. In pursuance of his plans, Martínez Campos ordered the protection of sugar estates, railroad trains, and other valuable property. His forces were ordered to convoy provisions to such towns as needed them and to attack Cuban forces when they were encountered.[48] With the emphasis on defense, the backbone of the Spanish general's strategy was the use of the *trocha*. A good insight into the magnitude of this device may be obtained from a description of the eastern *trocha*, a relic of the Ten Years' War when it effectively served to confine the rebels to the eastern province of the island. The *trocha* stretched from coast to coast at the narrowest part of the island from Júcaro on the south coast to Morón on the north. An eyewitness description of this *trocha* which constituted the most extensive fortified line ever constructed by Spain in the New World, pictures it as a broad belt across the island two hundred yards wide and fifty miles long. The space in the center had been cleared of timber, which was then placed in rows parallel to the two sides, "forming a barrier of tree trunks and roots and branches as wide as Broadway [in New York City] and higher than a man's head." Down the center of this cleared space there was a single-track military railroad, equipped with armor-clad cars, to facilitate movement from one point to another along the fifty miles. Telegraph communication wires stretched along the railroad. Along the sides of the *trocha* more than thirty forts of three types were constructed—big forts, little forts and blockhouses. The larger forts were placed at intervals of a half mile, with the blockhouses and smaller forts placed in between at strategic points. In addition to these obstacles, there was a maze of barbed wire placed so that "to every twelve yards of posts there were four hundred and fifty yards of wire fencing." Each of the fortified houses had adequate loopholes from which to observe and fire, and some of them were encircled by trenches on the outside. For armor the forts were equipped with iron or zinc roofs. As a final defense, bombs were placed at points most likely to be attacked, and these had wire attachments to enable their being set off in "booby trap" fashion.[49]

The eastern trocha was duplicated at other points in the island, and it is not difficult, therefore, to understand why Martínez Campos believed that this formidable system would enable him to confine the Cubans to the East, and as in 1878, overwhelm them by superior force. But he soon found that his plan of warfare was of no avail in this Revolution in the face of increased Cuban determination and better organization. Guerrilla warfare is a type of warfare demanding determined, disciplined, uncompromising and selfless rank-and-file soldiers and leaders. Cuba was fortunate, in her Second War for Independence, that her Revolutionary Army had these essential qualities. As we shall now see, this Army successfully fought an enemy five to six times greater and possessed of many advantages other than size.

CHAPTER III
The War in Oriente and Preparations for the Western Invasion

THE WAR for the liberation of Cuba was not characterized, as we have pointed out, by large armies campaigning in the field or by decisive engagements of a monumental nature. Few battles occurred in which there were more than two or three thousand men on a side because Cuban forces, adhering to the principles of guerrilla warfare, avoided conflicts when they were outnumbered. Nevertheless there were, from the beginning, innumerable daily small engagements, and by 1898 these clashes caused the total number of men killed in action to exceed the total number of Americans killed in the War of 1812, the Mexican War, the Spanish-American War, and the war to crush the Philippine insurrection.[1]

Gómez pursued the Cuban strategy effectively in Camagüey, attacking and destroying on June 17, 1895 the town of Altagracia, following this with attacks on the forts of El Mulato, and defeating Martínez Campos at San Jerónimo. But no one was a greater master of the technique of harassing the Spanish in daily small engagements than Antonio Maceo, commander of the Cuban forces in Oriente. The Spanish soldiers derisively sang:

> With the beard of Maceo
> We will make brooms
> To sweep the barracks
> Of the Spanish troops.[2]

But the Spaniards soon discovered it was easier to sing of defeating Maceo than to accomplish it. On May 23, 1895, during an interview in the field with a correspondent of the New York *Herald*, Maceo declared, "I march with five thousand well-armed men. I have received various small but excellent expeditions. I have two mountain cannons with sufficient ammunition and soon I shall begin operations on a large scale." [3] This was actually an exaggeration for the sake of propaganda. Maceo had the men he claimed, but they were not well armed and they had very little ammunition. He had no artillery; indeed, during one of his maneuvers, his troops came across a printing press. When he saw it, Maceo exclaimed, "That is the artillery of the Revolution." (He had the press installed in a secure place, and published *El Cubano Libre*.) Many of Maceo's attacks depended mainly on the use of the *machete*, and most of his arms came from the enemy.[4]

Although he had neither a large army nor sufficient supplies of ammunition and materiel to fight many large battles, Maceo, using whatever materials were available, conducted a series of raiding and harassing activities throughout Oriente which greatly alarmed the noncooperative property owners and caused the Spaniards much concern. It was the sort of warfare which kept the Spanish forces constantly moving from one valuable property to another trying to protect the interests of the economy and its principal benefactors.

"Tranquillity was not meant for me," Maceo wrote to his wife, María Cabrales, on June 30, 1895. "I live on a horse, running in every direction, organizing forces and prefectures. . . ."[5] During that month, the Negro general carried on repeated raids in the zones of Holguín and Gibara. It was the type of warfare in which he excelled; striking here and there, he kept constantly on the move, never giving the enemy a chance to pin him down, always keeping him guessing. For the most part the actions were small, but carried on day after day, their cumulative effect was felt by the Spaniards. With the property holders thrown into panic, the Spaniards were forced to place their main contingents in the region of Holguín. This enabled Gómez to ride across the deserted lines and pass safely into Camagüey.

In mid-July, Maceo scored a great victory over the Spanish army. While camped in Baraguá, where he had earned great fame in the Ten Years' War,* Maceo received word from his scouts that made him hopeful of once again engaging the famous Martínez Campos in

---

* See Philip S. Foner, *A History of Cuba and its Relations with the United States*, vol. II, 1845-1895, New York, 1963, pp. 267-70.

battle. He learned that the Spanish general Fidel Alonzo de Santocildes was in Manzanillo, waiting for the arrival of Martínez Campos in order to conduct an important convoy to Bayamo. At once Maceo broke camp and led his fifteen hundred men to a place between Veguitas and the town of Bayamo known as El Tanteo or Peralejo. Here he revealed part of his plan to his staff. In case the Spaniards came by the main road, as could be expected, they would set an ambush and launch a surprise attack. Accordingly Maceo placed the infantry of Jesús Rabí* in a favorable position alongside the road at one point and that of Quintín Banderas, a Negro veteran of the Ten Years' War, at another. To the rear of these positions he placed the *impedimenta* (the cooks and camp servants) along with forty men. At another position, a little further removed and out of sight, were the cavalry led by Maceo. Maceo's strategy was clear. The infantry, applying the first pressure on the enemy, would close on both sides. After the enemy responded, Maceo and the cavalry would move in and decide the conflict. He was confident that he would win a great victory over both Spanish generals —Martínez Campos and Santocildes, capturing them and their valuable supplies.

But an unforeseen development marred Maceo's carefully-laid ambush. While he was waiting for the enemy, two traveling salesmen were intercepted by Maceo's advanced guards. After a brief interruption, the Negro chieftain, to the complete surprise of his staff, allowed them to leave. It was a costly mistake, for they promptly warned the approaching Spaniards of the rebel ambush. The Spanish forces struck swiftly from the rear of the *impedimenta,* the weakest and most vulnerable point of the rebel positions. Thus the element of surprise upon which Maceo had counted was now with the enemy.

At once Maceo, with the quick decision for which he was famous, rallied his forces and redirected the formation. At the head of his cavalry, which he had hoped to employ only after the battle was well under way, he furiously charged the Spanish troops who were attack-

---

* Rabí was a descendant of the Siboney Indians who had inhabited much of Cuba when Diego Velázquez landed.
Among the members of the infantry of General Rabí was a contingent of Chinese *mambises,* a number of whom were veterans of the Ten Years' War. (Juan Jiménez Pastrana, *Los Chinos en las Luchas por la Liberación Cubana, 1847-1930,* La Habana, 1963, pp. 93-95.)

ing his *impedimenta*. The momentum of this wild, *machete*-wielding charge gradually rolled the Spanish infantry back and forced them to form a defensive square. With the pressure off his *impedimenta*, Maceo ordered Rabí and Banderas to execute a flanking movement to the right with their infantry and to place themselves between the enemy and the woods at the rear. By this maneuver, Maceo hoped to keep the Spanish foot soldiers in the open, a target for his cavalry charges.

Before the Spaniards realized the consequences of Maceo's maneuvers, they were caught in the fire from the two groups of rebel infantry on the one side and the charges of the cavalry on the other. The Spanish foot soldiers, seized with panic, were about to capitulate, when suddenly the sounds of furious firing came from the outposts. Unknown to Maceo, the Spanish forces had been divided into two parts; the main body had not been in the battle thus far and were now attacking from the rear of Maceo's cavalry. The Negro commander turned his horsemen around to charge the new attackers. Now the battle swirled back and forth, with Maceo's forces barely managing to hold their own. All at once, disengagement or destruction faced the rebel commander.

At this critical moment, Maceo learned of a new and unidentified cavalry force approaching in the direction of Poniente. He sent Lieutenant-Colonel Héctor (Mariano) Lora to determine whether the new soldiers were Cubans or Spaniards. For what seemed an interminable length of time, Maceo waited anxiously for the report. Finally it came: the troops were the Cuban cavalry from Guá. With the reinforced cavalry, Maceo charged a large detachment of Spanish infantry entrenched behind a tangled thicket. The thicket broke the momentum of the charge, and twenty-six of the horsemen were killed in front of the barricade. Promptly the cavalry squadron reformed, and stampeting a herd of cattle in front of them, they broke through the natural barrier. Maceo immediately ordered his infantry to advance in an irregular line against the entrenched Spaniards. The battle raged at close quarters, and the troops of both sides exhibited great spirit and courage. Shouts of "*Viva Cuba libre!*" and "*Viva España*" mingled above the sound of battle.

Without giving the enemy a chance to recover, Maceo ordered another *machete* charge against the Spanish troops on the heights of Peralejo. The charge succeeded in dislodging the Spanish soldiers. Now, in full command of the heights, Maceo could survey the positions of the Spaniards. He learned that General Santocildes had died in the general attack. Now with the expectation of capturing Martínez Campos and his whole column, he reorganized his forces for a final attack. Noticing that the enemy had begun to withdraw toward Bayamo before the attack could begin and wishing to prevent their escape, Maceo ordered an encircling movement; but he was informed that the infantry of Rabí had used up its ammunition.

The Spaniards retreated more rapidly now that the Cuban infantry had ceased firing. Maceo's cavalry followed the withdrawing enemy, but Martínez Campos' rear guard kept them engaged until the main body of the Spaniards could cross the river Mabay. With darkness falling, the Spanish column headed toward Bayamo in a forced march.*[6] A few days later, Maceo sent a message to Martínez Campos, informing him that the wounded Spanish soldiers left behind on the battlefield had been lodged in the homes of Cuban families living near the scene of the conflict. He assured the Spanish General "that the forces you may send to escort them back will not meet any hostile demonstrations from my soldiers. . . ."[7]

After the battle of Peralejo, Martínez Campos took no further risks. He remained in Bayamo until a large force was assembled, and then moved to Havana.

Although Maceo did not gain the complete triumph which seemed in the offing before the battle started, he did earn a great victory at Peralejo. As Gómez noted: "The personal defeat recently suffered by General M[artínez] Campos by Maceo's troops has resulted in his loss of credit and fame, and it is my opinion that the morale of his army is deeply hurt."[8] Maceo himself informed his wife that he considered the battle—along with the one at Sao del Indio†—"superior to all of

---

* One account has it that Martínez Campos escaped alive because, knowing that the Cubans never fired upon a gravely wounded enemy, he had himself slung in a hammock and carried on the shoulders of his men. (Clarence King, "Fire and Sword in Cuba," *The Forum*, vol. XX, Sept. 1896, p. 35.)

† The battle of Sao del Indio in Oriente in the last days of August, 1895, was a victory for the Cubans. Maceo defeated the Spaniards, and, in following up the retreating Spanish troops, inflicted heavy casualties on the enemy besides capturing a large quantity of horses, ammunition, arms, and other materials. (Maceo to María Cabrales, "El Jobito," Sept. 3, 1895, Gonzalo Cabrales, *Epistolario de héroes*, Habana, 1922, pp. 82-83.)

the past war, and . . . without equal in our fight for the independence of Cuba." He closed the letter: "The final contest will be in the port of Havana, where I will be within a few months." [9]

To the Spaniards, to the world at large, and even to most Cubans, talk of fighting around Havana was just rebel propaganda. In all of the ten years of the first war for independence, the rebels had not come close to the province of Havana, much less the capital city itself. But the Cuban revolutionists, led by Gómez and Maceo, were soon to surprise everyone.

As early as June 30, 1895, Gómez informed Maceo that he should prepare for a campaign into the western provinces where the Revolution had faltered. Gómez was anxious to begin as soon as the dry weather set in, and by attacking and destroying the plantations of the West in full harvest, reduce to ashes the wealth Spain principally depended on to wage the war.[10] The "Old Chinaman"—his slanty eyes gave Gómez this nickname—declared that he could never think of beginning such an invasion without the Negro chieftain's "valuable cooperation." Maceo replied, however, that such a campaign should not be undertaken until some sort of government for the Revolution had been settled. A few weeks later, when Gómez again asked Maceo to prepare for a western invasion, the Negro commander again hesitated, this time on the ground that he first wished to accumulate the substantial amounts he was collecting from sugar, coffee, and timber interests in Oriente in return for allowing them to continue production; with this money he planned to obtain "new elements of war." [11]*

At a conference with Gómez and Maceo at La Mejorana on May 4, 1895, José Martí had proposed calling a convention of all the civil and military leaders of the Revolution to form a civil government and to elect its officials.† On that occasion, Maceo had taken a strong stand

---

* During the summer of 1895, Maceo sent more than $100,000 in money orders and promissory notes to the Delegate in New York to be used to purchase arms and ammunition. (Estrada Palma to Antonio Maceo, New York, Sept. 25, 1895, *Antonio Maceo; documentos para su vida, op. cit.,* p. 148.) A small amount of the money he received from the levies upon planters, Maceo sent to his wife, including three hundred pesos for his son's education. (*Ibid.,* p. 142.) Maceo felt he was justified in providing his family with these modest sums since none of the officers of the Liberating Army received any pay.

† Whether the plans for the invasion of the West were discussed and decided upon at La Mejorana has been a point of much disagreement among Cuban historians. There is no direct evidence in support of either side of the controversy.

for a military *Junta* until victory was achieved. ("First the war and its victory; afterwards the government and its law."[12]) Although Martí was selected as supreme leader of the Revolution abroad and in non-military matters, the issue of civil versus military control of the war was not decided. Moreover, Martí's untimely death prevented the selection of representatives to form a government. Meanwhile, the delay in forming the government made foreign recognition of Cuban belligerency almost impossible, and caused the Cuban *Juntas* in the United States, engaged, as we shall see below, in campaigning for U.S. recognition of Cuban belligerency, a great deal of concern. These *Juntas* continued to urge upon the revolutionists in the island the necessity of a formal organized government. Meanwhile, Maceo had reconsidered his position and decided that a government of some sort was necessary or was unavoidable, even though he still feared that its officials would hamper the war effort, as they had in the first Revolution, by bickering among themselves and jealousy of the military commanders.* He made it clear, however, that he did not desire and would not accept any post in the government and would not even take part in the deliberations leading to its formation.[13] Salvador Cisneros Betancourt, the old and aristocratic revolutionist who had been second president of the Republic of Cuba during the Ten Years' War, wrote to Maceo, hinting that he might offer the Negro General some high government post if Maceo supported him for President. Maceo wrote back:

> Do not forget the nature of my temperament if it should again occur to you to speak to me of posts and destinies which I have never solicited. As you well know, I have the satisfaction of never having held a post through favor; on the contrary, I have exhibited manifest opposition to the slightest suggestion of such a thing. The humbleness of my birth kept me from placing myself at the beginning on the heights with others who were chieftains of the Revolution by birth.[14]

---

* At La Mejorana, Maceo had pointed out that the weakness, dissension, petty rivalries and incompetence of the civil government during the Ten Years' War had interfered with the prosecution of the Revolution, and had ultimately contributed to the collapse of the rebellion. He had argued that, in order to avoid this error in the new rebellion, the war should be conducted under the control of a small group of the highest military leaders. Martí, on the other hand, as he had always insisted, maintained that complete military control would be a very bad precedent for a post-war independent Republic. (Foner, *op cit.*, vol. II, pp. 356-57.)

One does not have to read between the lines to understand that Maceo was reminding Cisneros that he had been born a Negro and a poor Negro at that, and that the aristocratic, wealthy Cuban revolutionists had always looked down on him with some contempt. They had also feared Maceo's rise to prominence in the Revolution as enhancing the role of the Negro people in Cuban society. Rumors had circulated widely during the Ten Years' War that the "Bronze Titan" was seeking to set up a Negro Republic in Cuba after the example of Haiti. Despite Maceo's repeated denials, these rumors and fears of a Negro Republic persisted and continued even during Cuba's Second War for Independence, especially since the number of black *mambises* was greater in this struggle than during the previous war.*

On September 13, 1895, the Constituent Assembly, composed of delegates from Oriente, Camagüey, and Las Villas, met in Jimaguayú, Camagüey, to organize the Republic of Cuba and its government. Three days later, a new Constitution was approved, with a preamble which declared that the Revolution of 1895 was a continuation of the Revolution of 1868. It was a provisional Constitution, designed to last no more than two years unless the war for independence ended before this, when a final form of government would be adopted. The Constitution provided for a president, a vice-president, four secretaries, and four sub-secretaries endowed with supreme power in the Revolution, a government council, composed of the president, vice-president and four secretaries of state, to carry on the administrative duties of the government; and for a judiciary which was independent of the other branches. The government council was to have extensive powers necessary for the prosecution of the Revolution: it was to have control of taxes, expenditures, and policies of government, and was to exercise all legislative and administrative powers. The army was nominally under the civil government, which was to issue all commissions above that of colonel. But Article IV state: "The Government Council shall intervene in the direction of military operations only when in their judgment it shall be absolutely necessary to do so to realize high political ends." Article XVIII added: "All the armed forces of the Republic and the direction

---

* In his description of the make-up of the Cuban army, Flint wrote that "half the enlisted men as you saw them together were Negroes, with here and there a Chinaman." The officers were mainly of the planter class "with a trifling percentage of Negroes and mulattoes."

of the military operations shall be under the control of the general-in-chief, who shall have under his orders as second in command a lieutenant-general, who will substitute for him in case of vacancy."

The Constitution bound all Cubans to support the Revolution actively, and required all foreigners owning property in Cuba to pay taxes for the support of the Revolution so long as their respective governments did not recognize Cuban belligerency. All debts and obligations contracted by the chiefs of the army corps for the benefit of the Revolution since the beginning of the war until the promulgation of the Constitution, would be as valid as those which hereafter the government council might contract.

The officials selected by the convention were Salvador Cisneros Betancourt, President; Bartolomé Masó, Vice-President; Tomás Estrada Palma, Delegate Plenipotentiary and foreign representative of the Cuban Republic;* Máximo Gómez, General-in-Chief of the Army, and Antonio Maceo, Lieutenant-General.[15]†

As previously noted, the Constitution gave an automatic preponderance to the General-in-Chief in practice, although theoretically his actions were subject to the approval of the government council. As one contemporary Cuban noted, the granting of great power to the military authority was "justified in part by our experience in the last war in which, to tell the truth, much importance was given to the civil element with prejudice to the military, while in a revolution like ours, it is

---

* The only election that was at all close was for the presidency of the Cuban Republic. Salvador Cisneros Betancourt and Bartolomé Masó were nominated for this office, and it was agreed that the loser would accept the office of vice-president. In the balloting, Cisneros Betancourt received twelve of the twenty votes and was thus elected to the chief executive position, while his rival, Masó, filled the second post. (Tomás Estrada Palma to John Sherman, September 14, 1897, in *Notes from the Cuban Legation in the United States to the Department of State*, 1844-1906, National Archives, and Notes on the Constituent Assembly taken by José Clemente Vivanco, Secretary of the National Council and Chancellor of the Republic of Cuba, in Tomás Estrada Palma, "Memorandum Regarding the Causes Leading to the Cuban Revolution," National Archives, Folder E1079.)

† Upon being informed that there were rumors that he resented the fact that Gómez and not he himself had been elected General-in-Chief, Maceo replied, "I was the first one in exile to give him my vote and accept his authority because I recognized, as I now recognize, his indisputable authority and because that is my temperament of order and discipline." (Emilio Roig de Leuchsenrig, *Máximo Gómez el Libertador de Cuba y el Primer Ciudadano de la República*, La Habana, 1959, p. 17.)

undeniable that the latter should direct. . . ."[16] It is one thing, however, to attempt to suppress the seeds of dissension between the civil and military authority on paper and quite another to do so in practice.* At any rate, the government was now formed, and one of the two reasons Maceo had given for not preparing to go West no longer existed. He now intensified his efforts to remove the other reason—the acquisition of funds with which to obtain the badly needed war materials.

While his brother José Maceo commanded the balance of his forces, the Negro General busied himself with the collection of taxes from property owners. On September 22 he notified Estrada Palma that he was sending him a bank draft for more than ten thousand dollars, and urged the Delegate to hurry along, in return for this money, arms and ammunition required for the coming western campaign.[17] A few weeks later, he again wrote to Estrada Palma: "Please do your best to send us, as quickly as possible, the weapons and munitions ordered, in order to enable us to fight effectively the winter battles which our enemies are preparing for us with so much ostentation."[18]

Maceo was now ready to begin preparations for the western invasion. But now a new difficulty arose. In organizing the invasion, Gómez had called for eleven hundred men for each of the two corps of Oriente—the first headed by Maceo and the second headed by Bartolomé Masó. Masó had been designated by Gómez as commander of the second corps of Oriente with responsibility only to the General-in-Chief. As was to be expected, Maceo was upset; since he was commander of the whole province of Oriente, he supposedly had authority over all the troops of the area.† But Gómez, who was notorious for

---

* "The problem," Rafael María Portuondo wrote to Gonzalo de Quesada as early as June, 1895, "will be to decide what refers exclusively to the organization and operation of the Liberating Army and what should be left to the competence of the [Governing] Council." (Portuondo to Quesada, C[uba] L[ibre], June 11, 1895, *Archivo Quesada*, vol. II, p. 156.)

† The appointment of Masó as commander of the second corps of Oriente was a repudiation by Gómez of an agreement already made. Maceo's first general order on landing in Cuba had been to designate himself as the supreme commander of Oriente. In the conference at La Mejorana, this action had been confirmed by Martí. Therefore, the designation of Masó as commander of the second corps, responsible only to Gómez, angered Maceo. (Máximo Gómez, *Diario de campaña*, La Habana, 1940, p. 437.)

overlooking the sensitivities of his colleagues, had simply ignored the difficulties that were bound to arise.*

Maceo bore no grudge against Masó; indeed, he had favored his election as president of the new government and had expressed his preference to the delegates from Oriente.[19] The Negro caudillo set about readying the forces from his own corps, and he dispatched a message to Masó advising him to do the same. Maceo was now anxious to go West, and his orders to the various units under his command instructed them to be ready to move by October 17.[20] But as the days passed, Maceo received no answer from Masó, and this soon became common knowledge to the troops, causing uneasiness in the ranks over the ability of the Invading Army to operate effectively against the enemy.[21] A further concern was that Masó's recalcitrance might encourage the troops in the insurrectionary army to pull out of the invasion since many of the soldiers were afflicted with a strong sense of localism and provincialism, and were not too happy about having to fight outside of their own areas. Since the majority of the soldiers were peasants who, in the East especially, rarely traveled more than a few miles from their homes, their reluctance to fight in a strange area is perhaps understandable. But it complicated problems in 1895 as it had done in the Ten Years' War.[22]

To meet these problems, Maceo asked for permission to send additional men from his own units and for his brother José to send additional men from his unit. José did send soldiers, but most of them had only *machetes*.[23]

As Masó continued his delaying tactics, Maceo began to suspect that the Revolution was being confronted with a situation similar to the one it had faced towards the end of the Ten Years' War, and that Masó might actually be stalling in order to negotiate peace with the Spaniards. Although there was nothing concrete on which to base this suspicion, Maceo could not forget that very early in the present war, leaders of the Central *Junta* of the pro-peace Autonomist Party, along with representatives of other political groups, had met with Masó in order to halt the conflict. The meeting had taken place at La Odiosa where the delegation tried to convince Masó of the terrible consequences

---

* Since Masó was a man of considerable importance and influence among the *insurrectos*, Gómez may have found it necessary to obtain a post for him even though he must have been aware that it would anger Maceo.

of another civil war. The latter had asked for time to consult with other revolutionary chiefs, but the entire scheme collapsed when the Spanish commander at Santiago de Cuba refused to allow further delay and ordered his troops to attack the rebels.[24] Perhaps, Maceo now reasoned, Masó was trying to delay the western invasion while negotiations for a new Pact of Zanjón (which had ended the Ten Years' War) got under way.[25]

Meeting with President Cisneros and his cabinet in the area of Baraguá, Maceo gave the government a complete account of the problem and demanded that it order Masó to send the requested troops. But the government would only agree to send an emissary to Masó ordering him to attend a conference to discuss the situation.[26] To placate Maceo, Cisneros advised him to begin his journey West with the understanding that the troops designated from the second corps would join the column en route. The Bronze Titan, as Maceo was now called,* impatient to move, agreed. On October 22 the soldiers for the invasion of the West staged a review, and the famous journey began. Five days later, the column arrived in Pestán. Here Maceo received several letters from officers of the second corps which revealed that they had not acted on Maceo's previous requests because General Masó had intercepted the messages and had not delivered them. Maceo presented these letters to the government,† and once again demanded that it act. Rafael Portu-

---

* On October 10, 1895, the anniversary of the *Grito de Yara*, which opened the Ten Years' War, was celebrated in New York's Chickering Hall. Here, as one Cuban patriot after another spoke, the feats of Antonio Maceo in Oriente were hailed, and Manuel Sanguily gave him the name "The Bronze Titan." (He also applied the name to José Maceo, Antonio's brother.) The name was applied to Antonio Maceo thereafter. In a poem written at this time, R. Silva paid the following tribute to the Negro caudillo:

> "I call him a glorious fighter
> In the arduous business of life,
> Who in the fight for his beloved country,
> Is like the iron fist of a colossus.
> Of vigorous stature, on the radiant
> Stage of Cuba, he shows
> The uplifted face of a titan. . . ."

(José L. Franco, *Antonio Maceo: Apuntes para una Historia de su Vida*, vol. III, La Habana, 1957, pp. 238-39.)

† To Maceo's annoyance, the government had decided to accompany the column. Maceo did not want the responsibility for the government's safety. (José Miró y Argenter, *Cuba, Crónicas de la guerra; las campañas de Invasión de*

ondo, Secretary of the Interior, proposed dismissing Masó from his post as commander of the second corps, but President Cisneros and the rest of the cabinet considered this proposal too drastic. They suggested waiting for Masó's answer to the order already sent by the government.[27]

The fruitless deliberations caused two days' delay in the progress of the march to West. But the arrival of new units to swell the ranks of the invading column partly compensated for the loss of time. On the third day, Masó's answer came. He could not comply with Maceo's order since he had no troops to spare for the mission. Actually, Masó felt that his orders should have come directly from the General-in-Chief, and it is probable that the whole controversy could have been prevented had Gómez issued direct orders to Masó. But Maceo, as commander of all the forces in Oriente, had felt that he had sufficient authority, and enraged by Masó's refusal, he charged him with being in communication with José Ramírez, one of the Autonomist Party leaders who had been present at the La Odiosa meeting and who was still trying to arrange peace negotiations. When the government hesitated to take action, Maceo ordered Brigadier Rabí to take command of the second corps, to send General Masó forcibly to Maceo's headquarters, and then to fulfill the quota of men requested of the second corps. The members of the government were shocked at first by the order, but finally went along and gave it their approval.[28]* Nevertheless, they still refused to order Masó's dismissal, and continued him in his office until Gómez had been consulted and had rendered a decision. This, of course, put the problem where it belonged from the beginning, but meanwhile Maceo's invading column lacked the reinforcements of the second corps.

The conduct of the government in the Masó affair naturally revived Maceo's original opinion that a weak civil government would only hamper the progress of the Revolution. This feeling was buttressed by the action of the President and his Cabinet in reversing their previous

---

Occidente, 1895-1896, Habana, 1945, vol. I, p. 98. This masterful work, written during the actual events by Maceo's Chief of Staff, is the most important account of the celebrated invasion of the West.)

  * In a letter to Estrada Palma, November 2, 1895, President Cisneros condemned Masó for sabotaging the war effort and praised Maceo for his decisive action in the matter. (Archivo Nacional.)

stand on the question of collecting contributions from the sugar producers. They now ordered that all sugar-cane grinding should be prohibited without exception, a policy which greatly disturbed Maceo, partly because he feared that the expeditions financed by contributions would be ended,* and partly because he was concerned that his reputation would be jeopardized if the properties of the producers with whom he had made agreements were destroyed.[29] Although the government, in an effort to placate Maceo, agreed to review the whole matter, the Negro General's opinion of the civil arm of the Revolution did not change for the better. He obviously still clung to the views he expressed to Martí at the conference at La Mejorana. Thus he wrote to Manuel Sanguily in the United States:

> We have not been very fortunate in the make-up of the new government. Again we have been the victims of the vain effort of trying to give it the democratic forms of a republic already constituted when we have the enemy in front of us, and we are not the masters of the land we walk on. As you will understand, while the war lasts, there must only be soldiers and swords in Cuba, or at least men who know how to prosecute the war and how to achieve the final redemption of our people. When this is achieved, which is the objective to which our efforts are directed, the time will then be ripe for the forming of a civil government. Such a civil government should be eminently democratic and be capable of managing the public affairs with prudence and moderation, attentive to our own peculiar political and social requirements.[30]

Despite the bickering over the Masó affair, Maceo was moving westward. On October 30, he wrote to Estrada Palma, "I am on the way to Las Villas province leading the invading army. The troop spirit is excellent."[31] Actually, Maceo had moved toward Las Villas earlier than he had planned. Including his staff, his personal escort, a scouting unit, and a sanitary corps, the total number of the invading column he led was 1700 men. He considered this number inadequate, and was particularly anxious to have more cavalry, for the horsemen gave the mobility required for the hit-and-run operations he had in mind, and provided the rebels with an important advantage over the Spaniards who relied primarily on foot soldiers.[32] But Maceo could not wait

---

* Actually, Maceo exaggerated the extent of supplies coming through from expeditions.

for further reinforcements. The Spaniards had learned of the invading column's plan to head for Las Villas,* and since Maceo wanted to hide his movements as much as possible, this development forced him to put the column into immediate motion.[33]

Passing from the rough terrain of Oriente into the open plains of Camagüey province, Maceo was not able to hide his movements completely from the enemy. Thus he was vulnerable to a vastly superior opponent. Counting the volunteer native units, General Martínez Campos had nearly two hundred thousand soldiers at his disposal to use against Maceo's invading column. Yet in the first ten days of November, 1895, during the passage from Oriente into Camagüey, the Cubans had only two small though intense engagements with the enemy. "I am on my way to the western province, up to now without having faced any troubles," Maceo reported to Estrada Palma on November 21.[34]

As the column entered Camagüey, Maceo received two sensational reports from President Cisneros. One was that the government of the United States had just recognized the belligerency of the Cuban Republic. The other was that an American syndicate had offered a loan of three million dollars (*Trescientos millones de pesos*) "to meet the financial expenses of the war." This news was greeted with great joy by the government and the soldiers, but Maceo was more cautious. "I have viewed it with a certain reservation due to the fact that the United States Congress is not in session [and thus could not have acted on a recognition of belligerency], and because I belong to that group of men who say, If it comes, good; if not, it's just as well." [35] However, the Negro General was highly pleased by the more tangible event of November 10. On that day, General Rodríguez brought two well-equipped regiments of cavalry to the invading column.[36]

As Maceo's column moved westward, he encountered none of the expected enemy resistance. ("In this Revolution," he wrote to his wife, "there is hardly any fighting."[37]) Actually, he moved at such speed that the Spaniards were not able to catch up with him when they tried to pursue him. Again, the Spaniards were primarily concerned over the action of Gómez on his way West through the northern part of Camagüey. Alarmed western property owners, feeling for the first time

---

* Ironically, the Spaniards learned of it because the directors of Maceo's newspaper, *El Cubano Libre*, had indiscreetly published the news.

the effects of the "man of the torch," insisted that their plantations and mills be protected at all costs. In response, General Martínez Campos ordered the Spanish forces to be concentrated in Las Villas in an effort to block any further advance by Gómez. This left the path open to Maceo to advance without meeting resistance.[38]

The Spanish strategy did not even halt Gómez's progress. But this did not come as a surprise to Martínez Campos. He had from the beginning given up all hope of preventing Gómez from moving west. On June 8, 1895, he wrote to the Minister of Overseas Affairs that while he hoped to confine Gómez to the eastern provinces, "if he wants to pass, he will pass." He based this conclusion on experiences "from the other war and a knowledge of Gómez's methods."[39]

Maceo moved forward rapidly until on November 29 he found himself only five kilometers from Ciego de Avila through which passed the *trocha* stretching from Júcaro to Morón. This *trocha*, extending from one side of the island to the other, had been an obstacle to an invasion of the West during the Ten Years' War; and now, about 16,000 troops had been brought together by Martínez Campos to bar the rebels.

The effort to cross the line began during a dense early morning fog. Maceo ordered the local cavalry forces of Camagüey to execute a diversionary maneuver against one point of the line while Maceo's invaders crossed at another. Within forty minutes the fifteen hundred men of the invading column had completed the crossing without the loss of a man. The only shots fired were at the now retreating cavalry of Camagüey. The whole operation had been so swift that the Spaniards literally had no time to bring up reinforcements.[40]

In Lázaro López, still in Camagüey, but on the western side of the *trocha* and only a short distance from the province of Las Villas, the two great revolutionary commanders, Gómez and Maceo—"the fox and the lion" as the Spaniards called them[41]—had their long-delayed reunion. Maceo had come from Oriente in the extreme East without any significant losses to the enemy; Gómez had crossed the barrier further North without any losses on his journey from Sancti Spíritus. Together, the combined invaders had a total of 2,600 men. Maceo had been appointed commander of the Invading Army by the government, and now Gómez confirmed the appointment. With the force of 2,600 men, headed by Maceo, Gómez predicted Martínez Campos would be entombed in the West. Maceo added that at the end of the campaign, the Spanish General would be discredited as a military leader.[42]

During the first night of the reunion, the *insurrectos* celebrated with song and music provided by the Military Band of the Invasion. A military march, composed by Enrique Loynaz del Castillo was dedicated to Maceo, who named it "The Invading Hymn." It opened:

> The beloved memory of Martí
> Offers honor to our lives,
> And the resplendent sword of Maceo
> Guides us to the Invader's advance. . . .[43]

On the following day, November 30, Gómez, on horseback, spoke to all the assembled forces. In a harsh, fighting speech, he declared:

> Soldiers! The war begins now; the hard, pitiless war. The weak will fall by the wayside; only the strong and the intrepid will be able to stand the ordeal. In the full ranks which I see before me, death will open great gaps. Do not expect rewards, only suffering and work. The enemy is strong and tenacious. A day which has no battle will be a day lost or ill-spent. Victory will only be attained by the shedding of much blood.
> Soldiers! Do not be frightened by the destruction of the country. Do not be frightened by death on the field of battle. *Do* be frightened by the horrible picture of the future of Cuba if, by our weakness, Spain succeeds in winning the war. . . . I predict for Martínez Campos complete destruction, which already began for him in the savannahs of Peralejo, a prediction which will be fulfilled when the invaders reach the doors of Havana with the flag of victory. Soldiers! Let us reach the furthest limits of Occidente, wherever there is Spanish blood. . . ."[44]

Immediately after the address by the General-in-Chief, the campaign of invasion began. The combined forces of Gómez and Maceo marched toward Las Villas and the West. It was the beginning of some of the most glorious pages in Cuban history.

CHAPTER IV

The Invasion of the West

THE CAMPAIGN OF INVASION began on an auspicious note. On the first day, General Gómez disposed of the Masó affair by ordering his dismissal from command of the second corps. Thus notice was given that those who repudiated Maceo's command would not be tolerated.[1] This was to prove important when the invading column passed through Las Villas, where the tradition of localism was especially strong and had hampered the plan for a western invasion in the Ten Years' War.[*] In an effort to avoid a repetition of that difficulty, General Maceo directed a proclamation to all the people of Las Villas, calling upon them to think of the nation rather than the province. "Our mission is a high, generous, revolutionary one. We want the liberty of Cuba; we long for peace and the future well-being of all our children." [2]

The first problem facing Gómez and Maceo was how to cross the province of Las Villas without dissipating the invading force in the process. The Spanish high command was determined to destroy, or at least turn back, the invading column before it could enter the three western provinces. The Spaniards wished to confine the rebels to the East at all cost, convinced that as long as the destruction of income-producing property could be limited to Oriente, the *insurrectos* could not win the war. Consequently, Martínez Campos concentrated 25,000 troops in Las Villas in addition to the forces of the various garrisons and fortified estates already there. This Spanish force, under the command of General Suáres Valdés,[†] Fernando Oliver, Enrique Luque, Leopoldo

---

[*] *See* Foner, *op. cit.*, vol. II, pp. 234-35, 253-54, 260-61.

[†] Winston Churchill received his initial experience in war as a member of General Valdés' staff. "Here then was fighting actually going on. . . . Accordingly

Garrich and García Aldave, had to operate within an area of nearly 21,000 kilometers.³

Gómez and Maceo decided that the only way to prevent a Spanish blockade or encirclement was by diversionary tactics, and that Las Villas was large enough to carry out such tactics successfully. The plan decided upon was to divide the column into two parts at Trilladeritas: one thousand in infantry, under Quentín Banderas, would penetrate the mountain range around Trinidad to the south of Las Villas, while the main body of the invasion force would continue through the center of the province. The troops under Banderas would create as much destruction and confusion as possible in order to distract the attention of the Spaniards from the main body, and would also recruit new men for the Invading Army.* After crossing the province, the two groups would reunite in Matanzas or in the province of Havana. Both groups would be guided by Gómez's basic strategy: avoid any large-scale actions with the enemy.† This could be accomplished only by remaining constantly on the move, and never giving the enemy a chance to pin the invaders down.⁴

However, in the very first encounter with the enemy, this strategy went by the board. On December 3, the main body of the invasion crossed the Jatibonico river into the populous, rich, cultivated province of Las Villas. Shortly thereafter, Gómez learned from some local peasants that a Spanish column was escorting a well-supplied convoy not far from Iguará. Gómez immediately leaped at the opportunity to surprise the enemy and capture much needed materials in the convoy, and began to deploy his forces along the road over which the Spaniards had

---

it was to Cuba that I turned my eyes," he wrote later. He received permission to join a Spanish mobile column, and after an interview with Martínez Campos, was assigned to Valdés' troops. (Winston S. Churchill, A Roving Commission: My Early Life, New York, 1930, pp. 90-99.) A Cuban historian comments that Churchill was "making his initial political-military experience by fighting against the freedom of a people from whom neither he nor his country had received any harm." (Franco, Antonio Maceo . . . , vol. II, p. 262.)

* How well Quintín Banderas succeeded in the recruiting drive is illustrated by the fact that when he rejoined Maceo two and a half months later, he brought with him 4,000 well-disciplined and fairly well-armed soldiers.

† Although Maceo accepted Gómez's strategy of avoiding large and costly battles, he did so with a certain amount of reluctance, for he was ever anxious to defeat the Spanish army in the field in a major battle. However, he adhered to the fundamental strategy throughout the entire invasion.

to pass. However, the ambush was discovered before the trap could be sprung; still, Gómez decided to fight even though the Cubans would be fighting entirely without infantry. An intense battle between the troops began. The battle of Iguará soon developed into precisely the type of action Gómez had planned to avoid. Although the Cubans finally forced the enemy to retreat to the fort of Iguará and thus scored a victory, it was a costly one. Both sides had heavy casualties—the Spaniards left eighteen dead on the field and 54 rifles, 800 cartridges and twenty fully-equipped pack mules; the Cubans lost the services of thirteen men—but the Spaniards could better afford the loss of both men and supplies.[5]

The *insurrectos* buried their dead and moved forward. (At this point the government party left the Invading Army and turned northward. Before going, President Cisneros presented the column with a war flag embroidered by the women of Camagüey and directed Maceo to carry it to the westermost part of the island.) When they came to the beautiful valley of Manicaragua, the rebels, warmly greeted by the inhabitants, decided to take a period of rest. But this was not to be, for General Fernando Oliver was pursuing them. Gómez discovered that a large number of Spanish troops were approaching. The General-in-Chief ordered his soldiers to take better positions on the nearby heights of Manacal.

On the Manacal Heights, a battle began on December 10 which lasted three days with intervening nights of rest. The Spanish force consisted of some fifteen hundred men and the Cubans had almost sixteen hundred, but the Spaniards had cavalry, artillery, and infantry while the rebels had only cavalry. Cavalry was not effective in a fixed battle, but the Cubans did not propose to stand and fight; their aim was to outmaneuver the Spaniards while continuing westward. For three days the Cubans moved on with the Spaniards in hot pursuit. Finally, the rebels erected an adequate defence position in the mountains of Quirro. At daybreak on the following morning, December 13, General Oliver began an artillery bombardment of the rebel positions. The Cubans withdrew, leaving Maceo to fight a continual delaying action with ambush after ambush against the closely following enemy. Finally, by late afternoon, the pursuing Spaniards had had enough and decided to return to their base. The victorious but tired invading column spent the night in Siguanea.[6]

During the battle of Manacal Heights, Maceo had paused long enough to issue a moving proclamation to the people of the western provinces: "The war will be hard and desolating, but that is the way tyranny wants it. Yet there is more dignity and grandeur for the people in living free though poor, than rich and comfortable in a home besmirched by servitude and hatred."[7]

The battles of Iguará and Manacal Heights had practically exhausted the rebels' supply of ammunition. Discussing this desperate lack with Maceo, Gómez seriously questioned whether the western invasion could continue without more ammunition, especially in the face of the heavy concentration of Spanish troops the invading column was certain to encounter. But Maceo refused to consider the idea of abandoning the invasion. The invasion must go on at all costs, he told the General-in-Chief, and he, for one, would march to the extreme western tip of the island even if he had to open his way with the *machete*.[8] Gómez then turned to the ever-recurring problem of whether to let the sugar mill operators grind their cane. The old Dominican stood firm behind the policy of preventing all sugar production without exception, while Maceo argued for permitting mill operators who paid for the privilege to continue grinding. In addition to the usual argument that this would provide funds for the purchase of weapons and ammunition, Maceo also argued that if the *insurrectos* could show that it was they and not the Spaniards who controlled what the operators could or could not do, the campaign to win recognition of Cuban belligerency by the United States would receive a tremendous lift.* But Gómez brushed the new argument aside just as he had done all previous justifications for a flexible sugar policy. As far as he was concerned, all arguments had to give way before the primary consideration of revolutionary strategy. Moreover, the Cubans must not count on foreign governments for the victory; the only way they could defeat the Spaniards was by waging ruthless economic warfare.[9]

Maceo had to yield to the General-in-Chief's policy that the In-

---

* Maceo had advanced this argument in a letter to Estrada Palma, November 21, 1895, in promising to make collections in the West to send the Delegate. In reply, Estrada Palma agreed that demonstrating control over the sugar operators would help the campaign in the United States to achieve recognition of Cuban belligerency. (Antonio Maceo to Estrada Palma, Nov. 21, 1895, Archivo Nacional; Estrada Palma to Antonio Maceo, New York, Dec. 10, 1895, *Antonio Maceo, documentos* . . . , *op. cit.*, pp. 158-59.)

vading Army must ocntinue setting fire to the cane fields in its path, and he yielded without equivocation.* On the day after the conference with Gómez, Maceo was the first to order the burning of the cane fields of the large sugar plantation Teresa. The garrison offered no resistance to the destruction of the property which they guarded.[10]

Despite Maceo's determination to fight clear to the western tip of the island with only the *machete* if necessary, the fact was that he, like Gómez, was worried about the serious ammunition shortage. Yet the only way at the moment to obtain ammunition was to take it from the enemy. With this in mind, the two rebel leaders decided to attack a well-supplied Spanish force in nearby Mal Tiempo. Informed that there was no ammunition for their rifles and that they had to depend almost entirely on the *machete* to win the battle, the Cuban cavalry charged with such fury and wild abandon that before the Spanish foot soldiers were aware of it, the rebels were upon them. The battle became a whirling scene of flashing *machetes* and bayonets. "It was all frenetic confusion," Gómez recalled later. "There was no one who could give orders or receive them, nor were there orders to give. The bugle would not have been heard. This type of wild attack is the explicit privilege of the Cubans." The Mauser rifles of the Spanish infantry were of little use after the rebels, disregarding their losses in the charge, engaged the enemy at close quarters. The rearing, plunging horses of the Cuban cavalry with their *machete*-wielding riders spread first confusion and then terror in the Spanish ranks. The Spaniards were soon fighting in individual duels and isolated groups. Seeking hiding places in the short cane fields, the Spanish soldiers had only one thought in their minds —to save their lives. The enemy was completely routed; those who were not killed or captured were dispersed in all directions.

The Spaniards left behind 150 Mauser and 60 Remington rifles. (With these more than two hundred rebels could arm themselves.) In addition, there were six boxes of munitions with ten thousand rounds of ammunition, horses, mules, first aid kits and other articles. Even

---

* However, Maceo was pleased to learn at this time that the government had agreed to honor those contracts which he had already negotiated in Oriente and to exempt those sugar mill operators with whom Maceo had reached agreements from the prohibition against cane grinding. But even these exceptions from the general rule could be made only if the parties concerned paid promptly the stipulated contributions. (Miró, *op. cit.*, vol. I, p. 170.)

the regiment colors and archives fell in the hands of the rebels.* All in all, the Battle of Mal Tiempo was a decisive one for the campaign of invasion. If the Cubans had not acquired the ammunition in this battle, they probably, as Gómez realized, could not have continued the western penetration; indeed, they could not even have maintained themselves in Las Villas with only the *machete*. To be sure, even this booty was not enough to support the invasion to the westernmost extremes of the island, and more would have to be acquired before that goal would be achieved. But at least the Invading Army could move forward with confidence.[11]

During the second half of December, the forces of Generals Gómez and Maceo crossed the river Hanabanilla and advanced into the province of Matanzas, fighting only minor skirmishes on the way. The Revolution had now reached the western provinces. Along the way the advancing *insurrectos* were warned by the peasants, upon whom they always depended for valuable information, that Martínez Campos was preparing unusually heavy concentrations of military units to block their advance and that he was in the field to lead them personally. Accordingly Gómez and Maceo worked out a strategy to avoid being caught in enemy pincers. To make their escape, they relied upon information supplied to them by the people in the countryside and upon their own devices for camouflaging their movements. One of the devices employed by the rebels was that of sending out wide-ranging units from the main column to set fire to all the surrounding cane fields. Thus the burning of the cane served a tactical as well as a strategical purpose, since the billowing clouds of smoke created great uncertainty as to the positions of the insurgents. Invariably the tactic was successful.[12]

For two anxious days after crossing the border into Matanzas, the invading column was accidentally divided into two parts. Maceo led one column and Gómez the other. Both were fearful that the searching Spanish forces would isolate and destroy one of the two divisions. For two days three forces were in motion: two of them were Cuban forces searching for each other, and the third was a Spanish force searching for the other. Fortunately, by an amazing stroke of luck, the

---

* Included in the archives was an order from General Martínez Campos criticizing officers for concealing Spanish losses and boasting of "victories over the Insurgents, tales I have never seen verified in the reports sent in later." (King, *op. cit.*, p. 45.)

two rebel divisions reunited on December 23 at Caliseo just before the arrival of a powerful Spanish column commanded by Martínez Campos himself.[13] The accidental encounter with the 2500 Spanish troops, headed by the Spanish General-in-Chief, threatened to destroy the reunited Cuban divisions. For before the Cubans could adjust themselves to the sudden appearance of the Spaniards, the enemy attacked with unusual fury. Concentrating intense rifle fire on the rebels, the attackers managed to create considerable confusion in the Cuban ranks. Several of the officers who formed Maceo's escort were felled in the first hail of bullets, and the Negro caudillo had his horse shot from under him. Commanding another, Maceo organized a cavalry charge in an effort to drive the enemy back. But the Spanish fire was too intense and the charge was stopped. Realizing that they were at a disadvantage and seeking to avoid a major battle,* Gómez and Maceo sounded the retreat. Martínez Campos apparently mistook the withdrawal as an attempted flanking movement, and fearing repetition of a Peralejo, he failed to follow up his advantage. Consequently the Cubans were able to disengage themselves and to withdraw.[14]

Then began the famous Cuban countermarch. After the Cuban withdrawal, the Spaniards could not immediately relocate the *insurrectos*. However, they expected them to continue through the province in a northwesterly direction toward the province of Havana, passing through the large and important towns of Cárdenas and Matanzas. Hoping to intercept and trap the *insurrectos*, they concentrated their forces in the northern part of the province.[15] To avoid the trap, Gómez and Maceo executed a brilliant countermarch which lasted five days. Instead of turning to the right or north, they turned to the left and south and then back eastward until they had once more entered the territory of Las Villas.[16] When Martínez Campos learned of this development, he jubilantly notified his government that the rebels had been blocked and forced back to the East. The danger to the West had passed! *Diario de la Marina* of Havana carried this welcome news on January 1, 1896, and the Spanish element and their sympathizers, especially the wealthy property owners of the West, greeted the New Year with huge sighs of relief and joy.

---

* General José Miró does not classify the action at Coliseo as a major battle. Instead, he lists it as a skirmish. (Miró, *op. cit.*, vol. I, pp. 224-25.)

But with their deception completed, the Cubans turned suddenly and re-entered Matanzas, moving rapidly through the southern portion of the province. On January 1, 1896, the very day in which readers of *Diario de la Marina* were rejoicing over the knowledge that the Cubans had returned to the East, the Invading Army entered Havana province. Within a few days, the readers of the pro-Spanish paper were to learn that the rebels were actually in the capital province itself.

Martínez Campos had been completely outmaneuvered. Thinking that the rebels had gone eastward, he had broken up the powerful concentration of his troops in the eastern part of Matanzas province and had dispatched a large portion of his army eastward by sea to the port of Cienfuegos, hoping to confront the *insurrectos* in that area. Meanwhile, the Cubans passed rapidly through the province of Matanzas with only moderate opposition, destroying cane fields, communication wires, railroad stations, sugar mills, and other valuable property along the way. When they entered Havana province they had left a wide smoking path of desolation clear across Matanzas.[17]

The feat of the Invading Army was unprecedented. Still, the skillful maneuver had been costly. The ranks of the *insurrectos* had been greatly thinned by casualties. Many of the wounded had to be left behind in hastily improvised out-of-the-way places like the swamp peninsula of Zapata in Matanzas. By the time of their entrance into Havana province, a number of the best officers of Maceo and Gómez had been killed or wounded. Six officers had been wounded and four killed in action around Calimente in Matanzas on December 29, and after the skirmish the column carried with it 69 wounded soldiers.[18]

The *insurrectos* more than made up their losses in the province of Havana. In seven days, the first week of the new year, they covered 172 kilometers. In these seven days they not only destroyed some of the most valuable property in Cuba, but reinforced their ranks with men and supplies. The garrison of Güira de Melena, consisting of three hundred volunteers, surrendered to the rebels after a hard fight with all of their equipment intact. In a brief speech to the prisoners, Gómez contrasted Spanish and Cuban policy:

> Spaniards! If things were the opposite way and you were the victors, not a single one of us would remain alive to tell the tale.*

---

* There is a vast literature relating to Spanish atrocities against Cuban prisoners of war, both in Spanish and English, and it would require a small

But it is the Cubans who triumphed, and neither Antonio Maceo nor I can find it in our hearts to kill prisoners of war. Both of us respect the vanquished, especially when the enemy, as you were, is courageous. So then, Spaniards, remain at complete liberty in spite of having shed our blood through a misunderstanding of your own interests. Tell your companions, the Spanish merchants, that the great Cuban Liberating Army will respect the persons and interests of those who obey and respect our Revolution. But those who oppose it will be crushed....[19]*

In Alquízar all the arms and other war supplies were turned over to the rebels without a fight, and in Ceiba del Agua the *insurrectos* camped in the streets and were welcomed with band music.[20] On January 3, Martínez Campos sent a frantic cable to the Minister of War in Madrid: "The enemy keeps advancing through the lines North and South of Havana. A numerous separatist force is in San José de las Lajas, a town situated twenty-nine kilometers from Havana. It comes destroying all. They burn the railroad stations. There are also parties

---

volume to tell the full story. It is difficult to distinguish between atrocity stories based on fact and those manufactured by writers friendly to the Cuban cause or based on hearsay and imagination. (*Cf.* George B. Rea, *Facts and Fakes About Cuba*, New York, 1897.) The same might be said of Spanish atrocities against Cuban noncombatants. However, there is evidence that an unusual number of atrocities attributed to the Spaniards were true. (*Cf.* Lee to Olney, Havana, June 27, July 22, 1896, Consular Dispatches, Department of State, National Archives, Washington, D.C. Hereinafter cited as National Archives.) Grover Flint, whose reporting was respected by the Cubans, notes that most atrocities or brutal executions committed against noncombatants were done by Spanish irregulars or by a few Spanish units commanded by particularly notorious men. (*Marching with Gómez. A War Correspondent's Field Note-Book Kept During Four Months with the Cuban Army*, Boston, 1898, p. 33.) Some atrocities were committed by irregular Cuban units over which there was not sufficient control by the regular army.

* It is clear that Gómez realized that the revolutionary policy to be followed in the West, where revolutionary enthusiasm had always been weakest, had to be more lenient than that followed in other provinces. Thus on January 10, Gómez issued a public circular announcing that the Liberating Army would respect the peaceful population and agriculture. ("Máximo Gómez to the People of the West," Havana Province, January 10, 1896, Archivo Nacional.) By following a softer policy in the West, Gómez hoped to attract more support for the insurrection in that area. The invading columns could not long maintain themselves in the West without local help, and unless western recruits and enthusiasm were forthcoming, fighting in the West would die out when and if the invading columns were withdrawn.

in Guara. Similarly insurrectionary forces are in Melena del Sur not far from Batabanó. Numerous families reach Havana fleeing from nearby villages. The panic is extraordinary...."²¹

On January 6, Three Kings' Day, the Cuban forces entered Vereda Nueva, and were received with cheers "for the Liberating Army and for the chiefs who came from far-off Oriente...." Some of the Veredanos joined the insurrectionists; others turned over arms which they had been hiding, waiting for the arrival of the rebels. The few pro-Spanish volunteers who lived in the village escaped in time, some abandoning their arms and ammunition, which were turned over to the Cuban army. A delegation even arrived from Havana to see in person the mambises and their famed leaders, Gómez and Maceo.²²

Following Vereda Nueva, in quick succession, the villages of Caimito, Punta Brava and Hoyo Colorado likewise surrendered; again there was rejoicing in the streets, and again provisions, war supplies and various types of recruits for the rebel army were received by Gómez and Maceo.²³ "What's happening is really inconceivable," cried the *Heraldo de Madrid*. "The government should know that this situation cannot be prolonged."²⁴ In Havana itself, there was unusual excitement. For the first time since the outbreak of the Revolution, the inhabitants of the capital city felt that a serious war was in progress. Heretofore the wealthy had lived their usual gay lives as if nothing unusual were happening in the island. (American correspondents upon their arrival in Havana had been amazed to find cafés, shops, places of entertainment all doing a thriving business,* and the residents of the city acting as if times were normal.²⁵) Now that the rebels were within sound and sight, there was panic in the capital and demands were made that its defenses be strengthened.²⁶

Under increasing criticism in Spain for failing to stop the rebel advance, Martínez Campos declared a state of war in the provinces of Havana and Pinar del Río "in order to repel ultimately, rapidly and energetically any aggression whatsoever and to choke off every seditious internal movement...." He also dispatched eight columns of troops to combat the rebels, and strengthened the fortifications and the warning system around the city of Havana.²⁷ But try as he might, Mar-

---
* Like other large coastal cities such as Santiago de Cuba and Matanzas, Havana was able to receive sufficient supplies by sea to offset partially restricted trade with the interior.

tínez Campos simply could not cope with the situation. For one thing, he had to comply with the insistent demands for protection raised by alarmed property owners and to set aside troops to defend their holdings. For another, Spanish units sent to pursue the rebels were too slow to cope with the fast-moving, fast-striking *insurrectos*. On top of all this was the fact that valuable information and aid was given to the rebels by the country people. Consequently the *insurrectos* were better informed than their enemy. Finally, Martínez Campos was hampered by an inability to shift his forces about quickly owing to the rebels having destroyed the swiftest means of transportation. Early in the war he had authorized the Spanish army to assume command of the railways,* and they remained theoretically in the hands of the Spanish government. But practically they were controlled by the insurgents. Nothing but armored cars got through, and soon even those could not pass because of the destruction of rails and blown-out bridges. For the same reason, telegraph lines stayed down more often than up.[28]

The final result, as De Truffin, the Russian Consul in Havana, noted in a dispatch early in January, 1896, was that Martínez Campos' strategy ended "in a sad fiasco," and the General's "prestige has been considerably shaken. . . ."[29] About this time the following song ran through Cuba:

> Martínez Campos,
> Sweeping over the mountain
> With pieces of artillery,
> Believed that Cuba would belong to Spain.
> And Maceo said to him,
> "You go away to Havana,
> And I with my Cuban troops,
> With Máximo Gómez up front,
> Will make Cuba independent
> With American gunpowder."[30]

On January 7, 1896 Gómez and Maceo arrived near the northwestern border of Havana. Here the two rebel chieftains held a strategy conference. They agreed that Maceo should take part of the Invading Army and carry the invasion into the province of Pinar del Río, while Gómez with the largest portion remained in Havana, keeping the capi-

---

* The eastern provinces of Camagüey and Oriente were not yet connected by railroad with Havana.

tal province in a turmoil and preventing the Spaniards from sealing Maceo off in the western extreme of the island.* With this policy decided upon, all the soldiers were drawn up in review and the two leaders proceeded to choose their contingents.† The one agreed upon for Maceo consisted of slightly less than fifteen hundred men. With this force he was expected to march to the western end of the island, and to maintain an active campaign in Pinar del Río. It was an indication of Gómez confidence in the brilliant Negro General that he was given the difficult assignment of completing the invasion of the western provinces.[31]‡

But the Spaniards spread the word that Gómez had deliberately sent Maceo into Pinar del Río with a limited force "so that he might fall into a trap"; that Maceo resented this, and that a serious split had developed between the two generals. When the correspondent of the Washington *Star*, then in Cuba, asked Maceo if there was any foundation to the Spanish story, Maceo wrote to the editor of the paper:

> In the first place, there could not exist such a disagreement, a split as you wish to call it, between General Gómez and myself. He is the General-in-Chief and his laws are, as laws, accepted and respected by me. I am only the Lieutenant General of the Army, and at all times, and in whatever place and for whatever reason, I am subject to his orders. Our army is not composed of riff-raff

---

* At a previous conference after entering the territory of Havana, Gómez and Maceo agreed that the latter should take steps to reorganize and strengthen his depleted forces. Maceo then sent General Serafín Sánchez back to Las Villas to take charge of the war of devastation in that area, and he dispatched an order to General "Mayía" Rodríguez in Camagüey to bring a picked force of 200 men to Havana without delay. Finally, Maceo sent Colonel Roberto Bermúdez ahead with a small but well-armed force to act as a scouting and organizing unit. Bermúdez was ordered to enlist recruits, to destroy properties, to choose locations for making camp, to discover where supplies and arms could be obtained most easily and to collect any other information that might prove to be valuable. (Miró, *op. cit.*, vol. I, pp. 314-20.)

† An eyewitness at the conference described Maceo as "carefully groomed, neat, impeccably dressed in coarse linen, elegant, extremely clean . . . and mounted on a superior sorrel-colored horse of large build. . . ." Gómez was "a gloomy little old man, dried up, thin, with a white goatee and mustache, and seated on a little white mule of slight build. . . ." (Benigno Souza, *Máximo Gómez, el generalísimo*, La Habana, 1936, p. 238.)

‡ Another indication of Gómez's great respect for Maceo was the fact that he appointed the latter Chief of the Invading Army, Chief of the Western Department, and Chief of the Sixth Corps.

in which the man who shouts the loudest is the chief. It is organized under a plan of a modern military force in which order and discipline are maintained, and superiors are respected. But apart from the rules of military discipline, there is not a soldier in the Cuban army who for one instant would disobey the orders of Máximo Gómez. The whole army trusts implicitly his patriotism and his military ability. We who have known him and followed him in other wars are convinced of our comparative smallness compared to his knowledge and rectitude.

With respect to the assertion that he assumed the command and left for the province of Havana, abandoning us . . . in the "quagmire," I have nothing to say about this. We have our campaign plans in the Cuban war and it is not necessary for the whole world to know about them. The Spanish government would love to know why . . . we make certain moves and do not make others. When the Spanish authorities cannot see a plausible reason in some important movement of the rebel forces, they immediately invent some agreeable theory and throw it out to the four winds. However, we have no complaint if they receive some satisfaction from this, nor does it disturb us. We let them enjoy their theories. . . . Still they do not realize that they are making themselves ridiculous in the eyes of the world because what could people of good sense believe who, having read the official Spanish dispatches saying that the Revolution was insignificant, on the following day read in the newspapers that in Spain more troops were reembarking to reinforce the army of more than 100,000 men that they have here. . . .[32]

With his force of 1,500 men Maceo set out for Pinar del Río. He did not, however, move in the due West direction which was the shortest route to his destination. Instead, Maceo went on a reconnoitering mission in the northwest corner of Havana province and to the very outskirts of the capital city itself. The mission had two purposes: one was to search for the weakest points of the *trocha* across the narrow coast of the island near the border of the two western provinces, and the other was to determine if he could successfully invade the suburbs of the city of Havana.[33] Maceo, a keen student of public opinion, was aware that the whole world would sit up and take notice if the Liberating Army could put on a convincing demonstration within the suburbs of Havana and offer a serious threat to the capital city of the island. It was the sort of daring, spectacular venture which most appealed to Maceo.[34]

In scouting the possibilities of invading Havana, Maceo approached the city from along the western coast, passing by the beach of Baracoa and going as far as the edge of Marianao, the principal suburb of Havana. But there he learned that the city was too heavily garrisoned and fortified to afford even the calculated risk of an attack by a force so small as the one he commanded. In fact, it was only by skillful maneuvering that Maceo was able to prevent the entrapment of his troops. The Spanish General Prats had discovered Maceo's presence, and he tried energetically to pin him against the ocean between the beach of Baracoa and Havana. Maceo managed to escape the trap only after fighting a vigorous running battle with the Spanish troops, and at the cost of several wounded, including the serious wound suffered by Colonel Francisco Pérez Carbó, his chief of dispatch. When the Spaniards had been outdistanced, Maceo stopped at the sugar mill Luisa, whose owner, Señor Perfecto Lacoste, was sympathetic to the Revolution. There Colonel Pérez Carbó and the other wounded rebels were left to receive medical attention.[35]

Señor Lacoste told Maceo that the story making the rounds in Havana was that "if you pass the *trocha* of Mariel you will be greater than Hannibal." To this the confident General replied, "I do not know where that fortified line is, but give me tomorrow and I will be situated in Pinar del Río."[36] Of course, Maceo not only knew the exact location of the *trocha* of Mariel, but he had already figured out exactly how to pass through it. He knew that this *trocha*, like the others in the system, was surrounded by thick wooded areas, undergrowth and swamps, so that his troops could creep near the line before making their charge. (On an open terrain the Spaniards would have been able to detect his approach in advance.) Moreover, Maceo knew that he would have well-informed guides who would lead him to where the Spaniards would least expect him.* As good as his word, on the next day January

---

* When one considers the thoroughness with which the *trochas* were constructed, one wonders how the rebels could have passed through them with such apparent ease. Especially is this true of the line now facing Maceo, constructed between Havana and Pinar del Río provinces, the narrowest part of the island. Well-informed guides were vital to the rebel success. An American who actually crossed most of the western *trocha* explained how his small Cuban party accomplished the feat. From his experience the most important requirement for success in this endeavor was a well-chosen guide. This man needed to be so familiar with

8, Maceo passed through the trocha and was camped in Pinar del Río, Cuba's most western province.[37]

The Spanish authorities were not at first too alarmed by the news that Maceo was in Pinar del Río. For one thing, they were confident that they had only to concentrate enough troops, out of the nearly two hundred thousand men available in the narrow confines of Pinar del Río to crush the 1500 rebels led by Maceo.[38] For another, they were convinced that their propaganda would turn the people of Pinar del Río against the *insurrectos*. Spanish propaganda pictured Maceo as a crude, barbaric caudillo of the Negro people, who delighted in all sorts of barbarous practices forbidden in the recognized rules of warfare. Moreover, the Spaniards made ample use of the fact that Maceo was a Negro, and they hammered away at the theme that he was leading an invasion of predominantly Negro troops from the East who were bent on subjecting the white Cubans of the West to a reign of terror, rape, pillage and murder, with the ultimate objective of establishing in the island a Negro Republic headed by Antonio Maceo.[39]

Yet on both points the expectations of the Spaniards were not fulfilled. Maceo, by following a zigzag course through Cuba's western province, avoided contact with the superior forces pursuing him. Nor were the peasants of Pinar del Río frightened by the picture drawn by Spanish propagandists of the Invading Army and its leader. On the contrary, whenever news spread that Maceo was in the vicinity, group after group of peasants travelled miles by horseback just to see, speak to, and shake hands with the most celebrated and most fabled of all the *insurrectos*,[40] who had come all the way from Oriente, defying, defeating and humiliating Spain's best generals—generals in the military traditions of Europe, leading over two hundred thousand troops, with the finest rifles and unlimited war materials at their command. For the Negro peasants the opportunity to meet Maceo was the fulfillment of a life's dream. For Maceo was the idol of the colored people of Cuba and their acknowledged leader.

If the Spaniards believed that Maceo's march would be halted by resistance from the towns of the province, they were speedily disillu-

---

the area that an isolated spot could be selected at a time when no Spanish patrols were passing. (Flint, *op. cit.*, pp. 112-13.)

Later, as we shall see, the *trochas* were greatly strengthened, and passage was not simple, especially for large groups.

sioned. Time after time as Maceo's column approached a town, the municipal officials, either because of sympathy of the populace with the Revolution or because the wealthier citizens were anxious to avoid the expected pillage and destruction, gave him the keys to the community. In the few cases where the towns did not throw open the gates to him, Maceo sent a note to the authorities informing them what they could expect if his troops were not supplied with arms, ammunition, and supplies. Usually he got what the locality had to offer, for only strongly fortified and garrisoned municipalities could afford to resist the rebel chieftain.

Although Maceo burned some towns which resisted,* he proved that the Spanish propaganda depicting him as a ruthless conqueror was false. Realizing that the people of Pinar del Río were afraid that his troops would "destroy their tobacco harvest," Maceo saw to it that the column avoided passing through tobacco fields since their "passing through would have ruined them."[41] He countered the Spanish propaganda picturing him as a Negro leader bent on dominating the white population, by exercising extreme care in dealing with civilians and requiring iron discipline of his own troops. Whenever Maceo's column was welcomed into a town, the residents were surprised by the discipline of the troops. Maceo permitted no plundering, and his orders were followed to the letter.[42]†

"In Guane," wrote General José Miró in his famous account of the invasion, "no farms were destroyed nor were any commercial establishments occupied. No one was denied a safe conduct or the necessary documents for goods, and all work tools were

---

* Fifty-nine known towns in the four western provinces were burned and destroyed during the invasion of the West. Most were burned for resisting attacks or because they were being used as depots of supplies for Spanish troops. In some cases, like that of Cabañas, the Spanish troops demolished the towns to prevent the *insurrectos* from occupying them. (Gonzalo de Quesada, *The War in Cuba: The Struggle for Freedom*, Washington, 1896, p. 156.)

† An earlier example of Maceo's discipline occurred on December 27, 1895 in Las Villas during the famous false retreat from the West. Four of Maceo's soldiers invaded the home of the Colonel of the Spanish Volunteers, and when they threatened the family, the Colonel killed one of the rebels. The Colonel was brought before Maceo with the expectation that he would be executed. But when Maceo learned the facts of the incident, he congratulated the man who had killed one of his soldiers and ordered the three surviving *insurrectos* to be shot. The Liberating Army, he made it clear, must respect family homes. (Miró, *op. cit.*, vol. I, p. 259.)

respected. . . . Men of the highest importance talked with Maceo, measuring and admiring him, surprised to find themselves in his presence, and even more astonished that he was an affable and kindly man. . . ."[43]

During his two day stay in Guane, Maceo ordered that the municipal funds be used to pay the back salary of teachers of primary schools.[44]

On January 22, 1896, the ultimate goal of the Campaign of Invasion was achieved. Maceo's column left Guane in the morning, and at three in the afternoon arrived at Mantua, the westernmost town in the island of Cuba. The Invading Army was met on the outskirts of the town by an official body, headed by the Mayor. General Miró continues the story:

> One hour later, at four in the afternoon, the Liberating Army made its triumphal entry into Mantua, the last Spanish bulwark of the far West. . . . The glorious campaign of invasion was ended, and the wishes of our famous caudillo [Maceo] were fulfilled. . . . In the column entering Mantua, with the bells of the town tolling, there came men from the Sierra Maestra; from Bayamo; from Santiago de Cuba; from Manzanillo; from Holguín; from Mayarí; from Guantánamo, and from Baracoa. What an achievement! These men had changed horses in Camagüey, in Las Villas, in Matanzas, in Havana, and on the highway of Pinar del Río. . . . Only Maceo, first soldier of America, only he, audacious warrior, intrepid captain, tireless soldier, always in the lead, could have opened the road to victory and imposed his indisputable authority on these men from the Sierra of Guantánamo and the pine groves of Mayarí, wild and brave men like the peaks of these mountains.[45]

People congregated in the streets of Mantua to see the fabled caudillo and his soldiers, and Maceo, aware of the historic occasion, had his troops form a parade to make a grand entrance into the town. Aware also of local feelings, he wisely accorded his newly formed cavalry of natives of the province the honor of leading the procession. Immediately behind the cavalry of Pinar del Río, at the head of his veterans, came the proud General mounted on a splendid horse, stiffly erect, and as always perfectly groomed.[46]

Many Mantuans joyously greeted the Liberating Army, but the Volunteers and other Spanish sympathizers had fled the town, convinced that their lives would be extinguished and property confiscated by the

"Negro Devil." Maceo immediately dictated an order to his troops designated to maintain public order and respect for the lives and property of all classes. He also commissioned one of his officers to go to the neighborhood to which the frightened Mantuans had fled, and authorize them "to return to their homes with their arms or without them, with the security that they would not in the least be molested by any Cuban force." He urged them, moreover, "to dedicate themselves to the care of their families, separating themselves from their political work in which they had served to sustain an iniquitous and shameful enemy government. . . ." All returned to their homes and 50 rifles and more than 4,000 cartridges were turned over to Maceo.[47]

Those who had been taken in by Spanish propaganda were astounded by Maceo's behavior. Describing one scene, Miró writes: "The most important of the Spanish sympathizers, fearing Maceo and observing him carefully, were very surprised to find him conversing freely with them, and they appeared even more amazed at his fine manners and agreeableness. He spoke to them [about the Revolution] without reference to origins or opinions, all the while trying to draw them over to the cause of the Revolution, but without the slightest inferences of offense."[48]

On January 23, 1896, official ceremonies were held during which a document was signed by representatives of all classes in Mantua, the Parish priest and the heads of the Invading Army. It read in part:

> First, that the town of Mantua is situated at the extreme West of the island in the province of Pinar del Río.
> Second, that General Maceo, with the forces at his command, has occupied the town and municipal terminal: lives and goods of all kind having been respected by his troops, public order having been kept, and the authorities and employes which the Spanish government had placed there having been left in the exercise of their functions, and that the proceedings of the Liberating Army and its chief . . . will redound not only to the benefit of this region, previously impoverished by multiple exactions of which it has been the victim, but also to the benefit of the whole country which has been suffering from the same bad treatment. . . .

Following the signing of the document, the Mayor offered a champagne toast to Maceo. The General graciously declined the glass offered him, saying, "I do not drink any kind of liquor." Offered a cigar from

Vuelta Abajo, the area which produced the best tobacco in the world, he again graciously refused, stating, "I am sorry not to be able to please you, but I do not smoke." [49] On that note, the official ceremonies marking the final achievement of the great invasion of the West ended.

Writing to his wife, María Cabrales, Maceo noted with deep satisfaction: "The Invasion which here and abroad was thought impossible* has been realized and without great difficulties and with few losses despite hard fighting every three days." [50] In ninety days and in 78 marches from Baraguá to Mantua, the Invading Army had covered 1,696 kilometers; 27 battles were fought; 22 important towns taken; more than 2,000 rifles, 80,000 rounds of ammunition, and 3,000 horses captured; and in Mantua, two mountain cannons acquired. All this was accomplished by a few thousand devoted Cuban patriots, without help of any kind from outside the country, against an enemy who, in these three months, according to the official report of the Ministry of War in Madrid, had in Cuba 124 infantry battalions, 40 squadrons of cavalry, 16 batteries of field artillery, 6701 general and other officers, 183,571 individual line troops and more than 60,000 volunteers and guerrillas, a navy which controlled the coast, and an elaborate "system of defenses and trochas thought up by expert military engineers." [51] What is more, the last part of the invasion took place in areas favorable to the Spaniards. As De Truffin, the Russian Consul in Havana, correctly noted in a dispatch on January 8, 1896, "The part of the island which the insurgents have just captured is a vast cultivated plain without any forest at all. In these conditions the enemy who moves in columns of 2,000 or 3,000 men each, apparently ceases to be elusive. Nevertheless he is not routed, and apart from a few skirmishes in which he lost less than a few hundred men, nothing prevented him from advancing and leaving a trail of ruins. . . ." [52]

All told, the Campaign of Invasion was a remarkable achievement.

---

* The invasion of the West received much attention in the world press, and newspapers of many countries reported the progress of the *insurrectos* from Oriente to Pinar del Río. Editorially, the papers had expressed considerable doubt over the ability of the Invading Army to achieve its goal. With the success of the campaign, the fame of the Cuban rebels spread throughout the world, especially that of Maceo. Picasso recalls that Maceo was so famous that even children in Málaga, Spain, would assume his name when playing soldiers. (Interview with Juan Marinello, who received this information from Picasso.)

One military historian has compared it with "Hannibal in Italy, and the marches of San Martín, Sherman and Napoleon."[53] Clarence King, a leading American geologist and student of military history, describing the invasion in an article published in the *Military Review* of Brussels, called it "the most audacious military feat of the century."[54]*

While the invasion campaign as a whole gained worldwide admiration, the operation conducted by Maceo in Pinar del Río won special praise. Even the Spaniards themselves were amazed. Juan Ortega y Rubio, the Spanish historian, wrote: "Our historical impartiality obliges us to say that the campaign carried out by Antonio Maceo in the province of Pinar del Río is a glorious page in the history of that valiant caudillo.... With extraordinary activity and pursued always by our columns, Maceo went from one end of the province to the other...."[55]

Five days after the official ending of the invasion in Mantua, Maceo replied to a question posed by the Washington *Star* as to what had been accomplished by the campaign. "Much," he wrote. For one thing, the rebels had been able to march from the eastern end of the island to the other end "without a single hitch," proving to the Cuban people and to the world that Spain's boast that the Revolution had been crushed was a myth. Then again, they had shattered the Spaniards' bragging that the system of *trochas* would keep the Revolution confined to the eastern provinces and doom it to an early death. "We crossed them and rendered them useless forever." Furthermore, the revolutionary cause had gained numerous new supporters. "Since we reached this province, the Cuban army strength has grown twenty-five per cent in other areas. Ten thousand patriots have been recruited to our flag...." Unfortunately, the Liberating Army simply did not have enough arms for all who offered their services; indeed, as many as 35,000 men could have been recruited in the provinces of Havana and Matanzas alone. "But we lack sufficient arms to give them, and it is useless to say that we have them, since we do not gain anything throwing out boasts like the Spaniards. Our soldiers are not well armed by

---

* Clarence King wrote several accounts of the Campaign of Invasion based on material furnished him by General José Miró. One published in *The Forum* (vol. XX, Sept. 1896, pp. 31-52) had the title, "Fire and Sword in Cuba." The only biography of King (*Clarence King* by Thurman Wilkins, New York, 1958) says nothing of this aspect of his work. Nor does it do justice to King's great sympathy for the Cuban Revolution.

any measure. If they were, there would exist today not a single Spanish column outside of the cities of Havana, Matanzas and Santiago de Cuba." Nevertheless, the invasion had improved the *insurrectos*' capacity for fighting, and had demonstrated for all to see that the war could never be won by Spain.

As Maceo put it:

> It might last a few months or several years, I cannot say. But what is certain is that the red and yellow rag of Spain will never wave again over a Cuba enslaved. Cuba must be free. This oppressed people has consecrated its life to the work of emancipation, and God in heaven will strengthen its arm.[56]*

---

*In 1958 Fidel Castro commissioned his companion in arms, the hero of Sierra Maestra, Camilo Cienfuegos, to duplicate the legendary invasion by Antonio Maceo of the western province of Cuba. He named the column entrusted to Cienfuegos, "Antonio Maceo."

CHAPTER V
Weyler Versus Maceo

ON JANUARY 7, 1896, Martínez Campos resigned his post as Captain General of the island of Cuba. The Spanish government, furious over his failure to crush the *insurrectos*, agreed to accept his resignation, and announced the appointment of General Valeriano Weyler y Nicolau as his successor.* Sabas Marín became the acting Captain General until Weyler's arrival from Spain.

When General Maceo heard the news of Martínez Campos' resignation, he could not hide his emotion. The man who had defeated the revolutionists in 1878 had now been defeated completely by his old adversaries. Nothing could have demonstrated so completely to the world the strength of the Revolution as the failure of Spain's ablest general to subdue it with the great numbers placed at his disposal.[1] He also saw another advantage for the Revolution in the turn of events. Since Martínez Campos resigned in the midst of a great clamor in Madrid for sterner measures against the *insurrectos*, a more ruthless policy could now be expected from the Spaniards, especially since the man designated to apply this policy was General Weyler, who had gained a reputation for harsh military policies during his two years'

---

* Martínez Campos observed that he had been forced out of Cuba by "corner grocers" who wanted "the repetition of horrors, such as they asked for under these balconies, when they demanded the shooting of the students." ("Remarks made by Martínez Campos on his Departure," Williams to Uhl, January 21, 1896, U.S. Consular Despatches, Havana, National Archives.) The reference is to the eight medical students from the University of Havana who were executed in 1871. (See Foner, *op. cit.*, vol. II, p. 225.)

service as a subordinate general in the Ten Years' War.* Maceo felt that the new Spanish policy of repression might be beneficial to the revolutionists since it would force the autonomists and other Cuban neutrals to choose sides. In the type of war Weyler could be depended upon to launch—a war of extermination—there could only be Cubans and Spaniards. Now at last there was little prospect of a peace offensive such as might have been expected under Martínez Campos; this, Maceo feared, would have met with favorable response from the faint-hearted just as it had in the last stage of the Ten Years' War. Now there could only be total war![2]

Ever the daring warrior, Maceo was anxious to show the world that he could stage a demonstration at the very gates of Havana at the precise moment of the arrival of General Weyler. While en route to putting on his demonstration at the edge of Havana, Maceo looked forward to the opportunity of clashing with the enemy in a major battle even though this meant forsaking Gómez's basic strategy of avoiding large and costly engagements. Not only did he long to defeat the Spanish army in the field, but he believed that if he could win an important victory before reaching Havana, he would deliver a crushing blow to Spanish morale, already sagging as a result of the triumphant invasion of the West.[3]

Unknown to Maceo, however, his decision to engage the enemy directly coincided with a change in Spanish tactics. With the departure

---

* Upon the news that Weyler was to replace Martínez Campos, the following sonnet made the rounds of Cuba:

> "He has a face like a reptile, the
>   body of a dwarf,
> The instinct of a jackal, the
>   soul of a dog.
> Hypocrite! Coward! Vile and
>   obscene!
> Ruin, desolation, hunger and misery
> Are the works which this
>   horrible heap of vileness
>   dares to perpetrate.
> And it is such a monstrosity
>   whom Spain, with treacherous intent, puts
>   in charge of Cuba as the
>   nineteenth century expires."
>
>   (Emilio Roig de Leuchsenring, *Weyler en Cuba*,
>   La Habana, 1945, p. 175.)

of Martínez Campos, more Spanish columns were operating in the field on the offensive, and under persistent prodding from the home government, they were demonstrating more aggressiveness. This was to complicate Maceo's plans to achieve a decisive victory.

After an unexpected and unplanned encounter with the Spaniards at Paso Real in which the Cubans drove the attackers off after hard fighting, but sustained losses they could not well afford,* Maceo moved to attack and capture Candelaria, one of the two important fortified towns on the railroad line from the West. (The other was Artemisa.) Here Maceo hoped to obtain his important victory, and he launched a savage attack on the town. His determination to capture the town increased when he learned that many of its defenders were Cuban Negroes fighting with the Spaniards. Nothing infuriated Maceo more than to have his own people fighting with the oppressors of Cuba and while such cases were not frequent, they enraged the Negro General when he encountered them. Maceo, abandoning his usual chivalrous regard for enemy prisoners, gave the order for all the Negro defenders to be killed by the *machete* when Candelaria fell. Since his attitude toward them was well-known, the Negroes fighting inside the town put up a ferocious defense. Just at the point when the stubborn defense of the town was about to be overcome, strong enemy reinforcements arrived from Artemisa. The rebels were forced to retreat after twenty-six hours of intense fighting.[4]

Compelled to leave the scene at Candelaria, Maceo laid a trap for the Spanish column which had frustrated his chance to capture the fortified town. His plan was to catch the troops by surprise when they returned to Artemisa. It worked well and Maceo was again at the point of a decisive victory when Spanish reinforcements arrived on the scene. Furious at the prospect of having victory snatched from his grasp twice, the Negro caudillo refused to leave the scene of battle even in the face of mounting odds. Not even when his horse was shot from under him and he himself suffered a bullet wound in the right leg would he stop fighting. Mounting a new horse, whose fine performance

---

* The Spaniards suffered one hundred killed and wounded, and General Luque, the Spanish General, was seriously wounded. However, the Cubans lost fifty-five killed and wounded, and while their losses were less than the Spaniards, the latter were quite willing to trade losses at this ratio. (Miró, *op. cit.*, vol. II, pp. 27-35; Franco, *op. cit.*, vol. III, pp. 69-70.)

caused him to name the animal "Liberator," Maceo continued to lead personally repeated *machete* charges. With nightfall both sides ceased fighting, and the battle was over. The Spaniards left seventeen dead on the field of conflict in addition to the many wounded whom they carried away with them, but the Cubans this time had suffered more losses than the enemy. Maceo's determined stand, in the face of superior numbers and firepower, was an indication of his great courage. But it had been costly. During the battle his alarmed officers had agreed that prudence dictated a rapid retreat. But, as General José Miró later reported in his account of the battle, no officer dared to question Maceo's decisions while in the midst of a battle.

Before Maceo could move toward Havana, he learned that Weyler had already landed on February 10. The planned demonstration before the arrival of the new captain general had to be shelved. (Actually, the recent losses in battle, the shortage of ammunition, and the increased concentration of Spanish troops around the capital, had made the planned demonstration unreasonable.) None the less, Maceo led his column toward Havana determined to show the world that he was active in the vicinity of the capital despite the vaunted Weyler with his long and imposing military record.[5]*

As Maceo had predicted, the arrival of the notorious General Weyler initiated a new phase of Spanish military strategy. Weyler had only contempt for what he called "the benevolence" of Martínez Campos, and believed that he should have been selected to deal with the insurrection in the first place.[6] He decided to make up for lost time. While he continued the *trocha* policy and the holding of garrisoned towns and forts, he determined to remove one of the chief obstacles facing Spanish forces in cornering and annihilating the rebels—the aid the insurrectos received from the Cuban peasants. Reasoning that when there would be no large groups of country people to provide information to the rebels, as well as to assist them in other ways, Spanish forces would materially improve their own freedom of movement, Weyler decided that the peasants had to be removed from the countryside. He decided, too, that with the peasants gone, the rebels ought not to have the food products and other supplies remaining in the countryside;

---

* In addition to having served in the Ten Years' War in Cuba, Weyler had participated in the Santo Domingo campaign of 1865, the Carlist Wars, the Moorish war and the Philippine insurrection.

hence he initiated a campaign to destroy all crops, cattle, horses, empty houses, and all other materials which might furnish aid to the *insurrectos*.

Immediately after his arrival, Weyler issued innumerable proclamations touching nearly every phase of life in Cuba. The most important were embodied in the infamous *reconcentración* or reconcentration order. By this decree, all inhabitants outside of the fortified areas were given eight days to move into the towns occupied by the troops; the transport of food from one place to another was forbidden; all cattle were to be brought to the towns, and all people were to congregate in designated areas. The proclamation closed with an offer of clemency for insurgents who surrendered before the lapse of eight days, provided they brought in their arms and furnished information concerning the rebels.[7]*

The conditions and effects of these concentration areas will be discussed thoroughly below;† here it is only necessary to point out that Weyler's scheme, which was to earn him the name "Butcher," was brutal, and as Maceo had predicted, brought a total war, a war of extermination to Cuba.‡

Weyler reorganized the Spanish army in Cuba immediately after his arrival. He divided it into three corps and improved the Spanish

---

* The policy outlined in Weyler's orders was not applied immediately to the entire island. The first order named only the provinces of Oriente and Camagüey and the jurisdiction of Sancti Spiritus. (Valeriano Weyler y Nicolau, *Mi Mando en Cuba*, Madrid, 1910, vol. II, pp. 427-28.) The second concentration order of October 21, 1896 designated only the province of Pinar del Río. In practice, however, an effort was made from the beginning to apply the *reconcentrado* policy to the entire rural population of Cuba.

† See below, pp. 110-18.

‡ Many Spanish and American historians have justified Weyler's policies with the argument that he was applying a military strategy already put into practice by Máximo Gómez, was simply fighting fire with fire and outmaneuvering the rebels at their own game. But this ignores the fact that while he did move some women and children into the hills from towns, Gómez's policy was basically directed against an economy and not against individuals, against property not people, and that when they entered the western provinces, the rebels took care to protect the lives of the inhabitants of all towns they conquered, even those of the Volunteers and other Spanish sympathizers. Weyler's policy, on the other hand, made no distinction between people and property, and none between those who aided the rebels or were neutral. Certainly, the *insurrectos* did not prohibit anyone, least of all old people, women and children, from working the soil and keeping cattle in order to feed themselves.

Intelligence Service. Nevertheless, he did not abandon the primary defensive nature of Spanish strategy in the war. Spanish forces were still concentrated in the cities, towns, fortified areas, and especially along the *trochas*. Instead of placing his huge forces into the field, he sent relatively small task units in search of the rebels.[8] His fundamental aim was to compress the insurgent forces in the western provinces into a small area and then smash them against the anvil of the *trocha*. This process was then to be repeated between the western and eastern *trocha*, and finally with the enemy confined to the extreme East, the whole Spanish army could overpower him by sheer weight of numbers. All the time, meanwhile, the *reconcentrado* policy would work to deprive the rebels of support from the peasants, destroy their source of information and life, and by the misery created among them, diminish the will of the Cuban people to resist.[9]

On February 19, two days after Weyler issued his orders, Gómez and Maceo met in Soto. Discussing Weyler's decrees, both agreed that the plain people would now fully appreciate what Spanish rule meant and the importance of the rebel fight to overthrow it. (A few days before, Maceo had written to his wife, "The importance of the Campaign of Invasion had been understood by the foreigners and the Spanish militarists, but not by the plain people."[10]) Both agreed, too, that for the time being they must avoid encounter with the concentration of troops which Weyler was forming against them in that part of Havana. Both columns, therefore, should re-enter Matanzas and operate in that region.[11]

In fulfillment of this plan, General Maceo marched northward and General Gómez went southeastward through Havana toward Matanzas. According to agreement between the two commanders, Gómez would operate in the central provinces of the island and Maceo would continue to carry on the war in the western provinces. In neither area, and particularly the West, could the revolutionists afford to allow inactivity. Maceo's immediate assignment in this plan was to detract attention from the column under the command of Gómez. On February 23, Maceo was already operating in the province of Matanzas. The following day, his forces camped at the sugar mill *La Perla* in the valley of Guamacaro. Here they observed the first anniversary of the Revolution in a simple celebration.[12]

Maceo's disappearance from the province of Havana immediately produced a rumor that the Negro General was dead. But in the action at *La Perla* on February 25, the Spaniards sorrowfully learned that, like previous rumors of Maceo's death,* this was not true. Two days later, Maceo joined the cavalry regiment of General Francisco Aguirre at Cayajabos. After reviewing Aguirre's well-armed cavalrymen, the two Generals sat down to exchange information and discuss the progress of the war. Aguirre informed Maceo that since Weyler had assumed command, atrocities and war crimes had increased sharply, and that "mass acts of barbarism were committed daily by Weyler's troops." Enraged by this news, and "realizing the direction the war was going to take," if Weyler's policy was not reversed, Maceo wrote an open letter to the Spanish commander-in-chief.[13] He began by asserting that he had at first believed that the reports of atrocities and crimes committed at Weyler's command were being spread by enemies of the Spanish General. He had therefore expected Weyler "to give the solemn lie to your detractors," and to adopt toward the wounded and prisoners of war "the generous system followed from the beginning by the forces of the Revolution with the Spanish wounded and prisoners of war." But this was not to be. Not only had he learned of massacres of the wounded and prisoners of war, but that even civilians were being treated savagely. He went on to warn Weyler that while, in the interest of humanity and in keeping "with the spirit of the Revolution," he would never "take reprisals which would be unworthy of the prestige and strength of the Liberating Army," nevertheless "at the same time, I warn that such abominable conduct on the part of you and yours will provoke in the not too distant future, private vengeance which will be practiced without my being able to prevent it, even though hundreds of innocents may suffer from it."

Hence Maceo urged Weyler to reverse his policy and "reprimand with a severe hand those deeds, if they were committed without your sanction. In any case, avoid the shedding of a single drop of blood outside of the field of battle. Be kind to all those unfortunate noncombatants, and we shall proceed in the same way." [14]

Maceo's moving appeal was wasted on the Spanish General. An

---

* As early as May, 1895, the Spaniards spread reports that Maceo had been killed in battle. These reports continued, the only new touch being added was that the frequently-deceased General had committed suicide.

era of terrible human misery descended upon Cuba, and the Revolution rapidly grew into total war.

Confident that his policies would produce the desired results, Weyler, late in February, publicly prophesied that the province of Pinar del Río would soon be completely pacified, and he assured the sugar producers that they could begin grinding cane.[15] Maceo, as he phrased it, could not allow "Weyler's dreams to come true"; consequently, he issued orders for the destruction of all sugar crops in the two westernmost provinces. In a report to Estrada Palma in New York, he pointed out that he had to take this extreme step "and spread the necessary terror so that plantation owners are sufficiently frightened and do not develop their sugar crop." Maceo carried out his own orders; returning to Havana province, he created a wide path of destruction of sugar plantations and mills everywhere he passed. After making a devastating circle through the province of Havana, Maceo returned to Matanzas on March 5, 1896, outmaneuvering a powerful column which Weyler had sent against him.[16]

On March 10 Maceo joined General Máximo Gómez at El Galeón. It was the last meeting between the principal leaders of the Cuban Revolution. The two Generals agreed that Maceo would continue his campaign in the West, and Gómez would direct operations in the central part of the island. Both agree, too, that the tempo of destruction must be accelerated since it was becoming clear that Spain could not bear the tremendous financial burdens of the war much longer. In parting, Gómez promised to send Maceo desperately needed war supplies from the East.[17]*

Upon leaving El Galeón, Maceo set out for Pinar del Río to give the lie to Weyler's prediction that the province would soon be pacified. ("Due to the fact that many landowners were inclined to trust Weyler, I had to invade that province again . . ." he wrote to Estrada Palma.[18]) His rapid passage across the province of Havana could be traced by the fires along the way. By March 15 he was once more in the province of Pinar del Río, and on the following day, he announced his presence in a special proclamation designed to make Weyler's claims look ridiculous.[19] Maceo's presence was felt more concretely by the Spaniards in

---

* General Mayía Rodriguez accompanied Gómez for the specific purpose of bringing these war materials back to Maceo.

his battle with them on March 20 at El Rubí, where despite the lack of amunition, he forced a superior opponent to retire from the field. At the time of the battle, the Bronze Titan had only five hundred men with him. Wishing to foster general fighting in the entire province, he had split his forces into several parts.[20]

Despite the continuing scarcity of ammunition, the indomitable Maceo fought a series of clashes and continued his work of destruction in rich Pinar del Río through the last week of March and first week of April. He suffered only one defeat—at La Palma where a traitorous guide led his unit into a trap and he lost thirty-nine dead and eighty-eight wounded in battle—a heavy loss considering the small size of his unit.[21] Despite this setback, Maceo proudly reported to Estrada Palma that, even though he had "taken such necessary steps against my wishes," he had "successfully destroyed every piece of property that might be a source of revenue and assistance to our enemies," as well as effectively diminishing Weyler's reputation by making a mockery of his promise to pacify the province of Pinar del Río.[22]

Weyler was not one to take such an affront to his reputation lightly. He busied himself making extensive preparations to seal Maceo off in the extreme western province. Weyler was building a modernized *trocha*, equipped with electric lights, across the narrow waist of the island from Mariel to Majana on the border of the provinces of Havana and Pinar del Río. The captain general stationed fourteen thousand soldiers in fortified positions along this line in the hope of trapping Maceo.[23] Upon learning all this, Maceo, with typical audacity, wrote confidently to Gómez: "If I crossed *trochas* coming here, I can cross them again whenever I choose to do so. I am more worried about new Zanjones than trochas."[24]* He was referring, of course, to the Pact of Zanjón ending the Ten Years' War, which Maceo had bitterly opposed and refused to sign.[25] To prevent another Pact of Zanjón, Maceo issued orders promising the death penalty to any rebel officer or soldier who might initiate discussions with the enemy.[26]

Weyler was not content to build a wall at one end of the province

---

* Maceo's contempt for the Spanish *trochas* was widely known. Thus De Truffin reported: "Although being vigorously pursued, Maceo boasts that he is absolutely calm and . . . that he is not worried about the fortification line at all and will cross it whenever he likes." (De Truffin to the Russian Ambassador in Madrid, May 1, 1896, *International Affairs*, Moscow, March, 1964, p. 121.)

to contain the Negro rebel leader. Ignoring the war everywhere else in Cuba, he concentrated all his energy on crushing Maceo. Thus he sent three thousand veteran troops, under the command of General Suárez Inclán, to attack Maceo's forces which now numbered exactly 250 men! (As we have seen, Maceo had dispersed many of his troops throughout the province.) Yet the audacious Cuban, with only a few hundred men, without adequate ammunition, with a vastly superior enemy exerting every effort to trap and annihilate him, and with the Spaniards publicly predicting that they would finish him off in the month of May,[27] exuded his usual confidence. He wrote to Estrada Palma on April 14, 1896 that he could hold out "until Spain is exhausted." Three days later, he assured his wife that he would outwit the enemy, that Spain would see the hopelessness of her situation in the month of August and abandon the island.[28]

Until he could obtain more ammunition, Maceo decided to avoid the concentration of Spanish forces sent against him by taking refuge in the Tapia Mountain Range. The Spaniards attacked this natural defensive position repeatedly from April 18 to 26, but Maceo repulsed them each time. Learning of the landing of an expedition with war materials from the United States, Maceo left his retreat, outmaneuvered the enemy waiting for him, and hurried in search of the new arrivals.[29] At Cacarajícara he was delayed by the battle which his company, now down to 170 *mambises*, had to fight against a Spanish column of nearly one thousand soldiers led by General Suárez Inclán. At a critical point in this unequal conflict, Colonel Juan E. Ducasse, from the newly-arrived expedition of the *Competitor*, reached the scene with reinforcements, rifles, and ten thousand rounds of ammunition. With shouts of "*Viva Cuba!*" the rebels quickly forced the enemy column to retreat.[30]

The auspicious arrival of the reinforcements and the defeat of the Spaniards at Cacarajícara led Maceo to issue a communique declaring that victory was in sight and that economic necessity would soon force Spain to stop the war. At precisely the same time, De Truffin was writing to the Russian Ambassador to Madrid that the news of Maceo's victory "gives ground to assume that Spain's cause in Cuba is a lost one."[31]

Returning to his bastion in the mountains of Tapia, Maceo fought a series of small but fierce engagements. On May 23 he attacked the fortified town of Consolación del Sur and left it in flames. Two days later, he won a victory over the forces of General Suárez Valdés y Molina, the supreme commander of the province. In the fighting the Spanish General himself was badly wounded.[32]

The entire world now rang with paeans of praise for the Cuban Negro General. Poems ridiculing Weyler and hailing Maceo were published in all Latin American countries. From Havana, Colonel Charles E. Akers, correspondent for the London *Times*, sent the following dispatch which was printed in the British paper early in June, 1896:*

> In the province of Pinar del Río, at some eighteen miles from the center of the Spanish lines, is encamped since last March the rebel General Antonio Maceo with his army. Here are the rebels almost in view of 60,000 Spanish soldiers. There is no pretense of not knowing the position of Maceo since a Spanish General indicated to me the precise point where the insurrectionist encampment was. The frequently repeated Spanish boast that Maceo will not be able to cross the *trocha* is already worn out and useless. Undoubtedly whenever it suits the insurrectionist leader, he will succeed in breaking the line, and meanwhile, it is enough for him to stay where he is and compel more than a third of the entire Spanish army to remain on the defensive.[33]

Weyler now decided that the only way to retrieve his reputation was to enter the field himself. He organized a combination of forces made up of twelve thousand troops and twelve cannon to launch against the five hundred men fighting under Maceo's immediate orders. At San Gabriel de Lombello, part of these forces attacked the Negro General on June 19. For five days the battle raged back and forth as Maceo tried to keep the Spanish battalions from pinning him down. On June 24 Maceo received his twenty-fourth battle wound in his fight for Cuban independence. A rifle bullet broke a bone in the lower portion of one of his legs. With the general out of action, his troops again took refuge in the Tapia Mountains.[34]

Maceo was taken to the house of a rebel civilian in the Rosario Mountain range where for nine days he was treated by his medical aid. During his convalescence, Maceo wrote to Estrada Palma pointing

---

* The article opened: "With an army of 175,000 men, with materials of all kinds in unlimited quantities, beautiful weather, little or no sickness among the troops, in a word, with everything in his favor, General Weyler has been unable to defeat the insurrectionists." (London *Times*, June 6, 1896.)

out that to a large degree his actions against the Spanish forces of the West were fought with the arms he took from the enemy; he complained that favoritism was being shown in the East in the matter of military supplies, and demanded shipments of arms.* A few days later, Maceo learned of the arrival of the expedition of Colonel Francisco Leyte Vidal, and off he went to obtain the much-needed supplies. On September 18, he met Leyte Vidal, and from the expedition received 500,000 rounds of ammunition, one thousand rifles, two thousand pounds of dynamite, one cannon, and one hundred cannon shells. With the pneumatic cannon came three American artillerymen. Francisco (*Panchito*) Gómez Toro, the young son of Máximo Gómez, also came to join Maceo, his hero.[35]

The happy shouts and *vivas* of the *mambises* over the arrival of the war material abruptly ended when they noticed General Maceo's face. He had been handed a copy of the *Boletín de Guerra* of July 15 which featured the news that on July 5, José Maceo had been killed in battle at Loma del Gato in Oriente. It may seem incredible that it took so long for the news to reach Maceo. Actually, it was an indication of the indifference of the revolutionary government to their greatest warrior. They had simply neglected to inform Maceo. Indeed, the only communication Maceo received from government officials during the entire campaign in the West was not congratulations for his remarkable achievements against the enemy, but a criticism for making a number of appointments and conferring ranks "without first submitting them to the Governing Council for their approval."[36]

With the supplies from the Leyte Vidal expedition, Maceo, despite his sorrow over the death of his brother,† was ready to fight extensive battle. And this was precisely what he proceeded to do. On October

---

* This was not Maceo's first complaint on this score. On March 21, 1896, he had written to Estrada Palma that "the privileged ones" in the army were being favored, and that he was being neglected in firearms and equipment. (Antonio Maceo to Estrada Palma, March 21, 1896, Archivo Nacional.) It is not difficult to discern that Maceo was hinting that he was being discriminated against because he was a Negro. He was soon to discover that there was ample grounds for his suspicion.

† Maceo received hundreds of letters of condolence from his friends abroad, but with the exception of one or two replies, it was two months before he could bring himself to acknowledge receipt of these expressions of sympathy. (José Luciano Franco, *La vida heroica y ejemplar de Antonio Maceo*, La Habana, 1963, p. 112.)

14, De Truffin wrote: "At present being better organised and well supplied with arms and ammunition, they [the rebels led by Maceo] have altered their tactics, and are offering resistance to the royal troops. Five rather serious clashes have taken place in the last few days . . . the bitterness with which both sides fought is an indication that the war has entered an entirely new and more active phase."[37] Maceo's first combat after receiving the new supplies was at Montezuelo, September 23-24. Here he drove the Spaniards from the battlefield at the cost of sixty-eight casualties. On the next day, he had another clash at Tumbas de Estorino, and on October 1, he was momentarily trapped by three Spanish columns at Ceja del Negro. Making effective use of the new cannon, he not only broke out of the Spanish encirclement but forced the enemy to retreat. In three days of fighting at Ceja del Negro, Maceo won a notable victory. But it cost him two hundred and twenty-seven casualties, and he had only two hundred fighting men left after the battle was over. Nevertheless, the Bronze Titan had once again demonstrated his extraordinary skill and ferocious tenacity in fighting the enemy.[38]

Throughout the remainder of October, Maceo continued his work of destruction and his rapier-like thrusts at the enemy in Pinar del Río. On October 27, in San Cristóbal, he made what was to be his last address to the troops under his command. He urged them to take courage and to prepare for whatever sacrifices were necessary to win independence for their country. He assured the few score men that they could wear down the Spaniards in the West and open the way for final victory.[39]

But Maceo did not know, as he spoke, that his days of campaigning in the West were practically over. On October 29, in El Roble, he received a letter from Máximo Gómez urgently requesting him to break through the *trocha* and return to Camagüey.

This was not the first time Maceo had received a request from the General-in-Chief for him to stop fighting the enemy in the West and join him. During his convalescence in the Rosario Mountains, he had been asked by Gómez to leave for Camagüey. The reason for the request was the difficulties Gómez was having with the government.

There was really nothing new about this. For many months, certain members of the civil government had become extremely irritated at their own lack of importance because of Gómez's strong individuality; Gómez obstinately insisted on enforcing the policies he regarded as essential for victory. They had become increasing piqued over the manner in which Gómez summarily dismissed their plans for obtaining finances by making exceptions to his policy of destruction. The Supreme Commander stubbornly resisted all efforts to moderate what he considered the basic strategy for winning the war, that is to say, destruction of all wealth. For a time, the dispute even threatened to split the revolutionary leaders into two opposing camps. Gómez, however, dominated the dispute and his opponents gave in.[40]

But members of the civil government remained dissident over the basic question of authority. An issue which brought the conflict to a head involved the Maceo brothers, Antonio and José. José Maceo had been placed in command of the province of Oriente by Gómez. This action had infuriated President Cisneros who charged that the Maceos, one in the East and the other in the West, were trying to monopolize the Cuban Revolution. He further charged that the monopolization of key positions by the Negro brothers would enable the Spaniards to make more effective use of propaganda accusing the rebels of seeking a Negro-dominated Cuba. Furthermore, the campaign for United States recognition of Cuban belligerency would be seriously impaired if the impression spread in that country that the rebel cause was dominated by Negroes and being carried through mainly in their interest. Cisneros and other leaders in the government clearly revealed that they too had swallowed the Spanish propaganda, which was not too difficult since they had long harbored anti-Negro prejudices. The charge that Maceo was planning Negro domination of the future Cuban Republic was not a new one by any means; it had been spread by the Spaniards in the Ten Years' War, and was accepted then by too many elements in the revolutionary ranks.

At any rate, Cisneros decided to diminish the influence of the Maceos; he did this first by demanding that Gómez replace José Maceo with Calixto García, and secondly by stopping all efforts of Gómez to send replacements and material aid to Antonio Maceo in the West. Although Gómez refused to remove José Maceo, the latter resigned his post in favor of Calixto Garcia early in July, 1896 in order to prevent the dissension over his position from further hindering the war effort. His untimely death a few day laster in battle disposed of this issue as far as the government was concerned.[41]

Encouraged by its victory in the José Maceo case, the civil government began interfering with Gómez's conduct of the war by issuing military orders directly to the commanders in the field. Gómez expressed his opinion of this action in a note which he wrote on the back of a communication he had received from one of the leading government officials informing him that military commands would hereafter be issued by the governing body: "I believe we should be sensible and recognize that while Cuba is not free, we should recognize the military power as the only supreme power."[42]

This then was the background for Gómez's first message to Maceo asking the commander of the Invading Army to leave the West and join him, in order to prevent the Revolution from being destroyed from within.[43] But Maceo was not interested in becoming involved in political disputes, even though he was furious over Cisneros' treatment of his brother who had been made the victim of racial prejudice. In addition, as he informed Gómez, his departure "would prevent the realization of our plan to crown the work of the Invasion with a Cuban Ayachucho."[44]*

At El Roble, however, Maceo learned that the rebel government had dismissed Gómez from his post as General-in-Chief of the revolutionary armies, and had taken over the direction of the war.† Gómez now insisted that Maceo leave for Camagüey; the very existence of the Revolution depended on his return. Loath though he was to leave off fighting the enemy in the West, Maceo decided that he must return to the East as quickly as possible.[45]

It had not been easy for Gómez to order Maceo to abandon his campaign in the West. He was fully aware of the significance of what

---

* In the battle of Ayachucho in Peru, December 9, 1824, the Spanish forces were decisively defeated by the Latin American patriots under Simón Bolívar. This battle was the final blow to Spanish rule on the continent; only Cuba and Puerto Rico were left to Spain.

Maceo frequently referred to his desire to climax the invasion with a Cuban Ayachucho.

† On September 1, 1896, an addition was made to the Organic Military Law which was designed to restrict Gómez's powers. Article One of this amendment provided that the Commander-in-Chief could dictate "only military dispositions and general orders of the army." He was required to submit to the Council of Government his operational plans for its approval, except where military exigencies temporarily prevented this. (*Leyes de la república*, New York, 1897, pp. 43-45.)

was being accomplished by the Negro General. As he noted in a letter to Estrada Palma, the fact that the Spaniards had had to concentrate so many of their troops against Maceo had weakened them in many other strategic places, "thus giving us the opportunity and more time to prepare operations in areas like Santiago de Cuba, Guantánamo and Camagüey. . . ." Then again, Maceo had built an effective organization in Pinar del Río made up of "well-trained men," and had destroyed the myth of the invulnerability of the *trocha* system. These were important contributions "to the final triumph."[46]

In view of this analysis, it is clear that only a great crisis endangering the very existence of the Revolution could have led Gómez to plead with Maceo to abandon the important work he was accomplishing in the West. Knowing the old Dominican, Maceo must have realized that his decision came only after the most careful analysis of all the factors involved, and that he would have to yield to Gómez's judgment. As he told his officers, referring to the crisis in the Revolutionary government, "Whatever our sacrifices for independence and whatever the fate reserved for us in the future, however bad it may be, it is preferable to be resigned to it than to continue suffering the dishonor of being governed by unworthy people from a foreign soil."[47]

Just what Maceo had in mind to do after he rejoined Gómez is not known. But it is known that he did not intend to lead a revolt against the government, even though he had little respect for it. Eusebio Hernández, his old friend and advisor, who held a post in President Cisneros' cabinet, even urged Maceo forcibly to take over the direction of the Revolution, assuring him that he would have sufficient support to carry this through. Hernández overlooked two important facts: that Maceo prided himself on disciplined obedience, and that he had never revolted against the revolutionary government during the Ten Years' War, despite his opposition to many of its policies. It was thus typical of Maceo that he not only rejected Hernández' suggestion, but commented that his friend must be out of his mind to think that he would have responded favorably. He added: "We [rebels] are our own worst enemies."[48]*

---

* A few months later, Calixto García echoed Maceo, writing: "We Cubans, as in past times, are doing our best to lose the war in spite of the fact that everything is in our favor." He was referring to opposition to Gómez in the government. (Calixto García to Estrada Palma, Jiguaní, Jan. 3, 1897, Archivo Nacional.)

Immediately upon making his decision to join Gómez, Maceo began marching toward the *trocha* of Mariel, not far from the city of Havana. General Weyler's pet *trocha* was now a truly formidable military line equipped with electric lights, artillery, innumerable forts, and garrisoned by some fourteen thousand soldiers. Weyler, moveover, collected more than ten thousand troops to surround Maceo as he moved westward to pin him against the *trocha*.[49] Maceo, it appears, did not seem to realize how much strength Weyler was sending against him nor did he expect to encounter much difficulty in passing through the trocha.* As he moved toward the fortified line, he sent a message to Commander Baldomero Acosta in the province of Havana ordering him to prepare fresh horses for the long journey eastward. He advised Acosta to expect him on November 11.[50]

On November 9 Maceo encountered the advanced columns of Weyler's encircling force in the valley of Tapia. With great effort and skill he broke away from these columns, but lost seventy-seven of his two hundred and thirty men in the process. On the following day, he was almost completely encircled by the main body of the Spanish force, made up of eighteen infantry battalions and six battalions of artillery, a total of 6,000 men, all under the command of General Weyler himself. To oppose this formidable enemy, Maceo had exactly 153 men—but again the brilliant general managed to snatch his forces from the enemy's pincers.[51]

On November 11, the day on which he had expected to meet Acosta across the *trocha*, Maceo reconnoitered the fortified line in an effort to find the best place to cross. He became increasingly uneasy as he discovered the true strength of the *trocha* and realized that it would not be an easy matter to make a crossing. Nevertheless, he was still determined to break through the massive fortified line, and sent new orders to the rebel units of Havana ordering a concentration of forces at a predetermined place on November 27.[52]

While preparing for the task ahead, Maceo wrote a series of letters to friends in the United States, reaffirming his faith in ultimate victory

---

* On August 18, witnout firing a shot, Quintín Banderas, Maceo's Negro assistant, had passed through this *trocha* at the head of 100 men, and Maceo must have reasoned that he could duplicate this daring exploit. He did not realize that by November, when he was setting out to cross it, the *trocha* had been made much more powerful.

for the Cuban cause, but at the same time, not ignoring the problems still facing the Revolution. To Clarence King in New York, he wrote on November 22 thanking him for praising his military achievements,* but modestly stating that these were due more "to the abnegation and heroism of the Cuban army than to my skill which is very little." Maceo noted that the Cuban rebels still faced "very superior forces who are provided with all the elements of war," indeed: "No other people of the Americas, upon fighting for their independence, have had to confront the formidable obstacles facing the people of Cuba . . . not even the English colonies of North America. . . ." But even if Spain should triple the number of soldiers she put in the field against the Cubans, she could not succeed in forcing them "to submit to foreign domination."[53]

On November 25 Maceo talked to three soldiers who claimed knowledge of a weak spot in the *trocha*, but after questioning them for half an hour he was dissatisfied with their information. On the following morning, Maceo made another reconnaissance of the military line, seeking an escape route. He continued this until December 3 when he decided that the best plan was to go around the *trocha* by water at the port of Mariel. Carlos Soto, a local civil official in the revolutionary organization, agreed to furnish the boat and act as guide. Maceo then chose seventeen men to accompany him around the line and to the East.[54]†

At 11:30 on the night of December 4 Maceo and his men successfully circled the *trocha* within sight of a Spanish garrison. The feat required four trips of the small boat. Once on the other side, Maceo

---

* King expressed his "sincere admiration for the genius and courage you have demonstrated so brilliantly in the campaign of invasion." He could not forget that Maceo was "all alone in Pinar del Río, facing Weyler and the greatest part of the Spanish army," but he was confident, as were all admirers of Maceo in the United States, that he would be able "to hold your position in spite of all the forces which Spain might send against you. . . ." Since King's letter was written on August 20, 1896, it is clear from all that we have seen that this confidence was justified. As a token of his admiration for Maceo, King sent the Negro General a set of dishes. (José Antonio Portuondo, *El Pensamiento Vivo de Maceo*, La Habana, 1962, p. 99n.)

† José Luciano Franco, Maceo's biographer, records the fact that the men who had accompanied Maceo from Baraguá to Mantua and were not now selected to accompany their beloved leader around the *trocha* "wept and begged for the honor of accompanying him." (*La Vida heroica y ejemplar de Antonio Maceo*, La Habana, 1963, p. 115.)

could not locate the delegation appointed to meet him, and the small group took refuge in an abandoned sugar mill, *La Merced.* While several members of the party were trying to locate the rebel unit which was supposed to meet Maceo, the General remained in the sugar mill. On the morning of December 6 the horses for Maceo's group had still not arrived. By midday Maceo could wait no longer, and even though he had developed a high fever through aggravation of old and recent leg wounds from the long walking,* he gave the order to begin marching toward the sugar mill Garro. On the road they met the rebel contingent led by Lieutenant Colonel Baldomero Acosta with the long-awaited horses. Delighted, Maceo quickly placed his fine saddle, which he had brought with him, on one of the animals. The group continued to *Garro* and remained until nine o'clock that night. Then Maceo decided to join the forces of Colonel Silverio Sánchez Figueras, chief of the Brigade of Southern Havana, at San Pedro de Hernández near the border between Havana and Pinar del Río.[55]

In San Pedro the Bronze Titan revealed that he had a new plan. He had heard from Acosta and others that his actions in the West had caused so much concern among the officials in Madrid that an attack on any community around Havana would bring the removal of Captain General Weyler and possibly the end of his brutal policies. Before leaving the West and continuing towards Las Villas, Maceo wanted to deliver the blow that would hasten the departure from Cuba of the hated Captain General. Maceo's plan was to assault the town of Marianao on the outskirts of the capital itself, and he issued orders for all the rebel forces in the area to gather for the operation.[56]

After formulating his plans for that night's action in Marianao, Maceo, still suffering from his recent wound, stretched out in a hammock to rest. He asked José Miró to read from the *Crónicas de Guerra,* which his chief of staff was then compiling. He particularly wanted to hear Miró's account of the Battle of Coliseo. Maceo's revolver and *machete* were close at hand, and his horse was standing unsaddled. As Miró read, sudden sounds of gunfire startled the group. Before the Negro General and his companions could move from their positions, enemy bullets were whistling around them. Somehow the Spanish

---

* According to José Miró, Maceo could ride in the saddle for hours without ill effect, but his legs could not stand the strain of prolonged walking. (Miró, *op. cit.,* vol. III, p. 214.)

troops had evaded the rebel outposts. One of his aides helped the still-ailing Maceo out of his hammock. In a few minutes the General was astride his horse, armed with his *machete* and revolver. A group of Cuban cavalrymen from the regiment Santiago de las Vegas had heard the shots, and were now forcing the vanguard of the attackers back.

But the ever-daring Maceo was not content. He determined to pursue and annihilate the invaders. Sighting another group of enemy infantrymen behind a wire fence to his left, Maceo ordered the forty-eight men around him to charge. The horsemen were detained by the fence, and the Spanish foot soldiers concentrated heavy rifle fire against them. Maceo ordered Commander Juan Manuel Sánchez to cut the fence and sent Brigadier General Pedro Díaz with a small group on a flanking movement to the right. After giving these orders, Maceo leaned toward Miró and shouted, "*Esto va bien!*" (This is going well!) Those were his last words. A bullet struck him in the face. Dropping his *machete,* the caudillo fell heavily from his saddle while at the same time some twelve men from Commander Sánchez's escort likewise fell.

With the strength of the enemy fire increasing, some of the rebels tried to help Maceo, and others tried to drive back the Spaniards. Colonel Nodarse tried to put Maceo, still alive, on a horse to remove him from the scene. But as two men lifted Maceo to put him on the horse, the caudillo received another bullet wound—this time in the chest. The rider trying to hold Maceo was also shot from his saddle. Lieutenant Francisco Gómez Toro, the young son of Máximo Gómez, rushed to help. Nodarse and Gómez carried Maceo away by the arms and legs. When Gómez was shot in the leg, Colonel Nodarse ordered him to leave. But Gómez refused. The young lieutenant then was shot again and fell over the body of General Maceo. Nodarse was also wounded, but managed to escape the advancing Spaniards.

The body of the Bronze Titan was abandoned to the enemy. The Spaniards removed the clothes and other valuables from Maceo's body and those of the other rebel dead. The Spaniards evidently did not recognize the body of the fabulous Antonio Maceo, for they would have relished the opportunity to display the corpse in Havana. Before the Spaniards learned that one of the dead was Maceo, it was too late. The Cubans in the area reorganized, and after driving the enemy troops away, recovered the bodies. Maceo's body was taken to an abandoned house nearby. At three o'clock in the morning of December

8, 1896, the Negro hero of Cuban independence was buried together with *Panchito* Gómez Toro in a place called Cacahual, Santiago de las Vegas.⁵⁷

So Weyler had accidentally won the long struggle against Maceo. De Truffin, writing from Havana on December 14, 1896, noted: "Maceo's accidental death in a clash at the gates of Havana . . . is undoubtedly a great success for our Governor General [Weyler]. . . . It is not to be denied that the death of the most popular insurgent leader is a grievous blow to the revolutionary cause, because the deceased, quite apart from his military qualities, enjoyed great influence among his men. . . ." Still the Russian Consul quickly added the shrewd observation: "But it may be assumed that after the initial moments of confusion events will continue in their old course. The insurgents still have as their leader the old Máximo Gómez, and there is no doubt at all that it was he who laid the groundwork for the existing organization of the insurgent forces. . . ."⁵⁸

Actually, the Cubans had more than this. They also had the memory of two great martyrs to the cause of their independence, both slain on the field of battle: José Martí at the age of 42 and Antonio Maceo at the age of 52.* Like Martí, Maceo's entire adult life was dedicated to the cause of his country's independence, and he sacrificed everything—his family and opportunities to lead a life of ease and luxury—to this cause. Continuing resolutely toward his fixed goal, suffering insult and criticism because he was a Negro, sustaining twenty-five wounds, he fought bravely and brilliantly for his country, *and never once lost a battle.* Neither bullets nor sickness stopped him; as we have seen, at the time of his death, his body was racked with constant pain, and he could walk only with much effort. But his thoughts were on how best to defeat the enemy.

---

* The exact age of José Antonio de la Caridad Maceo y Grajales at his death is difficult to determine, since his birthday has not yet been fixed with entire certainty. Various authorities choose different days, months, and even years, each with certain evidence for support. The official and most commonly accepted conception is that the famous Maceo was born on June 14, 1845, in Majaguabo, San Luis, in the Province of Oriente. This is based on the baptismal entry made by the priest of the Church of Santo Tomás Apóstol where Maceo was baptized on August 26, 1845. According to this church entry, Maceo was born on June 14, 1845. A copy of the baptismal record, as certified by a church official, is in the Maceo Collection of Francisco de Paula Coronado, Archivo Nacional, Havana, Cuba.

Uneducated, and of humble circumstances, Maceo rose from obscurity to heights of great fame and prestige, and he accomplished this feat under the constant burden of race prejudice. Maceo's career as a revolutionary patriot began in a movement dominated by the white aristocracy —the élite of Oriente province. Yet against imposing obstacles he became a hero of his country and an idol of his people.

After the death of José Martí, Maceo, with Máximo Gómez, was the spirit of the Cuban revolutionary movement. The name Maceo was a household word among all Cubans wherever they lived, and in the *bohíos* of the peasants, his exploits were discussed again and again. Nor was Maceo only the uneducated fighting arm of the Revolution, as he has been pictured too often, even in Cuba.* His correspondence demonstrates how well his self-education, constantly pursued even in the midst of campaigns, had succeeded. His contributions to the ideology of the Revolution were of great importance. With his Protest of Baraguá, he kept alive the Cuban hopes of independence; indeed, when the rebel leaders wished to rekindle the Cuban spirit, they pointed to Maceo and his Protest. When Cubans, in the Second War for Independence, spoke of the unbeatable drive of their Revolution, they spoke of the undefeated Maceo, humiliating the Spaniards, who, though outnumbering the Negro General hundreds to one, with unlimited war materials at their command, could not cope with Maceo. They could not even confine him in an island averaging fifty miles in width. General after general was recalled and replaced because of Maceo's fabulous exploits, and even the feared and famed General Weyler was about to be summoned home when Maceo fell. In the Ten Years' War it was Maceo and the Protest of Baraguá which aroused world-wide attention. In the Revolution of 1895, it was Maceo and the western invasion, Maceo and the threat to the capital, Maceo and the campaign in Pinar del Río.

The fact that Maceo was a Negro made him an especially significant force in the revolutionary struggle even though it also caused him to be attacked by white supremacist elements in the revolutionary ranks, to say nothing of making him the target of Spanish insults. He was the symbol, the embodiment of the hopes of the Negro people of

---

* For a Cuban refutation of this viewpoint, see José Antonio Portuondo, *El Pensamiento vivo de Maceo*, La Habana, 1962, pp. 7-15.

Cuba, and he fulfilled their faith in him. In every utterance Maceo stressed two cardinal principles: independence for the nation and freedom and equality for the Negroes. He placed an equal emphasis on both ideas. He was thus able to rally to the revolutionary cause the great mass of the Negro people whose support was so important for the struggle against Spain. At the same time, by his discipline and refusal to place himself above the Revolution, he reassured those who feared that he might lead the Negroes to a place of dominance in Cuba. Maceo always insisted that there were no black and white soldiers: all were Cuban warriors and all should work together to establish and build the Republic.

Writing in the *Journal of the Knights of Labor,* official organ of the famed Order of the Knights of Labor, in its issue of December 17, 1896, J. Syme-Hastings, who had met Maceo in Cuba,* observed:

> I consider him the greatest hero of the nineteenth century— aye—even in history. Caesar crossed the Rubicon; Napoleon crushed the world; Alexander crossed Hellespont; William III caused the Boyne to run blood; Skobeloff forced leagues of rock-bound ravines and crossed the Balkans; but all had armies; all had arms; all levied strict discipline; all had room in which to operate. With a handful of untrained men, armed with machetes, without any discipline save loyalty to the cause, cut off from food, water and shelter, and operating in a few square miles of territory, Maceo routed the flower of the Spanish army again and again. He has gained control of the whole island again and again. With 20,000 men he has not only kept over 200,000 well trained, well disciplined and well armed men at bay, but he has routed and crushed them repeatedly and forced a passage from one end of the island to the other.
>
> To Maceo fear was a myth. He was absolutely devoid of the sense which we call fear. Every nerve, every sense, so tingled and vibrated with keen foresight, certainty of victory, and love for his country, that he never gave the slightest heed to personal danger. I have wondered if other great generals were like Maceo but history fails to show any light. I have crouched down behind a tree when the air was red with bullets, when showers of clipped leaves and pieces of bark fell on me like flakes, of snow, and I have watched Maceo's face as he sat firmly on his horse waiting for

---

* See *Journal of the Knights of Labor,* Nov. 5, 1896, and Philip S. Foner, "A Tribute to Antonio Maceo," *Journal of Negro History,* Vol. LV, Jan. 1970, pp. 65-71.

his ambushed, crawling followers to get close enough to the enemy to allow him to give the charge signal. Had I stood up I should certainly have been filled with Mauser bullets, because I feared them. But there was no fear on that face—the bright eyes roamed calmly from the ambushed enemy to where his men were, and back again, his horse restlessly snorted when the bullets singed him, but Maceo merely patted and calmed it. God! that was a memory; each moment I waited to see him fall with a hole in his high forehead, but it never came to pass. That is why the Cubans win their engagements, with such a noble figure for a leader, even a band of cowards could sweep all before them. . . .

I loved him best when the lion was dormant and he grew reminiscent. He was one of those immortal characters who cause one to forget for the time that he is but a man. His was a soul of strong magnetism and great character—poetical like all of his race—and ever surrounded by that strength of refinement which denotes genius. . . .

I have seen him carry five wounded men from the field after a battle and care for them with all the tenderness of a sister of charity—yet this was the same man whose cool, bloody fighting made each field after an engagement, look like a dissecting room in a hospital.

He was the life of every camp—was, in fact, one of the men—he would share his water and food with anyone who was short, often he wrote letters home for many of the 'Cubes' who were unable to do so. His heart was as big as his massive frame. Therefore, one cannot wonder that he was idolized and that his men would gladly die fighting under him.

Antonio Maceo was not only a great Cuban. He was one of the outstanding figures in the entire history of the Hispanic-American wars of independence. The Detroit *Journal* did not exaggerate when, upon learning his death, it called Maceo "the greatest colonial fighter since Toussaint L'Ouverture."[59]*

---

* The reference is to the Haitian Negro liberator. The Detroit *Journal's* evaluation of Maceo has not been followed by the vast majority of American historians who have either ignored or maligned the great Cuban leader. Outstanding in the latter category is *The Martial Spirit* by Walter Millis. After a brief sentence on the slaying of Antonio Maceo, Millis writes: "He [Maceo] had abandoned the remnant of his forces in Pinar del Río, and slipping out with a small escort, was making his own escape to the eastward when his party was accidentally intercepted." (New York, 1931, p. 61.) In other words, Maceo, who had most reluctantly left the campaign in the West on orders of Gómez, is described as running away to save his life from Weyler and the Spanish forces.

Black Americans in this country continued to honor Maceo long after his death. A leading guest house in New York's black community in the late 1890's was named Hotel Maceo. In the *Colored American Magazine* of November, 1900, S.E.F.C.C. Hamedoe described Maceo as "the greatest hero of the nineteenth century." In his speech accepting nomination as presidential candidate of the National Liberty Party in 1904, George Edwin Taylor, the first black American to be nominated for President of the United States, referred to "General Maceo, the greatest Negro soldier and general of modern times." In *The Crisis* (official organ of the NAACP) of May, 1931, Arthur A. Schomburg wrote: "I know of no man of military standing in the whole of America white, yellow or black that can excel the exploits of Antonio Maceo in the field of battle, as a soldier, during the past hundred years. . . . Toussaint L'Ouverture had Wendell Phillips to enlighten an English speaking world to his greatness . . . yet the world knows little of Maceo, the ablest and noblest of American-born cavalry leaders, unsurpassed by any which the new world has produced."[60]

In his general order of December 28, 1896, announcing the death of Maceo, Máximo Gómez, doubly grief-stricken by the death of his son as well as of his comrade-in-arms,* wrote: "The army is in grief and with the army its General-in-Chief. Now the country mourns the loss of one of its most mighty defenders, Cuba the most glorious of its sons, and the army, the first of its generals."† Gómez pledged that the Liberating Army would not rest until it had achieved the goal for which Maceo had laid down his life—a free and independent Cuba.[61]

On the previous page, Millis describes Maceo as having "been shut up in Pinar del Río by a military cordon and was being harried through the province. . . ." (p. 60.) Actually, of course, Maceo was harrying the Spaniards who could never defeat him.

* Gómez did not mention his son's death in his general order. But to María Cabrales, Maceo's widow, he wrote: "Weep, weep, María, for both, for you and for me, since for this unhappy old man, the privilege of relieving his innermost grief by letting go a flood of tears, is not possible." (Franco, *op. cit.,* vol. III, p. 420.)

† All over the world, and particularly in Latin America, men and women who believed in freedom shared the Cuban people's grief over the news of Maceo's death. (See Franco, *op. cit.,* vol. III, pp. 410-19 for tributes to Maceo in various countries.)

CHAPTER VI

The People, the Economy, and the Revolution

THE SUCCESS OF THE REBELS in Oriente, in the invasion of the West, and in the campaign in Pinar del Río against a vastly superior enemy could not have occurred without the support of the majority of the Cuban people, who assisted the revolutionists in spite of every form of suppression designed to break that support. The Spaniards claimed that the rebels did not represent the Cuban people—and this claim has been echoed by many historians—but they could not explain how the rebels could succeed as guerrillas if the population opposed them. It is true, as we have seen in the previous chapter, that the Revolution was organized by a relatively small group outside of the island.[1] The success of the movement, however, depended from the beginning on the support it would receive from the people inside Cuba.

Of the approximately 1,600,000 people in Cuba when the war began, about 200,000 were Spaniards, about 500,000 were Negroes, over 800,000 were white Cubans, and an undetermined number were Chinese and others. With some notable exceptions, particularly among the clergy,* the Spaniards were united in opposition to the Revolution.

---

* The majority of the Spanish priests were blindly loyal to Spain, but a minority did support and assist the revolutionaries. Father Escambre was shot because he blessed a Cuban flag, and under the pseudonyms of Virgilio and Fabio Rey, Monsignor González Arocha aided the Cuban forces, sending them medicines, provisions and clothing. Some priests even lived with the *mambises*. (Charles M. Pepper, *Tomorrow in Cuba*, New York, 1899, pp. 253-54; Manuel I. Mesa Rodríguez, *Monseñor Guillermo González Arocha, Patriota y Ciudadano*, La Habana, 1945, pp. 17-23.)

During a visit to Manzanillo in 1960, I was told by a number of old Cubans who had lived through the Second War for Independence that some liberal Spaniards in the community used to send food and other supplies to the rebels by hiding them in coffins which were supposedly on their way to burial.

On the other hand, the Negroes (again with some exceptions) were enthusiastically united in its support from the beginning, partly because the revolutionists had been leaders in the movement to abolish slavery, partly because Negroes themselves were prominent revolutionists, and partly because they felt that their future was linked to a victory over Spain. "They hoped," wrote a contemporary, "that under a new regime they would have better conditions, and stimulated by the example of Haiti, they fought for a realization of their dreams—a Cuba Libre."²*

The 800,000 white Cubans were divided in their loyalty. The white peasants, like the Negroes, generally supported the Revolution. The hostility of the peasants, particularly in the eastern zones, toward the large estates, especially those of Spaniards and foreigners, was eloquently voiced by Máximo Gómez. Indeed, the emphasis which Gómez placed on the importance of building a Republic in which the poor man would receive his proper share, long overdue in Cuba, had a strong appeal to the peasants. Finally, peasants of all types, Negro and white, had an admiration for such men as Gómez, the Maceos, and Calixto García because of their heroic deeds in the Ten Year's War.

Those who had property, position or wealth of some kind were generally opposed to the Revolution in the beginning, and many remained so throughout the entire war.‡ They were frightened by a Revolution which had such wide support from the poor people, and felt that their future in Cuba was safe only under Spanish rule. This does not mean that the wealthy class of Cubans was content under this rule. For years, they had been chafing under Spain's rigid control of Cuba's economic life; this dissatisfaction had reached a high point after the economic depression of 1893, the collapse of the sugar market and the cancellation of favorable commercial arrangements with the United States.³ Nevertheless, a majority of the manufacturers, planters and property-holders, especially in the West, were opposed to armed conflict because they feared the destruction of their wealth, and were

---

* "Who freed Cuba? Black men," wrote W. E. B. Du Bois, the distinguished leader of the Negro people in the United States, militant crusader for full freedom and equality for his people. (*The Horizon*, April, 1908.)

‡ Groyer Flint exaggerated when he wrote that of the entire Cuban population "less than one per cent favors the continuation of Spanish rule in any form." (*Op. cit.*, p. 274.)

suspicious of a Revolution which had among its top leaders men who had no great respect for wealth and property. In addition, while their commercial activities were hindered by Spanish government regulations, they did not relish losing the protection or privileges which they, on the other hand, did receive.

In an effort to check the revolutionary movement, the Autonomists and Reformists,* spokesmen for the manufacturers, planters and property holders, set out to petition and negotiate with the government in Madrid, hoping to persuade Spain to make concessions to Cuba which would deprive the revolutionists of popular support. In March, 1895, forty-three manufacturing firms of Havana sent a telegram to the Colonial Ministers and the Cuban deputies to the Cortes (the Spanish legislature) asking for economic reforms, and reminding the Spanish that if such reforms were not forthcoming, more Cubans would be driven into the revolutionary ranks.[4] The appeal brought no real results, but the Autonomists were successful in obtaining the so-called Home Rule Bill of 1895, which was passed by the Cortes on March 15, 1895, but was never applied in Cuba because the Revolution was then in full swing. It is generally conceded by all students that even if the measure had come earlier it would not have halted the Revolution, since in spite of its gesture toward granting Cubans a greater voice in government, the real power still remained in the hands of the Governor General. In essence, the measure gave Cuba constitutional provisions on paper, but in reality the authority of the Governor General remained final, and the Spanish bureaucracy remained in control of all important offices.[5]

Even though the gesture toward home rule never went into effect, the Autonomists acted as if it had made the Revolution unnecessary, and they vowed, in a circular published on April 4, 1895, that they did not intend to abandon their efforts to dissuade those who planned "to ruin the land and darken the prospects of our future with the horrible spectre of poverty, anarchy and barbarism."[6] As revolutionary strength increased, the Autonomists became more desperate. In October,

---

* The Reformist Party was primarily Spanish in its composition, and it generally cooperated with the Autonomist Party in its endeavors. However, it was willing to accept less in the way of home rule than its collaborators. Mainly it desired a streamlining of the existing system. (Varona Guerrero, *op. cit.*, vol. I, pp. 245-46.)

1895, the Party sent an exposition to the Peninsula requesting complete home rule for Cuba as the only means that could keep the Revolution from spreading. But Spain was deaf to all such appeals.* And while the Autonomists and Reformists continued their futile efforts to obtain relief from Spain, the revolutionists were daily gaining fresh adherents, and gaining them from all sections of the Cuban population. On August 20, 1896, the London *Times* declared:

> The nature of the rebellion is quite at variance with nearly all such revolts hitherto, not only in Cuba but in all the former Spanish colonies in America. Here the movement began amongst the lower stratum of the population, and essentially the predominating element in the beginning of the insurrection was the Negro. Gradually the flood swelled upward and engulfed the middle and upper classes to such an extent that the sympathy of practically the whole population of Cubans is now on the rebel side. In the fighting ranks of the insurgents today the proportion is, in round numbers, 70 per cent of white and 30 per cent of Negroes. The Spaniards still assert positively and repeatedly that the war in Cuba is a war of races—black against white. It is now nothing of the kind. It has become a war between Cubans and Spaniards, and in this sense may be called a war of races if the latter so wish to characterize it; but to say that the question of color is the chief feature in the struggle is to convey a completely false impression.

One may argue that the *Times* was exaggerating the degree of support for the Revolution among the upper-class Cubans. But a document signed in June, 1896 by a number of Cuban lawyers, professors and owners of sugar plantations indicates that such support was definitely increasing. The signers denied the Spanish Government's assertion

---

* The Romero-Abaruza Bill which passed the Spanish Cortes in late summer 1895 was about as far as Spain was willing to go. Under its terms the Cubans were guaranteed an elective deliberative body and a council of administrative departments responsible to the Cuban assembly, but did not even meet the Autonomist demand for complete home rule. In Havana, *La Discusión*, an Autonomist newspaper, complimented the Spanish government on the "good principles" embodied in the bill, but commented caustically that "good principles are no longer enough." It presented a six-point critique of the bill which closed with the observation that "only deficiencies are observable in the Romero-Abaruza Bill." ("The Romero-Abaruza Reform Bill," *La Discusión*, November 16, 1895, enclosed in Williams to Uhl, November 19, 1895, U.S. Consular Despatches, Havana, Department of State, National Archives.)

"that we hate the Revolution and condemn our brothers in arms, whereas we are known to the patriots as united to them in heart, having the same ideals as those fighting for the liberty of their country. . . ." They could not, of course, express "our opinions openly and formally, for he who dares, whilst living in Cuba, to protest against Spain, would undoubtedly be made a victim, both in his person and property, to the most ferocious persecution at the hands of the government. . . . But that does not mean that, in heart and soul, they are not with their country to the same extent as those who defend her and fight for her liberty against the Spanish army. They can say nothing because a gag prevents them from speaking, but whoever penetrates into their inmost souls can see that there is no difference between them and the combatants."[7]

There was, of course, a distinct difference between the signers of this document and the *mambises* in the battlefield. Nevertheless, the document is significant in indicating the success of Martí's mission to include every section of Cuban society in the revolutionary movement.*

In general, there was a difference in the reactions of the eastern and western portions of the island. Although the peasant classes, Negro and white throughout the island, supported the Revolution as did the Chinese,† those in Oriente were more sympathetic and cooperative with the insurgents.‡ Many eastern men of wealth supported the Revolution from the outset, while those in the West were almost un-

---

* In this connection, the comment of one North American observer, the well-known journalist Richard Harding Davis, is interesting even though he exaggerated the degree of support for the Revolution in upper-class Cuban circles:

"The last revolution was organized by the aristocrats; the present one is a revolution of the *pueblo*, and, while the principal Cuban families are again among the leaders, with them are representatives of the 'plain people,' and the cause is now a common cause in working for the success of which, all classes are desperately in earnest." (Richard Harding Davis, *Cuba in Wartime*, New York, 1897, p. 11.)

† "In the war of 1895," writes Juan Jiménez Pastrana, "many Chinese performed valiant services for the Revolution, lending themselves to entering the villages and cities with the object of collecting food, medicine, clothing and shoes for the *mambí* soldiers." (*Los Chinos en las Luchas por la Liberación Cubana, 1847-1930*, p. 99.)

‡ A special census conducted by members of the revolutionary government in Oriente claimed 120,000 rural supporters in that province (Bartolomé Masó to Tomás Estrada Palma, Oriente, Dec. 31, 1897, Archivo Nacional).

animously opposed and only gradually changed from hostility to support. Again, at no time did the townspeople view the Revolution as favorably as did those in the countryside. Still each town, even though under Spanish control, had a number of rebel sympathizers, and their numbers increased as the war continued. The Spaniards struck back with wholesale arrests, most often without any evidence, merely because of suspicion.* The fate of these suspects was more often than not unknown; however, many were sent to the penal colony at Ceuta in Africa. De Truffin repeatedly referred in his dispatches to "the numerous arrests and the deportations to Africa for hard labor. . . ."[8]

In Havana the trade unions were suppressed because a number of their members had joined the Liberating Army and all of the others were correctly considered in sympathy with the Revolution.[9]† Santiago Iglesias, a Spaniard who came to Havana just before the outbreak of the Revolution, became active in the Cuban labor movement and was Secretary of the *Círculo de Trabajadores* (Workers' Circle), described the conduct of the Spanish authorities:

> About two years after the Grito de Baire, I had to leave Havana. Some of my companions had already been deported and others had joined the Revolution. My situation in Havana had come to be very difficult and dangerous. The room in which I lived had been subjected to repeated searches, and all the books, documents and papers had been confiscated by the police who carried an order of arrest against me. They accused me of work-

---

* Forty-seven arrests on suspicion were made in Pinar del Río in a period of five days shortly after the arrival of General Weyler. In Jovellanos, in Matanzas province, 600 people fled because 36 were arrested on suspicion in two days. Whenever the *insurrectos* captured a town, they freed the prisoners held by the Spaniards. Maceo liberated thirty such prisoners in Jaruco. To prevent their liberation by the rebels, the Spaniards would convey prisoners from various towns, under a strong Spanish column, to Havana. One such column included fifty suspects from Cienfuegos, 37 from Matanzas, and an undetermined number from Santa Clara, Santiago de Cuba, Candelaria, and Marianao. (Quesada, *op. cit.*, pp. 114-15.)

† Enrique Creci, a tobacco worker employed in Tampa when the Revolution began, joined an expedition to his native land, enlisted in the Liberating Army and rose to the rank of Captain. He was killed in battle. On November 19, 1899, his remains were carried to Havana, and in a funeral attended by thousands of Cuban workers from all over the island and delegations of various trade unions, he was buried with full honors. (José Rivero Muñiz, *El Movimiento Obrero durante la Primera Intervencion: Apuntes para la historia del proletariado en Cuba*, Universidad de Las Villas, 1961, p. 159.)

ing for the revolutionaries. The order of arrest could not be served on me because I evaded it with every effort.

Around December, 1896, when General Weyler was in command of the island, the prevailing policy of military repressions against those under suspicion of being in favor of independence reached also those Spaniards of liberal ideas and democratic spirit. In fact, free men could not exercise their functions as citizens. Civil restrictions were very severe, and all residents who fell under suspicion were subjected to persecution and harrassment. They were accused of being "laborantes" (conspirators in favor of the Cuban Revolution). In view of the extraordinary circumstances I have described, the activities in the workers' organizations were suspended. But not before some of its leaders, both Cubans and Spaniards, had been deported. To remain in Havana was certainly dangerous, and it was then that I decided to leave the Cuban capital and head for Barcelona and London.[10]*

Despite the support of a majority of the Cuban people, the revolutionists were not able to finance their struggle from within the island. The rural peoples did provide aid to the insurgents throughout the conflict, but it was in the form of food and clothing and valuable information about the enemy rather than financial contributions which they could not afford. To be sure, under arrangements worked out by Maceo with sugar mill owners in Oriente, which allowed them to grind cane and produce their product for export in exchange for contributions regularly paid, the Revolution received financial support from property holders in that province from the earliest stages of the war. (In October, 1896, the sugar planters of Manzanillo paid the revolutionists at the rate of thirty cents a bag, in addition to a bonus, ranging from $3,000 to $5,000 depending upon the size of the crop.[11]) But this source of income soon dried up; first, because of Gómez's insistence upon ending these arrangements, and upon destroying all production that would assist Spain economically; second, because of Spanish destruction of the properties of those landowners who had made financial arrangements with the rebels; and finally, because of the widespread destruction of roads, railroads and many other facilities essential for economic activity.

---

* Actually, Iglesias did not return to Europe. He stopped en route in Puerto Rico, participated in the struggle for independence in that island, and later became a leader of the Puerto Rican labor movement and Socialist Party.

In its January 1, 1896 issue, *Sugar Cane,* the international magazine of sugar interests, wrote: "There is no doubt whatever that the Spanish troops are able to put down this insurrection of the Negroes, but it is doubtful if this can be effected before the first of January, by which time all the factories should be at work." But this optimistic prediction changed quickly. Economic affairs in the island took a sharp turn for the worse early in 1896 when Gómez and Maceo invaded the West. Railroads were interrupted, commerce was reduced to practically nothing, and the burning of cane fields and destruction of building and machinery eliminated all prospects for the sugar crops of that year. Many owners of plantations abandoned their estates as the rebels advanced westward, and sought refuge in the fortified garrisons and cities. In April, 1896, *Sugar Cane* reported dismally: "Of the 380 factories or plantations on the island only about 25 are working, and these are either strongly garrisoned by Spanish troops or have made arrangements with the insurgents. Most of the rest have to stand idle until 1897, the insurgents have in many cases burnt nearly all their canefields."[12]

With Weyler's assumption of the office of Captain General, the hopes of the planters rose. The manager of the Guaibaro estate owned by Edwin F. Atkins, the American capitalist, wrote to Atkins "that Weyler is the man. . . . Let us try some one who can inspire these people with the fear of God and the devil at the same time." He forecast a quick recovery of sugar production. Instead, the economy of Cuba still further deteriorated. Weyler ordered the planters to continue operating and promised them protection.[13] But of course, he could not keep his promise, and many owners of sugar mills tried to negotiate with the insurgents. In doing this, however, they were subject to reprisals by the Spaniards for dealing with the enemy. Indeed, upon passing estates spared by the insurgents, Spanish troops burned them in the belief that the owners undoubtedly paid taxes to the Revolutionary government. Many owners, faced with this dilemma, simply gave up in despair. Others who tried to work their mills soon found that it was impossible to do so because of the scarcity of laborers and lack of railroad transportation. *Sugar Cane* reported on October 1, 1896 that the Cuban situation was "apparently becoming more and more hopeless as regards the probability of production of cane sugar."[14]

There were 380-400 mills in operation when the Revolution began, but gradually many of the owners gave up for the duration of the war, and fled to the cities. Only 175 to 200 mills were even making efforts to operate by mid-1896. While it is true that the decrease in the number of mills was partly due to reorganization within the industry, the major cause was the impact of the war.[15]

The result of this situation is clearly reflected in statistics. From January 1, 1895 to March 1, 1895, 249,049 tons of sugar were exported from the island, while for the same period of 1896 only 103,453 tons were exported. And this was before the invasion of the West with its thorough destruction. In 1894 there had been 1,054,000 long tons of sugar produced in Cuba with a valuation of $62,100,000; for 1895 the figures were 1,004,000 and $45,400,000, and for 1896, 220,000 and $13,000,000.[16] The utter collapse of the sugar industry was also reflected in Willet and Gray's *Statistical Sugar Trade Journal*. Crop receipts by February 20, 1896 were but 22,196 tons as compared with 234,812 tons the previous year. By mid-April it was apparent that the total crop would approximate only 200,000 tons, scarcely a fifth of the 1895 production.[17]* What these statistics meant for the island's economy was briefly but vividly pointed out by the American consul general in Havana:

> With the loss of the sugar production of the Island, all the minor industries—the very links of the commercial chain of Cuba—will die for want of the vivifying current that flows from this prodigious and abundant spring, the sugar industry of Cuba.[18]

For a while the tobacco trade did not suffer equally with the sugar industry. Pinar del Río was not invaded until 1896, and even then, as we have seen, Maceo took precautions not to destroy the crops. But in May, 1896, General Weyler forbade the export of leaf tobacco to foreign countries. All tobacco was thereafter to go to Spain, thus eliminating all competition and sharply reducing the income of the tobacco growers. Only ten days were given for fulfilling contracts made before May 16, 1896, and violators of the proclamation would

---

* Although most of the decline was attributed to the rebel program of destruction, part of the loss was due to a disastrous hurricane which destroyed thirty per cent of the crop in the Cienfuegos district. (*See* Willet and Gray's *Statistical Sugar Journal*, Oct. 24, 1895.)

be considered as "abettors of the rebellion. . . ."[19] The consequent decline in tobacco production accelerated after Maceo began destroying property on a wide scale, in an effort to disprove Weyler's assurance that Pinar del Río would soon be pacified.

The general economic picture in Cuba was vividly portrayed in the London *Times* of June 6, 1896: "The economic condition grows daily worse and more acute. . . . Poverty and misery are everywhere apparent throughout the length and breadth of Cuba. Families who were in comfortable and even wealthy circumstances a year ago now wonder where they can obtain the wherewithal to buy the necessities of life. The next few months foreshadow naught but famine and pestilence throughout the whole country."

With the sugar industry practically destroyed and the tobacco growers suffering serious reduction in income, the revolutionists could not expect much financial support from within the island. (At the same time, Spain's source of revenue in Cuba was also drastically reduced.*) The *insurrectos* depended mainly on Cubans and sympathizers in foreign countries to finance the Revolution. Monetary contributions were made by sympathetic Cubans in Mexico, Santo Domingo, Colombia, Venezuela, Costa Rica, and other Hispanic-American countries, together, to a lesser degree, with donations by the natives of those countries who sympathized with the revolutionary cause.[20]† From France, where a number of wealthy Cubans resided, the General Agency, organized under the supervision of Dr. R. E. Betances, sent some valuable contributions for the Revolution.‡ The most generous of the donors was Marta Abrei de Estévez. On July 10, 1896, she wrote to Estrada Palma:

---

* The collection of revenues from import duties by the customs houses of Cuba for the month of February, 1895 were $1,220,941.94 and for February, 1896, $763,341.80, a decrease of $457,627.14 (*El Boletín Comercial*, Havana, April 14, 1896.) This decline intensified as the war continued.

† The local revolutionary clubs represented the chief source of funds for the Cuban Revolutionary Party; over two-thirds of the entries in the Party's ledgers came from the local clubs. (Marshall M. True, "Revolutionaries in Exile: The Cuban Revolutionary Party, 1891-1898," unpublished Ph.D. thesis, University of Virginia, 1965, p. 166.)

‡ Not all of the contributions from Paris came from the wealthy. One Cuban resident in that city fasted one day each week to contribute his few francs to the Cuban revolutionary movement. (Ramon Betances to Estrada Palma, Paris, September 29, 1896, *Correspondencia diplomatica de la delegacion cubana en Nueva York durante la guerra de independencia de 1895 a 1898*, La Habana, 1943-46, vol. III, pp. 70-71. Hereinafter cited as *Correspondencia diplomatica*.)

"A letter of our compatriot Raimundo Cabrera has informed me that the Revolution needs some fifty thousand pesos in order to purchase arms and munitions of war in abundance for our valorous soldiers and, complying with my duty as a good Cuban, I am hastening this day to dispatch a telegram authorizing twenty thousand pesos to your account."[21] In all, this lady contributed about seventy thousand pesos.[22]*
After they received news of General Maceo's death, the Cuban colony in Paris contributed $100,000 to the Revolution in memory of the Bronze Titan.[23]*

By far the most important financial source for the Revolution was the Cuban population in the United States, especially the tobacco workers in Florida. The Cuban Revolutionary Party appealed to the Cuban workmen to contribute ten percent of their wages, and the workers in Tampa and Key West regularly turned over a minimum of a day's work a month throughout the entire war.[24] Many Cubans in the United States contributed regularly as much as a tenth of all their earnings,‡ and J. A. Huau, Cuban delegate in Jacksonville, con-

---

* According to Horatio S. Rubens, her contributions were anonymous and only revealed after her death. (*Liberty, the Story of Cuba*, New York, 1922, p. 282.)

† Maceo's death brought a flood of contributions to the revolutionary treasury. In Chile, Eugenio Maria Hostos's article "Quien era Maceo" aroused widespread interest in the great Cuban Negro General and many contributions followed. (Hostos described Maceo as a man who "above all and more than all was a citizen . . . a precursor of Independence, father of his country and founder of a nation." (Enrique Maria de Hostos, *Obras Completas*, Habana, 1939, vol. X, pp. 159-61.)) Antonio Rosado, a Cuban Negro working in the nitrate plants of Iquique, upon learning of Maceo's death, contributed 1,000 chileons, his life savings, and the services of his twenty-year-old firstborn son, Francisco. Francisco Rosado joined Estrada Palma in New York where he translated articles from New York newspapers into Spanish for publication in the Cuban press. (Aristides Aguero to Estrada Palma, Lima, January 4, 1887, *Correspondencia diplomática*, vol. II, pp. 77-80.)

The tiny Cuban settlement in Managua, Nicaragua collected 135 American dollars as a special tribute to Maceo. In Paris a Cuban named his newly born son Antonio Maceo to "conserve the name and soul of Maceo." (José Maria Izaguiree to Estrada Palma, Managua, Nicaragua, December 18, 1896, Ramón Betances to Estrada Palma, Paris, December 18, 1896, *ibid.*, vol. IX, pp. 71-72; vol. VI, p. 86.)

‡ A Cuban stevedore in New York City came into Juan Fraga's shop every Friday with his hard-earned and ill-spared dollar. (Rubens, *op. cit.*, p. 283.) This was typical. Horatio S. Rubens noted that "the constant sacrifice of the Cubans abroad to supply the patriots in the field with arms and ammunition, is as re-

tributed his entire fortune of approximately $150,000 to the Revolution.[25] An undetermined amount of money and goods was donated by non-Cuban citizens in the United States who became interested in the revolutionary cause.*

Not until the middle of 1896, when the Revolution had progressed considerably, did the wealthy Cubans abroad begin to respond financially. Until then the revolutionists subsisted mainly on contributions from property owners in Cuba in return for permission to produce and on thousands of small contributions from ordinary Cuban emigrants. Even afterwards, it was the tobacco workers in Tampa and Key West who made the most important contributions to the revolutionary treasury. Emilio Roig de Leuchsenring, the noted Cuban historian, points out that these workers practically sustained the Revolution by themselves during its entire course.[26]

The collapse of the Cuban economy had many other important effects, of course, besides limiting the financial support the revolutionists could find in the island. Hunger and unemployment were felt as early as the summer of 1895.[27] Agricultural laborers left plantations which were burned by both sides in the war. By October, 1895, there

---

markable as it is touching. These men who have been called cowards, have proved themselves to be endowed with the highest moral courage and capacity for self-sacrifice, and they are an indispensable part of the revolutionary movement." ("The Insurgent Government in Cuba," *North American Review*, vol. CLXVI, May, 1898, pp. 561-62.)

* It is difficult to determine exactly how much came from the United States in the way of contributions. Varona Guerrero, who examined the books of the Cuban Revolutionary Delegation in the United States, puts the figure of receipts at about two million dollars, but this does not include the receipts obtained separately by some clubs, groups and individuals. (Varona Guerrero, *op. cit.*, vol. I, p. 428.) I have examined the record of receipts from the United States in the Archivo Nacional in Havana, Cuba, but they are too fragmentary to enable one to arrive at an exact figure. However, the income recorded in the Account Book of the Cuban Revolutionary Party reveals only $91,083.65, and if we assume that each revolutionary club kept its fifty per cent share of the money collected, the amount should then be doubled to $180,000, but still far from the figure cited by Varona Guerrero. According to *Patria*, the Cuban Revolutionary Party collected, in round numbers, $187,000 for the year ending February, 1896, $108,000 for the year ending February, 1897, and $163,000 for the year ending February, 1898, or a total of $448,000. ("Nuestra Tesorería," *Patria*, February 24, 1896, 1897, 1898. This issue came out annually on the anniversary of Marti's "Manfiesto de Montecristi.") For the account books of the Cuban Revolutionary Party, see Archivo Nacional, *Inventario general del Archivo de La Delegacion del Partido Revolucionaria en Nueva York, 1892-1898.*)

were reports that peoples of the towns and villages were finding it difficult to obtain food, that is, those who did not have much money which was the largest proportion.[28] This was due in part to the effect of Gómez's decree that no animals or food stuffs could be transported into the towns and garrisons occupied by Spanish troops.

On February 25, 1896, the *Diario de la Marina* of Havana conceded that "all trade of this Island feels the precarious situation brought on by the war." It warned that something had to be done quickly to relieve the desperate situation of the people in the overcrowded towns. And this was before the advent of General Weyler's brutal *reconcentración* policy!

From February 24, 1895 to February 24, 1896, the respective Spanish Captains General, Emilio Callejas, Arsenio Martínez Campos, and Sabas Marín, had permitted the rural population, the great majority of the Cubans, to live (with more or less respect for their life, property, and honor) in their habitual rural residences. To be sure, the farmers suffered from the loss of sources of meat, as both Cubans and Spaniards slaughtered cattle whenever they felt hungry,[29] and from the prohibition against trade with towns occupied by Spanish troops, since they had always depended upon this traffic for many of their household staples. However, despite these other difficulties, the situation of the residents in the Cuban countryside in the first year of the war was endurable.

All this changed when Weyler decided that since it was the country folk who helped the revolutionary cause the most, they should be removed from the country. In this way, he felt he could score several military points at one stroke: (1) deprive the *mambises* of the means of subsistence; (2) deprive them of knowledge, through the peasants, of movements of the Spanish troops; (3) limit the spread of revolutionary propaganda to those already involved in the war; (4) prevent men, kept by force in urban centers, from joining the rebels; and (5) demoralize the rebel soldiers since many would have relatives in the concentration camps and would be influenced, in order to end their misery, to favor a halt of hostilities.[30] With these objectives in mind, Weyler introduced his infamous program which has become known in Cuban history as "la reconcentración," under which hundreds of thousands of men, women and children were forcibly removed from their homes in the countryside and herded into the towns and cities. Weyler's proclamation read:

> 1. All inhabitants of rural areas or areas outside of the lines of fortified towns will be concentrated within the towns occupied by troops at the end of eight days. All individuals who disobey this order or who are found outside the prescribed areas will be considered as rebels and judged as such.
> 2. The extraction of food products from the towns and their transfer from one town to another by sea or land is absolutely prohibited without the permission of the military authority at the point of departure. Violators will be judged and punished as auxiliaries to the rebels.
> 3. The owners of cattle are required to conduct them to the towns or their environs where they can be given convenient protection.[31]

There was no lack of directives by General Weyler to provide for the reconcentrados. The areas of confinement were supposed to be chosen with a regard for considerations of sanitation, housing, water, and other necessary requirements insofar as conditions allowed. Likewise, plots of ground were to be set aside in the immediate environs of the guarded areas in order that *reconcentrados* could cultivate them for their own sustenance.[32] But apart from the fact that Weyler made little effort to see that his orders were carried out, there were simply not sufficient facilities for the miserable peasants and their families who flocked into the overcrowded towns. Every effort was made in practice to apply concentration immediately to the entire rural population of Cuba even though on paper, it was not supposed to be instituted immediately and uniformly throughout the entire island.[33] An article in *El País* described the situation in Sancti Spíritus on April 5, 1896, as the program was just getting under way:

> Within the last few days the pictures of despair presented by people flocking into the city have succeeded each other at intervals of *seconds* of time. . . .
> The situation of the concentrated people is going to be difficult from all points of view, and the more so from a measure of this military district in obedience to a superior order, which prohibits the planting of corn and plantains, and will also surely embrace sugar cane, which is of double use—the tops as fodder for cattle and the stalks for the manufacture of sugar; the same

measure limits its cultivation within the radius of 500 meters of the forts, which is an extremely limited space when taking into consideration the fact that the furthest fort is just outside the city and the number of people ordered in from the country is large.[34]

From the start of the concentration then, a leading pro-Spanish newspaper warned that the orders issued by the Governor General were too vague and that tragedy for the rural people lay ahead. But this warning was ignored both by the Spanish governing officials and the urban authorities. The result was soon evident. Food was already insufficient in most of the towns for the people resident there before the arrival of the *reconcentrados*. Moreover, all available housing was overcrowded, and unemployment was high. It is not surprising, therefore, that urban residents viewed with great displeasure the arrival of thousands of people who could only add to their own difficulties. While some, out of pure humanity, were disposed to aid the new arrivals, there were many, particularly among the wealthier and official classes, who viewed the *reconcentrados* as deserving of their plight, since by aiding the rebels they had prolonged the armed conflict.[35]

Small wonder that the *reconcentrados* underwent terrible suffering. Housing was uniformly bad. Old warehouses, abandoned buildings, and improvised shelters were used in most cases, but quite often the overflow was so large that old men, women and children were forced to sleep in courtyards, doorways or wherever the slightest protection against the elements could be found. A contemporary observer described a concentration point in Havana as consisting of an old abandoned warehouse resting insecurely on partially decayed stilts over an odorous body of water in the dock area. The floor was weak and full of holes; the roof had large gaping holes; and there were no partitions separating men and women; no toilet facilities and no beds. A resident of Havana wrote of the situation in that city: "Sickness among these families increases each day. Spanish troops occupy so many buildings that no suitable lodging is left for excess peoples. The living quarters of the *reconcentrados* are little more than pigstys, and the people are not breathing the clean fresh air to which they are accustomed. This, along with the scarcity of food, is resulting in hundreds of deaths."[36] William J. Calhoun studied the plight of the *reconcentrados* in five towns during his residence in Cuba from May 13 to June 7, 1897, personally visiting the camps on the outskirts of Matanzas several times. He wrote on June 22:

> I went into the huts, talked with the people, and saw evidence of destitution and suffering that made my heart bleed for the poor creatures. . . . We saw children with swollen limbs and dropsical appearance; this, I was told, was caused by want of sufficient food. . . . There is no use to dwell on the sad and grewsome [sic] picture. It is my opinion if the present policy is continued it must result in the gradual but sure extinction of these people. I talked with many unprejudiced and disinterested people from different parts of the island and they all told the same story of suffering and death on the part of the helpless *reconcentrados*.[37]

On November 8, 1897, the head of John F. Craig & Company of Philadelphia wrote to Secretary of State John Sherman:

> The advices we receive from business correspondents and friends in Cuba present an extreme of destitution and suffering of the country people driven into large cities under the "Concentration" decrees, that the dictates of humanity call for most prompt succor & well considered relief. Men, women and children are crowded together by thousands in roofless pens, and without sufficient food, clothing or medicines and in utter disregard of sanitation, [and] are dying in large numbers daily.[38]

If the *reconcentrado* had any comfort at all, he provided it for himself. From the government which had forcibly transferred him to the towns he could expect very little. Food was irregularly supplied by the authorities and amounted to only what was left over from the mess of military garrisons. Observers reported seeing starving people fighting over this meager fare like animals. Thousands of emaciated, sick and dying people moved like ghosts through the streets of Cuban cities and towns looking for scraps of food and begging from Spaniards and foreigners and often dying on the sidewalks. Young girls sold their virtue to Spanish soldiers and civilians for a morsel of bread, medicine and clothing. Although concentration zones were supposed to be guarded to prevent the internees from returning to the country, some Spanish commanders urged the *reconcentrados* to go into the country in search of food, reasoning that if they were killed by Spanish troops for violating Weyler's orders, their misery would be ended much sooner.³⁹*

Graft played a considerable part in the treatment of victims of the reconcentration policy,† and Spanish officers, petty officials and black market dealers accumulated small fortunes by supplying food and other necessities to those who arrived at their stations with personal belongings and money. Once they had disposed of the possessions, these unfortunate people were left to starve.⁴⁰ Corruption was also evidenced in the distribution of necessities for the *reconcentrados*,

---

* One Cuban soldier reported that when some *reconcentrados* who had slipped out of camp, encountered his unit at breakfast and were offered some food, they replied that "they preferred some fried sweet potatoes in order to take them to their small children who had not yet eaten rather than stop to eat themselves." (Quoted in Varona Guerrero, *op. cit.*, vol. II, p. 79.)

† While in Cuba in 1960, I had the opportunity to interview a former *reconcentrada*, Rosalía Conde. Born in 1883, she was thirteen years old in 1896 when she was taken from her home. Her father and mother had died, and she, a relative, two sisters, one brother and a nephew who was only a baby lived on the family farm near Peralejo. One day in 1896, the Spanish troops came and informed the family that they had to evacuate the farm and house by 6 o'clock that evening. If the Spaniards returned and found anyone on the farm that night, they would kill them. They shot the parrot to show what would happen. Rosalía and her family, together with the farm laborers, left and went to Veguitas as *reconcentrados*. The family was relatively fortunate because Rosalía's father had owned a house in Veguitas, and they managed to stay with the tenants. But they had nothing to eat because of the shortage of food. Rosalía obtained a job as a washerwoman at the Spanish hospital, washing bandages and sheets in the river, and with the money she bribed some Spanish officers to give her food for the family. In addition, she was able at times to get some left-overs from the hospital. In this way, the family just managed to survive, but eventually the eldest sister died of tuberculosis contracted while she was a *reconcentrada*. (Interview with Señora Rosalía Conde, Havana, October 20, 1960.)

The following account of an interview with *reconcentrados* by an American, written on August 1, 1898, is significant:

"While waiting this morning I talked with two white women who had been *reconcentradas* but had managed to escape from Ciego de Avila and hide out in the woods. The description which one of them gave of the march to that town at the reconcentration was harrowing. The poor wretches of women and children and old men were herded by Spanish soldiers and driven at the point of the bayonet along trails worse than any we had traversed. Those who tried to carry food or clothing or furniture through the knee-deep mud exhausted themselves and fell by the wayside to die. Little children were borne by their mothers until they died in arms or were dropped from sheer exhaustion in the last effort to keep moving before the bayonets. Only the strongest reached Ciego de Avila— and they reached there only to starve under guard." (N. G. Gonzales, *In Darkest Cuba: Two Months Service under Gómez Along the Trocha from the Caribbean to the Bahama Channel*, Columbia, South Carolina, 1922, p. 222.)

government officials keeping most of the limited supplies for sale on the black market. A resident of La Rosa in Matanzas province reported to the American Consul General that this practice had caused "great want" in such towns as Jovellanos and Cimarrones. "This government pretends to distribute rations to those in need, but according to the *alcaldes* [mayors] themselves, they receive about one half of what is alloted." [41]

How many people were brought from the countryside to the concentration zones is difficult to determine accurately. Stephen Bonsal, an acute American observer,* estimated in 1896 that "By the first of December, 1896, 400,000 non-combatants . . . were concentrated in stations, which, whether they were chosen with the object in view or not, have proven admirably adapted to the realization of a policy of extermination." [42] Others place the number of people in the concentration zones at between 500,000 and 600,000. [43]

There are also different estimates regarding the number of deaths among the *reconcentrados*. (No official lists containing numbers or names were kept, and the dead were quickly buried.†) Carlos M. Trelles y Govín, the Cuban historian, states that "*la reconcentración*" caused the death of "not less than 300,000 Cubans," [44] but this probably includes urban residents who were not concentrated and those killed trying to evade the order. On one statistic most authorities agree: in the province of Havana alone 50,000 perished. [45] According to the reports of American consuls in Cuba, during July, August, and September, 1897, the Cuban death rate doubled and trebled. In December, 1897, Consul Lee estimated that 200,000 *reconcentrados* had already died, and that the remaining 200,000 were starving. The Central Cuban Relief Committee also estimated that 200,000 people had died, and they based their calculation solely on available Spanish sources. [46]

Whatever the exact figure, it is clear that the death rate within the

---

* In his excellent *Historiografía de Cuba*, José Manuel Pérez Cabrera describes Bonsal's book, *The Real Condition of Cuba Today* as "a pathetic description, deeply felt, of the misery, anguish and unimaginable misfortune of the peasants population of Cuba under the iron command of General Weyler." (Mexico, 1962, p. 290.)

† The Nazis were more efficient; they kept accurate records of all who died in their concentration camps.

concentration centers was appalling.* For the most part, the *reconcentrados* were peasants who were used to living in relatively sanitary homes and were completely strange to close confinement in unhealthy surroundings. Consequently, they were as susceptible under concentration to diseases of an epidemic nature as were Spanish soldiers fresh from the Peninsula.[47] When on top of this was added the low quality and quantity of food, it is not surprising that the *reconcentrados* died in such large numbers. In one of the better stations, the Cascorro hill in the city of Matanzas, which was comparatively healthy with good natural drainage, twenty-five to thirty inhabitants of the colony of three thousand *reconcentrados* died each day in March, 1897, of malnutrition and other causes.[48] One can imagine the daily death rate in stations which did not have even these facilities.

Despite the evils of concentration life, the Cuban peasant found it hardly a less dangerous course to remain in the country. To be caught in one's home evading concentration camps meant certain death. Emulating the Indians when they tried to evade the Spanish *conquistadores*, Cuban peasants in 1896-1897 sought out the more inaccessible parts of mountains, forests, and swampy areas and began cultivation of little gardens in the more secluded places, on a temporary basis. In some cases they managed to bring a few animals to these hidden places. These people, of course, ran grave risks. After reconcentration started, the Spanish patrols took special pains to seek out evaders.[49] While in the eastern provinces of Oriente and Camagüey, and in parts of Las Villas and Pinar del Río, the nature of the terrain was such as to enable evaders to escape the notice of Spanish patrols, unless they were betrayed by spies, the provinces of Matanzas and Havana, the western part of Las Villas, and the southern portion of Pinar del Río offered few such sanctuaries. In Oriente province, primarily, and in other provinces to a lesser extent, there were groups of peasants who escaped

---

* Walter Millis, for whom Weyler is practically a misunderstood humanitarian who was simply meeting Gómez's tactics with his reconcentration policy, dismisses the idea that undue suffering and wholesale deaths were a result of this policy, and calls this merely propaganda by circulation-seeking newspapers, Cuban propagandists in the United States, and a result of reports by naive American consuls in Cuba. (*The Martial Spirit*, pp. 59, 76.) For an effective Cuban analysis and refutation of Millis' viewpoint, see Herminio Portell Vilá, *Historia de la Guerra de Cuba y los Estados Unidos Contra España*, La Habana, 1949, pp. 54-55.)

from the concentration camps into regular defensive colonies. These were formed under the direction of revolutionary civil officials and were organized so as to effect mutual protection. They maintained scouts and posted guards who kept the colonies well informed in advance of Spanish patrols. Enough of the men were provided with arms of one sort or another to conduct delaying actions in case of too rapid Spanish movement before a protective rebel unit could arrive. Since many young men had already joined the rebel army, the colonies consisted mainly of old or very young men, physically handicapped persons, only sons of fatherless families, and women and children.[50]

Spanish patrols wandering through the countryside destroyed all crops and animals they encountered. They cut down fruit trees, and contaminated water supplies. The chief of a rebel cavalry unit recorded a typical description of the situation in Havana province in 1897: "In the countryside here one sees nothing but debris and ashes. In many places sown fields have been uprooted completely. The few cattle remaining are dead from Spanish guns because they did not want them to be of use to the Revolution. It is a great pity to see families who have escaped from the concentration zones looking for food for their children." [51]

In his report, William J. Calhoun, an American government official in Cuba, wrote:

> I travelled by rail from Havana to Matanzas. The country outside of the military posts was practically depopulated. Every house had been burned, banana trees cut down, cane fields swept with fire, and everything in the shape of food destroyed. It was as fair a landscape as mortal eye ever looked upon; but I did not see a house, man, woman or child, a horse, mule, or cow, nor even a dog. I did not see a sign of life, except an occasional vulture or buzzard sailing through the air. The country was wrapped in the stillness of death and the silence of desolation.[52]

On numerous occasions, Spanish patrols killed civilians on the supposition that they were rebels in disguise or serving as spies for the Revolution.* The truth is that after concentration began, Spanish

---

* One Spaniard, dismayed by the cruelty unleashed under Weyler, revealed to United States Commercial Agent Barker that a young Spanish officer had told him: "Go ahead, execute every person you believe to be in sympathy with the Cubans, but make no report of your action—the idea is to exterminate and conceal your method of doing so." (Barker to W. W. Rockhill, May 5, 1896, U.S. Consular Despatches, Sagua la Grande, Department of State, National Archives.)

forces regarded all farmers as enemies even if they professed pro-Spanish sympathies.[53] They had good reason to reach this conclusion. The suffering of their wives and children had only strengthened the peasants' determination to rid the island of Spanish domination. Gómez reported from Camagüey in September, 1896 that the Cubans who had succeeded in evading concentration "are living in the country and are aiding the Revolution more each day."[54] About the same time, De Truffin reported to the Russian Ambassador to Madrid that Weyler's inhuman policies had backfired:

> . . . the suspension of agricultural operations and the concentration of peasants around the Spanish garrisons creates the conditions for a great number of supporters joining the revolutionary army. In addition, such a mass concourse of the poor worsens sanitary conditions in the island, which are sufficiently bad as it is. Herded together like cattle, without any means of assistance, many of our unfortunate peasants prefer to join the insurgent detachment rather than die of poverty and starvation in the towns and villages.[55]

As we shall now see, the military events of 1897 demonstrated that Weyler's barbarism had utterly failed to weaken the ability of the Liberating Army to continue the war successfully for the independence of Cuba.

CHAPTER VII

The Military and Political Scene in 1897 and Early 1898

SHORTLY AFTER Antonio Maceo's death, General Weyler jubilantly announced the crushing of the insurrection in Pinar del Río. Within another month, he announced the "almost complete" pacification of Havana and Matanzas provinces.[1] Yet reports even in the fiercely pro-Spanish *Diario de la Marina* showed that Pinar del Río, Havana and Matanzas still contained thousands of active insurgents.[2] On January 15, 1897, De Truffin wrote to the Russian Ambassador to Madrid: "As I had foreseen, Maceo's actual or supposed death has had very little effect on the general course of the insurrection. The insurgents are still masters of almost the entire island. Whatever General Weyler says, Pinar del Río Province has not been pacified in any way.* The numerous insurgent detachments are still hiding out in its mountains and this is easily tested by a short trip into the interior. . . ."[3]

The *insurrectos* in Pinar del Río, now led by Major General José María Rodríguez, who had disembarked on July 25, 1895 with the Roloff-Sánchez expedition, and later by General Pedro Díaz, made repeated sorties from their mountain retreats against Spanish columns and burned property and lines of communication. In Matanzas and Havana, where the abundant communications, great population centers, the small size of the provinces and the topography of the

---

* Walter Millis, however, showed he had swallowed Weyler's boasts when he wrote in *The Martial Spirit*: "After Maceo's death the situation in Pinar del Río had been pretty well cleared up. . . ." (*Op. cit.*, p. 66.) Consul General Lee reported to Washington that Weyler issued false reports which left even the Spanish government unaware of the true situation in Cuba. (Lee to Sherman, March 17, April 13, 1897, Consular Letters, Havana, Department of State, NA.)

terrain favored the Spanish troops, the *mambises* fought the enemy ferociously throughout 1897, and reached Marianao and Guanabacoa, that is to say, the very doors of the capital of the island. On July 15, 1897, De Truffin summed up the situation accurately:

> ... the whole island is not what you might say occupied but rather infiltrated by the insurgents, and never a week passes without their making their presence known by some bold sortie, be it a derailed train, a blown-up bridge, a sacked village or a ransacked transport.... Such is the present situation in the country and such are the successes in pacifying the island of which General Weyler is wont to speak.[4]

Yet even this was only part of the whole story. From January 2, 1897 until April, 1898, when the United States entered the war, the troops under the command of Máximo Gómez, numbering no more than 3,000 men, had 41 encounters with the 40,000 Spanish soldiers, cavalry and infantry, concentrated south of Las Villas. From the *trocha* to Cienfuegos, in a territory of no more than 500 square miles, the rebels, commanded by Gómez, moved about freely without the Spaniards being able to dislodge them or inflict decisive losses on them. In the campaign of La Reforma, Weyler was decisively defeated by Gómez, even though he had 34 battalions and four regiments of cavalry plus the all-important artillery.[5]

With the exception of Santiago de Cuba and other seaport cities, and two or three large cities of the interior which were well fortified and protected by garrisons, the eastern provinces of Camagüey and Oriente were "under the absolute control of the Liberating Army, led by General Calixto García." All military operations were initiated by the Cubans, and the Spaniards were forced to remain on the defensive, setting themselves the task of protecting a few key positions. In repeated skirmishes, the troops of García, Cebreco, Rabí, and other Cuban chiefs reached the suburbs of the key cities, and captured them after sieges. Bayamo, which had a few thousand inhabitants when the war began,* was besieged by García throughout the entire year of 1897 and captured early in 1898; Jiguaní was attacked and bombarded

---

* Bayamo had been destroyed by the Cubans themselves early in the Ten Years' War to prevent it from falling into the hands of the Spaniards, and rebuilt after the war.

by García's forces in March, 1897 and also taken early in 1898; Guáimaro was assaulted and taken. Equipped for the first time with a few cannons, of United States origin for the most part, the forces of García, even though hampered by lack of ammunition and quinine, made a series of daring and well-organized attacks on other towns and cities under Spanish control.[6]

Captain Aníbal Escalante Beatón, who served under General Calixto García, has given us an analysis of the great Cuban military leader's strategy in capturing a town defended by the Spanish army. He points out that García planned his attack with "chronometric perfection," training his small forces so thoroughly that they were able to overcome a powerful enemy. "He was not dismayed at any stage in the battle, slowing it down when necessary, but always keeping himself on the offensive."[7] These characteristics were brilliantly exhibited in Calixto García's great triumph and one of the Cuban's most dramatic successes —the capture of Las Tunas, also called Tunas de Bayamo. The Spaniards had given it still another name—Victoria de Las Tunas. For the city had always been the center of the most intransigent pro-Spanish sentiment, and while it had often been attacked by the Cubans during the Ten Years' War, the attacks had always been repulsed. Hence the Spaniards bestowed upon the city the honor of being called Victoria de las Tunas.

Although it had suffered losses in population because of Weyler's reconcentration policy, Las Tunas in August, 1897 still contained a civil population of over 2,000 inhabitants and a permanent Spanish garrison made up of a series of forts guarded by a battallion of infantry, an artillery with several Krupp cannon of 12 pounds, a section of the Civil Guard, a company of volunteers and one of military administrative forces. In all, it had well over 1,000 effectively armed soldiers, and possessed sufficient supplies and equipment to resist the attack of a powerful adversary. The forces in the fortified city were under the command of Lieutenant Colonel José Civera.

Having determined to capture Las Tunas, Calixto García prepared the attack. He gathered together a force of 700 infantry and 200 cavalry and several pieces of artillery from various parts of Oriente, and instructed his men meticulously in the plan he had worked out for the siege. On the morning of August 28, 1897, General García gave the signal for the attack. The dynamite cannon and the Hotchkiss cannon went into action, and the rebels invaded one fort after another, capturing each one in hand-to-hand combat. The dynamite cannon put the Spanish Krupp cannons out of action, and the first day of battle ended with the Cubans occupying the streets of the city. The next day opened with a four-hour artillery attack on the forts still holding out. When August 30th dawned, General García entered the city with several of his aides and a cavalry escort. After some severe fighting, Spanish Lieutenant Mediavilla appeared carrying a white flag as an emissary from Commander Civera, with instructions to discuss terms of surrender.[8]

> "I offered him liberty for himself and his comrades," Calixto García wrote to Gómez. "The surrender was verified by the turning over of the remaining forts. . . . I have taken more than a thousand rifles and a million bullets. . . . In addition, I have obtained 10 wagon loads of medicine, many *machetes*, several cannons, and an infinity of cavalry supplies plus supplies of clothing, edibles, etc. . . . The prisoners consist of a chief, two doctors, ten officers, 380 soldiers plus 100 odd non-combatants and volunteers who were armed and fought during the siege. . . . I have sent some of the prisoners to fortified areas, others to Holguín, still others to Camagüey, and some to Bayamo, with the object that the enemy should not be able to hide the fierce blow it has suffered."

García closed his report to the Cuban Commander-in-Chief with the proud observation, "I cannot help from showing that I am highly satisfied with the conduct of the officers and soldiers who took part in the operations of Las Tunas. I feel true satisfaction in telling you that all of them knew how to stay at their posts with no exception whatsoever."[9] The Cubans had suffered 83 losses in the attack on the city. Colonel Mario García Menocal, who had distinguished himself in the battle, was elevated to the rank of Brigadier-General.

One incident gave General García special satisfaction. He described it as follows in a letter to Estrada Palma from the captured city: "A great part of the triumph is owed to the dynamite cannon which performed prodigious feats. The Spanish soldiers and officers were astounded by the destruction it created with its shots, and asked to see the artillery which they believed was 'Yankee.' You don't know the pride with which I presented to them the boy who is today Comandante Juan Miguel Portuondo, saying to them, "Es Cubano." [He is Cuban.]"¹⁰*

The capture of Victoria de las Tunas after a 48-hour siege was proof that the Cubans dominated Oriente; the Spanish troops in the province were totally incapable of coming to the aid of the besieged city.† It proved further that given the proper military equipment, the rebels could fairly quickly have put an end to the Spanish domination of Cuba. As Calixto García put it in a letter to Estrada Palma in the summer of 1897: "If this were not the case, we would have already won.‡ The weaknesses of the Spanish are every day more obvious. Their action these days is none other than to avoid fighting, and to remain inside with the barracks tightly closed." ¹¹

Another indication of the extent of Cuban control was the large vote cast in every province for representatives to the General Assembly to chose a successor to President Cisneros whose term was about to expire. From the provinces of Havana, Pinar del Río and Matanzas, which Weyler had reported as permanently pacified, more than 14,000 votes were cast. "We have carried out the elections without the slightest trouble," Calixto García reported jubilantly to Estrada Palma in the summer of 1897.¹²§

Spain's efforts to crush the rebellion in Cuba were being hampered by an insurrection in the Philippines. (She also faced a threatened uprising in Puerto Rico in May, 1896.) Like Cuba, the Philippines had long been the scene of unrest and dissatisfaction with Spanish rule. Forced labor, abusive treatment by both civil and church officials, and other outrages against the people resulted in revolts. But these uprisings

---

* The Hotchkiss cannon was operated under the command of the American Frederick Funston. Funston himself had learned how to operate the twelve-pound field gun from the firm in the United States, Hartley & Graham, from which it had been purchased. (Frederick Funston, "To Cuba as a Filibusterer," *Scribners*, vol. XXXVIII, September, 1910, p. 316.)

† Five days after the surrender of the city, García wrote to Gómez that the Spaniards in the region had still made no effort "to attack me." (Calixto García to Máximo Gómez, Tunas de Bayamo, Sept. 3, 1897, Archivo Nacional. See also Capitán Aníbal Escalante Beatón, *Calixto García, Su Campaña en el 95*, La Habana, 1946, p. 262.)

‡ On December 6, 1896, García had written to Estrada Palma: "I am between Cauto and Bayamo and if I had cannon bullets those towns would be mine before long." (Archivo Nacional.) They were eventually taken.

§ The Assembly met at Guaimarillo. A new Council of Government, presided over by General Bartolomé Masó, succeeded the Cisneros administration.

failed, owing to lack of concerted action on the part of the rebels. The year 1896 marked a turning point. Inspired by the writings of Dr. José P. Rizal and other Filipino intellectuals, the nation arose in rebellion against tyranny.* The immediate cause of the Revolution was the discovery by the Spanish authorities of the *Kataastaasan Kagalanggalangang Katipunan Ng Mga Anak Ng Bayan* (Highest and Most Respected Association of the Sons of the Country), often referred to simply as the *Katipunan*. It was organized in 1892 by Andrés Bonifacio as a secret revolutionary society; its birth and rise signalized the end of a long crusade to secure reforms from Spain by means of peaceful propaganda. Its discovery on the night of August 19, 1896, resulted in a meeting of the *Katipuneros* in the hills of Balintawak, north of Manila. Bonifacio took out his *cedula* certificate, a symbol of vassalage, and tore it to pieces. Everyone followed suit. This was the so-called *Grito de Balintawak,* and like the *Grito de Baire*, in Cuba, it reverberated throughout the land. Rafael Guerrero, in his contemporary account of the insurrection in Cuba, notes that the uprising in the Philippines "had much in common and was analagous to the first *grito* of independence given by the Cubans two years ago, and . . . [is] almost an extension of the same movement."

Spain used terror to try to crush the uprising, arresting and jailing suspected revolutionaries in the military jails of Manila. In the dungeons of Fort Santiago "men died and were borne away by the carloads." Over a thousand Filipinos were exiled to Guam, the Mariannas and to other Spanish penal colonies in Africa. Large numbers were executed after summary trials. But the Filipinos, like the Cubans, fought back ferociously. On November 11, 1896, insurgent General Emilio Agui-

---

* Dr. José P. Rizal occupies in the Philippines the same position that José Martí occupies in Cuba. He founded the *Liga Filipina* on July 3, 1892, with the specific purpose of using it to unite the entire country against Spanish oppression. His two novels—*Noli Me Tangere* and *El Filibusterismo*—inspired the Filipinos to fight for freedom. Author, scientist, scholar, physician, poet, novelist, historian, musician, painter, sculptor, educator, farmer, engineer, and linguist, he was one of the remarkable figures of the nineteenth century. He studied in Spain and at Heidelberg in Germany, and visited the United States. Asked about his impressions of the United States, Dr. Rizal replied, "America is the land par excellence of freedom, but only for whites." (José Alejandro, *The Price of Freedom*, Manila, 1949, p. 7.) From 1892 until shortly before his execution by the Spaniards for treason at Bagumbayan, Manila on December 30, 1896, Dr. Rizal lived in exile.

naldo engaged General Ramón Blanco and forced him to withdraw, and the victory further fanned the flames of revolt. By the end of the month, Manila was hemmed in by provinces in revolt and the patriotic cause was spreading to other regions that had been considered loyal to Spain. On December 13, 1896, Blanco was replaced by General Camilo de Polavieja, and the repression was increased. With the execution of Dr. José Rizal, who had not taken part in the armed uprisings, the Revolution surged to greater fury. ("Spanish bullets destroyed Rizal," Filipinos proudly assert, "but his ideas destroyed the Spanish empire in the Orient.") The Spanish authorities organized concentration camps, as in Cuba, forcing the country people to live in them, intensified summary imprisonments, executions, and deportations. But it was not until December 14, 1897 that the organized rebellion ended.* Yet even after this the island was not at peace. In a report dated February 22, 1898, the American Consul General at Manila wrote:

> Peace was proclaimed, and since my coming, festivities therefore were held; but there is no peace, and has been none for about two years. Conditions here and in Cuba are practically alike. War exists, battles are practically daily occurrences, ambulances bring in many wounded, and hospitals are full. Prisoners are brought here and shot without trial, and Manila is under martial law. The Crown forces have not been able to dislodge a rebel army within 10 miles of Manila, and last Saturday, February 19, a battle was there fought and 5 dead left on the field.[13]

Thus throughout 1897 and continuing into 1898, Spain had to fight a two-front war requiring her to send troops to the Philippines that were scheduled for Cuba, and further weakening her already unstable economy. Developments in Spain reflected the increasing pressure upon her resources and her inability to crush the rebellion in Cuba. Catalonian factories shut down due to the loss of much of the Cuban market, and unemployment rose in many other Spanish cities. Many people in Spain who maintained themselves on rent from Cuba had

---

* On December 14, 1897 an agreement was reached which has come to be known as the Pact of Biac-na-bato. Under the terms of this treaty, the Spanish government purportedly agreed to six important concessions designed to improve the lot of the Filipinos. Emilio Aguinaldo, head of the insurgents, and some forty insurgent leaders went into exile. (W. Cameron Forbes, *The Philippine Islands*, Boston, 1928, pp. 57-60.)

to cut expenses drastically. Spain found it more and more difficult to raise funds for the war.[14]*

Small wonder that the government of Prime Minister Cánovas del Castillo experienced increasing opposition to his Cuban policies. In late May, 1897, Práxedes M. Sagasta, leader of the Liberal Party, announced that his party would no longer support the conservative program which was leading the country to ruin in Cuba and the Philippines, and was encouraging civil war at home. In order to obtain a vote of confidence, Cánovas resigned on June 3 and was reinstated a few days later by the Queen Regent. During the ministerial crisis, the liberals showed a great deal of strength among all classes in Spanish society, and it became clear that if Weyler did not succeed soon in fulfilling his repeated boasts that the island was being pacified, Sagasta would come to office and bring changes to Spanish colonial policy. Toward the end of June, Sagasta released a manifesto for the Liberal Party which pledged to adopt political reform as well as military force to end the Cuban Revolution, indirectly criticizing Weyler for handling Cuban affairs so clumsily. He called for the abandonment of Weyler's "policy of excessive severity and repression . . . for that system is not calculated to improve the prospect of pacification which we earnestly desire." Though firmly opposed to the independence of Cuba, Sagasta believed that with the rebels gaining in strength, with the failure of Spanish arms, and with the failure of repression to curb the rise in revolutionary sentiment in Cuba, only concessions could save the island for Spain. It is clear that Spain was moving toward another ministerial crisis on Cuban policy.[15]

Then in August, 1897, Cánovas was assassinated by the anarchist

---

* As early as April, 1896, the American Consul General in Havana wrote that it was already being reported in that city that Spain was having great difficulty "in supplying the funds to be needed . . . in the suppression of the Cuban insurrection. . . ." (Williams to Rockhill, Havana, April 10, 1896, Consular Despatches, Department of State, National Archives, Washington, D.C. Hereinafter cited as National Archives.)

"The Cuban revolution," writes Tedoro A. Agoncillo, "had been eating up Spanish resources in men and materials, to such an extent that those pressed for the Philippine campaigns were nothing more than 'boys, ignorant of the use of arms, ill clad, badly fed, and with months of pay in arrears.'" Spain, he notes, "was at the end of the rope." (*Malolos: The Crisis of the Republic*, Quezon City, Philippines, 1960, pp. 11, 81.)

Angiolillo.* Azcárraga, who became Premier, announced that Weyler's conduct of affairs in Cuba had his full confidence, and that he planned to back the Captain General until the rebellion was crushed. But the Azcárraga Ministry fell within a few weeks after this announcement. The Queen Regent called upon Sagasta to head the new Ministry. In October, 1897, shortly after becoming Prime Minister, Sagasta declared that he would completely reverse Spain's policy in Cuba since the outbreak of the Revolution. "I will fulfill my program, establish autonomy in Cuba and recall Weyler. . . . The Liberal Party is prepared to grant Cuba all possible self-government, a broad tariff and every concession compatible with inflexible defense of Spanish rule and sovereignty in the West Indies." [16]

Segismundo Moret, Sagasta's Colonial Minister, announced the reforms to be introduced in Cuba. The Cubans were to elect municipal and provincial councils and an insular parliament of two chambers. The colonists were to have complete control of domestic affairs, including control of education, tariff regulations, customs, charity, public works, agriculture, and industry. Spain was to retain control over international relations, military and naval organizations, the law courts, and relations between church and state. Cuba was to continue to elect deputies to the Spanish Cortes.[17]

As we shall see, pressure from the government of the United States played an important part in Spain's decision to remove Weyler and to grant Cuba autonomy. But most American historians have tended to mention this as the only influence, ignoring the fact that the failure

---

* Angiolillo declared that he had acted in retaliation for the execution of a group of anarchists convicted of bombing a religious procession in Barcelona. Nevertheless, a number of Spanish papers charged that there was a direct connection between the Cuban insurrection and the assassination. Actually, although the death of Cánovas was to benefit the Cuban cause, the rebel leaders did not look with favor on individual acts of terror. While predicting that Spain would be seriously weakened, Gómez noted: "If it had occurred to Angiolillo to escape after his attempt against Cánovas and seek refuge in our ranks, hoping to save himself, he certainly would have been mistaken because here justice, which must be the choice of civilized men, would have been done as it was done in Madrid. We cannot rub elbows with those guilty of common crimes because that would be defiling the flag of liberty and order which we have unfurled in this field of glory. The Spaniards, on their part, show no regard for honor and decency when they used this incident against the Cubans." (Máximo Gómez to Estrada Palma, Sept. 18, Dec. 18, 1897, Archivo Nacional. See also Emilio Roig de Leuchsenring, Máximo Gómez el Libertador de Cuba . . . , op. cit., p. 34.)

of Spain's military operations in Cuba was a decisive factor.* As the Madrid *Heraldo* conceded on November 17, 1897: "It is now evident that there is no such thing as pacification in any of the island's provinces, and also that if General Weyler and his policies had continued in Cuba we would have lost our colony." [18]

While the promises of reform and autonomy were being dangled before the Cubans in order to disrupt the increasingly successful drive for independence, Sagasta made it clear that military activity against the insurgent armies would continue. He announced that beginning in November, the new Captain General, "equipped with every possible means of pacification," would push the campaign vigorously in Santiago de Cuba and Puerto Príncipe. Reinforcements numbering twenty thousand men would leave for Cuba before the end of November. The Spanish army in the island was to be maintained at a strength of at least 145,000 men until pacification of the entire island was achieved. One aspect of the Sagasta policy was not announced publicly. This entailed the expenditure of considerable funds for the bribery of rebel leaders to induce them to support the program of autonomy and lay down their arms.[19]

It soon became clear that the insurgent leaders both in Cuba and in the United States would not fall for Sagasta's bait.† Cuban leaders in New York announced that only independence would end the war: "The Cubans are more determined today than ever to accept nothing short of independence." Estrada Palma announced: "We Cubans will never accept autonomy or reform. We are fighting for independence and we will accept peace only on the condition of separating completely from Spain. . . ." [20] In Cuba, Máximo Gómez and Calixto García issued a statement listing twenty facts to prove that Spain had completely failed to crush the rebellion, which was flourishing better than

---

* Millis is especially guilty of this tendency; typically, he bases his conclusion that Weyler was winning the war against the rebels solely on the Captain General's own pronouncements, which no contemporary believed. (Millis, *op. cit.*, pp. 79-80.)

† As early as June, 1896, when Maceo learned that the United States and Spain were discussing the possibility of granting Cuba autonomy, he wrote to Perfecto Lacoste: "The [North] Americans and Spaniards can make whatever agreements they wish, but Cuba will be free inside of a short while and can laugh at the negotiations which do not favor its independence." (José Luciano Franco, *La Vida heroica y ejemplar de Antonio Maceo*, La Habana, 1963, p. 110.)

ever. Among them was cited the election of the Assembly which met at Guaimarillo, "without the Spanish Army still in Cuba being able to prevent it"; the siege and capture of Victoria de las Tunas by the Liberating Army; the complete civil and military organization maintained by the Republic of Cuba from Cape Maisí to San Antonio; the fact that only 70,000 Spanish combatants remained in Cuba "out of the 260,000 soldiers which were so arrogantly and fruitlessly sent to our fields to fight against us"; the "daily desertions of the brave Spanish soldiers"; the "notorious failures" of General Martínez Campos and General Weyler, thus revealing that neither the former's policy of "moderation" nor the latter's policy of "pitiless and cruel war" could achieve the defeat of the Cubans; the "absolute paralyzation imposed by the Army of the Republic upon agricultural and industrial labor in the sugar-making districts"; and the total and complete failure of Spain, despite the overwhelming superiority in men and materials, "to extirpate the sentiment and idea of independence." Gómez and García then expressed contempt for the policy of autonomy as "characteristic of Spain's treachery and its impotence to prevent by force of arms the irresistible and near advent of the independence of Cuba. . . .":

> . . . it is inapplicable, useless, inefficacious, unworthy and absurd that any solution but the independence of Cuba can sensibly, satisfactorily, and definitely resolve the political problems of this country. . . . Under no consideration shall we treat with the oppressors of our country except solely and exclusively on the basis of the absolute independence of Cuba.
> No; Cuba cannot, must not and does not wish to continue any longer under the sovereignty of Spain. . . . Cuba cannot accept Autonomy, not only under the Spanish form, but not even with the amplitude enjoyed by Canada and the Australian colonies. The epic pages of the Revolution are not written in our glorious fields, with the blood of our heroes, in order that upon the termination of such a prodigious work the unworthy record of errors of our patriotism be read. The names of our champions who have fallen and those of the 150,000 defenseless Cubans pitilessly murdered by General Weyler would condemn us from Heaven if we were to treat with Spain. . . .[21]

Despite these rebuffs, Sagasta went ahead with his plans. Weyler was removed as Captain General and replaced by Ramón Blanco, a veteran army man.* Weyler's reconcentration policy was modified, but the system was not abolished and deaths of helpless civilians continued. Owners or lessees of farms who could prove they possessed "the elements of resources to help themselves" were permitted to return to their homes. Agricultural laborers were permitted to return to work "provided they reside in the farm or plantation where they work, that they pass the night within the fortified place of said farm or plantation, and that they always carry with them their proper personal documents." For the destitute *reconcentrados* unable to take advantage of these orders, an elaborate plan of relief was announced. Government funds were promised and an official appeal was made for private contributions. Civil authorities (provincial governors, mayors, and deputies) were to head relief boards, and were to be aided by the military commandants, parish priests, municipal physicians, and such "proprietors, merchants, traders and agriculturists, whom the president of each board may designate." Destitute rebels invoking pardons were to be aided by the boards. Bi-monthly reports were to be submitted by each relief board. General Blanco was authorized by Madrid to sign a credit of one hundred thousand dollars to be devoted to the immediate relief of sufferers.[22]

It all sounded impressive on paper; but despite the lofty-worded proclamation, Spain was financially unable, and perhaps also unwilling, to give sufficient direct relief, and the condition of the *reconcentrados* grew worse, as did that of the regular residents of the cities, for the spread of diseases of one sort or another greatly increased the death rate of the city as a whole.[23] By December, 1897, the death-rate in the camps was higher than ever—probably half of the *reconcentrados* had perished by then—and the relief allotments from Spain were woefully insufficient. Blanco did make his grant of $100,000, but it amounted to nothing when distributed among thousands in the camps. $12,500 was allowed for relief in Havana Province, but this amounted to only seventeen cents per person if distributed to each living *reconcentrado*.[24]

Some real aid began early in 1898, when the Spanish military authorities gave permission to the Central Cuban Relief Committee to operate among the *reconcentrados*. The Committee was founded at the instiga-

---

* Don Ramón Blanco y Arenas, Marquis de Peña Plata, had served in the Carlist War and as Captain General of the Philippine Islands from 1894 to 1896. He had acquired his title after a victory over the Carlists.

tion of Clara Barton, head of the Red Cross. Returning from Cuba she reported, "The murders of Armenians in Armenia shine mercifully in comparison with what I saw in Havana."[25] Alerted by her report, the American National Red Cross founded the Central Cuban Relief Committee, through which appeals went out to all Americans for supplies and funds to aid the *reconcentrados*. The first shipment of relief made by the Committee arrived in Cuba on January 4, 1898. It consisted of 160 cases of condensed milk. The second shipment consisted of 39 tons of food, clothing and medicine.[26] In February, Clara Barton was in Cuba with several assistants supervising the distribution of medicines, clothing, food supplies, fresh milk and fruit among *reconcentrados* who were in the worst conditions, particularly those in the smaller towns.* There were tremendous difficulties to be overcome. On February 23, 1898, J. K. Elwell, one of Miss Barton's assistants, wrote from Havana to the office of the Central Cuban Relief Committee:

> To tell you the honest truth we have not been received as warmly as I expected by the [U.S. Consul] Gen'l [Lee]. We have hardly got the support it is his duty to give us. Every time we try to talk to him on business subjects, he is in a great hurry, is always very busy & yet he seems to find plenty of time to devote to his large circle of lady friends here. When we arrived he knew no more about the supplies on hand than "the man in the moon" & as yet, to my knowledge has never been inside the warehouse. Of course you will consider the part of this letter in relation to the Consul Gen'l private. But it makes me furious to see him act so. It makes it so hard for Miss Barton. Under the best of circumstances it is hard enough for her.[27]

In Santiago de Cuba the Spanish merchants opposed relief distribution on the ground that "it greatly injures their business," and they were joined by Spanish officials who called the relief activities "Amer-

---

* On February 5, 1898, J. K. Elwell, Clara Barton's assistant, wrote from Havana that there was an imperative need "to immediately get the supplies out into the country, Habana is doing well enough. The country towns are the ones that need succor and need it desperately." (Elwell to Stephen E. Barton, Feb. 15, 1898, Clara Barton Papers, Box 51, Library of Congress.)

There are 34 boxes of the Clara Barton Papers in the Library of Congress dealing with relief work in Cuba.

ican intervention and interference." In the Custom House, relief supplies were held up for weeks while the Collector of the Customs opened all packages to determine which of the supplies should pay duty. "All new clothing, shoes, canned goods & medicines he put to one side and declared they should pay duty as it was evidently intended to smuggle & sell them." [28]

Even where the Spanish authorities cooperated, not a few military commanders and local officials followed their usual practice, diverting supplies for the *reconcentrados* for their own use and profit. In March, 1898, after corresponding with Clara Barton, the chairman of the Central Cuban Relief Committee wrote that "she is far from satisfied with the method of local distribution and she believes that the whole benefit of our generosity is not reaching those for whom it is intended." [29]

In time, Miss Barton and her co-workers succeeded in bringing much-needed relief to the *reconcentrados*, distributing hundreds of tons of food and medicine, helping to set up clinics, dispensaries, and hospitals for the refugees.* But improvements came slowly. In February, 1898, the commanding officer of the U.S.S. *Montgomery*, then visiting Matanzas, wrote from that city: "Fourteen thousand people without food or shelter. The people are suffering from famine." [30] When Senator Redfield Proctor of Vermont visited Cuba in late February and early March, 1898, he found thousands of families living in towns in huts of about ten to fifteen feet, in sanitary conditions that were "unmentionable." "Torn from their homes, with foul earth, foul air, foul water, and foul food or none," he declared in his celebrated speech in the Senate on his return to the United States, "what wonder that one-half have died and that one-quarter of the living are so diseased that they cannot be saved? Little children are still walking about with arms and chest terribly emaciated, eyes swollen, and abdomen bloated to three times the natural size. The physicians say the cases are hopeless." [31]

On November 15, 1897, the Queen Regent signed three decrees of the Liberal Ministry for political reforms in Cuba. The first two, imme-

---

* One Cuban writes: "The activities of Clara Barton for the victims of the reconcentration lasted two years. During this time hundreds of thousands of persons whom she helped to survive these horrors learned to bless the name of their protector. . . ." (A. Garden, *Clara Barton, protectora de los reconcentrados Cubanos*, La Habana, 1954, p. 19.)

diately operative, extended to the island the rights of Spaniards and established the electoral laws of Spain. The third, setting up the actual machinery of autonomous government, was not effective until the Cortes had consented. It provided for an Administrative Council of thirty-five and a popularly elected House of Representatives to be chosen by qualified voters of the island. Seventeen of the Council were to be elected; eighteen were to be appointed by the Governor-General, who was still to be named by the Crown. The Insular Parliament had the power to legislate on matters concerning the departments of justice, interior, treasury, public works, education, agriculture, civil administration, provincial, municipal, and judiciary apportionment, public health, public credit, banks and the monetary system. It had exclusive power over the local budget of expenditures and revenue and tariff schedules. Legislation involving taxation and public credit was to originate in the House of Representatives. The Governor-General, who commanded the military and naval force and supervised the administrative machinery, could initiate colonial laws; he could suspend the insular parliament for a maximum period of three months; he could defer consideration of any bill "affecting the national interest" until the Madrid government had had the opportunity to render its opinion, and he appointed the department heads, who were responsible to the House of Representatives. The home government retained the right to determine the "sovereign expense" of the island. Treaties of Commerce affecting Cuba were to be made by Madrid "with the cooperation of special delegates duly authorized by the colonial government." The apportionment between Spain and Cuba of the present national debt, as well as that still to be incurred in the suppression of the insurrection, was to be determined by the Spanish Cortes. Cuba and Spain were to have equal power in settling mutual tariff reductions.[32]

It is obvious that for all the fanfare preceding the Liberal Ministry's concrete proposals for political reforms in Cuba, the final program fell far short even of the form of government enjoyed at that time by Canada. As one can see, the Governor-General was still an executive and administrative dictator who could dissolve the legislature at will, appoint the administrative officers, veto any act of the legislature, and even revoke the guarantees of the constitution. In case a member of the parliament too ardently opposed the governor's policy, he could be arrested. The insular parliament could not deliberate on fiscal affairs of the island until provision had been made for the payment of its tribute to Spain, tribute which was to be determined by the Spanish Cortes. Finally, since the Cubans elected only eighteen of the thirty-five members of the Council, the Governor could easily defeat undesired legislation without resorting to a veto. Thus, on all questions, the final authority remained with Spain.

But even if Spain's concessions had been more truly in keeping with the principles of self-government, they still would have come too late and been insufficient. The truth is that Autonomy was dead in Cuba; the party that had worked for it had withered away, and it was said that not fifty persons in Havana favored its platform. As Máximo Gómez correctly noted in an article in *El Yara,* published in Key West, Spain had turned to the autonomists "to save her from the abyss towards which she is rolling, without realizing that these people are without influence, since the Cuban people, having battled the enemy effectively . . . consider the autonomists as sick pigmies." [33]

Blanco's efforts to bribe the rebels into accepting Autonomy and laying down their arms were completely unsuccessful.* As Herminio Portell Vilá points out, "It was absurd to expect that those who had gallantly fought against the Spanish army would have surrendered for a few and cleverly worded political reforms." [34] Offers of payment of money and the grant of ranking positions in the Spanish Army were scornfully rejected. General Gómez, who regarded the offer of autonomy as "the final insult which comes to profane the decency and honor of the Cuban people,"† and, as between Weyler and Blanco, did not know "which of the two is the most unworthy," issued an order that Spanish emissaries tempting insurgent chiefs with bribes were to be executed.[35] Colonel Joaquín Ruiz, who sent by General Blanco to make known to the insurgents the concession of the Spanish government, was cap-

---

* According to reports in the American press, Blanco drew $380,000 from the Bank of Havana with which to purchase the Cuban leaders in Santa Clara province. (George W. Auxier, "The Cuban Question as Reflected in the Editorial Columns of Middle Western Newspapers, 1895-1898," unpublished Ph.D. thesis, Ohio State University, 1938, p. 130.)

† "I cannot accept autonomy," Gómez wrote in February, 1898, "because I believe that its only goal is to divide the Cubans. Those who are truly interested in our Cuba must reject this form, hypocritically conceded by Spain. It is neither prudent nor sensible to trust the sincerity of Spanish governments." (Emilio Roig de Leuchsenring, *Máximo Gómez, El Libertador, op. cit.,* p. 48.)

tured and ultimately executed, although he carried the rights of immunity as an envoy!³⁶

Even though her program had been rejected on all sides, Spain went ahead with her plan to form an autonomous Cuban government. The first cabinet, composed of members named by Ramón Blanco, took office on January 1, 1898. Blanco, hoping "to show the Cubans in arms that Autonomy was instituted for their benefit and protection," excluded members of the ultra-Spanish, pro-Weyler Conservative Party.³⁷ The gesture failed; it was scorned by the *insurrectos* and only antagonized Weyler's supporters, the extreme Spanish conservatives. On January 12, the new experiment in government collapsed. Outbreaks of serious rioting occurred in Havana as mobs, led by Spanish officers, roamed the city crying, "Death for Blanco," "Death to Autonomy," "Viva Weyler," and attacked the offices of several newspapers which had advocated autonomy as well as those of the American consular representatives whom they considered responsible for Spain's concessions.³⁸

On leaving Cuba, Weyler boasted of his achievement in pacifying the four western provinces, and predicted the early restoration of complete Spanish sovereignty throughout the island.³⁹ The derisive scorn that greeted this statement in many countries increased when Blanco disclosed that "of 192,000 regular troops received by General Weyler only 84,000 fit for duty remain," and that, as a result, Spanish military activity had been virtually suspended.* But Blanco himself aroused a

---

* The exact number of soldiers Spain had in Cuba in late 1897 and early 1898 is a matter of some dispute. In rejecting autonomy, it will be recalled, Gómez and García had stated that only 70,000 Spanish combatants were in the field. In a report from Cuba, January 25, 1898, Lee, the U.S. Consul at Havana, estimated that "there are possibly 55,000 Spanish troops 'fit for duty' scattered over the Island, exclusive of some 9,000 volunteers or local troops now in Havana—a lesser number than I supposed." (Report attached to R. A. Alger to William R. Day, March 8, 1898, William R. Day Papers, Library of Congress.) On the other hand, José A. Medel, in his work, *La Guerra Hispano-Americana y sus Resultados,* puts the total number of Spanish forces at 278,457 men. (La Habana, 1929, pp. 86-87.) But Benigno Souza in his biography of Máximo Gómez places the number at 119,500 men. (*Máximo Gómez,* La Habana, 1936, p. 287.) Herminio Portell Vilá asserts that "Spain had more than 200,000 soldiers of all classes in Cuba." (*Op. cit.,* p. 213.) On the other hand, he cites an article in the British medical journal, *The Lancet,* which reported that 201,000 Spanish soldiers had passed through the military hospitals in Cuba during the early months of 1897. (*Ibid.,* p. 61.) Thus even if Spain had the number of soldiers Medel and Portell Vilá indicate, a large percentage of them were not "fit for duty."

storm of laughter when he announced that he would succeed in the field against the rebels where Martínez Campos and Weyler had failed.[40]

Rebel victories in November and December, 1897 proved that Blanco would be no more successful than his predecessors. The year 1898 began on an ominous note for Spain. General Pando, attempting a series of military operations at the Cauto River, was completely checked by the forces of Calixto García and forced to return to Santiago de Cuba.[41] In the West, large insurgent forces began a new invasion of Matanzas and Havana provinces, and increased rebel activity started in Pinar del Río. In February, 1898, Blanco sent a large army to overwhelm and destroy Gómez's forces in the vicinity of Sancti Spíritus in Las Villas. The campaign ended in a fiasco. On March 1, Gómez wrote, "The enemy is crushed and in complete retreat from here, and the time which favored their operation passes without their doing anything." [42]

This report by the Cuban Commander-in-Chief will undoubtedly come as a surprise to students of American history who are convinced that the Cuban Revolution was in such desperate straits in the early months of 1898 that it would have collapsed if the United States had not intervened militarily against Spain. Yet even the United States government knew better. On March 1, 1898, the same day Gómez wrote his letter in Las Villas, the U.S. State Department sent Stewart L. Woodford, Minister to Spain, its evaluation of the military situation in Cuba. It emphasized first, that "the Spanish armies have not achieved any success over the Cubans in more than two months"; second, that the campaign of General Blanco against General Máximo Gómez has "failed absolutely"; third, that "the Cubans continue to dominate the Eastern half of the island, and its columns are operating in the Western provinces without the Spaniards being able to stop them." The report also noted that Autonomy was "an utter and complete failure," that "the social and economic situation of the country is worse than ever, and the national rehabilitation work appears more than the forces of the autonomous regime can cope with." [43]

Everything points to the fact that by 1898 the Spaniards were facing an impossible situation in Cuba. To be sure, they more or less dominated towns, cities, garrisoned areas and the seaports. But their armies were unable to win any victories in the field. The rebels were in complete possession of the countryside outside the fortified areas, winning skirmishes and battles, continuing the tactic of isolating the towns and cities from the countryside, and threatening Spanish control of the more populated areas. When the Spanish armies ventured from the fortified regions, they still faced the danger of being shot at from all sides, ambushed on any road, and attacked without prior notice. The Spanish Army had never learned how to fight guerrilla soldiers. Many Spanish officers were still unwilling to accept the fact that they were not fighting novices in warfare, but well-trained, disciplined, even though frequently poorly-armed, guerrillas, fighting in a national revolution.

In some regions, mainly around the cities, Spain still exercised more or less effective control, and the Revolution was represented only by clandestine cells. But in the other regions, over three-fourths of the island, Spanish forces seldom if ever penetrated.* These areas were steadily expanding, and in them it was the Republic of Cuba that ruled, its government the only one that functioned. Besides maintaining an army of 30,000 men in the field, the Revolutionary government levied and collected taxes, disbursed large sums of money, and conducted a postal system which carried mails throughout the island and even into the Spanish fortified cities. When Benjamin J. Guerra, sub-treasurer of the Cuban Republic, appeared before the United States Senate, he showed the Senators books reporting more than $470,000 collected by the Republic's tax collectors throughout the island and transmitted to him as revenue, every dollar of which had been accounted for by an official receipt.† In addition to a postal and fiscal system, a school system was in operation in the areas occupied by the Republic of Cuba. A

---

* On December 14, 1897, Consul Lee wrote: "I think I speak advisedly when I say that in this end of the island (Oriente) at least there are many thousand square miles where the foot of the Spanish soldiers have never trod." On December 28, 1897, Consul Parker wrote from Santa Clara: "It is over a month since the planters were officially advised of Spain's inability to provide protection in order to operate their mills. This leaves the sugar growers entirely in the hands of the Cubans in revolt, as to whether they will be allowed to grind without hindrance or fear of total destruction of their property." (55th Congress, 2nd Session, *Senate Document No. 230*, p. 35; *House Document No. 406*, p. 50.)

† Guerra testified further that "There is no Cuban in the service of the Republic who receives any salary." Senator Foraker then asked, "Every man works simply for—?" and Guerra replied, "For patriotism." (55th Congress, 2nd Session, *Senate Report 885*, p. 534.)

compulsory system of education was begun and every child up to the age of eight required to attend school. A public printing press at Cubitas, the capital of the Republic in 1898, printed school books which were distributed throughout the island.[44]

On March 25, 1898, Walter B. Barker, an American businessman, wrote from Sagua la Grande, Cuba: "Spain's status—actual authority—in Cuba to-day is of a nature to render her sovereignty—in my humble judgment—more tentative than real." [45] In the towns and cities, the Spanish troops had to depend upon shipments of supplies brought in by strong military convoys. The contents of most of the convoys which managed to escape rebel ambushes did not suffice for the needs of the garrisons. (In the few cases where there were sufficient foodstuffs and goods available, they ended up in the black markets under the operation of graft-ridden municipal boards or Spanish military officers.) Thus in addition to the rebel military operations, hunger and fever took their toll in the morale and nerve and lives of the Spanish army. An article in *El Socialista* of Madrid in April, 1898, referred to the Spanish Army as made up of

> numerous soldiers who walk about in Cuba on crutches, too weak, through hunger, to stand up alone . . . mere spectres doing duty on the Cuban fields, weakened by fever, hunger and thirst . . . soldiers who garrison the towns that are the depots of food, and yet are kept below half rations . . . soldiers who lie in the hospitals, taken thither wounded and famishing . . . cripples and almost corpses that return home piled up in our transatlantic convoys, genuine funeral hearses. . . . [46]

The more clear-sighted Spaniards were at last aware that the war could not make any headway without first winning the Cuban people. But there was no way to do this. Brutal repression had failed. Autonomy had failed. Military strategy had also failed. The strategy of reinforced *trochas* and concentration camps to deprive the rebels of civilian support and eventually grind them down, had failed. Thus the war in Cuba was frustrating to official Spain, to the military leaders on the scene, and to the poor Spanish soldiers. Expedient action in Cuba and the constantly changing programs had developed from unworkable policies, and no policy existed that might be more successful in the future.

On the other hand, Gómez's strategy of making the island economically undesirable for Spain had had overpowering effect. Nearly all economic production was at a standstill, and practically everything of value in the island was devastated. "Productive work outside of Havana had ceased; unemployment was universal; thousands were deprived of food and clothing; disease was rampant, and chaos was predominant throughout the Island. . . ."[47] Writing from Madrid on March 31, 1898, Stewart L. Woodford, American Minister to Spain, informed President William McKinley that most people in the Spanish government were of the opinion that the devastated island was not worth further sacrifices.[48] But even if they had been willing to make additional sacrifices, it is difficult to see how Spain, weakened by tremendous financial and manpower drains and with her economy devastated, could have continued to hold out in Cuba much longer. Gómez's strategy had been based from the beginning on the theory that time was on the side of the Revolution and that the Spaniards would gradually find it economically and morally impossible to continue the war. Everything points to the fact that by the winter of 1898, his prediction was coming true. The war might still drag on for an indefinite period, but the Cubans were bound to win.

For many years Cuban historical works, especially the history texts used in Cuban schools, praised American intervention in La Guerra Hispanoamericana (the Spanish-American War) of 1898 as essential for the defeat of Spain and the achievement of Cuban independence.*
While a number of distinguished Cuban historians challenged this view,† the major contribution in revising the traditional interpretation was made by Dr. Emilio Roig de Leuchsenring. From 1912 when he won first prize in a contest with his work *Se puede vivir en la Habana sin un centavo?* Dr. Roig published books until his death in 1964, and in many of them he challenged the traditional view that Cuban inde-

---

* This interpretation was advanced in the most widely used text on Cuban history in the elementary schools of Cuba, Vidal Morales', *Naciones de historia de Cuba*, especially the chapter, "La Guerra Hispano-Americana."

† Several Cuban historians, however, continued to adhere to the traditional view. See especially Cosme de la Torriente, *Fin de la dominación de España en Cuba*, La Habana, 1948, and Julio Morales Coello, *La importancia del poderío naval-positivo y negativo-en el desarrollo y en la independencia de Cuba*, La Habana, 1950.

pendence was largely the result of North American intervention.*
Dr. Roig insisted that the struggle for independence was not a series of wars but one continuous struggle of thirty years' duration; that there was never lacking in the United States friends of Cuban freedom, but that the North American government was consistently opposed to Cuban independence; that the entry of the United States into the struggle in 1898 was not necessary for Cuban victory because the Cuban patriots had Spain practically defeated by that time, and that the name "The Spanish-American War," which gave the Cubans no credit for their contribution, should be changed.†

For many years Dr. Roig served as Historian of the City of Havana, and he used the office of City Historian to launch a series of historical conferences open to the public, and to sponsor several series of historical publications. By 1950 more than one hundred volumes of historical studies had been published by the Oficina del Historiador de la Ciudad de la Habana.‡ In 1940, Dr. Roig organized the Sociedad Cubana de Estudios Históricos e Internacionales, and two years later, this society and the office of the City Historian joined in promoting the First National Historical Congress of Cuba. The Ninth Historical Congress of 1950 stated flatly:

> Cuba does not owe its independence to the United States of North America, but to the efforts of its own people, in their firm, unbreakable will to put an end to the injustices, biases, discriminations, and exploitations that they suffered under the despotic colonial regime, and to achieve liberty, democracy, justice, culture and

---

* See especially Dr. Roig's works *La Guerra Libertadora Cubana de los Treinta Años, 1868-1898*, La Habana, 1952; *La Guerra Hispano-Cubano-Americana fue ganada por el Lugartemiente General de Ejército Libertador Calixto García Iñiquez*, La Habana, 1955, and *Cuba no debe su Independencia a los Estados Unidos*, 3rd edition, La Habana, 1960.

† Largely as the result of the work of Dr. Roig and his associates, the Cuban Congress passed a law in May, 1945 making official the name "La Guerra Hispano-Cubanomericana." (*Gaceta oficial de la Republica de Cuba*, May 22, 1945.)

‡ These included the popular series, *Cuadernos de Historia Habanera*, no. 41 of which was Herminio Portell Vilá's *Historia de la Guerra de Cuba y Los Estados Unidos Contra España*, with a "Nota Prelimina" by Emilio Roig de Leuchsenring, La Habana, 1949. No. 72 (La Habana, 1960) contains a complete list of the collection with other publications down to 1960. From an evaluation of the publications down to 1955, see Davon C. Corbitt, "Historical Publications of the Oficina de Historiador de la Ciudad de la Habana," *Hispanic American Historical Review*, vol. XXXV, Nov. 1955, p. 498.)

civilization. Convinced that it was impossible to obtain these things under Spanish sovereignty, they decided to win them by means of revolution, and after numerous conspiracies and expeditions, a national consciousness was developed. Then broke out the great *Thirty Years War of Liberation* which in its final phase (1895-98) had the support of the majority of the people of the island, of the groups of Cuban exiles on the Continent, and, through the power of the Liberating Army, due to superior military capacity of its leaders and the spirit of discipline, heroism, disinterestedness, and sacrifice of its soldiers, was able to destroy the economic and military power of Spain and defeat the best of its military forces, although it had against it at times the indifference, and at others the hostility of the North American State; having brought about even before the intervention of the United States in the Cuban-Spanish conflict the complete exhaustion of Spain's "last man and last peseta," the limit indicated by the leaders of her political factions in Spain as the extreme to which it would go in the battle against the Revolution. . . ."[49]

Early in 1966 I sent a series of questions to several Cuban historians asking for their views.* One read: "What is the current opinion among Cuban historians as to whether Cuba could have defeated Spain in the Second War for Independence without the intervention of the United States?" Professor Sergio Aguirre of the Department of History, University of Havana, wrote in reply:

> In 1898 Spain was facing an economic collapse so that not even the ministers of the Queen could believe in victory. . . . Cuba was winning the war. . . . It is obvious that it is not possible to project how long the war could have gone on without North American intervention in view of the angry resolution of Spain "to the last man and the last peseta." In my judgment, the important thing is that the Invasion [of the West] had no Spanish counter-strike which was comparable to it. Why presume that this counter-strike would have been able to appear in 1898 or after? There is no doubt that the United States hastened the final decision, introducing into the struggle the "knockout" punch. But victory for the Cubans would have come in the end even without the intervention of the United States."[50]

---

* I also discussed this and other questions with Cuban historians while in Cuba during the summer of 1966.

Aníbal Escalante Beatón, author of *Calixto García, su Campaña en el 1895* and himself a veteran of the Second War for Independence, wrote:

> Yes, we could have defeated Spain without the intervention of the United States. . . . From every standpoint it was clear in 1898 that Spain could not keep Cuba; that her forces were wilting, and that we *mambises* were stronger all the time. When the United States intervened in the hispano-cubana war, victory was on the side of the Cubans. In Oriente and Camagüey, we dominated the field, and the Spanish army was only in charge of the cities. In Las Villas our forces had the Spaniards in check, and in Matanzas, Havana, and Pinar del Río, the *mambi* units harassed the enemy continually." [51]

Although he notes that there is more research to be done on this subject, Blas Roca, member of the Comité Central, Partido Comunista de Cuba, is convinced that "the Cuban revolutionaries could have defeated Spain without the military intervention of the United States." He added:

> The liberating Revolution, two years after it had started, had been extended up to Pinar del Río, thanks largely to the invasion of the East to West, conducted by Maceo, which demonstrated the impotence of the Spanish armies to defeat it by military means. Extensive regions had been won by the Cubans and were administered by the Government-in-Arms to which the sugar mills, cane colonias and plantations raising other crops had to pay tribute.

Although the Revolution had suffered two serious blows militarily and politically with the deaths of Martí and Maceo, nevertheless, despite this, "even in 1898 the war advanced without even the new policy put into practice by Spain being able to weaken it. The war of independence probably would not have been able to achieve victory in 1898, but the conditions existed so that it would have achieved victory sooner or later without the intervention of the United States." [52]

Professor Julio Le Riverand, formerly Professor of History at the University of Havana and at present assistant director of the Academia de Ciencias de Cuba, feels that while there is still work to be done in the Cuban and Spanish archives to answer definitively the question as to whether the Liberating Army could have defeated Spain without the intervention of the United States, there is much justification for the viewpoint that such an outcome would have resulted. Not only was the Spanish army unable to crush the Revolution, but the mother country "was maneuvering to establish the autonomous regime because she was convinced she was not able to conquer the Revolution by force of arms. . . . Any revolutionary movement which succeeded in consolidating itself in the face of such powerful enemies, obliging them to maneuver, is on the way to victory. This is a universal experience." [53]

The vast majority of American historians have a different interpretation of the situation in Cuba in 1898. They contend that the rebel strategy from the beginning was based on the theory that time would work in the Revolution's favor by eventually involving the United States in the war and winning it for the Cubans; that by the winter of 1898, the rebels were merely holding on the best they could, hoping and praying for the intervention of the United States against Spain, without which they could never possibly win independence.* That there were some revolutionists who favored such intervention is true. But the more clear-minded among them, and all the Cuban leaders in the island fighting the Spaniards, did not want U.S. troops. They merely wanted recognition and credit for supplies.

As we have seen, José Martí had feared U.S. intervention, knowing from personal experience derived from his long residence in the United States, that among the North Americans were influential economic and political forces who sought increased profits through direct annexation of indirect control of Cuba. Martí was determined to keep Cuba free from all foreign domination, domination by the United States as well as domination by Spain. Hence he had timed the outbreak of the Second War for Independence so as to prevent "the annexation of Cuba

---

* It is impossible, for lack of space, to cite all the American historians who have advanced this thesis, but the following, both published recently, is fairly typical: ". . . . they [the insurrectos] saw a chance to win the war with the aid of American intervention; all they need do was to keep it going." (David F. Healy, The United States in Cuba, 1898-1902, Madison, Wisconsin, 1963, p. 17.) "Gómez destroyed property to keep the [Cuban] issue alive in the United States and to provoke American intervention." (H. Wayne Morgan, America's Road to Empire: The War with Spain and Overseas Expansion, New York, 1965, p. 9.) Professor Morgan does not even know that the opponents of Gómez's policy among the revolutionists argued that his "policy of the torch" would hold back U.S. recognition of Cuban belligerency, and that the old Dominican took the position that revolutionary strategy should be based on hurting Spain's ability to wage war and not on reaction to it in the United States.

to the United States." As for U.S. assistance for the Cuban Revolution in the form of armed intervention, Martí expressed his opinion tersely: "Once the United States is in Cuba, who will get it out?" [54]

The majority of the leaders of the Revolution shared Martí's determination to keep Cuba free from all foreign domination, and after "the Apostle's" death, they continued to uphold his principles. Henry A. Himley, a New York merchant who was interested in the Occitania estate in Cuba and had had frequent discussions with the leaders of the Revolution, made this point clear in a letter to U.S. Secretary of State Richard B. Olney, April, 1896:

> . . . the insurgents not being annexationists (neither the ones who are in Cuba, nor those who are in the United States) they do not see that in case a war did arise between the United States and Spain and that the first came out victorious, it would have been foolish in them to have spent their money and spilled their blood in order to make a present to the United States of the Island without reaping any benefit from the conflict. . . . [55]

None of the revolutionary leaders were more determined to follow Martí's principles on the question of United States intervention than the military commanders in the field. Antonio Maceo favored a declaration by the United States recognizing the belligerency of the Republic of Cuba, realizing how important this was for the acquisition of military equipment as well as for its moral effect. But this was where he stopped. "All I want to obtain from the United States is the recognition of the belligerency of the Cuban Republic," he wrote shortly after he landed in Cuba. He informed the New York World: "I should not want our neighbors to have to shed their blood for our cause. We can do that for ourselves if, under the common law, we can get the necessary elements to overthrow the corrupted power of Spain in Cuba." [56]

Maceo made it clear from the beginning of the Second War for Independence that he feared that the future Republic would be born a cripple if its freedom was achieved through the military intercession of any other country. Only by wresting freedom through her own power could Cuba develop as a truly independent nation. Other nations could help by assisting Cubans financially to purchase war equipment and allowing them to transport it to the island. But the fighting itself had to be done by the Cubans.[57] So important did Maceo regard this issue that in the midst of continual fighting against the enemy, he repeatedly took time out to press his point of view on Cuban officials in the island and in the United States. Writing from Pinar del Río on April 4, 1896, Maceo informed Estrada Palma that he was worried by reports in newspapers that there was widespread discussion in the United States "whether the U.S. should or should not go into the war so that the war may end soon.* And I suspect that you, inspired of course by motives of patriotism, are working restlessly to achieve for Cuba all you can. But I dare say that we do not need any intervention to obtain victory in more or less time. Do you really want to cut the war down? Bring Cuba 25,000 to 35,000 rifles and a million bullets. . . . We Cubans do not need any other help." [58]

On July 14, 1896, Maceo wrote to Federico Pérez Carbó: "From Spain I never expected anything. She has always despised us, and it would be undignified to think otherwise. Liberty is won with the edge of the machete; it is not asked for. To beg for rights is the domain of cowards incapable of exercising these rights. Neither do I expect anything from the [North] Americans. We must all depend on our own efforts. It is better to rise or fall without help than to contract debts of gratitude to a neighbor so powerful." [59] And two days later, he wrote to José Dolores Payo, Delegate of the Revolutionary Government in Key West: "Why do they insist so much on foreign intervention which we neither need nor wish? Cuba is winning its independence by the arms and hearts of its sons. She will be free in a short time without needing any other help." [60] The same day Maceo developed this theme more fully in a letter to Dr. Alberto J. Díaz then residing in Louisville, Kentucky:

---

* Perhaps it was this expression of concern by Maceo that led James Street, in his novel *Mingo Dabney*, set in Cuba during the Second War for Independence, to include the following dialogue between Maceo and Mingo Dabney, an American who was with the Liberating Army:

"'However, [said Maceo], some of us are afraid that sooner or later, your country will intervene.'

"'Afraid?' Mingo gasped at the general, amazed that a little neighbor like Cuba should fear the United States. 'What's there to be afraid of?'

"His artlessness was apparent and the Cuban shrugged.

"'The money lords of your country have determined on a policy of aggressive imperialism. They call it manifest destiny and speak of service to the weak.'" (New York, 1954, pp. 181-82.)

The official recognition of our belligerency does not seem to me to be such an important thing, if in order to achieve it we have to concentrate so much of our effort in that direction. Nor is American intervention so advantageous to the future of Cuba as most of our compatriots think. I believe rather that the secret of our final triumph is intertwined with the efforts of Cubans who are working for the independence of our country, and that only if the final triumph is achieved without this foreign intervention will it bring us complete happiness.[61]

This was Maceo's last word on the subject before his death several months later, and, as the history of Cuba after U.S. intervention in the war against Spain was to prove, it was a truly prophetic analysis. The same theme was struck by Máximo Gómez in his frequent proclamations to the Liberating Army and in his correspondence. Like Maceo, Gómez felt that the leaders of the Revolutionary Government were too much concerned with maneuvering to gain United States recognition of Cuban belligerency, and while he did not underestimate the importance of such an achievement, he felt that it should not determine the policies the Revolution must follow.* Throughout the long and bitter struggle, Gómez had only one request of the United States: to speak out against Weyler's reconcentration policy. "Say to the Spaniards," he wrote to President Grover Cleveland in February, 1897, "that they may struggle with us and treat us as they please, but that they must respect the pacific population; that they must not outrage women nor butcher innocent children." But he assured Cleveland that he did not wish the President to regard this appeal "as a request for intervention in our affairs." The Cubans had thrown themselves into the struggle for independence, "confident in our strength," and they did not require others to do the fighting for them.[62]

Gómez's confidence in the ability of Cuban troops to win the War for Independence without the help of foreign soldiers was shared by Calixto García. Although he conceded that it would take longer for the Cubans to win without American armed intervention, García was

---

* Grover Flint reported that "Gómez had long since ceased to count on assistance of any kind from the United States. Concerning recognition I heard him say, 'I have a mind to forbid any man's speaking that word in camp. Recognition is like the rain; it is a good thing if it comes, and a good thing if it doesn't come.'" (*Marching with Gómez: A War-Correspondent's Field Notebook During Four Months with the Cuban Army,* Boston and New York, 1898, p. 152.)

convinced that it was in Cuba's best interests that victory should come through her own efforts. A few days before the outbreak of war between the United States and Spain, García wrote to Estrada Palma from Oriente, expressing his opposition to sending foreign troops, either "Yankees or a single South or Central American." With the proper supplies, "the veteran troops of Cuba" would finish the job and expel the Spaniards from the island.⁶³*

In Gómez's view, Cubans who favored intervention by the United States as a means of achieving independence, and ignored "the North American Republic's absorbing aspirations" were "morally" in the Spanish camp.† There was only one way to make Cuba truly free: freedom had to be won by the Cubans' own sacrifices. "Cuba must not be beholden for its independence in any way, to foreign good graces." "We must trust only in our own arms and in our own resolution. Supplies yes; troops no!" ⁶⁴‡

To be sure, a number of Cuban revolutionists feared that a victory over Spain without the presence of American troops and power could easily lead to a situation in which the most radical elements would become dominant, and privately they preferred to have the United States intervene in order to prevent such an outcome. Lacking confidence in and respect for the capacity of the Cuban people to govern themselves and admiring the United States and its institutions, these elements in the Revolutionary camp felt that intervention not only had the virtue

---

* García added a reassuring note: "Don't worry about Oriente. Here nobody even speaks about autonomy, but on the contrary, so many people come out of the towns to unite with us that we don't know where to put them." (García to Estrada Palma, Potosí, Tunas, March 22, 1898, *Boletín del Archivo Nacional*, Havana, vol. 34, 1936, pp. 102-03.)

† Gómez was by no means the only one in the Liberating Army to be so concerned. Anibal Escalante recalls that the prospect of "intervention by the United States filled us with concern because many of us in the Liberating Army knew the historical fact that our neighbor had wrested from Mexico an immense fertile territory including California, Arkansas, Arizona and New Mexico, and before this had annexed the province of Texas. We sincerely believed that this intervention would result in danger for Cuba, and many of us preferred not to have this help and to keep fighting without it since sooner or later we would have had to defeat Spain." (Letter of Anibal Escalante Beaton, La Habana, marzo 16 de 1966, in possession of author.)

‡ Even after the United States had declared war on Spain, Gómez urged it not to send troops to Cuba, assuring the North American government that if it would supply him with arms, the Liberating Army "will yet drive the Spanish into the sea." (*The Nation*, vol. LXVI, May 12, 1898, p. 354.)

of shortening the war but also of imbuing Cuba with the North American way of life and laying the foundations for financial assistance from U.S. capitalists to a Cuban government. Probably the outstanding exponent of this viewpoint was Tómas Estrada Palma, the Delegate of the Cuban Revolutionary Party stationed in the United States.* Though an active worker for the Cuban Revolution in the first and second wars for independence, Estrada Palma had grave doubts about the ability of the Cubans to establish a "stable" government with "law and order," believed that without this, independence was worthless, and that semi-independence under the control and guidance of the United States with its civilizing influences, was the best way out for Cuba. In a letter to Perfecto Lacoste in Havana, January 29, 1898, Estrada Palma wrote glowingly of the purposes of the United States in intervening in the war against Spain, "through which, without the necessity of annexation, absolutely, the government of the United States will have in the Republic of Cuba an indirect intervention which will serve to impress morality on the administration of our finances, and give us credit with the capitalists who may lend us credit. I don't want to be more explicit. . . ."[65] Several weeks later, on March 9, 1898, Estrada Palma spelled out even more explicitly what he understood to be the purposes of the struggle in Cuba: "that the only possible solution to end the Cuban war is absolute independence from Spain in order to constitute in the island an independent republic which in some way, without affecting our national sovereignty, may be under the moral protection of the United States, as a guarantee of order, of internal peace, and to give confidence to American capitalists, who may lend us the money necessary for the reconstruction of the country."[66]

---

* A number of contemporary Cuban historians feel that Gonzalo de Quesada, charge d'affaires for the Cuban Revolutionary government in Washington, also favored the intervention of the United States. Indeed on January 19, 1898, Estrada Palma, while congratulating Quesada upon his activity in Washington, particularly his work in cultivating "the good spirits of our friends of Congress and the Senate," cautioned him: "But it is not good to excite them toward violent procedure." (Papers of Estrada Palma, Archivo Nacional, Havana.) Evidently Quesada was pushing for U.S. intervention more actively than Estrada Palma thought wise at that particular time.

Dr. Enrique H. Moreno Plá, who has spent several years working on the Quesada archives, denies that Quesada favored intervention of the United States. (Letter of Enrique H. Moreno Plá, Havana, March 1, 1966, in possession of author.)

THE MILITARY AND POLITICAL SCENE IN 1897 AND EARLY 1898   149

From this point of view Estrada Palma never swerved. In a letter to a friend in October, 1906, he wrote:

> I have believed, since the time I took active part in the Ten Years' War, that independence was not the final goal of all of our noble and patriotic aspirations—the aim was to possess a stable Government capable of protecting lives and property and of guaranteeing to all residents of the country, natives and foreigners, the exercise of natural and civil rights, without permitting liberty ever to become pernicious license or violent agitation, to say nothing of armed disturbances of public order. I have never feared to admit, nor am I afraid to say aloud, that a political dependence which assures us the fecund boons of liberty is a hundred times preferable for our beloved Cuba to a sovereign and independent republic discredited and made miserable by the baneful action of periodic civil wars.[67]

This, of course, was the language used by the annexationists in the United States and by every Cuban advocate of annexation for nearly a century. It was also the excuse used by American imperialism to justify depriving the Cuban people of real independence.* With this outlook, Estrada Palma, for all his services to the Revolution, logically came to favor American intervention to prevent the Revolution from becoming too revolutionary.

But publicly, even Estrada Palma and those who shared his views did not dare to call for more than recognition of Cuban belligerency and/or independence, and the right of the Cuban Republic to purchase arms in the United States. On April 9, 1898, just ten days before the war between the United States and Spain, *The State*, published in Columbia, South Carolina and edited by N. G. Gonzales, who was on intimate terms with leaders of the Cuban Revolution in the United States, issued the following challenge:

> Let somebody quote us, if he can, a word of appeal from representatives of the Cuban republic for "help" from the United States, one request that it "settle the Cuban troubles." We chal-

---

* In his letters to Perfecto Lacoste, Estrada Palma practically outlined the status Cuba would occupy as a Republic under the terms of the Platt Amendment. He failed, of course, to explain how it would be possible for Cuba to function under such an arrangement "without effecting our national sovereignty." The Platt Amendment will be discussed below.

lenge the proof in full confidence that it cannot be adduced. In no way and at no time has this government been solicited by the Cubans of Cuba Libre for aid or intervention. They feel quite competent to drive Spain from the island without assistance. They only ask for recognition of an independence maintained by arms during three years.

The challenge went unanswered. But the absence of proof has not prevented American historians from picturing the Cubans as beseeching the United to intervene with its troops.

"Supplies yes; troops no!" said Gómez, voicing the viewpoint of the Cuban Revolution. But, of course, United States troops did come. The course of events leading to their coming and why they came will be the theme of the next chapters.

CHAPTER VIII

Latin America and the Cuban Revolution

IN A LETTER TO *Patria,* July, 1895, Máximo Gómez called for "a frank presentation of our revolutionary aims throughout the hemisphere."[1] Tómas Estrada Palma decided to act on Gómez's suggestion, and to promote the Cuban cause in South America, approached the distinguished orator and historian, Manuel Sanguily. Sanguily regretfully decided that he had to decline in order to represent his brother, Julio, who had recently been arrested by the Spanish authorities and sentenced to Morro Castle.[2] Thereupon, Estrada Palma sent two young Cubans, Aristides Agüero and Nicolás de Cárdenas to Peru to open diplomatic negotiations with the governments of various South American countries.[3]* The Delegate of the Cuban Revolutionary Party also sounded out Enrique José Varona, who had assumed the editorship of the revolutionary organ *Patria* after the death of Martí, about sending him to the countries of the Rio de la Plata. Varona, pleading that his health and his duties as editor would not allow him to leave the United States, refused. But his conversations with Estrada Palma were not wasted. On October 23, 1895, Varona published a pamphlet entitled *Cuba contra España manifiesto del Partido Revolucionario Cubano a los Pueblos Hispano-Americanos (Cuba Against Spain, manifesto of the Cuban*

---

* Estrada Palma also appointed diplomatic agents to other nations of the hemisphere: Costa Rica, El Salvador, Mexico, Peru, Bolivia, and Chile, Nicaragua, Honduras, Colombia, Haiti, Uruguay, Venezuela, and Argentina. This action was later ratified by the Governing Council and an order of November 21, 1895 officially recognized the diplomatic representatives appointed by Estrada Palma, both to the Latin American countries and to Great Britain, Belgium and France. (Salvador Cisneros Betancourt to Estrada Palma, November 21, 1895, "Notes from the Cuban Legation in the United States to the Department of State, 1844-1906," National Archives.)

Revolutionary Party to the Latin American People). Varona appealed to the governments and people of Latin America to give the Cuban Revolution the same kind of enthusiastic sympathy and support they had rendered the revolutionists during the Ten Years' War.[4*] The Governing Council followed up Varona's appeal by naming a special committee to establish and maintain relations with the republics of the Antilles and Central America. At the same time, Antonio Maceo wrote identical letters to the presidents of Venezuela, Mexico, and several other Latin American countries in an effort to obtain a joint loan of one million dollars from these nations and the recognition of Cuban belligerency.[5] On November 24, 1895, Maceo wrote enthusiastically to General José Manuel Capote and Jesús Rabí:

> All the news which Senor Estrada Palma has communicated to me and which I have read in the foreign newspapers is most promising. The recognition of belligerency appears an assured thing when the American Congress inaugurates its session which will be the 4th of the coming month. In Latin America there have been large demonstrations of sympathy for our cause; in Caracas, a meeting of 5,000 persons took place under the statue of Bolívar. Chile and Peru have openly shown their desire to intervene in the question. The President of Costa Rica has been urged to convene the government heads of the rest of the Republics to agree on a collective intervention for the purpose of recognition of the independence of Cuba by Spain.
>
> As you see by the news, we are travelling with the wind behind us and everything makes us believe that it won't be long before the Revolution triumphs.[6]

Maceo's joy over recognition of Cuban belligerency by the United States soon vanished, but according to General Miró, this neither surprised nor disappointed him too much, for he felt that Cuba could rely more upon the Latin American Republics collectively "than upon the big power of the North [the United States]."[7] Unfortunately, the kind of support Maceo envisaged receiving from Latin America never materialized.

Two forces operated in Latin America during the period of Cuba's

---

* For the attitude of Latin America toward the Cuban Revolution during the Ten Years' War, see Philip S. Foner, *History of Cuba and Its Relations with the United States*, vol. II, New York, 1963, pp. 198-99, 247-51, 351.

second war for independence. One was sympathy for the Cuban struggle for independence; the other was solidarity with Spain. For several years prior to the outbreak of the Cuban Revolution, the Pan-Hispanic movement had been fostered by a group in Spain whose object was to promote solidarity between that country and the Hispanic nations of America, largely for the purpose of combatting the growing aggressiveness of the United States. The methods used included diplomatic overtures, distribution of books exposing American imperialism in Latin America and the founding of newspapers friendly to Spain in Latin American countries. The founding of the Ibero-American Union and the celebration of the fourth centenary of the discovery of America in 1892, marked the high point in the efforts of the Pan-Hispanists.[8]

But it was the imperialist expansion and policies of the United States before and during the Cuban Revolution that made the propaganda of the Pan-Hispanists influential. During these years, as Walter La Feber points out, "the American business community began systematically opening Latin American markets. . . . American investment composed mainly of surplus capital accumulated from the home markets' collapse [during the depression which began in 1893], flowed into Latin America in increased amounts during the 1893-1898 period. New steamship lines, heavy investments in Latin American railroads, the movement of American bankers into Santo Domingo and the expansion of the Guggenheim interests in Mexico exemplified this southward advance of the dollar."[9] United States arrogance toward Latin America intensified the fears created by the "advance of the dollar."

Political strife in Chile in 1891 resulted in a serious international incident between that country and the United States, in which the latter's role infuriated Latin Americans. The Chilean internal struggle was one between the President of Chile, who, supported by the feudalists, wished to become a dictator, and the Congressional Party, supported by the laboring classes and peasants, which aimed to enforce the Constitution. During the struggle for power, the American minister to Chile, Patrick Egan, openly sided with the President and feudalists, thus making himself unpopular with the victorious Congressional Party and its revolutionary supporters. The United States Government, through illegal detention and ultimate seizure of the *Itata*, a vessel bearing arms for the revolutionists from the United States, by the American warship, *Charleston*, increased the antipathy of the revolutionists towards the North American state.

A climax in Chilean-American relations was reached in October, 1891 when more than a hundred American sailors were given shore leave in Valparaiso at the time anti-American sentiment was at its highest. The outcome was a street battle in which two American sailors were killed and a number wounded. Putting the blame for the incident on the sailors, the Chilean revolutionary government simultaneous demanded the recall of Minister Egan. But the United States, dispatching the cruiser *Boston* to Chile and threatening to follow it up with troops, forced the government to acknowledge that it was to blame and to pay indemnity.[10]

The hostility of all Latin Americans, not only Chileans, to its meddling in Chile's domestic affairs, was intensified in January, 1894 when President Grover Cleveland used the Navy to block a revolution in Brazil. This operation was undertaken to preserve the recently negotiated reciprocity treaty with the existing government of Brazil (which favored American exporters), and to forestall further European economic penetration in South America. Since the revolutionaries did not want to become too dependent on American goods, the United States put on a display of naval force to compel the landing of these goods. The presence of the American Navy, and the threat of force, caused the collapse of the revolution.[11]

But it was the United States' role in the British-Venezuela boundary dispute in 1895 that especially frightened Latin America. In his note of July 20, 1895 to the British Prime Minister Lord Salisbury, Secretary of State Richard B. Olney interpreted the Monroe Doctrine as reserving Latin America exclusively for the United States. "Today the United States is practically sovereign on this continent, and its fiat is law upon the subjects to which its confines its interposition." [12] When the British challenged these claims, Cleveland reaffirmed them in his special message of December 17, 1895, and warned that unless Great Britain settled the boundary dispute to the satisfaction of the United States, it would regard this "as a willful aggression upon its rights and interests." [13] In the final settlement of the boundary dispute, England recognized Olney's claim of American dominance in the Western Hemisphere.

Latin America was deeply disturbed not only by the broad interpretation of the Monroe Doctrine in the Venezuelan dispute, but also because during all the negotiations, the United States had acted unilaterally. Venezuela was not consulted or included, and the State Department revealed that it "cared little for Venezuelan opinion or advice, and hoped to benefit American interests primarily, not Venezuelan. . . ." [14] Latin America thus became an area to serve the interests of the United States.

To many Latin Americans then, not only the large and wealthy Spanish colonies in the Latin American countries, it appeared that Spain could be an ally against the threatening Yankee colossus. Especially was this true after they become convinced, partly through Spanish propaganda, that the United States was intent upon seizing Cuba, and that all its concern for pacifying Cuba in the interests of humanity, civilization, and the protection of American citizens was simply a cloak for American imperialism. Hence there was a distinct difference in the attitude of Latin America toward the Cuban Revolution of 1895-1898 and the attitude toward the Cuban Revolution of 1868-1878. Although several Latin American Republics had recognized the Cuban government during the Ten Years' War and even cooperated in an effort to force Spain to relinquish Cuba (a move frustrated by the opposition of the United States*) the situation was quite different in the Second War for Independence. No Latin American Republic recognized Cuban belligerency this time; many of them showed themselves indifferent to the independence of a sister Republic struggling for independence, and one, Argentina, was openly on the side of Spain. In 1895, Eloy Alfaro, President of Ecuador, sought to convene a special Pan-American Congress in Mexico to discuss aiding the Cuban Revolution. But the response from the Latin American governments was so cool that the project was abandoned.

In all Latin American countries clubs were formed which carried on propaganda for the cause of Cuba, and collected and sent funds to the Cuban Revolutionary Party in New York.† But the contributions

---

* See Philip S. Foner, *History of Cuba and Its Relations with the United States*, vol. II, pp. 247-51.

† Caracas, Port-au-Prince, Buenos Aires, Bogota, San Jose (Costa Rica), Vera Cruz and Mexico City not only had a Cuban colony but also had newspapers published by the Cubans. (J. Llaverias, "Martí y los periodistas," *Boletin del Archivo Nacional*, vol. 49, January-December, 1950, pp. 651-52.) Manuel de la Cruz, a Cuban exile in Buenos Aires, wrote a weekly column on the progress of

were never as much as the revolutionists had expected. Partly this was due to the scarcity of money among the lower classes who sympathized most with the Cubans.[15] But the main reason was that where there was sympathy among the people, the government was hostile. On November 8, 1896, responding to Spanish pressures, President Miguel Caro of Colombia prohibited all fund-raising programs or solicitations for the insurrectionary cause, except for the wounded.[16] Dominican President Ulises Heuraux blocked real aid for Cuba despite the wholehearted support of the Dominican people for the Cuban revolution, and worked with the Spanish minister to prevent money for Cuba from leaving the country. (Dominicans and Cubans friendly to Cuba were afraid that if they did not cease their activities, they would be jailed and turned over to the Spanish authorities.[17]*)

Despite the unceasing efforts of the friends of Cuba in Chile, they were never able to persuade the Chilean Congress in Santiago to recognize the belligerency of the Revolutionary Government. Venezuelan opinion in favor of Cuba was strong and was shared by President Joaquin Crespo, so that when meetings in favor of the Revolution in Caracas in August 1895 were protested by Spain, the protests were ignored. But as the other Latin American Republics did nothing for Cuba, the Venezuelan government became more receptive of Spanish protests, and pro-Cuban meetings were limited.[18]

Peru had an important Cuban colony which organized clubs to aid the Revolution as early as June, 1895. They worked tirelessly to obtain recognition of Cuban belligerency and to acquire arms and munitions

---

the insurrection for Buenos Aires' *La Nación*. (Juan J. Remos, "La Literatura," in Ramiro y Sánchez, *Historia de la Nacion Cubana*, Havana, 1952, vol. VII, p. 351.)

* The role played by President Heuraux is a confusing one. As we pointed out in the preceding discussion, he had loaned Máximo Gómez 2,000 pesos to help the Cubans launch the Revolution of 1895, and while he complied with Spain's request that he arrest Gómez, Martí and the other Cubans who were planning to leave Santo Domingo for Cuba in March, 1895, he managed to issue the order for their arrest after they had left on April 1. It is possible that he was playing the same dual role during the War for Independence, favoring the Cuban cause while seemingly appeasing Spain by pretending to suppress real support for Cuba. But the reports of the Cuban agents in Santo Domingo stress Heuraux's actions in blocking support for Cuba.

from the Peruvian government. But in spite of their activities, nothing concrete was accomplished beyond a modest collection of funds.[19]*

In Costa Rica the Congress debated the motion for the recognition of Cuban belligerency. Although the friends of Cuba pointed to the great achievements of the Invasion of the West and declared that "if Costa Rica had two generals like Gómez and Maceo, it would pride itself on being one of the foremost nations in the world," the motion was defeated.[20]

In Uruguay, the Cuban veteran of the Ten Years' War, Ramón Valdés, published for several years the weekly paper, *Cuba Libre,* which organized popular support for the Revolution. But Valdés informed Estrada Palma that despite the sympathy for Cuba, the economic relations between Uruguay and Spain, "would make difficult resolute action from the Montevideo government leading to recognition of belligerency, at least before the other Republics less commercially involved with Spain." The situation remained the same throughout the entire war.[21]

A nucleus of pro-Cuban sympathizers existed in Argentina, but the government was so decidedly on the side of Spain that it even permitted the recruiting of troops to help the Spaniards crush the Revolution. It also sponsored a public collection to raise funds to enable Spain to purchase a battleship, the cruiser *Río de La Plata.*[22]

Mexico had a long history of sympathy for Cuba's struggle for independence, going back to the 1820's during the administration of President Guadalupe Victoria.† This tradition was continued during Cuba's Second War for Independence by the people of Mexico, but their attitude was not reflected by the emerging dictatorship of Porfirio

---

* Jorge Basadre, the noted Peruvian historian, sadly concedes that Peru showed little interest in upholding "the noble tradition of continental nationalism" by assisting Cuba in her struggle. He attributes much of this to the feeling in the country, following the war with Chile, "that Peru should dedicate itself only to its national affairs. The gale wind of the war with Chile had left the country worried by its immediate problems, that is, spiritually reduced." (*Historia de la Republica del Perú,* Tomo VII, Lima, 1963, pp. 3224-25.) See also Virgilio Ferrer Gutierrez, *Perú en la independencia de Cuba, y otros temas Americanos,* Habana, Cuba, 1944.

† See Philip S. Foner, *History of Cuba and Its Relations with the United States,* vol. I, 1492-1845, New York, 1962, pp. 154-62. See also *Un Esfuerzo de México por la Independencia de Cuba,* con prólogo por Luis Chávez Orozco, México, 1930. Copy in Johns Hopkins University Library.

Díaz, which vacillated from favoring Cuba's remaining under Spanish domination, to supporting annexation of the island to the United States, to maneuvering for its annexation by Mexico. In a letter of September, 1895, to Estrada Palma, Don Nicolás Domínguez Cowan, Cuban agent in Mexico, summed up the situation:

> It is very certain that there are many Mexicans whose sympathies are with the Cuban Revolution, but because of the passivity of the inhabitants of this country, because of the policies which the government follows, and above all because of the ridiculous propaganda which has been circulating for some time in favor of annexation of Cuba to Mexico, the enthusiasm of the sons of this Republic in favor of our independence has become somewhat lukewarm. The Cuban, Carlos Américo Loria, anonymously started this thinking, and I suspect he was supported by the President, General Díaz and the Minister of Foreign Relations, Don Ignacio Mariscal. The enclosed articles will give you a perfect idea of the opinion of some newspapers of this city. I have believed it advisable not to answer, because I have not wished to wound Mexican sensitivity as well as because I do not wish to stir up the Spanish colony which is influential, numerous and wealthy.
>
> Mexico threw off the yoke of the Spanish oppressor, but it continues to feel the pressure of the Spanish element. . . .[23]

A few days later, Domínguez Cowan wrote that "there are good wishes and sympathies [here] in favor of Cuba, but on reaching the doors of Congress, some vacillate and others weaken."[24] Estrada Palma voiced the opinion of all Cuban revolutionaries when he replied, "The attitude of Mexico toward our conflict with Spain is deplorable. Mexico appears to have abdicated from the high and noble position which the Venezuelans, Chileans, Peruvians and Ecuadorians have occupied. . . ."[25]

But worse was yet to come. Domínguez Cowan's effort to organize a meeting celebrating the anniversary of the *Grito de Baire* was prohibited by President Porfirio Díaz after the representative of Spain had registered a protest. Estrada Palma, on learning of this, wrote to the Cuban agent in Mexico, "It does not surprise me. It seems today the American Republics have forgotten that yesterday they were oppressed like us, and that the same reason has obliged us to rise up in arms. They too became rebels in order to convert their sons, enslaved colonials, into citizens, masters of their sovereignty."[26]

Delegate Estrada Palma stressed the same theme in May, 1896 in an extensive note to President Salvador Cisneros Betancourt dealing with the state of foreign support for the Cuban Revolution. One paragraph read:

> *Latin American Republics.* The attitude of these governments is inconceivable, some indifferent, others even hostile to the liberating revolution of Cuba. And it is not that they do not know the development and the huge proportions which our way of independence has attained. They also are not ignorant of the causes which have produced it and know that justice is on our side. They know well that these causes constitute, in the perennial process of Spanish domination in America, the same grievances which obliged the Hispanic people of this continent to liberate themselves by force of arms from the Iberian yoke. But the number of Spanish residents in many of the Republics and the influence which they have in the governmental sphere, especially in some of them, for example, Mexico, Colombia, Argentina, have contributed powerfully to weaken the natural sympathy which all of our race in the world of Columbus must feel in favor of a people which struggles heroically to break the chains which enslave and degrade them. . . .[27]

Estrada Palma was only partly correct in his analysis. While it is definitely true that the government and governing classes in many of the Latin American countries, and especially in Mexico,[28] were in favor of Spain to a great extent because of the influence of Spanish residents, he did not appear to understand that Latin Americans were now more concerned with liberating themselves from the increasing dominance of the United States than from "Spanish domination in America," and viewed Spain as an ally against a common enemy—emerging American imperialism. This was clearly set forth in the accounts of Aristides Agüero, who pleaded the Cuban cause in the South American countries. Everywhere he went, he reported to Estrada Palma, he found "Yankee-phobia" a force to be reckoned with in winning support for Cuba's struggle for independence.* He warned Estrada

---

* Agüero reported that everywhere he went in South America the workers and students supported his pleas for Cuba, but that the conservatives were cold. In part, he explained, this was due to the fact that the conservatives were frightened by the Spanish press which painted a lurid portrait of a Negro Revolution in Cuba, dominated by freemasonry, to wrest political control from the Catholic Spanish. The Maceo brothers were accused of plotting to set up another Haiti in

Palma that great care should be taken to prevent the United States from determining the policy of the Cuban insurgents since this would only feed the flames of anti-American prejudice in South America. Agüero even felt that United States recognition of Cuban belligerency would only complicate Cuba's problems in the Spanish-American nations who "still have great respect for their ancient Senora and Duenna." [29]*

Agüero's comment on his experience in Brazil sums up the general attitude he found everywhere in South America. "This country," he wrote to Estrada Palma, "characteristically talks a great deal, offers much, puts on grand demonstrations and exaggerates her adjectives and her promises, but when the time comes to act, all her promises are reduced to words and nothing more." [30] In a bitter letter from Bolivia, Agüero wrote that "America, through her cowardice and egotism, is treacherous and disloyal to us." [31]

In August, 1896, the Provisional Government of the Republic of Cuba issued a moving appeal to the Republics of Latin America. Pointing out that 'the military success of the Revolution has surpassed all expectations," it noted with pride the invasion of the West. "The march of the Invading Army through the territory of Occidente was

---

Cuba for the benefit of their race. But the most effective Spanish propaganda was the charge by Spanish writers that the Colossus of the North was seeking to annex Cuba to use it as a base against the domination of all of Spanish America. (Aristides Agüero to Estrada Palma, Chile, September 30, October 16, 1895, Correspondencia diplomática, vol. II, pp. 26, 27-29, 31-33.)

Interestingly enough, the Spanish propaganda that the war in Cuba was a race war to establish another Haiti worked for the Cuban cause in Haiti. (Ulpiano Dellundo to Gonzalo de Quesada, Port-au-Prince, August 10, 1895, Correspondencia diplomática, vol. IV, pp. 9-10.)

* At the same time, however, other Cuban agents in Latin America were emphasizing that the failure of the United States to recognize Cuban belligerency was seriously retarding their efforts to secure such recognition from the Latin American nations. For if the powerful North American government did not see fit to recognize the belligerency of the Cuban Republic, how could the small Latin American Republics take such a step on their own? (See, for example, Correspondencia diplomática, vol. II, pp. 39, 43, 125, 163.) Of course, during the first war for independence (1868-1878), several Latin American nations did recognize Cuban belligerency even though the government of the United States refused to do so. But many of the Latin American governments had grown more conservative in the intervening years and were less inclined to look with favor on a revolutionary movement to overthrow an established government—even a Spanish government—in Latin America, probably fearing this might inspire their own people to take similar steps.

a true triumphal passage. The population hurried to meet our soldiers and the adherence of the people in the districts which were considered the bulwark of the sovereignty of Spain has crowned the military success with the most complete political triumph. Before this result which would be astonishing if the causes which had produced it were not obvious, it is impossible to ignore that the people of the colony have the firm wish to change their political condition completing their historical development, such as the sister nations of the continent completed it in their day, and elevating themselves to the dignity of a state."

"This being the case," the appeal concluded, "the government of the Republic of Cuba, has believed it its duty to direct itself to the other American states which have the same origin, to explain to them the grave motives which have caused them to go to war in order to constitute themselves and to express to them their fervent hopes that they will find in them a great moral force which will effectively aid in putting an end to the bloody conflict in which they are involved. From the wisdom of the free people of Latin America they await the recognition that will unite the community of origin of history and of language as well as the similarity of customs and beliefs from which this community is derived. Since the peace and prosperity of an American people are important factors in the life of all, it is obvious that the concept of American solidarity should not be an empty one." *

This plea was no more effective than had been previous ones. In his *Cuba y América,* published in 1897, L. G. del Portillo, a Cuban revolutionist, reported sadly that while "the heart of the people of Latin America beats in unison with ours and declares for the triumph of the flag which symbolizes the final victory of Hispano-American

---

* The appeal was published in *El Cubano Libre* of January 15, 1897 and was preceded by the following introductory comment: "We are suspending our editorial today to give space to the wise and well-written manifesto which in August of last year was written by Secretary of Foreign Relations, Rafael Portuondo, to the Latin Republics of America. It arrived late to our hands, nevertheless we are publishing it with true pleasure so that our readers may know a document which, given the spirit of truth and justice which animates it, carries notable importance for Cuba, and surely will provoke in the spirit of Latin American powers a favorable reaction to our cause." (A facsimile of the page of *El Cubano Libre,* containing the appeal and the introduction, is reproduced in Thomas W. Steep, "A Cuban Insurgent Newspaper," *Metropolitan Magazine,* vol. VIII, May, 1898, p. 148.)

independence," the hands which directed the governments of these Republics "abandoned a sister people which fights heroically to free itself. . . ."[32] The Spanish Queen was not far wrong when she boasted that the sympathies of most of the governments of Latin America were with Spain in the Cuban revolt.[33]

Thus it was that the Republic of Cuba had to depend solely upon the United States for assistance in arms and ammunition with which to liberate the island—had to depend, in short, on a government which had, even before the outbreak of the Cuban Revolution, made it clear that its interests and its interests alone would determine the course of events in Latin America. Perhaps if José Martí had not died at the very outbreak of the Cuban Revolution, struck down by the Spaniards as he moved into battle with the enemy, the course of Cuban-Latin American relations during the course of the War for Independence might have been different. For Martí was a man of considerable influence in Hispanic America and this might have produced results beneficial to the Cuban cause. In any case, the time was to come when Latin America realized how mistaken it had been in failing to support the Cuban Revolution effectively, leaving the door open for the United States to enter the war before the Cubans had succeeded in achieving victory by their own efforts. Although he was defending the continuation of Spain's despotic rule over Cuba, Juan du Bosc, a member of the staff of the Spanish Embassy in Washington, made a significant point when he asked the Latin American nations: "If the United States should triumph [in Cuba], whose turn will be next?"[34]

CHAPTER IX

The American People and Cuban Independence

IF ONE READS the majority of American historical works covering the period February, 1895 to April, 1898, one gets the distinct impression that the Cuban Revolution was fought not by the Liberating Army in the island but by a *Junta* in the United States. It was not Máximo Gómez, Antonio Maceo, Calixto García and the *mambises* they led who fought the Spanish Army, but Tomás Estrada Palma, Gonzalo de Quesada, Horatio S. Rubens and others associated with the Cuban *Junta* in the United States who did whatever fighting was carried on by the Cubans, and did so in the form of "news releases" to reporters describing battles in the island that never occurred and telling of rebel victories that never existed in fact, but were manufactured by the *Junta* in the United States.*

There was, of course, a Cuban delegation, or *Junta* as it came to be called, functioning in the United States. It was first officially appointed in September, 1895, by the Constituent Assembly at Guáimaro that

---

* A contemporary attitude which expressed a similar viewpoint appeared in the Cincinatti *Times-Star* of March 2, 1895. The paper sneered: "The insurgent forces seems to be mainly composed of newspaper correspondents armed with pencils, kodaks, and like deadly weapons." (Quoted in George W. Auxier, Jr., "The Cuban Question as reflected in the Editorial Columns of Middle Western Newspapers, 1895-1898," unpublished Ph.D. thesis, Ohio State University, 1938, pp. 4-5.)

Probably many Americans believe this today as a result of the famous telegram Frederick Remington sent William Randolph Hearst from Havana: "Everything is quiet. There is no trouble here. There will be no war. I wish to return." To which Hearst replied: "Please remain. You furnish the pictures and I'll furnish the war." In the movie *Citizen Kane*, based on the life of Hearst, a reporter named Wheeler wires from Havana: "There is no war in Cuba," and Kane replied: "I'll provide the war."

formed the insurgent government; the Constituent Assembly at the same time elected Tomás Estrada Palma its Delegate and chief representative abroad with authority to carry on diplomatic relations with other countries. For the last-mentioned purposes, it set up a Cuban Legation in Washington, with Gonzalo de Quesada as Cuban Revolutionary Chargé d'Affaires, Ricardo Díaz Albertini as Secretary, and Benjamín Guerra, Treasurer. The general headquarters of the Cuban *Junta* was located at 120 Front Street in New York City, but Estrada Palma operated mainly from the office of Horatio S. Rubens, a prominent New York lawyer, who was sympathetic with the Cuban Revolution and had assisted José Martí as early as 1893.[1]

The *Junta* proper consisted chiefly of nationalized Cubans, many of them cigar makers who lived in Tampa, Key West, Jacksonville, New Orleans, New York and other cities. The Cuban League of the United States, formed early in 1892,* offered membership to "bona fide American citizens whose pro-Cuban sympathies led them . . . to organize affiliated clubs throughout the United States."[2] The two organizations—the regular *Junta* and the League—had as their primary task the providing of material and moral aid to the rebels who were fighting the war on the island. This was to be accomplished through securing contributions to the Cuban cause, fitting out filibustering expeditions to the islands, organizing public sympathy for the revolutionary cause, and, most important of all, securing recognition of Cuban belligerency and independence from the United States so that the Revolutionary Government could obtain the means to wage war successfully.

Though officially subject to the Revolutionary Government, the Cuban *Junta* actually exercised a great deal of independent authority. To a large extent, its policies were determined by Tomás Estrada Palma. The distinguished Cuban was born in Bayamo, Oriente, in 1835, studied law at the University of Seville in Spain, lived several years in France, and upon his return to Cuba in 1868 became active in the

---

* The Cuban League was organized by William O. McDowell, a New York businessman, who devoted himself to the Cuban cause after he met Martí. He was described as a man who labored many hours in behalf of the Cuban cause with "his only reward being the knowledge of the large part he has had in bringing . . . happiness to these Liberty-loving people." (R. Martinez to José Ignacio Rodriguez, New York, May 26, 1902, José Ignacio Rodriguez Papers, Box 14, Library of Congress.)

revolutionary movement. He took a prominent part in the Ten Years' War against Spain and in 1877 the revolutionary Cuban Congress named him president, but he was soon captured and sent to Spain in chains. He was released in 1878 following the peace of Zanjón, and went to Honduras, where he taught school and later served as Postmaster General. While in that country he married the daughter of Santos Guardiola, then President of Honduras. After his wife's father was assassinated, Estrada Palma went to the United States and made his home there for some twenty years. For a number of years he taught in a boys' school in Central Valley, New York, and while there he continued to work for Cuban liberty. When the Cubans, led by José Martí, again started the struggle for independence in 1895, Estrada Palma took a leading role in assisting the movement in the United States. Upon Martí's death, he was elected Delegate of the Cuban Revolutionary Party, became head of the Cuban Junta, moved to New York City and took up leadership of the New York revolutionary clubs.

"Don Tomás," as Estrada Palma was often addressed by the Cuban revolutionary leaders,* was in close contact with the men who led the revolution on the island. But Maceo, Gómez and other revolutionists did not always see eye-to-eye with Estrada Palma. They felt that while he worked indefatigably for the cause of Cuban independence, he placed too much stress on the importance of American recognition of an assistance to the Revolution and was willing to use methods to secure this which might compromise the struggle. They did not share his growing doubt as to the ability of Cuba to achieve a military victory without American intervention.† They felt, too, that he was not

---

* In 1895 Estrada Palma was sixty years old. With a flowing white moustache and carefully combed white hair, he cut an impressive figure. (See Carlos Marquez Sterling, *Don Tomas, Biografia de una Epoca*, Habana, 1953.)

† In April, 1896, Antonio Maceo wrote to Estrada Palma criticizing his policy of seeking United States support for the Cuban rebellion: "Already I read in the papers a discussion on whether the United States should intervene in this war to bring it to a swift end, and I suspect that you, inspired by patriotism, are working without tiring to do all for Cuba that you can, but as I see it, we do not need intervention in order to win this war. If we want to reduce Cuba in a few days, send us 25 or 30 thousand rifles, a million rounds of ammunition and one, or at the most two expeditions." Maceo concluded by pointing out that if the United States were genuinely interested in Cuba's welfare, she would—even if tacitly—give her full support to this program. (Maceo to Estrada Palma, El Rubi, Pínar del Río, April 14, 1896, in *Documentos para su vida*, p. 137.) Maceo always doubted that the government of the United States was genuinely inter-

entirely opposed to annexation of Cuba to the United States, and that if an independent Cuba became too revolutionary, he might favor such a solution in order to achieve "law and order." As we shall see, Estrada Palma gave evidence later that there was justification for this feeling among the Cuban revolutionists.[3]

As early as August, 1895, Estrada Palma wrote frankly to Antonio Maceo: "The United States is disposed to our favor, and I can count on help from people in influential posts in the government.[*] With the employment of bonds in certain cases, I think I can get recognition of belligerency from the Executive Power, or at least the recommendation on the part of the Federal Congress that the President make the recognition opportunely. In such an event the Revolution could then get all the money it needed."[4] Just how many bonds the Junta issued and to whom they were distributed to advance the campaign to win recognition of Cuban belligerency will be discussed below. Here we may note that many revolutionists in Cuba did not favor this type of activity. Actually, the *Junta* itself did not regard this phase of its work as particularly effective. It was mainly through mass meetings, carnivals, public addresses, Cuban-American Fairs,[†] publication of its own news-

---

ested in Cuba's welfare. He told J. Syme Hastings that while he did not doubt the sympathy of the American people, he feared that "your Government may doubt the discretion of recognizing our belligerency." When Hastings remarked that Americans had had to fight for their liberty, Maceo smiled: "Ah, yes, but I doubt if we will have a Lafayette to aid us in this unequal struggle." (*Journal of the Knights of Labor,* Nov. 5, 1898.)

[*] Gonzalo de Quesada, whom Estrada Palma appointed as the representative of the Cuban Revolutionary Party in Washington, was the man who had most of the contacts with "people in influential posts in the government." Quesada, who spearheaded the Cuban campaign on Congress, had valuable contacts in Washington, including Senator John T. Morgan from Alabama, Senator Wilkinson Call from Florida, and Senator Henry Cabot Lodge from Massachusetts. Quesada received considerable help from the Mexican Minister to the United States, Matias Romero, in establishing these contacts. (Gonzalo de Quesada to Horatio S. Rubens, Washington, D.C. (September, 1895), *Correspondencia diplomática,* vol. V, p. 28.)

[†] A handbill announcing the "Grand Cuban-American Fair" at New York's Madison Square Garden, May 25 to 30, 1896, carried on top the slogan: "Cuba Appreciates Sympathy—She Must Have Assistance." (The original document is in the Hoes Collection at the Library of Congress. A facsimile is published in George W. Auxier, Jr., "The Propaganda Activities of the Cuban Junta in Precipitating the Spanish-American War, 1895-1898," *Hispanic American Historical Review,* vol. XIX, Aug. 1939, p. 295.)

papers, *Patria** and *El Porvenir*,† distribution of thousands of copies of scores of pamphlets,‡ feeding daily reports to American newspapers, especially those on the East Coast, and establishing contacts with leading Washington political figures, that the Junta conducted its massive campaign to win support for recognition of Cuban belligerency. This campaign attracted the support of many Americans who sincerely sympathized with the Cuban revolutionists, wished to see them achieve independence, and believed that they were entitled to the recognition of belligerency. But, as we shall see, it also attracted elements in the United States who viewed the Revolution as an issue suited to their own purposes, such as American traders and investors who were directly

---

* *Patria* was founded in 1892 by José Martí. In its first issue it announced: "This newspaper has been founded . . . to contribute, without delay or rest, to the organization of the free men of Cuba and Puerto Rico, in accord with the actual conditions and needs of the island." ("Nuestras Ideas," *Patria*, March 14, 1892.) For six years, until December 31, 1898, through 522 issues, *Patria* reiterated its conviction that "the actual conditions and needs "of the islands" of Cuba and Puerto Rico demanded independence. Setero Figuero, a Puerto Rican Negro and President of the club El Borinquen, was editorial assistant, under both Marti and Varona, on the staff of *Patria*. Figuero played a leading role in allying the Puerto Ricans with the movement for Cuban independence. In a speech delivered to a meeting in March, 1896, Figuero concluded: "We seek, not the affirmation of an isolated determined band of patriots, but the unanimous voice, the spontaneous manifestations of all the emigre centers of the United States to free our enslaved native lands." (*Patria*, March 26, 1896.)

Patria's importance to the revolutionary movement would be difficult to exaggerate. It was, José Maria Izaguirre pointed out, "essential for the centers of emigration—for news and for inspiration." (Izaguirre to Estrada Palma, Managua, November 26, 1896, *Correspondencia diplomática*, vol. IV, p. 68.)

† Enrique Trujillo's paper, *El Porvenir*, was published for the Cuban emigres in New York. Although opposed for a time to Martí's leadership, insisting that "Key West is trying to dictate to New York," his paper was important because Trujillo, a close friend of Antonio Maceo, published the Negro General's firsthand reports on the war. (For the rift between Trujillo and Martí, see *Patria*, March 26, 1892.)

Rafael Serra's *Doctrina de Marti* was also published in New York. (*True*, *op. cit.*, p. 155.)

‡ The following pamphlets in the Hoes Collection in the Library of Congress were among those published and distributed by the Junta: Enrique José Varona, *Cuba vs. Spain*; *Manifesto of the Cuban Revolutionary Party to the People of the United States of America*, n.p. 1895; Fidel G. Pierra, *Facts About Cuba*, n.p. 1895; *The Cuban Question in Its True Light* by "An American," New York, 1895; *Address of Tomás Estrada Palma to the American People*, n.p., c. February, 1897; Senator John T. Morgan, *Belligerent Rights for Cuba*, Washington, D.C., 1897. There was also a whole group published in the *Cuba Must Be Free* Series.

connected with Cuban affairs and wished to protect their trade and investments in the island; expansionist elements who were seeking foreign markets for manufactured goods and for the investment of surplus capital; businessmen and politicians who cared nothing for the revolutionary struggle in Cuba but saw in it an opportunity to divert popular thinking away from the economic and social problems arising from the depression which had begun in 1893, and newspaper publishers who saw in the Cuban Revolution an opportunity to boost circulation. In the latter category, the "yellow press" of William R. Hearst (New York *Journal*) and Joseph Pulitzer (New York *World*) was most important, although most newspapers in the United States played a part in this campaign. The news releases of the Cuban *Junta* published in Hearst's *Journal* and Pulitzer's *World*, were picked up by all newspapers belonging to the Associated Press and passed on to their readers.[5] Actually, Hearst did not take active control of the New York *Journal* until November 6, 1895, by which time many other newspapers had already been publishing releases of the Cuban *Junta*.

That there were influential forces in the United States which had reasons of their own for espousing the Cuban cause should not obscure the fact, as it does too often in historical works dealing with this period, that a majority of the American people supported the Revolution, wished to assist it themselves, and desired to see their government give it the recognition they believed it was entitled to. Sympathy for Cuba was expressed in editorial columns, plays* and pamphlets, preached from the pulpit and platform, and voiced in poetry. One poet wrote on the European amazement at American sympathy for the rebels:

> Amazed, perhaps! But wondering Europe, know
> That this republic of the free and freed
> Can pity the oppressed, view human woe
> And speak a sympathy that's more than greed!

---

* Some of the plays written and produced in the United States during the Cuban War for Independence were: G. A. Kastelic, *Cuba Libre*, Chicago, 1895; James A. McKnight, *Cuba Free*, New York, 1896; R. G. Taber, *A Cuban Rebel*, Greatkills, New York, 1895; Henry J. Pain, *Cuba*, New York, 1896; Charles W. Russell, *Cuba Libre*, n.p., 1897; James F. Milliken, *The Cuban Patriot*, New York, 1897. A collection of these plays is in the Hoes Collection, Library of Congress.

Another poem, published in a mid-Western newspaper in December, 1896, went:

> Arise! ye lovers of the right;
> Strike fast, O sons of liberty!
> United in your purpose, smite,
> And bleeding Cuba will be free!⁶

It is common for American historians to assert that this sympathy did not express the real feelings of the people but was the product of a well-organized campaign of individuals and groups who had their own reasons for generating support for Cuba. Such influence did play its part, but at the root of the nationwide support for Cuba was admiration for a people struggling for freedom against overwhelming odds. "The failure of the revolutionary movement can safely be predicted," an American newspaper declared when the uprising began in Cuba. Another commented in November, 1895 that "out of stores and ammunition, shoeless, coatless, gunless and discouraged, the soldiers [in Cuba] battling for liberty and right cannot hope to master their enemies." ⁷ The ability of the *insurrectos,* although vastly outnumbered and greatly inferior in equipment, not only to maintain the Revolution but to spread it and to defeat the Spaniards, was a major reason for American sympathy for the Cuban cause. An added factor, of course, was the continual record of Spanish cruelty against Cubans, soldiers and civilians alike.

Granted that many accounts of this cruelty in the "yellow press," particularly those involving women,* were either fabricated or exag-

---

* "How long," asked the New York *World,* "shall women passengers on vessels flying the American flag be unlawfully seized and stripped and searched by brutal, jeering Spanish officers, in violation of the laws of nations and of the honor of the United States?" (Feb. 13, 1897.) Consular General Lee reported from Havana to Assistant Secretary of State, W. W. Rockhill that ladies on American steamers had on two occasions been searched by men before women were employed in that capacity, but the "yellow press" made it appear that this was the regular procedure by the Spanish authorities. (Lee to Rockhill, Feb. 18, 1897, Department of State, Consular Letters, Havana, National Archives, Washington, D.C.) The most celebrated case involving a woman was that of the Cuban girl Evangelina Cosío y Cisneros whom Hearst's representative in Cuba freed from prison and brought to the United States where she was hailed as "The Cuban Joan of Arc," especially in the New York *Journal.* (W. A. Swanberg, *Citizen Hearst: A Biography of William Randolph Hearst,* New York, 1961, pp. 116-30.)

gerated, it is still difficult to see how the terrible effects of the reconcentration policy could have been distorted. The reaction of the American people to the war of extermination waged by Weyler—who was given such names as butcher, wolf, mad dog, human hyena—was to rally behind the struggle for Cuban independence.

In a letter to Secretary of State Richard B. Olney, Daniel E. Sickles, United States Minister to Spain during the Ten Years' War, expressed the sentiments of thousands of American citizens:

> . . . my sympathies are . . . warmly interested in behalf of the heroic struggle made by the insurgents to emancipate themselves and their Island from Spanish rule. Spain has only herself to blame for the present insurrection. That Government pledged itself to the United States, as you will see in my correspondence [in the State Department] to grant the most ample concessions to the legitimate demands of the Cubans for a large measure of self-government. . . . None of these pledges have been kept. Cuba has been and is the worst governed spot on this continental hemisphere. I hope . . . that the President, in his annual message, may recognize the claims of this struggle for freedom upon the attention of our government, as it has already won the admiration and sympathy of our people. . . . Our independence was founded on the right of insurrection. . . . [8]

Support for the Cuban cause was expressed by men and women in all classes of society, and in all sections of the country. Estrada Palma received telegrams from "Cuban sympathy" meetings such as the one which read: "A public meeting representing the business, labor, religious and political interests of this city sends you greetings. May the merciful Father of all prosper the cause of liberty on your beautiful island. Long live the Republic of Cuba." From the West came telegrams assuring Estrada Palma that the farmers viewed the Cuban Revolution as "another case of liberty struggling against an oppressive European despotism," and hailed the Cuban insurgents "who are making a heroic fight for their freedom and independence." [9]

The Negro people of the United States held mass meetings in support of the Cuban Revolution at which they especially expressed pride in the exploits of Antonio Maceo. But American Negroes were suspicious of the fact that Southerners, who deprived Negroes of their freedom, were among the most enthusiastic supporters of *Cuba Libre*.

"Is it better," asked a group of Massachusetts Negroes, "to be Cuban revolutionists fighting for Cuban independence than American citizens striving to do their simple duty at home? Or is it better only in case those American citizens doing their simple duty at home happen to be Negroes residing in the Southern States?" [10]*

A number of labor and Socialist groups were suspicious of joining in support of *Cuba Libre* along with businessmen, doubting the latter's sincerity.† Nevertheless, it was from the American labor and Socialist movements that the cause of Cuban independence received some of its greatest support. Soon after the Cuban people took up arms to secure their independence, the labor press in the United States reported that

---

* The opponents of Cuban independence made a telling point in stressing the contradiction between the Southern support for Cubans fighting for liberty, many of whom were Negroes, and the treatment of Negroes in the South fighting for liberty. The New York *Tribune* asked the Southern Democrats who supported recognition of Cuban belligerency whether they "do not know that more than one-fourth of the Cubans including some of the foremost leaders, are what they politely term 'niggers,'" and asked sarcastically, "Can it be that they regard 'niggers' in Cuba more favorably than in Georgia or Mississippi?" It twitted the Southern Democrats for "loving the 'nigger' in Cuba," and "lynching the "nigger' in the South." (Dec. 19, 1897.) Senator Orville H. Platt of Connecticut (a name later hated in Cuba as the author of the "Platt Amendment") declared in opposing recognition of Cuban belligerency: "Men whose love of humanity was not fluttered when in Texas about a year ago a negro was covered with kerosene oil and burned to death on a public platform in the presence of 7000 yelling people, are shedding tears over the sad fate of [Antonio] Maceo." (Louis A. Coolidge, *An Old-Fashioned Senator—Orville H. Platt*, New York, 1910, pp. 265-66.)

Manuel de la Cruz wrote "The Cuban Revolution and the Colored Race," a pamphlet which pointed to the opportunity for advancement that the Revolution offered to the Negroes of Cuba and which had a fairly wide circulation in Negro circles in the United States. (See Juan J. Ramos, "La Literatura," in Ramiro Guerra y Sánchez *Historia de la Nacion Cubana*, Havana, 1952, vol. VII, p. 351.)

* The affiliation of Andrew Carnegie, the iron and steel millionaire, with the Cuban Liberty League—he was one of its vice-presidents—aroused the suspicion of *The Coming Nation*, a Socialist paper. "The gentleman has found patriotism very profitable—human liberty under the competitive social system has proven very profitable to the philosopher of Homestead. So Mr. Carnegie unloosens the bonds of his sympathy and lets it affiliate with the struggle. The religious philanthropist makes armor plate for battleships . . . and of course his sympathies [for Cuba] are not born of a desire that this country and Spain should go to war." (Jan. 2, 1897.) The reference to Homestead is to the breaking of the steel strike of 1892 at Homestead, Pennsylvania by the Carnegie Steel Company. (See Philip S. Foner, *History of the Labor Movement in the United States*, Vol. II, New York, 1965, pp. 206-19.)

meetings were being held "in all parts of the country to discuss the Cuban revolution," and that "in most cases labor organizations are taking the initiative passing resolutions of sympathy for the insurgents."[11] American Socialists joined them with similar resolutions, although some, like *The People*, organ of the Socialist Labor Party and edited by Daniel De Leon, expressed a willingness to aid Cuban attempts at freedom on only one condition: "If by 'freedom' is meant freedom of the Cuban toiler from subjection to the thrall of another human being held in the pursuit of his living; if it meant his freedom to hold and enjoy the full fruits of his efforts without the compulsion to pay tribute to others for the boon of life." On the other hand, if freedom meant merely a "change of masters," from Spanish to Cuban or American,* "the game would not be worth the candle." There was, therefore, only one way for the Cuban revolutionists to win the support of the Socialist Labor Party; by demanding "the overthrow of wage slavery and thereby freedom from capitalism. . . . If they do not, they prove themselves either incompetent, or political deceivers trying to catch the people with a snare and a delusion, in either of which cases, so far from being entitled to our aid, they are entitled to our condemnation."[12] It never seemed to have occurred to the Socialist Labor Party that if the Cuban revolutionists had raised, as their major objective, the overthrow of capitalism, their support in Cuba would have been confined to the small body of Socialists.

Six months after the Cuban rebellion broke out, the *Journal of the Knights of Labor* declared that "the revolution is one of the most righteous ever declared in any country and *should be supported by every lover of liberty and free government in this country.*" A week later, denouncing the government's interference with filibustering expeditions to Cuba, it urged that "Cuba needs freeing from the tyrants more than

---

* District Assembly No. 1 of the Socialist Trade & Labor Alliance, the trade union body of the Socialist Labor Party, asked the Cubans if anything would be gained by changing Spanish for American masters; yet this was precisely what would happen if the revolutionists were not careful. "The insurrection is eagerly watched by the American Sugar Trust, the American Tobacco Trust and other American sharks, ready to take actual possession of the island in the name of King Dollar." (*The People*, Sept. 20, 1895, Aug. 9, 1896, Jan. 17, 1897.) See also *The Socialist Alliance*, January, 1897. Copy in University of Chicago Library and "Are We Better Off Than Cubans?" *Journal of the Knights of Labor*, Oct. 31, 1895.

the American colonies did, yet American men-of-war guard our southern coast, in the interest of tyranny and oppression, to prevent Cuba from becoming the land of the free and home of the brave." [13] The official organ of the Knights of Labor expressed an unqualified confidence that "the native forces cannot possibly be subdued," and on the basis of all available facts, concluded that "if we should simply refrain from helping Spain, Cuba would be free within a year. All we should have to do would be to remove the embargo our government is now enforcing on private assistance to insurgents and the revolutionary camp would bristle with rifles. 'For every gun,' remarked one of the rebel chiefs recently, 'it is easy to find a man.' We are now doing Spain the service of keeping guns out of Cuba." Recognition of Cuba as a belligerent by the United States would guarantee her independence![14]

The *Journal of the Knights of Labor* outlined specific procedures by which American labor could give effective aid to the Cubans:

1. "Let us have a series of mass meetings in every city, town and township in the United States, demanding in thunder tones that the President and Congress of the United States act, and act at once, to the end that this savage war be stopped at once, the armies of Spain withdrawn, and independence of Cuba be conceded by the Spanish government."

2. ". . . that all Knights of Labor and all other friends of Cuba and liberty should take the money which they intend spending this year for the usual fourth of July fireworks and contribute the same to a fund to buy either guns and ammunition for a warship to be presented to the Cuban revolutionists. . . . What Cuba needs today more than anything else next to the recognition of her independence by the United States government, is one or two first-class fighting ships on the sea. Let Americans make the glorious Fourth truly glorious this year by such a gift. . . ."

3. All friends of Cuba were urged to buy the souvenir silver dollar which the Cuban *Junta* was planning to issue and which would give the Cubans a sixty percent profit. "Hurrah for Cuba Libre! No better or more practical method could be found to show you[r] sympathy for the suffering Cubans than to buy one of these souvenir dollars. Keep it and carry it with you and hand it down to your children. It will be to them a certificate of your patriotism and your practical sympathy

and help for the cause of freedom in the Western Hemisphere." The *Journal* announced that it was prepared to accept these coins in payment for subscriptions.

4. "Labor all over the country should vote against all Congressmen who have not supported the Congressional resolution for recognition of Cuban belligerency, for recognition of belligerency is all the help the Cubans really need from the United States. This will give the Cubans the right to purchase munitions of war, and in three months from the time Congress recognized her independence, those gallant patriots will drive the Spanish troops from the Island without any further assistance from this country." [15]

At its 1895 convention, the American Federation of Labor adopted a resolution sympathizing with "the Cubans and the poor and oppressed of all nations." The following year it passed, by a vote of 60 to 9, a resolution stating: "That the example of the people of France in giving recognition and aid to the Fathers in their struggle to secure the independence of the colonies is worthy of imitation, and we hereby call upon the President and Congress to recognize the belligerent rights of the Cuban revolutionists." [16] The Atlanta Federation of Trades, affiliated with the A. F. of L., hailed this stand and pledged its "moral and financial support to the patriots of Cuba who are now engaged in their final struggle for liberty and independence." [17]

Still the A. F. of L. did not permit the jingoistic elements to convert its sympathy for Cuba into support of a war against Spain. At its 1897 convention, the Federation reaffirmed its previous stand of sympathy for the Cuban people, but rejected a strongly-worded resolution which urged that Congress should "waste no time in useless debates and diplomatic chicanery, but should take such immediae action as [might] tend to put an end to the indiscriminate murder of the common people of Cuba by the Spanish soldiery." The majority of the delegates expressed their sympathy for the Cuban struggle for freedom, but argued that by adopting the proposed resolution, the labor movement would only be adding fuel to the fire of jingoism which would involve the United States in war. Recognition of Cuban belligerency, they continued, would enable the Cubans to win the war without American intervention.[18]

"The sympathy of our movement with Cuba is genuine, earnest and sincere," Samuel Gompers, President of the A.F. of L., wrote in a private letter, summing up the Federation's position, "but this does not for a moment imply that we are committed to certain adventurers who are apparently suffering from Hysteria but who simply assume the role to attract attention to their unworthy selves."[19] Gompers, a cigar maker himself, had become acquainted with Cuban cigar makers in New York, many of whom were identified with the Cuban revolutionary movement.[20] His own union, the Cigar Makers' International Union, the largest union affiliated at that time with the A.F. of L., led the trade unions in support for Cuban independence. Apart from their support for a people rebelling against economic, political and social bondage, the union wanted the revolution to succeed so that American cigar makers might be protected against cheap labor competition. It was practically impossible for a labor movement to be organized under Spanish rule, but independence could lead to improving the bargaining position of Cuban workers, thereby aiding American labor. In addition, the Cigar Makers' Union in the United States was making slow headway in organizing the Cubans who had emigrated to Key West and Tampa, many of whom had had no previous trade union experience. Thus, support for freedom for Cuba would work in two ways for the benefit of the American union. "American labor," writes John C. Appel, "would help the Cubans gain their independence of Spain and thus open the way for favorable legislation in Cuba. Besides, Cubans in the United States might be more interested in cooperating with the unionization activities if it meant American aid to 'Cuba Libre.'"[21]*

In whatever way they could, many Americans assisted the Cuban

---

* Although he concedes that "Union labor seemed to take intense interest in the Cuban cause," Ernest R. May leaves the impression that this was largely the result of pressure by the Cigar Makers' Union. ". . . cigarmakers' locals were soon passing resolutions of sympathy, and their leaders were obtaining similar declarations from municipal trade assemblies and state federations of labor." (*Imperial Democracy: The Emergence of America as a Great Power*, New York, 1961, p. 70.) May offers no proof of this influence, and a study of the discussions at conventions of trade unions, national, state and city federations of labor, indicates that the vast majority of the labor organizations needed no persuasion by leaders of the Cigar Makers' Union to voice their sympathy for the Cuban Revolution. (See John C. Appel, "The Relation of American Labor to American Imperialism, 1895-1905," unpublished Ph.D. thesis, University of Wisconsin, 1950, pp. 23-31.)

Revolution. The most common form, apart from contribution of funds, was the adoption of resolutions and the signing of petitions demanding the recognition of the belligerency of the Republic of Cuba. To describe these activities as tantamount to jingoism and a desire for war or to view them as solely the result of the propaganda and machinations of the Cuban *Junta,* the "yellow press," and the expansionist forces in the United States, is to denigrate the American people.

CHAPTER X

Cleveland Stands Against the Cuban Revolution

IN 1947, THE CONGRESS of Cuban Historians declared: "On renewing the Liberation struggle in 1895, the Cubans again encountered the hostility of the North American state, represented at this time by President Grover Cleveland, Secretary of State Richard B. Olney, and their allies, the foreign investors in Cuba. . . . This anti-Cuban attitude of the North American state was in open opposition to the sentiment and feelings and demands of the North American people, nobly favorable to Cuban independence."[1] This evaluation is correct.

Despite considerable popular feeling for the Cuban Revolution, on June 12, 1895, President Grover Cleveland proclaimed the neutrality of the United States in the conflict between Cuba and Spain. He warned American citizens against accepting commissions, enlisting men, fitting out and arming vessels, and starting or aiding military enterprises in the United States for the purpose of assisting the Cuban Revolution. Assuring all offenders that the government would prosecute any violation, Cleveland called on federal employees to prevent infringement of the proclamation and to bring to trial all violators.[2] Cleveland's action, of course, meant that the United States would permit trading in arms with Spain, but would use its entire forces to prevent aid reaching the revolutionists. On July 11, 1895, the Secretary of the Treasury instructed collectors of customs to prevent the formation of filibustering expeditions to Cuba. More than two thousand employees of the department were put on guard by this letter of instruction. Eight vessels were engaged in the revenue cutter service in the Atlantic, and practically all the efforts of this fleet were spent in trying to prevent the shipment of arms and other supplies to the Cuban rebels.[3]

177

From the beginning of the Cuban Revolution, the Spanish and U.S. governments cooperated to stop filibustering expeditions. The former placed agents in many American cities and ports who reported to the Department of State any shipment of arms and munitions and any movement of ships suspected to be destined for Cuba. In all cases, the department turned the information over to the proper officials for legal action. The Spanish Ministers to the United States, Marugua and his successor Enrique Dupuy de Lôme, operated an extremely complex net of detectives and spies with the help of which they were able to keep the U.S. State Department informed of the plans of the Cubans to organize expeditions.[4]* With the aid of Spanish spies, the U.S. government kept Cuban-Americans under constant surveillance, arrested and prosecuted those against whom evidence of lending aid to their embattled brethren in Cuba was furnished by the Spaniards.[5]

Thus while Spain was freely buying from U.S. factories all the arms and munitions she needed in her effort to crush the Revolution, the government of the United States was doing all that was possible to prevent the Revolution from provisioning itself. This policy was a far cry from the strict neutrality proclaimed by President Cleveland and described by most American historians as representing his policy in the Cuban crisis.[6] Basically, it was a continuation of the policy pursued by the government of the United States throughout the Ten Years' War, a policy of helping Spain defeat the Cuban Revolution. This conclusion is not affected by the fact that Spain frequently complained that the United States was not stopping filibustering activities and not preventing expeditions from reaching Cuba. For Spain's grievance was directed not so much against the President, the State and Treasury Departments as it was against the Courts.†

---

* Dupuy de Lôme, who succeeded Marugua as minister to the U.S. in September, 1895, pointed out in *Harper's Weekly* that the difficulty faced by Spanish representatives in securing observance of the President's neutrality proclamation was due more to "lack of co-operation of the local authorities than to any lack of zeal on the part of the State Department." He expressed his "profound gratitude" to Cleveland for "the measures adopted by the Government of the United States to prevent infringements of the law and attempts against the peace and security of a friendly nation." (*Harper's Weekly*, vol. XXIX, Sept. 1895, p. 330; De Lôme to Olney, June 14, 1895, *Papers Relating to the Foreign Relations of the United States*, Washington, 1895, part 2, p. 1195. Hereinafter cited as *Foreign Relations*.)

† Although the federal government cooperated fully with Spain in arresting

CLEVELAND STANDS AGAINST THE CUBAN REVOLUTION

The crucial issue was whether the United States would give diplomatic recognition to the Cuban revolutionary government by recognizing the Cubans as belligerents. For at least six months after the revolt began, the Cleveland Administration did not even concern itself with the question. But on September 25, 1895, following a conversation with Paul Brooks of Vermont, owner of Los Canos estate at Guantánamo, valued at $800,000 and employing 800 people, Richard B. Olney, Cleveland's new Secretary of State, did propose to the President an investigation of the uprising to determine whether it was made up of bandits or substantial elements of the community attempting to gain better government:

> The Spanish side is naturally the side of which I have heard, and do hear, the most. It is, in substance, that the Insurgents belong to the lowest order of the population of the Island, do not represent its property or its intelligence or its true interests, are the ignorant and desperate classes marshalled under the leadership of a few adventurers, and would be incapable of founding or maintaining a decent government if their revolution against Spain were to be successful.* . . . There are, however, grounds for questioning the correctness of this view. The Cuban insurgents are not to be regarded as the scum of the earth. . . . In sympathy and feeling, nine tenths of the Cuban population are with them. . . .

---

filibusterers, the courts were more lenient. In the early part of the Cuban Revolution, the courts held that an expedition was legal unless the government could prove that it was militarily prepared in the United States to fight Spain, and officered and equipped for immediate hostile operations when it landed in Cuba. In nearly all of the early cases, one of these requirements was lacking and the Treasury Department's case was defeated. But more than a year after the Revolution began, the Supreme Court ruled that expeditions might be illegal even when poorly organized and lacking some elements of a military force. Cleveland promptly incorporated the new interpretation into a second neutrality proclamation in July, 1896, but in the same month, a federal judge dismissed a case because the various elements of the expedition had combined outside the three mile limit of American jurisdiction. But a year and a half later, a federal judge ruled that any person violated the neutrality laws who knowingly aided or took part in an expedition, no matter how crudely organized or indirectly routed to Cuba. (*The Laws of Neutrality of the United States with Reference to the Cuban Insurrection*, Washington, 1896, pp. 27-36.)

* A good example of what Olney was referring to is the letter of Dupuy de Lôme in *Harper's Weekly* of September, 1895: "The American people is made to believe that there is in Cuba a nation fighting for liberty! instead of a few thousand adventures taking for the moment advantage of the rainy seasons." (Vol. XXIX, p. 330.)

The property class to a man is disgusted with Spanish misrule, with a system which has burdened the Island with $300,000,000 of debt, whose imposition in the way of annual taxes just stop short of prohibiting all industrial enterprise, and which yet does not fulfill the primary functions of government by insuring safety to life and security to property.

Although Olney was relaying Brooks's evaluation of the status of the Revolution rather than his own, he placed great emphasis upon the fact that the Vermonter had told him that the Revolution, "just in itself," was "capable of issuing in an established, constitutional government," and that Spain would never be able to suppress the rebellion. The revolutionists, he felt, were "at least entitled to claim one thing of us, and that is an investigation of the fact." If Brooks, in whose "intelligence and . . . honesty," he had great faith, was proved to be correct, the United States would have placed itself "in a position to intelligently consider and pass upon the question of according to the insurgents belligerent rights, or of recognizing their independence." Olney then reminded Cleveland that "travel [between the U.S. and Cuba] as well as a large and important commerce between the two countries is seriously affected by the prevailing hostilities . . . and that the United States will surely be called upon in numerous instances both to protect the persons and property of its citizens and to exact indemnity for injuries actually inflicted upon them." He therefore recommended the dispatch of an agent to Cuba "empowered to investigate and report on all the features of the present Cuban situation so far as American interests are affected by them."[7]

It was characteristic of a wealthy corporation executive and lawyer like Olney to judge the Cuban Revolution by the standard of what it meant to property holders and to the future of industrial enterprise in the island, and to condemn it if it expressed the will and served the interest of "the lowest order of the population of the Island"—the workers and peasants, Negro and white. Nevertheless, his proposal for an investigation of the exact status of the Revolution, even though belated, was justified, as was his conclusion that if it had the support of the majority of the people, the United States should seriously consider recognition of belligerency or independence. But Cleveland had reached the conclusion that the Cuban people were incapable of self-government by United States standards,* even though he conceded that he was "impressed" by Brooks's evaluation of the status of the Revolution.[8] At any rate, nothing came of Olney's proposal. The Spanish authorities were understandably relieved.

Brooks's evaluation of the Cuban Revolution was confirmed by a report Olney received late in November from Cuba, submitted by Henry A. Himley, a New York merchant who was interested in the Occitania estate in the island. The report stated that matters were "in a much more serious condition that they were a couple of months previously," that the Revolution was making steady progress, had widespread popular support, and that the Spanish troops were completely incapable of dealing with the situation.[9] But Cleveland's annual message to Congress, delivered on December 2, 1895, showed no influence of the reports from responsible sources as to the real status of the Revolution. He conceded that the Revolution was "more active than the one preceding it from 1868-1878 . . . threatening to extend itself," and that the Cuban people "appears to be fighting to achieve the possession of a major part of liberty." He did express horror at the "cruelties which seem to characterize especially this ferocious and bloody war." But he dismissed the fact that the sympathy of the people of the United States was with the Cuban people who were struggling for greater freedom, and he cautioned individual citizens to remain impartial in the conflict. He then reaffirmed U.S. neutrality, and the administration's determination to prevent use of American territory as a base for expeditions hostile to Spain. (Nothing was said about the use of American territory as a base for supplying Spain with the military equipment to wage war against the Cuban people.) Finally, Cleveland offered the good offices of the government of the United

---

* On three separate occasions, Cleveland expressed his contempt for the Cuban people. On July 16, 1896, he wrote, explaining his opposition to the purchase of Cuba: "It would seem absurd for us to buy the Island and present it to the people now inhabiting it, and put its government and management in its hands." On April 26, 1898, after the outbreak of the Spanish-American War, he wrote: "In the meantime, we, who have undertaken war in the interest of humanity and civilization, will find ourselves in alliance and co-operation with Cuban insurgents—the most inhuman and barbarious cutthroats in the world." Finally, on March 26, 1900, he wrote: "I am afraid Cuba ought to be submerged for awhile before it will make an American state or territory of which we will be particularly proud." All three letters were addressed to Richard B. Olney, and are in the Olney Papers, Library of Congress.

States for the settlement of the Cuban question on the basis of autonomy.[10]

Less than a week later, Tomás Estrada Palma, representative of the Cuban Revolutionary government in the United States, addressed a long letter to Olney outlining clearly why the Cubans rejected autonomy, and why the United States should grant the rights of belligerency. He explained that the causes of the Revolution of 1895 were substantially the same as those of the rebellion of the decade of 1868 to 1878, which terminated with the Spanish government promising Cuba would be granted such reforms as would remove the grounds of complaint on the part of the Cuban people. However, the Spanish promise had proven absolutely without character, and events had fully demonstrated that there was no hope in autonomy. Only independence would now satisfy the Cuban people, and they expected that a government, itself born in Revolution, would support their desire for real self-government.[11]

But the Secretary of State paid no attention to Estrada Palma's plea. The Department of State was now being guided in its Cuban policy by an American planter in Cuba who was to play an increasingly influential role for the remainder of the Cleveland Administration. He was Edwin F. Atkins of Boston, owner of the Soledad estate at Cienfuegos, whose father, Elisha Atkins, was an old friend of Olney's.* Since Cleveland had not bothered to send an agent to Cuba to collect facts on the Revolution, Atkins supplied much of the information for the Secretary of State. ("Mr. Olney," Atkins wrote later, "was always willing to listen to what I had to say upon the Cuban situation and he requested me to make confidential reports to him from time to time. This I did, and one of my reports was embodied almost verbatim in his report to Congress as Secretary of State."[12]†) Atkins' large sugar

---

* Atkins was recommended to Olney by Charles Francis Adams who had passed considerable time at Soledad, as "thoroughly informed as to the whole situation in Cuba. . . . I do not believe there is any quarter to which you could go for outside information and depend so entirely upon the judgment and knowledge of the informer, as to Mr. Atkins in matters connected with Cuba." (Adams to Olney, June 27, 1895, Olney Papers, Library of Congress.)

† Olney did not display such care with reports from spokesmen for the Cuban revolutionists. He wrote to Cleveland on March 21, 1896: "I have not had time to read fully either the letters of the consuls or the papers sent in by Mr. Quesada on behalf of what is called the 'Cuban Republic.'" (Grover Cleveland Papers, Library of Congress.)

plantations near Cienfuegos, developed at the cost of approximately $1,000,000, were under special protection of the Spanish government, but he was constantly seeking more adequate armed protection. Hence he was alarmed at the growing sentiment in the United States in favor of recognizing the belligerency of the rebels in Cuba. It was of vital importance to many American property owners in Cuba, for whom Atkins was the leading spokesman, that such a step be forestalled, for Spanish obligations to protect their property would cease with such recognition of the insurgents.[13] Charles F. Rand, president of the Spanish-American Iron Company and representative for the Bethlehem Steel-owned Juraguá Iron Company, wrote to Olney, "It is very clear that our interests will be jeopardized if belligerency is recognized, as the protection of troops will be withdrawn, which means the immediate closing of our mines, and the probable destruction of our properties, particularly the railway and the dock and harbor improvements." [14]

Atkins accordingly launched upon a vigorous campaign in Washington to convince the administration and leading Senators and Congressmen of the "folly" of recognizing Cuban belligerency. Typical of Atkins' method is the following evaluation of the Revolution he sent to Olney:

> The Cuban insurgents have neither government nor seat of residence for it, no revenue of any kind; they have neither a seaport in their possession nor any organs of communication with the external world. They have no organized army beyond some guerrilla bands who with torch and dynamite set fire to everything and blow up factories, buildings, railroad trains, tracks and costly bridges in their path of destruction everywhere when they have an opportunity, relying solely on this method of warfare and desolation of the island, as the forlorn hope of accomplishing their final victory. . . .[15]

That Atkins, an agent for the Spanish government, should have ignored the fact that the kind of warfare the rebels were waging, and waging successfully, prevented some of the prerequisites usually associated with a formal government is hardly surprising. But for the government of the United States, which had recognized many governments with far less of the standards demanded of the Republic of Cuba, to accept Atkins' evaluation, speaks volumes for the so-called neutrality policy.

When Atkins learned in mid-December, 1895 that Estrada Palma and several of his colleagues were planning to call on Olney and plead their case for recognition of Cuban belligerency, he arranged to see the Secretary of State and pointed out that the members of the delegation were actually American citizens residing in New York City,* and that they sanctioned the devastation of American-owned property in Cuba. When Estrada Palma, accompanied by Gonzalo de Quesada and Benjamín Guerra, was received unofficially at the Department, the result of Atkins' visit to Olney was immediately apparent. Atkins reported jubilantly:

> Mr. Olney, who was always an outspoken man, after listening to what they had to say, asked [Estrada] Palma if he was an American citizen. [Estrada] Palma replied that he was proud to acknowledge his citizenship. Mr. Olney then asked the same of the others, and he received the same reply. He then asked if they had given orders to destroy the property of other citizens in Cuba, to which [Estrada] Palma answered that while he had not done so, he knew and approved of such orders as a war measure in their struggle against Spain. Mr. Olney said: "Well, gentlemen, there is but one term for such action. We call it arson." With that he terminated the interview.[16]

Obviously Olney had paid no attention to the explanation Estrada Palma had advanced in his letter of December 7, 1895 justifying Gómez's policy of preventing production favorable to Spain: "The reasons underlying this measure are the same which caused this country [the United States] to destroy the cotton crop and the baled cotton in the South during the war of secession." [17]†

There is no doubt that Atkins, who reflected the Spanish point of view, contributed materially to reinforcing the conviction already shared by both Cleveland and Olney that the Cuban "bandits" were not entitled to recognition of belligerency.[18] But he could not prevent the American people from voicing their sentiment in favor of such

---

* Many Cubans in the United States became naturalized American citizens after the Ten Years' War.

† Olney did concede that since the American owners of property in Cuba had "invested their capital in a country in which a rebellion has broken out," they would have to take "the inevitable consequences." (Olney to Cleveland, March 21, 1896, Cleveland Papers, Library of Congress.) This, however, did not affect his attitude that the revolutionists were "bandits."

action. Petitions from all parts of the country flooded both houses of Congress when the first session of the Fifty-Fourth Congress met in December, 1895. The petitions came from so many different groups that it would require many pages to list all the petitioners. But among them were Ministerial Associations, City Councils, State Legislatures, Veterans' Associations, Mass Meetings, Universities, Boards of Trades, Trade Unions, National Granges, Peace Societies, Professional Men's Organizations, Chambers of Commerce, and so on. Generally, the petitions announced: "That we extend our sympathy to the Cuban people in their struggle for freedom and independence, and we call on the Congress and the President of the United States and request them to grant belligerent rights to the Cuban Republic and ask our Representatives and Senators in the Congress to vote for securing the same. . . ." [19]

Representatives and Senators sent eighteen resolutions to committees for action, half of them calling for recognition of Cuban belligerency and others calling for recognition of "the revolutionists of Cuba . . . as composing an independent nation and possessing the rights thereby according to the law of nations." [20]

The Senate Committee on Foreign Relations took the first step toward granting belligerent rights to the Cubans on January 28, 1896. John T. Morgan, Democrat of Alabama,* acting for the majority, reported the following resolution out of committee: "Resolved, by the State (the House of Representatives concurring†) that in the opinion of Congress a condition of public war exists between the government of Spain and the government proclaimed and for sometime maintained by the force of arms by the people of Cuba; and that the United States should maintain a strict neutrality between the contending powers, according to each all the rights of belligerents in the ports and territories of the United States." Following this, Don Cameron, Republican from Pennsylvania,‡ representing the minority of the committee,

---

* Morgan was an influential Southern Senator who was an ardent advocate of annexation of Hawaii and the construction and ownership by the United States of a Nicaraguan canal as a necessary step toward expanding U.S. economic interests in Latin America and Asia.

† A concurrent resolution is an expression of Congressional opinion. It should not be confused with a joint resolution which has the status of law and must go to the President for his approval or veto.

‡ When the Cuban *Junta* sent a man to Washington, his first contact with the

presented a second resolution which he proposed to add to the majority proposal: "Resolved, further, that the friendly offices of the United States should be offered by the President to the Spanish Government for the recognition of the independence of Cuba." Both men supported their resolutions with long reports which were printed and given to the Senators. The resolutions were placed on the calendar and came up for debate a month later.[21]

The committee reports, submitted by Morgan and Cameron, contained most of the arguments which were later presented in debates favoring the recognition of Cuban belligerent rights and independence. The majority report advocated recognition of belligerent rights on various grounds, but the essential reason given for the resolution was that war in Cuba was an international fact which compelled recognition. While accepting the majority report's reasoning for recognition of belligerency, the minority members advanced, in addition, the precedent established by Spain herself in early recognition of the Confederate States during the Civil War.[22]

The resolutions raised two questions: what effects would their passage have on America's relations with Spain; and did Congress or the executive have the constitutional right to recognize belligerency? In a lengthy speech, Morgan examined and gave his answer to both questions. He assured the Senate that recognition of belligerency would not involve the United States in war with Spain nor would it be taken by Spain as a hostile action, and he argued that the sole power to recognize belligerency resided in Congress. His constitutional reasoning was rejected by students of constitutional law—even ardent advocates of belligerency did not accept it—and most supporters of the majority resolution took the position that recognition of belligerency was shared by the executive and legislative branches of the government.[23]

The opponents of the committee resolutions, led by Senators Stephen M. White, Democrat from California, George F. Hoar, Republican from Massachusetts, and Eugene Hale, Republican from Maine, attacked them as unconstitutional, contrary to international law, and more favorable to the Spanish than to the Cubans. Even if the Cubans were entitled to recognition of belligerency, which they denied, it belonged to

---

Senate was Don Cameron. (Horatio S. Rubens, *Liberty: The Story of Cuba*, New York, 1932, pp. 1106-07.) Cameron was closely allied with such expansionists as Henry Adams and Henry Cabot Lodge.

the executive and not to Congress; and even if the President should favor it, he should not proclaim it, since it would be harmful to the interests of the United States, for Spain could not then be held responsible for the destruction of property owned by Americans. As to recognition of belligerency aiding Spain more than the Cubans, it would do so by allowing the Spaniards to inspect all ships on the high seas for contraband, which would tighten the blockade of Cuba. Similar rights would go to the Cubans, but they could not take advantage of them for they had no ships to prevent Spanish vessels from carrying munitions from the United States.[24]

Some scholars of international law agreed with the opponents of the resolutions that the Cubans would gain no rights while Spain would be strengthened. But other scholars pointed out that recognition of belligerency would have been a moral boost to the Cubans, and would have made it easier for them to borrow money and buy equipment for their poorly-armed soldiers. The spokesmen for the Cuban Republic in the United States dismissed the argument that Spain would benefit more than Cuba, emphasizing that, given the equipment, the Liberating Army would soon end Spanish rule in the island.[25]

The voting in the Senate indicated overwhelming support for recognition of Cuban belligerency.* On February 28, the Senate passed the combined Morgan and Cameron resolutions by the decisive vote of 64 to 6. The Republicans gave the resolutions the most support with 35 votes, while the Democrats were not far behind with 25, indicating bipartisan support for recognition of belligerency. The vote as a whole demonstrated that Cuba was not a party issue and only to a minor degree sectional. Except for the coastal states, all sections and every party expressed America's sympathy for the embattled Cubans.[26]

The Senate forwarded the resolutions to the House where they

---

* In all, three votes were taken, two on substitute resolutions that had been submitted in debate and the third on the Morgan and Cameron resolutions as a unit. One of the substitute resolutions, offered by William V. Allen, Populist from Nebraska, an ardent Cuban sympathizer, called for direct recognition of Cuban independence. Although it was defeated 52 to 17, the vote showed a substantial body of Senators for government action in favor of Cuban independence. Thirteen of the votes for the Allen resolution came from the trans-Mississippi West, and were cast by Republicans and Populists. (*Congressional Record*, 54th Cong., 1st Sess., p. 2256.)

disappeared in the House Foreign Affairs Committee. On March 2, the Committee reported a different resolution with three clauses:

> Resolved, That in the opinion of Congress, a state of public war exists in Cuba, the parties to which are entitled to belligerent rights, and the United States should observe a strict neutrality between the belligerents.
>
> Resolved, That Congress deplores the destruction of life and property caused by the war now waging in the island, and believing that the only permanent solution of the contest equally in the interest of Spain, the people of Cuba, and other nations should be in the establishment of a government by the choice of the people of Cuba, it is the sense of Congress that the Government of the United States should use its good offices and friendly influence to that end.
>
> Resolved, That the United States has not intervened in struggles between any European Governments and their colonies on this continent; but from the very close relations between the two peoples the present war in entailing such losses upon the people of the United States that the Congress is of the opinion that the Government of the United States should be prepared to protect the legitimate interest of our citizens, by intervention if necessary.[27]

The first two clauses were similar in meaning to the resolution passed by the Senate but dressed in different terminology, while the third clause suggested that the United States directly intervene in Cuba to protect property in the island owned by Americans.

The arguments presented in favor of the first two parts of the resolution—mainly advanced by Robert R. Hitt, Republican from Illinois, chairman of the House Foreign Affairs Committee, and Robert Adams, Jr., Republican from Pennsylvania, chairman of the Cuban Affairs Subcommittee—were generally similar to those given earlier in the Senate. But in stressing the need for passage of the intervention section, major emphasis was placed on the fact that the Cuban war threatened American interests. Hitt maintained that the United States should protect, by force if necessary, menaced American life and property. He estimated United States investments in Cuba at over $20,000,000,* and noted that his committee had moved slowly during the first year of the

---

* As pointed out in a previous volume, (Foner, *History of Cuba and Its Relations with the United States*, vol. II, p. 297), the exact total of American investment is difficult to determine. Richard B. Olney estimated American invest-

insurrection, for it believed that Spain could be held responsible for destroyed American property if the Cubans were not accorded recognition as belligerents. New information from the State Department indicated that Spain might not be responsible, so the committee now favored passage of the intervention clause, along with the other two, as a safeguard.[28]

The arguments against the House Resolution were based on the position that too little was known about actual conditions in Cuba, that many supporters of the resolution were doing so because they hoped some day to annex Cuba, and that the passage of the resolution would lead to war. The House rejected these arguments in its vote: the vote —262 yeas to 17 nays—was as decisive as the Senate vote had been. Like the upper House, the Representatives exhibited a nearly nonpartisan vote. Eight of the votes cast in opposition came from New England and the rest were scattered through the South from Virginia to Texas.[29]

Since the chambers had passed different resolutions, a conference committee, composed of House and Senate members, convened and decided to send the House resolution to the Senate for approval. Here, after some bitter debate, the House Resolution was dropped, and the original combined Morgan-Cameron resolutions were passed. Finally, on April 6, 1896, the House responded enthusiastically in favor of the Senate resolutions, with 247 votes cast in the affirmative and 27 in the negative. The majority of the votes in the negative came from Massachusetts and New York, and may have reflected the influence of financial interests who believed they would lose their property in Cuba if the Cubans were given belligerent rights. However, Pennsylvania, where such interests were also influential, did not cast a single vote in the negative. It was reported in the press that Edwin Atkins from Massachusetts influenced that state's heavy negative vote.[30]

Thus after more than two months of debate, the Congress of the United States had gone on record as recognizing Cuban belligerency and proposing that the executive extend American good offices to Spain to effect peace on the basis of Cuban independence. Undoubtedly the passage of the resolutions was a victory for the Cuban *Junta,* but it

---

ment at $50,000,000, but recent scholarly studies indicate that investment in sugar production amounted to from $10,000,000 to $30,000,000 and that about $10,000,000 was invested in manufacturing.

was not the result, as many American historians have baldly stated, solely of its propaganda activities and contacts with members of Congress. To be sure, individual Senators and Representatives had motives other than a desire to support the Cuban struggle for freedom in voting for the resolutions. Senator Henry Cabot Lodge, an avowed imperialist, showed this clearly when he declared during the debate in Congress: "Our immediate pecuniary interests in the island are very great. They are being destroyed. Free Cuba would mean a great market for the United States; it would mean an opportunity for American capital invited there by signal exemptions; it would mean an opportunity for the development of that splendid island. . . . But we have also a broader political interest in the fate of Cuba. . . . She lies right athwart the line which leads to the Nicaraguan Canal. . . . But Mr. President, I am prepared to put our duty on a higher ground than either of those, and that is the broad ground of a common humanity." * Little wonder that Representative Gillette of Massachusetts, who opposed the resolutions, complained, "I do not especially object to ambition for aggrandisement, but I think if the United States is going to be actuated by ambition she ought to say so, and not say she is actuated by philanthropy. I think hypocrisy is a vastly worse vice than ambition or greed of territory." [31]

Nevertheless, the fact remains that the majority of the Congressmen who voted for the resolutions were truly expressing the feelings of their constituents, the American people. As one student, who condemns the Congressional action, concedes: "Congressional interest was merely a reflection of general public interest. . . ." [32]

Passed by impressive majorities, the Congressional resolutions ac-

---

* The following account by Atkins throws considerable light on Lodge's sincerity. Atkins was lobbying against the resolutions, and relates his conversation with Lodge: "I called upon Lodge in the evening at his house by invitation and went over the whole ground. He discussed the matter quite carefully and asked me this question: 'Mr. Atkins, do you think that if the Cubans obtain their independence they could establish a stable government?' I answered without hesitating that I did not believe the Cubans capable of maintaining a stable government. Whereupon he brought his hand down upon the table where we were sitting, and said: 'I am glad to hear you say that, for it is exactly my opinion.' I naturally left him feeling encouraged; but within a few days he was supporting and advocating a bill for recognition of belligerence in Cuba." (Edwin F. Atkins, *Sixty Years in Cuba*, Boston, 1926, p. 212. See also Karl Schriftgeisser, *The Gentleman from Massachusetts: Henry Cabot Lodge*, Boston, 1945, p. 152.)

complished little, for only the President could give them effect. At a cabinet meeting near the end of February, recognition of Cuban belligerency was "nervously discussed," and Olney resurrected the idea of sending a commission or special agent to Cuba. Others did not think the plan feasible, so the matter was dropped. Cleveland, meanwhile, had determined in his own mind that he would not be deterred from his policy of non-recognition regardless of any action Congress might take.[33] Thus, precisely at a time when the Cuban Revolution was demonstrating its power against Spain, especially in the great invasion of the West from Oriente to Pinar del Río,* and Congress, reflecting widespread public opinion, went on record in behalf of granting the revolutionists belligerency rights, Cleveland refused even to send an emissary to the island to find out what was taking place so that he might make an intelligent decision. He had made up his mind to oppose recognition of belligerency regardless of the facts. And this has been pictured by nearly all American historians as proof of Grover Cleveland's courage![†] The *American Federationist,* official organ of the A.F. of L., spoke the truth when it observed: "Is it not indeed a sad commentary

---

* Olney actually had in his possession an English translation of the account by General Miró, Maceo's Chief of Staff, of the Negro Commander's operations during February and March, 1896. It was entitled, "Extract of the Military Operations of the Army of Invasion under the Command of Lieutenant-General Antonio Maceo, from the 9th of February to the 19th of March, 1896." It had been sent to Olney by Gonzalo de Quesada, who accompanied it with the note that it went with "the confidence of the Cuban people that justice shall be done them by the country which you so well represent." (*See* Olney Papers, March 19, 1896 for Miró's account and April 18, 1896, for Quesada's letter, Library of Congress.)

† That Allan Nevins, the biographer of Cleveland, should take this position is understandable since Professor Nevins praised the stand taken by Hamilton Fish during the Ten Years' War in opposing, in every possible way, the independence of Cuba. (*See* Allan Nevins, *Grover Cleveland: A Study in Courage,* New York, 1933, pp. 715-17. For Fish's role, see Foner, *History of Cuba and Its Relations with the United States,* vol. II, pp. 201-23, 240-58, 262.) But for the progressive American historian, William A. Williams, to take a similar position is surprising. Professor Williams treats Cleveland and Olney as heroic figures for refusing to be "panicked" in the face of pressure for recognition of Cuban belligerency, and he hails Cleveland as truly standing up for the best interests of the United States in standing "firm against the jingoes." ("Cuba: The President and His Critics," *The Nation,* March 16, 1963, p. 227.) Professor Williams does not bother to consider just what was heroic about Cleveland's refusal even to order an investigation of conditions in Cuba to determine whether the rebels were entitled to belligerent rights.

upon our existing conditions that even the resolutions of Congress, almost unanimously adopted, favoring the recognition of Cuba, are ignored by the president and his government." [34]

The policy followed by the Cleveland Administration during and immediately after the debate in Congress was to strengthen Spain. On March 20, 1896, following a conversation with Olney, Dupuy de Lôme cabled his government that the Secretary of State had told him

> . . . that reports from Cuba are to the effect that it will be impossible for Spain to win, short of a protracted struggle, and that it is unlikely that the rebellion will in the future attain a degree of effectiveness greater than it now has; for which reason it appears that Cuba is threatened with complete ruin, to the great loss of many Americans who have interests in that Island; that he wishes to help Spain bring peace to Cuba; *that he would oppose any step which might be considered as unfriendly to our [Spain's] sovereignty* . . . but that he was sure that if Spain would put into effect reforms of a sort which the American public would regard as adequate, and which would evoke a declaration to this effect by this [the U.S.] Government, *in that case the insurrection would be shorn of the moral support it now has in this country, and the task of suppressing it would be easier, because public opinion in the United States would be arrayed against it and would force abandonment of arms by the Cubans, or facilitate their complete rout.*[35]

Thus the whole autonomy scheme, as proposed by the Cleveland Administration, was simply a device to prevent the Cuban revolutionists from obtaining their goal of independence. If Spain were wise enough to cooperate in the scheme, the American people would be fooled into believing that the grievances of the Cuban people had been met, and they would quickly abandon their support of the revolutionary cause. Obviously Olney, despite all the proof to the contrary he was receiving from Cuba, shared the Spanish view that without the support they were receiving from the American people, the rebels would collapse and the war would be over.

Is it any wonder that the Congress of Cuban Historians labelled Cleveland and Olney as enemies of Cuban independence and allies of Spain?

On April 4 Cleveland and Olney decided to follow up the interview with the Spanish Minister with a note to Spain. The note was ready on April 7, but at Cleveland's suggestion it was pre-dated to April 4 since the President wished to avoid the appearance of having issued it in response to the resolutions passed by Congress on April 6.[36] It was a long note, embracing the Cleveland Administration's evaluation of the Cuban Revolution and suggesting what Spain should do to crush it.

Olney began by assuring Spain that the United States had no designs on Cuba; it only wished to see permanent peace in the Island. But America was deeply involved in the conflict because of humanitarian, geographic, democratic, commercial and financial reasons, and it would not tolerate another Ten Years' War. Already the sugar industry was in a ruinous state; the insurgent policy of destruction "cripples the resources of Spain on the one hand, and drives into their [the rebels'] ranks the laborers who are thus thrown out of employment."

> The result is a systematic war upon the industries of the island and upon all the means by which they are carried on, and whereas the normal annual product of the island is valued at something like eighty or a hundred million, its value for the present year is estimated by competent authority as not exceeding twenty millions. Bad as is this showing for the present year, it must be even worse for the next year. . . . Some planters have made their crops this year who will not be allowed to make them again. Some have worked their fields and operated their mills this year in the face of a certain loss, who have neither the heart nor the means to do so again, under the present even more depressing conditions.

Clearly, the Cleveland Administration understood, even if it did not approve of, the strategy dictating Gómez's policy of the torch, and the devastating effect it was having on Spain's ability to conduct the war. Moreover, Olney conceded "the rapid growth and progress of the Revolution," and the "discipline" of the Liberating Army. He pointed out that the insurgents appeared to command a larger portion of the island than ever before; that their men, estimated a year ago from ten to twenty thousand, were at this time conceded to be two to three times as many; their ability to operate offensively had improved; their supply of modern weapons and equipment was much larger, and their confidence in themselves greatly enhanced. In short, the insurrection, instead of being quelled as Spain repeatedly reported, was more formidable than ever, and was entering upon the second year of its existence with decidedly improved prospects of successful results.

All this would seem to lead to the logical conclusion that a condition of war existed entitling the rebels to recognition as belligerents. But Olney argued that the insurgents had no centralized or functioning government, and to this he added the point that Cuba would be better governed under Spanish sovereignty since there was a real danger of a social upheaval in Cuba in the event that Spain withdrew or was defeated:

> There are only strong reasons to fear that, once Spain were withdrawn from the island, the sole bond of union between the different factions of the insurgents would disappear; that a war of races would be precipitated, all the more sanguinary for the discipline and experience acquired during the insurrection, and that, even if there were to be temporary peace, it could only be through the establishment of a white and a black republic, which, even if agreeing at the outset upon the division of the island between them, would be enemies from the start, and would never rest until the one had been completely vanquished and subdued by the other.[37]

Olney was only paraphrasing the analysis of the Cuban Revolution sent him by Dupuy de Lôme on January 10, 1896, when he argued against recognizing a state of belligerency.* The Spanish Minister wrote that Spain represented "civilization" in Cuba while the rebels stood for equality of the Negroes, and indeed their dominance in the island:

> In this revolution, the negro elements has [sic] the most important part. Not only the principal leaders are colored men, but at least eight-tenths of their supporters. The black population of

---

* Olney was probably influenced by an article by Winston Churchill which made the same point stressed by the Secretary of State. Churchill conceded that Spanish rule in Cuba was "intolerable," that the rebels had the support of the people, and could not be subdued by Spain. But he insisted that everything should be done to help Spain uphold her sovereignty over the island. "A grave danger represents itself. Two-fifths of the insurgents in the field, are negroes. These men, with Antonio Maceo at their head, would, in the event of success, demand a predominant share in the government of the country. Such a claim would be indignantly resented by the white section and a racial war, probably conducted with bitter animosity and ferocious cruelty, would ensue, the result being, after years of fighting, another black republic, or, at best a partition of the island as in San[to] Domingo." ("The Revolt in Cuba," *The Saturday Review*, vol. LXXXI, Feb. 15, 1896, p. 165.) *See also* "The Insurrection Does Not Represent Cuban Sentiment. Cuban Independence Would Mean a Black Republic," *The Independent*, vol. XLVII, Dec. 5, 1895, p. 1641.)

the Island forms a little more than one-third of the 1,600,000 Cubans, but they are strong and numerous in the Eastern part, and the result of the war, if the Island can be declared independent, will be a secession of the black element and a black Republic on the part of the Island. . . . The principal feature of the revolution is a racial war.³⁸

It is not surprising that an administration which had "approved the virtual disfranchisement of the Negro" in the Southern States³⁹ should have been alarmed by the prospect of a Republic less than a hundred miles off the coast of Florida in which the Negroes would occupy a prominent place. The maintenance of Spanish sovereignty was thus of vital importance, and Olney proposed that Spain give Cuba autonomy in the near future, for the longer the insurrection continued, the harder reconciliation would become. He left it to Spain to suggest a plan, but if one were presented that would be acceptable to the United States, he promised it would receive the complete support of the Administration. He closed by offering "to cooperate with Spain for the immediate pacification of the island, on the basis of such a plan as, leaving Spain her rights of sovereignty, shall yet secure to the people of the island all such rights and powers of local self-government as they can reasonably ask." ⁴⁰

One would think that in 1896 the request of the people of Cuba for independence was reasonable enough!

Thus one day after Congress recognized Cuban belligerency and proposed that the President extend American good offices to Spain to effect a peace *on the basis of Cuban independence,* the Cleveland Administration advised Spain that she could ignore this action and that the United States was, unknown to the people of the country,* extending its good offices to effect peace on the basis of a program which had already been rejected by the Cubans themselves. The purpose was clear. It was to maintain Spanish sovereignty over the island and defeat the Revolution. Little wonder Dupuy de Lôme was pleased with the Administration's attitude. In a letter to the Spanish Minister of State, the Duke de Tetuán, accompanying Olney's note, he wrote that

---

* Olney assured Dupuy de Lôme that the United States had no intention of publishing the note. (*See* letter of April 10, 1896, Olney Papers, Library of Congress.) The note was not printed until 1897, when it appeared in *Foreign Relations, 1897,* pp. 452-58.)

the Secretary of State's communication was "very satisfactory" because of its "explicit recognition of the sovereignty of Spain," and for its intelligent appraisal of the insurgents' objective of Negro domination of the island. He also expressed his admiration for Cleveland's position toward Spain, especially "when one considers the numerous resolutions of the Houses of Congress, the popular agitation, the attitude of the press and what it has been asking." [41]

On May 2, 1896, while the Spanish government still deliberated about replying to Olney's note, Atkins arrived in Washington from Cuba, to convince the Administration of the practicability of autonomy as a logical way to crush the rebellion. This conclusion Atkins had reached after talking with Spanish Generals, Havana merchants and bankers, Spanish and Cuban planters, and "working and country men of both classes." While he found that "the Spaniards do not think the Cubans would accept anything short of independence," and that the Cubans did not "believe the Spaniards would grant any concessions," yet individuals on both sides had indicated clearly that they "favored autonomy as a solution." Even among the rebels, "only the Negro element," and "the adventurers," both of "who[m] are seeking power from Spain, are not inclined to settle the matter short of absolute independence of the Island." But one Cuban influential in the council of the insurgents had assured Atkins "that the better classes of the white population now with the insurgents, would lay down their arms were autonomy granted by Spain. . . . He took occasion to state that he personally, and many of his associates who were in arms, would not press for independence, as they were fully aware of the incapacity of the people of Cuba to maintain a Government at the present time." [42]

Atkins' report was precisely what the Cleveland Administration wanted to hear since it confirmed the President's and the Secretary of State's conviction that the Cubans were not capable of operating as an independent nation,* especially since the Negroes, whom they regarded as the dominant element in the Revolution, would occupy an important place in the Republic once its independence was achieved. The significance which Olney attached to the communication is apparent in his

---

* Louis V. Placé, a prominent Cuban shipping agent of French extraction, had also confirmed Atkins' view in a letter to Olney: "In depence [sic] wont do—the Cubans are not prepared to govern themselves." (Placé to Olney, March 20, 1896, Olney Papers, Library of Congress.)

reply to Atkins: "I beg to acknowledge your valuable and instructive communication. . . . It furnishes information respecting affairs in Cuba, and states views respecting the solution of the present problem which have not been received, by me at least, from any other source, and which I hope I may use to the advantage of both public and private interests." [43] Atkins communication actually formed the basis for the policy which characterized the remaining ten months of the Cleveland Administration, a policy openly designed to help Spain defeat the Cuban Revolution. Indeed, when Atkins' view received corroboration from Charles E. Akers, a correspondent for the London *Times* in Cuba, Olney, who had had an interview with Akers, wrote to Cleveland: "The contents of Mr. Akers' note are all the more significant in that he is—or was when I talked with him—clearly Spanish in all his views and sympathies." Akers had emphasized that the establishment of a Cuban Republic, free from Spanish control, must be avoided at all costs since the Negroes would be an influential force in this government. "The negro elements are acquiring a taste for blood and incendiarism which will be difficult if not impossible to eradicate for many years to come." Akers hoped that the United States, "acting in conjunction with the Spanish Government," would act on the Cuban issue before the Negroes became dominant.[44]

The Cleveland Administration's hope that autonomy was the solution to the Cuban problem met with quick rebuffs. On May 14, 1896, Estrada Palma issued a manifesto declaring: "It is useless to speak of reforms and even of a large autonomy. To hold such language would be to create illusions and lose time which could be profitably used to avoid the ruin and devastation of the Island. The revolution is powerful, it is incarnate in the Cuban people, and there exists no power, either Spanish or human, which can arrest it in its course." [45] It was clear now that despite Atkins' optimistic assurance, the revolutionists, and not merely the Negro rebels, were interested in only one thing—independence.

On June 4, Olney received a virtual refusal from Spain in answer to his note of April 4 urging concessions in Cuba. The Spanish minister regarded the note favorably, but used its reply to deliver a sharp defense of Spain's Cuban policies. The Duke de Tetuán denied that Cuba had suffered at Spanish hands, and boldly declared that the island had "one of the most liberal political systems in the world, being enjoyed there now as well as before the outbreak of the insurrection." (This was dated Madrid, May 22, 1896, five months after Weyler's brutal policy of terror and extermination had been put into effect.) He recognized America's property loss, but declared that Spanish losses were greater and that foreign interests would suffer more if Spain abandoned Cuba and anarchy prevailed. The note reaffirmed Spain's belief that the only way to secure permanent peace was through force. Spain would be willing to grant some local government, but not until Cuba was pacified and not through the good offices of the United States. The Cleveland Administration was told that if it wanted to aid in bringing the Cuban revolt to an end it could tighten its neutrality legislation and swiftly enforce it; put an end to the Cuban *Junta*, and convince the American people that Spain was right so they would not aid the Cubans. If the revolutionists were certain that the United States was unsympathetic, Spain was confident that the revolt would easily collapse.[46]

Finally, in his first comprehensive report at the end of June, 1896, Fitzhugh Lee, the newly-appointed consul-general in Havana, stated that autonomy was impossible. "I secured the impression in interviews with you and the President," Lee wrote to Olney, "that a solution of the intricate problems involved in the consideration of Cuban affairs, might probably be found, by promoting indirectly the plans and purposes of the Cuban Autonomist Party, and by seeking to aid them in a quiet way to formulate reforms in the government. . . . Matters have progressed so rapidly since my arrival that today there is no autonomistic party." Lee concluded that the only real solution was independence, and suggested that the United States should attempt to purchase the island. Cleveland promptly rejected the idea of independence for Cuba, whose people he felt were simply incapable of maintaining a government by themselves. To purchase the island and turn it over to the Cubans was to invite anarchy! [47]

The Cleveland Administration actually had a simple way of ending the conflict in Cuba had it really been interested in this objective. This was to recognize the belligerency of the Cubans and allow them to obtain the arms and munitions needed to end the war. That this would be the result if the revolutionists had the means with which to fight more effectively was brought home to the Administration in the report of its own selected agent in Cuba.

There had been so many exaggerated newspaper accounts of the situation in Cuba that Secretary Olney, in order to obtain a more accurate picture of overall conditions in the island, arranged with Edward Marshall of the New York *Journal* to have its correspondent, Frederick W. Lawrence, submit a statement of his observations during his stay in Cuba. Since many newspaper correspondents in Cuba had to secure the services of interpreters, most of whom were Cuban-born Americans and sympathetic to the rebels, Olney had insisted on a man like Lawrence who could speak Spanish.

Lawrence submitted his report to Olney on May 18, 1896. He first advised the Secretary of State that he had gone to Cuba entirely unprejudiced and with instructions to exercise the utmost care in preparing his telegrams and letters, and to avoid giving favor to one side at the expense of the other. He had considered it the duty of a newspaper man, as well as that of a diplomat, to sift rumors and ascertain exact facts; this, he insisted, he had done. One of the first things he observed upon his arrival was that information coming in from the field to Havana would be changed by Spanish officials before being released to the press. And even after the correspondents had made up their news dispatches from these revised government reports, the dispatches were subjected to the most rigid scrutiny by the press censor, who further changed the facts so that they were in complete conflict with the truth. This was most noticeable when the strength and operation of the insurgents could be belittled thereby, or the successful operations of the Spanish troops magnified. (On the other hand, it was quite true that unreliable information and exaggerated reports were continually being offered to the representatives of the press by the insurgents and those who sympathized with them.) For example, he cited the operations of General Maceo in the province of Pinar del Río, which according to the Spanish authorities had resulted in a defeat for the Cubans, with great losses of rebel soldiers. He accepted the Spanish Government's statement as true and cabled it to the *Journal*, only to find a few days later from reliable sources that General Maceo had won a complete victory, "the Spanish garrison having been driven from the town in a demoralized condition. The Cuban loss did not exceed fifty men while three hundred Spaniards were killed."

This introduction over, Lawrence presented Secretary Olney with one of the best accounts of the military situation in Cuba by an American citizen. The complete report is too long to quote in full, but the following extract is especially significant:

> Enough people in this country to command respect believe that the Spaniards represents the only real army in Cuba from a soldier's point of view, and that the army of the Cuban Republic is composed of mere wandering bands of destroying outlaws led by men who respect and are subject to no law whatever. This is untrue. The Spaniards are in point of numbers superior to their opponents but the leaders of the Army of the Republic have exhibited superior brains, courage and military genius.
>
> Landing on the Island with only a small following last February a year ago, Generals Gómez and Maceo have now under their command in the neighborhood of one hundred thousand men whose numbers would be largely increased if the men who desire to join them could pass through the Spanish lines. The Republic is in possession of almost the whole interior of the island. . . . The only portions of Cuba which the Spaniards have managed to hold are the capital, Havana, and other towns on the seacoast where they have been favored with the protection of Spanish gunboats. *With their men as well armed as are the Spaniards, the Cubans could unquestionably overcome that advantage and hold the entire island against any force Spain might send against them.* . . .
>
> The Cubans are in a position to maintain the present state of affairs for the next twenty years if Spain can find resources to keep up her end of the war for that length of time. Up in the mountains the leaders of the Army of the Republic have established ranches where men are engaged in breeding and raising cattle for food purposes. The raising of vegetables is also encouraged by the Cuban commanders and in addition to this means of subsistence they have the native food plants that grow in wild profusion all over the island. From this it will be readily understood that no matter how long the war should last or how much privation they should suffer in other directions, the Republican Army will never suffer dangerously from lack of food. And with the Cubans in position to stop all agricultural pursuits, except what they choose to indulge in themselves, Spain will undoubtedly soon find her shortage of food a serious drawback to the campaign and will also have to depend upon importing their rations from some other country. . . .

In discussing the destruction of sugar cane, mills and plantations, Lawrence pointed out that in a great many cases, the plantations had been destroyed with the consent of the owners and that some owners had even gone so far as to invite the Cubans to do so because they did not want to grind their cane and thereby supply revenue to the Spanish Government. The fact that wealthy men cherished such hostility to Spain and were ready to help the Cubans in their fight, Lawrence informed Olney, "should be sufficient refutation of the charge that the war for Cuban freedom is only backed by the ignorant classes and Negroes. I find that nearly three-fifths of the population of the island are either actively engaged in the war on the Cuban side or that the revolution enjoys their active sympathy and support." [48]

The Cleveland Administration now had in its possession a factual and objective account of the conditions existing in Cuba* which demonstrated beyond all doubt that the Revolution had, by the spring of 1896, gained the support of the vast majority of the Cuban people,† and that the Liberating Army was in a position to end the war with victory for the cause of Cuban independence by receiving the necessary arms and ammunition. All that President Cleveland had to do was to put into effect the resolutions, overwhelmingly passed by both houses of Congress, which reflected the viewpoint of a majority of the American people. The Cubans would then do the rest as they always said they would, without the necessity of intervention by the United States. But the Cleveland Administration was blind to the logic inherent even in the reports it had commissioned itself. Instead, it continued to pursue the will-o-the-wisp hope that the Cuban Revolution could be bought off with the promise of autonomy, so that the island could still remain under Spanish sovereignty.

The issue of Cuba diminished in importance on the American politi-

---

* Walter Millis (op. cit., pp. 42-43.) dismisses Lawrence as a typical Hearst reporter who fabricated his reports, and W. A. Swanberg (Citizen Hearst: A Biography of William Randolph Hearst, New York, 1961, p. 118) calls him "one of the greatest Münchausens." But neither analyzes his report to Olney nor disproves the evidence he submitted to the Secretary of State. It is significant that Lawrence's evaluation of the situation in Cuba was corroborated by reports appearing at the same time in the London Times from its Cuban correspondent who, as we have seen, was friendly to the Spaniards.

† Olney had other evidence of this fact in his possession, such as an excerpt from the London Times of August 20, 1896 quoted above (p. 100) and the statement signed by a number of lawyers, professors, owners of sugar plantations, etc. in Cuba, also cited above (pp. 100-02). For the first, see Olney Papers, vol. 62, p. 10998, and for the second, see ibid., vol. 56, pp. 9914-15, Library of Congress.

cal scene in the summer and fall of 1896, the months of the presidential campaign. At the Republican and Democratic nominating conventions, however, some interest in the issue was still in evidence. The Republicans took a strong stand on the Cuban Revolution by adopting a plank in their platform which proclaimed: "We watch with deep and abiding interest the heroic battle of the Cuban patriots against cruelty and oppression, and our best hopes go out for the full success of their determined contest for liberty." The platform called upon the Government of the United States to "actively use its influence and good offices to restore peace and give independence to the island."* Although many of the delegates to the Democratic convention had come to Chicago with strong pro-Cuban resolutions prepared, the party platform contained only a simple declaration of sympathy for the Cuban people in "their heroic struggle for liberty and independence." [49]

But the Cuban issue was all but ignored in the campaign itself as free silver obliterated the concern for free Cuba. During the entire campaign, William McKinley, the Republican presidential candidate (and also the candidate of the wealthy corporations who financed his campaign), never mentioned Cuba. Instead, he repeated over and over again the different aspects of the money and tariff questions, and especially the need to prevent the "radical," "communistic," and "subversive" forces allied together in the Democratic Party from gaining the day.† William Jennings Bryan, the Democratic candidate, concentrated almost entirely on free silver, low tariffs, and the need to end injunctions issued by the courts in labor disputes.

---

* In general, on foreign policy the Republican platform expressed the expansionist policy of the business interests the party represented. It urged "continued enlargement of the Navy," a "firm, vigorous and dignified" foreign policy which would guard American property and lives in all parts of the world. It also laid out a policy of expansion in the Western Hemisphere that involved purchase of the Danish West Indies, control of the Hawaiian Islands, and construction of the American-owned Nicaraguan canal. The plank was written by Senator Henry Cabot Lodge.

† The presidential election of 1896 has been called a manifestation of the class struggle in American society, but as Dr. Rayford W. Logan has noted, "the class struggle [so far as the election was concerned] did not involve a commitment by either party to introduce legislation for the protection of the political and legal rights of Negroes, the most submerged class." (*The Negro in American Life and Thought, The Nadir, 1877-1901*, New York, 1954, p. 87.) For a discussion of the class forces in the presidential election of 1896, see Foner, *History of the Labor Movement in the United States*, vol. II, pp. 332-42.

While McKinley, the victorious candidate, was organizing his new Administration, the departing Cleveland Administration maintained its position of firm opposition to recognition of Cuban belligerency. In his final annual message to Congress, December 7, 1896, Cleveland examined in turn each of the ways which had been suggested for settling the Cuban question—the possibility of American intervention, purchase of the island, and recognition of Cuban belligerency or independence— and rejected all as impracticable. The Republic of Cuba was "a government merely on paper," its functions were shadowy, and the real direction of the rebellion came from generals in the field and the Cuban *Junta* in New York. Cleveland reaffirmed his belief that a Spanish grant of autonomy to the Cubans remained the best solution, even though he conceded that everything pointed to the fact "that the insurgents have gained in point of numbers and character and resources, and are none the less inflexible in their resolve not to succumb without practically securing the great objects for which they took up arms," in other words, independence. Written by Olney, the section of the message dealing with autonomy stated that there "should be no just reason why the pacification of the island might not be effected on that basis." The United States stood ready to extend its good offices to guarantee any satisfactory measure of home rule, should that facilitate a solution. Cleveland, however, added a warning to Spain. He declared that Spain must act soon, for when the struggle proved that Spanish sovereignty was extinct and prolongation of war meant useless destruction of life and property, then a situation would exist "*in which our obligations to the sovereignty of Spain will be superseded by higher obligations, which we can hardly hesitate to recognize and discharge.*" [50]

Accompanying the message was a special report by Secretary Olney which practically conceded the right of the Cuban Revolution to be accorded recognition of belligerency and independence. Despite rebel inability to obtain possession of a prominent seaport, the revolutionists had enormously increased their strength, a fact which was attributed to widespread support of the movement in the island, together with the tactical and military ability of its leaders:

> The insurgent armies represent the intelligent aspirations of a large part of the people of the whole Island. From every accessible indication it is clear that the present rebellion is on a far more formidable scale as to numbers, intelligence and representative fea-

tures than any of the preceding revolts of this century; that the corresponding effort of Spain for its repression has been enormously augmented; and that, despite the constant influx of fresh armies and material of war . . . the rebellion, after nearly two years of successful resistance, appears today to be in a condition to indefinitely prolong the contest on its present lines.[51]

And this with supplies to the rebels from the United States largely cut off by both Spanish and American agents cooperatively seizing suspicious cargoes in ports. Small wonder that Estrada Palma observed that all that Olney omitted was that the rebellion had only to be given the right freely to obtain "material of war" in the United States, through the recognition of its belligerency, to end the contest, with independence for Cuba! Autonomy, he warned, was no solution. "Cuba has decided to get rid forever of the Spanish rule." [52]

Although Minister De Lôme was satisfied with Cleveland's message because it "proposes to aid Spain in maintaining her sovereignty," [53] the Madrid press was concerned that Cleveland's warning to Spain foreshadowed a distinct change in American policy and early intervention in Cuba. For what did the President mean by his reference to a "situation will be presented in which our obligations to the sovereignty of Spain will be superceded by higher obligations, which we can hardly hesitate to recognize and discharge"? Behind this vague phraseology was there not the obvious implication that the United States was waiting for the time when it would best suit its interests to step in and take possession of Cuba?[54]

Cuban historians also interpret Cleveland's warning to Spain in this light. The Congress of Cuban Historians declared in 1947 that it meant that the United States would not intervene in Cuba as long as Spain was capable of protecting American interests, but when that ceased, it would step in.[55] Emilio Roig de Leuchsenring links the warning to the "fruta madura" policy,* meaning that it meant the United States was "sitting patiently at the foot of the tree, waiting for the apple to

---

* The "fruta madura" policy was first outlined by Secretary of State John Quincy Adams in April, 1823. It called for the United States to support Spanish sovereignty over Cuba until the time when the island by "the laws of political . . . gravitation" would fall into the hands of the United States. (See Philip S. Foner, *History of Cuba and Its Relations with the United States*, vol. I, New York, 1962, pp. 144-45.)

fall," an event which would occur when Spanish control was no longer possible in Cuba.[56]

Whatever interpretation may be placed on Cleveland's warning to Spain, there can be no question that the Spanish government had been given notice that it had better crush the rebellion and pacify the country shortly or the United States would intervene.* Meanwhile, for the remainder of his term in office, Cleveland was determined to prevent any assistance the American people and the Congress were prepared to offer in behalf of the Cuban Revolution. Immediately upon assembling in December, members of the second session of the Fifty-Fourth Congress began sending to committee resolutions on Cuba.† In the previous session, the majority of the resolutions called for recognition of belligerency, but in December, 1896, most of the resolutions demanded immediate recognition of Cuban independence. The Senate Committee used the resolution submitted by Don Cameron as the basis for action, for it was typical. It read:

> Resolved by the Senate and House of Representatives of the United States of America in Congress Assembled, that the independence of Cuba be, and the same is hereby, acknowledged by the United States of America.
> Be it further Resolved, That the United States will use its friendly offices with the Government of Spain to bring to a close the war between Spain and the Republic of Cuba.[57]

---

* As originally written by Richard Olney, the paragraph dealing with the proposed time limit read: "It would seem safe to say, however, that if by the coming of the New Year, no substantial progress has been made towards ending the insurrection either by force of arms or otherwise, the conclusion that Spain is incompetent to successfully deal with it would be almost inevitable." (Olney Papers, Nov. 1896, Library of Congress.)

† Four states sent memorials to Congress requesting action on Cuba. The General Assembly of Louisiana sent a resolution requesting belligerent rights for the Cubans. The Senate of Nebraska and the Wyoming Legislature both petitioned for recognition of Cuban independence and the South Carolina Legislature asked for recognition of the Cuban Republic. The Michigan Legislature, following an address to its joint session by Gonzalo de Quesada on February 14, 1897, unanimously passed a resolution asserting "that Cuba ought to be free and independent." (*Congressional Record*, 54th Cong., 2nd Sess., pp. 130, 1088, 1419 1638; Raymond A. Detter, "The Cuban Junta in Michigan," *Michigan History*, vol. LVIII, March, 1964, pp. 36-37.)

The Senate Committee drew up a report favoring the resolution.*
Since the Cameron resolution was a joint resolution, it required presidential action in the form of a signature or veto, and it could be passed over a presidential veto, thereby recognizing Cuban independence. But the Cleveland Administration moved quickly to proclaim its opposition to the resolution and its determination not to recognize the Cuban Republic even if it passed over the president's veto. Olney speedily called an imprecedented press interview, in which he announced to the nation that any resolution passed by the House and Senate would "be regarded only as an expression of opinion by the eminent gentlemen who vote for it," and that "the power to recognize the so-called republic of Cuba as an independent state rests exclusively with the Executive. The resolution will be without effect and will leave unaltered the attitude of this Government toward the two contending parties in Cuba." Countering Olney's interview, Cushman K. Davis, Republican Senator from Minnesota, replied for the committee, through the press, that all precedents proved Olney wrong, and that Congressional measures *did* have meaning for recognition.[58]

But Olney had done his work for Spain well, and he was assisted by Edwin Atkins who was in Washington lobbying against American recognition of the Cuban Republic.[59] Although the Senate committee reported the Cameron resolution to the Senate two days after Olney's interview, and the resolution was placed on calendar for January, it never came before the Senate for debate. The fact that the President would not recognize the Cuban Republic even if it passed over his veto convinced many Senators that it would be a waste of time to discuss something that would not produce results.[60] In any event, Dupuy de Lôme boasted (prematurely as it turned out) that "the Cuban question may be considered dead so far as the Congress and public opinion in America is concerned."[61]

Unknown to the members of Congress were the Cleveland Administration's attempts to settle the Cuban question on the basis of the

---

* Henry Adams, the noted American historian and a leading expansionist, took an important part in preparing the Cameron resolution. He and Elizabeth Cameron, wife of the Senator, wrote the first part of the report, which was sent out of committee to accompany the resolution. (Henry Adams to Elizabeth Cameron, April 10, 1898, in W. C. Ford, editor, *The Letters of Henry Adams, 1858-1918*, Boston, 1938, vol. II, p. 166.)

discredited autonomy plan. Aided by Atkins, Oscar B. Stillman, manager of the Trinidad estate and a neighbor of Atkins in Cuba, and Consul-General Lee, Olney established contact with Juan B. Spotoron, who assured the Secretary of State early in 1897 that autonomy guaranteed by the United States would prove acceptable to "the great majority of those now bearing arms in the field," as well as to the sympathizers in the towns and to the propertied Spaniards.[62] Since Spotoron had represented the insurgents in signing the Pact of Zanjón in 1878 which ended the Ten Years' War, the Cleveland Administration felt that the rebels were now ready for another Pact of Zanjón. (Lee, however, confessed he was not so sanguine about Spotoron's assurances as were Atkins and others.[63]) But when De Lôme was approached to notify his government to take steps to proclaim reforms for Cuba which were to be put into effect once the rebellion ended, the Spanish Minister insisted that it was necessary to get some expression of opinion from the rebels first as to the acceptability of peace overtures.[64] On February 18, 1897, Lee informed Olney that Gómez would not accept the proposed terms and that none of the rebels "in the hills" would "touch reforms."[65]

Thus, as it was destined to, Olney's project had come to naught. The Cleveland Administration ended as it had begun so far as its Cuban policy was concerned, a policy which consisted of doing everything possible to sustain Spanish sovereignty over the island, everything possible to prevent a victory for the Cuban Revolution.*

---

* Ernest R. May admits that "during the first year of the war, the [Cleveland] administration can be said to have made a fair trial, insofar as it could, of helping Spain to smother the insurrection." (op. cit., pp. 87-88.) He fails to understand, however, that this continued to be the Administration's policy for the remainder of its tenure in office.

CHAPTER XI

McKinley Prepares to Crush the Cuban Revolution

AS WILLIAM MCKINLEY prepared to assume the Presidency, the friends of Cuba in the United States and the revolutionists in the island recalled the plank in the Republican platform relating to Cuba. Willett and Gray's journal of the sugar trade predicted that "the new administration will no doubt be more favorably disposed toward recognition of Cuban independence." The New York *Sun* agreed: "Major McKinley is not the man to cast away his platform when he becomes President. He will be a President who will stand for Cuban independence." [1]

But standing for Cuban independence was furthest from McKinley's plans. Before his inauguration, McKinley had said nothing whatsoever about the Cuban situation in public,* stating that he was without full knowledge of the facts. However, he sought the advice of a number of Republican leaders on how to deal with the issue. From Henry Cabot Lodge, who visited him in Canton, Ohio, he received the advice to declare war on Spain immediately and annex the island. From Whitelaw Reid, publisher of the New York *Tribune*, the leading Republican paper in the nation, he received a more cautious suggestion on how to achieve this objective. "Some day," Reid wrote to the President-elect

---

* According to N. G. Gonzales, McKinley did make a commitment in private. "I learn from Buttari," Gonzales wrote on August 9, 1898, "that a great many Cubans were going to vote for Bryan in the election of 1896, but on its eve T. Estrada Palma, the Cuban delegate in New York, had an interview with McKinley in which the Republican candidate promised to intervene in behalf of Cuba, and Mr. [Estrada] Palma thereupon sent out a secret circular to the Cubans urging them to support McKinley, which they did. Buttari has seen the circular." (N. G. Gonzales, *In Darkest Cuba*, op. cit., p. 260.) There is no evidence of such an interview in the William McKinley Papers in the Library of Congress, nor does any biographer of McKinley mention it.

on December 5, 1896, "we will have Cuba, as well as the Sandwich Islands [Hawaii]. To that extent I believe in Manifest Destiny. To get both, in your administration, would put it besides Jefferson's in the popular mind, and ahead in History." The task of getting Cuba without war, he felt, was "possible, but delicate and difficult." The best procedure would be to keep Congress in check for four months, holding back any "recognition of independence," until "the next sickly season, suspending Spanish operations again, might bring them so near exhaustion as to be willing to consider parting with 'the ungrateful island' in payment of our claims or otherwise." Until that happy event, the administration's policy should be to uphold Spanish sovereignty over the island.[2]

There was no reference in the advice given to McKinley by these leading Republican spokesmen to the party's platform pledge "to give independence to the island." Nor was there any in the first public statement by John Sherman after the announcement that the Ohio Senator would be McKinley's Secretary of State. "So far as I can learn at present," declared the prospective cabinet member on January 16, 1967, "the Spanish government intends granting extensive reforms in Cuba. Thus the insurgents are to have practical autonomy in all matters vital. If this is done, as I am led to believe it will be, that is all that is necessary. The war will be settled. . . ."[3] Yet less than a month before, Sherman had voted in the Senate for a resolution recognizing Cuban independence! When, in mid-February, Sherman was asked by McKinley for advice on "the Cuban question," he told the future chief executive that the government's policy *"must be controlled by commercial interests rather than by sympathy with a people struggling for liberty."*[4] Yet the Republican platform had pledged the party to support "the [Cuban] people struggling for liberty."

In his inaugural address, McKinley made no direct reference to the Cuban question. In general terms, he committed the government to non-interference in the affairs of other powers which should be allowed to settle their own internal problems. In more specific language, he promised to be ever watchful of the nation's honor and its citizens' rights, but he avowed: "We want no war of conquest. We must avoid the temptation of territorial aggression."[5] This pledge, like the plank in the Republican platform urging recognition of Cuban independence, was all too soon to be forgotten.

Included among McKinley's Papers in the Library of Congress is a statement of policy on Cuba, unsigned and undated, that probably was prepared for the inaugural address and not included.* In the document, the President noted: "Our traditions teach, and the instincts of humanity prompt us, to deeply sympathize with those unfortunate [Cuban] people. During the protracted struggles for independence by the Spanish colonies in South and Central America, a period of nearly twenty years, our Government frequently expressed its sympathy with the insurgent and recognized their rights as belligerents,† a course that is now popular with Congress and our people as to Cuba. What action the future may require at our hands is largely conjectural, but I am sure that for the present, having in mind both the humane desires and material interests of our people in the proper settlement of the question, we should content ourselves with a policy of non-intervention and refrain from any threatening warlike movements. . . ."[6] It is significant that McKinley, after acknowledging that the American people and Congress favored recognition of the belligerent rights of the Cuban rebels, fell back on the "policy of non-intervention," as if recognition of belligerency meant any more intervention in 1897 than it had in the 1820's. What the President really meant was reported by Olney to De Lôme after the inauguration: "An hour and a half's talk with the new President the night before I left Washington convinced me of his thorough desire to maintain the same attitude towards your government that the last administration aspired to. . . . While sudden aberrations on the part of subordinates would not be surprising, the strong probability is that they will not be approved and will not be allowed to do real harm."[7] The only "real harm" that could then be expected from the new administration was to the Cubans' hope for recognition of their belligerency and independence.

The New York *World* of April 5, 1897 carried two items which

---

* In an undated Memorandum in McKinley's hand, there is the following explanation: "My information in relation to the conflict now going on in Spain [sic] is necessarily limited to that which is furnished by the public press and therefore unofficial and I have not deemed it advisable without full knowledge of all the facts in possession of the Government, to consider this important subject in this address." (McKinley Papers, Library of Congress, Volume IV.)

† McKinley exaggerated the speed with which the Government of the United States acted to express support of the revolutionists of South and Central America and grant them belligerent rights. (See Foner, *History of Cuba and its Relations with the United States*, vol. I, pp. 131-34.)

told much about the Cuban Revolution and McKinley's attitude towards it. The first was a letter by Salvador Cisneros y Betancourt, President of the Republic of Cuba, to President McKinley congratulating the latter on his inauguration and assumption of office. The Cuban leader informed McKinley that "in two years we have accomplished much more than we did in the entire last war, which continued ten years." He pointed out that "with the exception of several towns," the province of Oriente was entirely under the control of the Cuban Republic, and that in other provinces the people were paying taxes to the revolutionary government rather than to Spain. But he was especially proud of one development:

> An important feature of the civil government has been the issuing of books and the establishment of schools. Early in the war the government took up education, realizing that knowledge meant strength and liberty. In various sections of Santiago and Puerto Príncipe school-houses have been erected under the supervision of the Government, and native teachers have been appointed.

The President of the Cuban Republic appealed for recognition of his government, but he assured McKinley that failure to receive this from the new American administration would not change the results. "The struggle may go on for years and Cuba may continue to fight the battle against fearful odds alone, but so long as there is a God to give us courage we will cling to the banner of right and freedom and never falter until victory is won."

The same issue of the *World* carried the news that a boat loaded with arms for the Cuban revolutionary army had been seized by the U.S. cruiser *Vesuvius*. That same day McKinley announced that his administration would maintain an energetic policy of preventing filibustering expeditions to Cuba.[8] A month later, the President indicated that he did not favor the Morgan resolution being debated in the Senate which sanctioned recognition of Cuban belligerent rights.[9] Although it was passed by a vote of 41 to 14, a three to one vote, it was not as impressive a victory for the Cuban cause as the previous session when it was six to one. The main reason was the presidential opposition to the resolution. In the House, for the same reason, the Morgan resolution was killed by being referred to committee.[10]*

---

* Congress did pass and McKinley signed a bill appropriating funds for relief of native-born Americans in Cuba. This was based upon consular reports indi-

But McKinley's opposition to recognition of Cuban belligerency did not mean that the administration was going to sit by and watch the Revolution continue to grow. A vigorous plea for ending the insurrection came in May, 1897 from American shipping firms and business houses which were seriously affected by the destruction of the island's sugar industry and the consequent disruption of commerce. The memorial, addressed to the Secretary of State, came from over 300 prominent bankers, merchants, manufacturers, and steamship owners and agents in Boston, New York, Philadelphia, Baltimore, St. Louis, Savannah, Charleston, Jacksonville, New Orleans, and other places.* It recalled the former great volume of American commerce with Cuba and the serious decline in the year 1896, and continued:

> Many of your subscribers . . . have large interests in Cuba, either as property holders or holders of mortgages or in the shape of business credit advances, and your subscribers see these interests already seriously injured, now threatened with total annihilation.
> In order to prevent further losses, to reestablish American commerce, and also to secure the blessings of peace for one and a half millions of residents of the Island of Cuba now enduring unspeakable distress and suffering, the United States might take steps to bring about an honorable reconciliation between the parties to the conflict.[11]

The fact that the petition called upon the President to bring about an "honorable reconciliation between the parties in conflict" was interpreted in the press as a request for the United States to intervene in Spanish-Cuban affairs. The *New York Times,* reporting the memorial, quoted the memorialists as having requested John Sherman to "use his influences with the President to have the United States interfere"

---

cating the presence of destitute American citizens among the suffering *reconcentrados* in Cuban towns. (Washington *Evening Star,* May 12-15, 1897; *Congressional Record,* 55th Cong., 1st Sess., pp. 108, 1203; Lee to Day, May 25, 1897, Consular Letters, Department of State, Havana, National Archives.)

* Among the 79 New York signatories were Laurence Turnure & Co., Mosle Bros., August Belmont Co., Hugh Kelly (agent for Central Teresa), the Munson Steamship Line, James E. Ward, Jr., Osgood Welsh, and Bartram Bros. Fifty-one signed from Philadelphia, including the Baldwin Locomotive Works, John W. Brock (Sigura Iron Co.), John B. Hamel, Jr. & Co., Penna Sugar Refining Co., and many tobacco importers. Millers were predominantly represented among the 71 signatories from St. Louis. S. S. Pierce Co. signed in Boston.

to stop the war before the economic resources of the island were totally destroyed.[12]

Even before the petition was submitted, McKinley had begun to move in this direction. In April, he urged William R. Day of Canton, his lifelong neighbor, friend and advisor, to investigate the entire Cuban situation. But before he could leave for Havana, Day was offered the job of Assistant Secretary of State, which he promptly accepted.[13] (Day actually took over most of the Cuban diplomacy from the aged and almost senile Secretary of State Sherman.*) Therefore McKinley named William J. Calhoun, a judge from Danville, Illinois, to make a judicial investigation of the entire Cuban problem.[14]†

Calhoun's general Cuban report‡ severely condemned Spanish rule in the island, and found just cause for the Cuban Revolution. Spanish mercantilism, its arbitrary trade regulation and prohibitory tariffs, and Spanish politics, with its heavy military emphasis and corruption which, "like a mildew seems to cover the whole framework of society," were cause enough for revolution. But social factors also existed, and Calhoun reported that "the division between them [the Spanish and Cubans] is as well marked and defined as though they were of separate and distinct races," each despising and disliking the other.

Calhoun, in his study of the Revolution's development, ridiculed Weyler's claim that Cuba was almost pacified. Judging the insurgent strength to be 25,000 to 40,000 troops, and the Spanish forces to be 250,000, of which 50,000 were incapacitated, Calhoun believed that while the rebels, lacking arms, especially artillery, might not win a decisive victory in the immediate future, Spain could never defeat the insurgents. McKinley's agent, who confessed that he had thought the

---

* "Even the lowest servant in the State Department knows and talks about it [Sherman's senility]. It is pitiable in the extreme," wrote a contemporary. (John Foster to John Porter, Aug. 11, 1897, in McKinley Papers, Library of Congress.)

† Calhoun was also to investigate the death of Richard Ruiz, a naturalized American found dead in a Cuban cell after two weeks of solitary confinement. The "yellow press" charged that Ruiz had been murdered. (Joseph E. Wisan, *The Cuban Crisis as Reflected in the New York Press, 1895-1898*, New York, 1934, pp. 224-26, 280.)

‡ Calhoun also submitted a report on Ruiz's death in which he stated his opinion that Spain's responsibility in the case was clear. (William J. Calhoun report on the Ruiz death, June 10, 1897, Special Agents, Department of State, XLVIII, National Archives.)

Cuban forces to be largely formed from the lower classes, related with surprise that their "army [was] representative of all classes and conditions of Cuban society." In concluding his military survey, Calhoun declared, "Both [Cubans and Spaniards] are weary and breathless, and the [military] result is largely a matter of endurance."

After describing the horrors of the reconcentration policy, which we have cited above, Calhoun examined three possibilities for a peaceful settlement of the revolt, but found all disappointing. One possibility, suppression of the rebellion by Spanish arms, he believed almost impossible; this would come, if at all, only after "the almost total ruin and destruction of both life and property." A second way might be a grant of liberal autonomy to the Cubans, but it would be difficult to carry out, since most of them were ignorant and were unable to govern themselves. The Autonomist Party was quite small and powerless, and its leading exponent did not believe that autonomy could succeed unless it had a long period of time to develop. Cuban independence, a third possibility, was not any better, since it also required a politically active population which did not exist. In some ways, it was even worse. Calhoun emphasized that independence would result in class and racial warfare in the island with the danger of Negro domination always present. Nearly all the wealthy elements of the population, Spanish and Cuban, with whom Calhoun spoke, he reported, opposed independence as opening the gates to a vast social upheaval, and preferred annexation to the United States in order to maintain a stable society.[15]

Calhoun obviously did not see any contradiction in first reporting that the Liberating Army fighting for independence was "representative of all classes and conditions of Cuban society," and then concluding that all the wealthy Cubans, like the Spaniards, favored annexation to the United States. But, despite this contradiction, the report had an important influence on the McKinley Administration. McKinley, like Cleveland, had in his possession an analysis of the Cuban situation which demonstrated that, given the proper military supplies, the Revolutionary Army could fairly quickly end the war with a victory over Spain. This indicated that a logical way to achieve peace in the island was to recognize Cuban belligerency and make it possible for the Revolutionary Government to purchase the necessary war material to defeat the Spaniards and win independence. But independence, Calhoun had emphasized, threatened to bring class and racial warfare in its wake, and this was something neither the government of the United States nor the business interests who wanted to rebuild and expand their investments in, and commercial relations with Cuba, would tolerate.

The McKinley Administration had plans for dealing with the Cuban situation, but these did not include independence for the island. Following the receipt of Calhoun's report, the Administration abandoned the non-intervention policy, and began to dictate to Spain its solution for the Cuban crisis. The influence of the memorial from over 300 American shipping and business houses was evident in the first Cuban note the McKinley Administration sent Spain, dispatched four days after receiving Calhoun's report. Spain was accused of the "cruel employment of fire and famine to accomplish by uncertain indirection what the military seems powerless to directly accomplish. . . . The inclusion of a thousand or more of our own citizens among the victims of this policy, the wanton destruction of the legitimate investments of Americans to the amount of millions of dollars, and the stoppage of avenues of normal trade—all these give the President the right of specific remonstrance."[16]

But it was in the instructions to the new minister to Spain, General Stewart L. Woodford, that the administration's new approach to the Cuban question was most clearly evidenced. Before his departure for Europe, Woodford received from Sherman a lengthy note, dated July 16, 1897, intended for his own and Spain's guidance, outlining specifically the position of the Administration. Since McKinley himself took the time to "carefully" edit these first instructions for Woodword, they clearly reflected the President's policy.[17]

The note pointed out the spread of the rebellion despite Spain's unprecedented efforts, the disastrous effects upon the island of a policy of "mutual destruction and devastation," the subsequent loss of "capital and intelligence contributed by citizens of the United States and other countries," the dwindling of commerce, the difficulties of maintaining the treaty rights of U.S. citizens in Cuba. Fear was expressed that "some untoward incident may abruptly supervene to inflame mutual passions beyond control and thus raise issues, which, however, deplorable, can not be avoided." Woodford was instructed to show America's deep interest in securing a settlement of the war, because the revolt "keeps up a continuous irritation within our borders, injuriously affects the normal functions of business, and tends to delay the condition of prosperity to which this country is entitled." Although the United States had refrained from interfering in the revolt, Spain was warned that America could not do so much longer, since Congress and the people wanted to recognize the insurgents as belligerents. Spain's delay in restoring order had injured the United States, and a nation injured through such delay need only wait a reasonable time before "alleging and acting upon the right which it, too, possesses."

> Assuredly Spain can not expect this Government to stay idle, letting vast interests suffer, our political elements disturbed, and the country perpetually embroiled, while no progress is being made in the settlement of the Cuban question.

Woodford was requested to ask the Spanish government to stop the war by offering "proposals of settlement honorable to herself and just to her Cuban colony and to mankind," and if Spain would offer acceptable proposals, the United States would stand "ready to assist her and tender good offices in that end." The instructions ended with a threat of more energetic action if the offer was refused:

> You will not disguise the gravity of the situation nor conceal the President's conviction that, should his present offer be fruitless, his duty to his countrymen will necessitate an early decision as to the course of action which the time and the transcendent emergency may demand.[18]

The note to Spain and the instructions to Woodford were clear indications that McKinley's policy was being controlled by what Sherman had called "commercial interests rather than . . . sympathy with a people struggling for liberty." American investors in Cuba and those doing business with the island were being increasingly injured by Spain's failure to defeat the rebels, and the struggle in the nearby island was delaying business recovery in the United States. The implication was clear: if Spain could not wind up her Cuban problem, the United States would do it for her.

The Administration did not present concrete plans, but obviously independence for Cuba was not contemplated among the "proposals of settlement . . . just to her [Spain's] colony and to mankind." But annexation was not ruled out. Woodford was to be McKinley's personal agent, sending not only regular dispatches to the State Department, but also communications marked, "To be handed unopened to the President by his direction." * In several of these private reports, the Minister mentioned that McKinley had spoken to him about sounding out the possibility of annexation of Cuba. From London, en route to Spain, he reported on August 10 to McKinley that the English would not oppose American annexation of Cuba if it came as a natural outcome of events.[19]† A week later, Woodford reported to the President that time favored this ultimate solution, for Spain was running more heavily into debt and with the insurgent military strength growing, she might soon agree to United States acquisition of Cuba. The McKinley Administration, in short, could afford to wait.[20]

Woodford orally presented his instructions to Spain on September 18, and gave the Duke of Tetuán up to November 1 for the re-establishment of peace in Cuba, after which date the United States would proceed on its own course.‡ On October 23, the Spanish government,

---

* Woodford's "confidential" correspondence to the President is filed separately in a small volume in the State Department files in the National Archives. Herminio Portell Vilá, the Cuban historian, writes that he discovered the "confidential" volume in 1932, and asserts that he was "the first investigator of any nationality to have consulted this volume." (*Historia de la guerra de Cuba y los Estados Unidos contra España*, La Habana, 1949, p. 95.)

† Woodford informed Secretary of State Sherman that after investigating public opinion in England, France, and Germany while en route to Spain, he had come to the conclusion that these countries had but little interest in Cuba. (Woodford to Sherman, Aug. 30, 1897, No. 10, Department of State, Spain: Dispatches, National Archives.) Evidently Germany was suspicious of U.S. intentions, for Andrew D. White, the American Ambassador to Berlin, undertook the task of assuring the German government that his country was not attempting to encroach on Spain. He pointed out that the U.S. had been in a position to annex Cuba had that course been desired. Only the desire to extend slave territory had caused agitation for annexation in the first half of the century, but the death of the slave system had carried with it the death of Cuban annexation propaganda. (White to Sherman, Oct. 4, 1897, No. 115, Department of State, Germany: Dispatches, National Archives.) White was either naive or deliberately misleading the German government, for he must have known that the press in the United States was full of editorials and speeches calling for annexation of Cuba.

‡ Between the time Woodford presented his note to the Duke of Tetuán and the formation of the Liberal cabinet on October 6, 1897, the British, French, Russian and German ministers in Madrid called upon the new American minister, inquiring as to the position the McKinley Administration was taking, and proposed to take, in the future toward Cuba. To the four he individually pointed out that "the United States does not seek to annex Cuba nor to form a protectorate over her, but only peace." (*Foreign Relations*, 1898, p. 580.) Yet in

headed now, as we have seen, by the Liberal cabinet under Sagasta, gave its reply, pointing out in its note that Weyler had been removed and replaced by Blanco, and that although committed to pursue a vigorous policy in Cuba, Spain would conduct the war humanely and offer the island autonomy. For its part, the United States could help put an end to the revolt by strengthening its neutrality laws and suppressing the Cuban *Junta.* This request brought a quick reply from Woodford, who denied that the United States was lax in enforcing the neutrality law.[21]

On May 12, 1897, Estrada Palma had sent Sherman a note entitled, "Independence the only solution," in which he notified the McKinley Administration: "The Cubans never will accept autonomy or reforms. They are fighting for independence and will only accept peace upon condition of complete separation from Spain. . . . It is vain to ask us to surrender, in the strength of our armed organization, won by so much sacrifice and blood, and to accept what we know will never solve our problem. . . . We Cubans have made our choice, we have taken our position and we will maintain it. . . ."[22] Despite this, and despite all newspaper reports from Cuba suggesting that autonomy would not succeed—few autonomists existed in the island and the rebels made it clear that they would accept nothing less than independence*—the McKinley Administration decided to support the autonomy plan.[23] Woodford personally doubted that the promise of Cuban autonomy would work out successfully because the "Cubans, long under the shadow of our institutions and with their young men and women educated for the last fifty years in American schools and colleges, seek American autonomy and not the Spanish counterfeit." But he was ready to go along with the Spanish plan only so that peace could be estab-

---

his "confidential" communications to McKinley, Woodford was constantly writing about annexation.

* This view was shared by the Cubans in the various emigre centers. Estrada Palma used his regular column in *Patria,* "To the Delegation," to ask the different centers if they wanted to accept Spain's plan of reforms. ("A la delegación," *Patria,* October 14, 1897.) The answers were invariably negative. The answer sent by José Antonio Frias, the agent of the Cuban Revolutionary Party in Santo Domingo, was typical. Frias reported that "The Cuban emigres in Santo Domingo are absolutely opposed to negotiating with Spain except on the basis of absolute independence." (José Antonio Frias to Estrada Palma, November 7, 1897, *Correspondencia diplomatica,* vol. IV, pp. 105-06.)

lished. For, he informed McKinley, peace was the shortest route to annexation of Cuba:

> Peace could bring annexation as its necessary end. I hope that annexation will not arrive until the Cubans have learned to govern themselves, and until there have gone to Cuba enough Americans to constitute a dorsal spine of intelligent citizenry who can be trusted. But let there be peace today and the rest will come in its own time logically and surely.[24]

On November 7, 1897, Woodford crowed to McKinley that within a month of his arrival in Spain, Weyler had been removed from Cuba and Spain was committed to civilized warfare and autonomy. The United States was now in the driver's seat, for if Spain broke her pledges or played false, "her last attempted defense against our immediate and effective intervention [would] be gone."[25] A week later, he assured McKinley that the time was approaching for the application of the John Quincy Adams "law of political gravitation."

> If they [the Spaniards] now secure pacification through the realization of humane methods and efficient reforms, I do not see any possible ultimate result except that Cuba will gradually become accustomed to self-government and so will fully be fit for self-government. *When the apple is ripe it will drop from the tree...*.[26]

Autonomy was thus to be a training school to fit the Cubans for annexation to the United States!

In one of his "confidential" reports to McKinley, Woodford reported "an interesting conversation" he had had with Drummond Wolff, British Ambassador to Spain, on October 19, 1897. Wolff, Woodford reported, "mentioned a telegram or letter which has recently appeared in some or more of the Madrid papers and which stated that a Mr. McCook from New York was negotiating for some agreement with the Cuban insurgents and the Spanish authorities by which some large capitalists were to advance monies for the payment of the Cuban debt and were to be secured in some way by sale of the Government lands and mines in Cuba and by some control over the Cuban custom duties. He added that the account stated that Mr. McCook was a person of great influence and high standing in New York and had close relations and much influence with President McKinley. . . ."[27] Behind this "interesting conversation" is an interesting, if little known, aspect of Cuba's struggle for independence.

In the spring of 1897, the American press carried frequent reports that an American banking syndicate was organizing a scheme for the purchase of Cuba from Spain by the insurgents, with money borrowed by the syndicate acting under the supervision of the United States government. These newspaper reports were intensified in the last week of May by the visit to the White House of John J. McCook and Robert A. C. Smith. McCook, a wealthy and influential New York corporation lawyer of the firm of Alexander & Green, was, among other activities, a general manager of the Ward Line Steamers which traveled between the United States and Cuba, and a representative of American business interests in Cuba.* Smith was a multi-millionaire New Yorker who had investments in electric generating plants in Cuba, and also in the Ward Line. McCook had made his position on the Cuban question clear as early as January, 1896 when, in a letter to Senator J. B. Foraker of Ohio, he pointed out that "Cuba, with Porto Rico, stands sixth on the list of our exports to all countries in the world and third on the list of imports," and added, "How long would Great Britain put up with a condition like that existing in Cuba (even ignoring the humanitarian view), which affected its commercial interests to such an extent as this war does ours?" [28]

McCook and Smith told the press that they believed Spain would sell Cuba, which brought a response from Dupuy de Lôme that his country would never agree to such a settlement. Undaunted by this rebuff, the syndicate went ahead with the plan for the purchase of Cuba from Spain by the insurgents. A formal agreement to achieve this was concluded in New York City on August 5, 1897, signed by Tomás Estrada Palma, Delegate of the Republic of Cuba, and Samuel Janney of Christy & Janney, representing the syndicate† The key

---

* McCook was also interested in expanding American trade in China and in the construction of railroads, financed by American capital, in that country. He was repeatedly urging that American capitalists move into the China market before Russia and Great Britain gained a dominant influence. (John J. McCook to James H. Wilson, July 10, 25, Aug. 12, Nov. 11, 17, 1896, James H. Wilson Papers, Library of Congress.)

† There is some confusion among Cuban historians as to the exact date on which the contract was signed. Both the National Congress of Cuban historians and Emilio Roig de Leuchsenring set it as August 5, 1896, but a letter from

figure in the syndicate was McCook, who was a close friend of Mc-Kinley and had been considered by the President for the posts of Attorney General and Secretary of the Interior.[29]*

According to the contract, Janney and his associates would offer to pay a part of the huge debt incurred by Spain in Cuba, in return for her complete withdrawal from the island and her formal recognition of Cuban independence. For this, the syndicate was to receive bonds of the Cuban Republic to the amount of one hundred and fifty million Cuban dollars, paying interest at 4 per cent per annum, the principal to be paid off within fifty years. These bonds were to be secured by a lien on half of the Cuban customs receipts during the first fifteen days of each month. Their servicing and collection was to be under the supervision of the United States government, which was to act as financial trustee. McCook committed himself not only to obtain from the U.S. government an agreement to act as trustee, but also to induce Spain to accept the whole arrangement and to act as guarantor for the fulfillment of the terms by all parties. The Mercantile Trust Company of New York was named as fiscal agent for the transaction. The amount to be paid by the syndicate to Spain was not specified; the syndicate reserved the right to make the best arrangement it could with Spain, keeping as profit the difference between what it paid and the one hundred and lfty million Cuban dollars plus interest.†

The contract would be nullified if the Cuban Council of Government did not ratify it or if the Spanish troops were not evacuated from Cuba by October 1, 1897.‡ The October first deadline passed, but was

---

Estrada Palma to Samuel L. Janney, June 5, 1897, indicates that the terms of the contract were still under discussion. (*Correspondencia diplomática de la delegación cubana en Nueva York durante la guerra de independencia de 1895 a 1898*, La Habana, 1943, vol. I, p. 122.) Since the majority of the members of the syndicate were leading Republicans, the drawing up of the contract before McKinley's election would not make much sense.

* The Attorney Generalship went to another party, and McCook turned down the Department of Interior.

† Cuban dollars were worth somewhat less than United States dollars.

‡ According to David F. Healey, the only American historian to discuss the agreement, the contract would be voided if McCook failed to enlist the support of the McKinley Administration by October 1, 1897. (*The United States in Cuba: 1898-1902*, Madison, Wisconsin, 1963, p. 15.) But none of the Cuban accounts of the contract mention this provision, referring only to the withdrawal of Spanish troops from Cuba by October 1.

extended to November 1 while McCook sought to persuade the McKinley Administration to support the syndicate's plan.* Actually, it was not until December, 1897, that the Cuban Council of Government approved the contract with the modification that the Republic of Cuba would not be obliged to pay any of the debts incurred by Spain in Cuba or be responsible for the damages and losses suffered as a consequence of the war by foreigners residing in the island.[30]

McCook devoted much of his time during the fall of 1897 to a persistent campaign to convince the McKinley Administration that the rebels could never be defeated; that the Cuban Republic was entitled to recognition as a belligerent, and that under no circumstances would the revolutionists accept autonomy or any other reforms short of independence. He repeatedly furnished Assistant Secretary of State William R. Day with clippings from American, Spanish and Cuban papers —all supplied him by the Cuban Junta†—which were designed to buttress his argument that only independence for Cuba would end the war. When, late in November, 1897, the Spanish government announced its reforms for Cuba—autonomy—and provided for the first autonomous government to take office January 1, 1898, McCook predicted to Day that the program would fail, since "the Cubans will not

---

* In November, Janney and Estrada Palma signed a second contract under which the syndicate was to receive Cuban bonds worth $37,500,000 "if independence is achieved, Spanish troops evacuated from Cuba, the independence of the island of Cuba recognized by the United States, all of this without paying indemnification to Spain. . . ." The new contract, however, was to be "null and void if the result is obtained by reason of the first contract." The Council of Government approved the new contract on January 27, 1898. According to Healy, the provision in the second agreement that nothing was to be paid to Spain was evidence that "the syndicate now meant to buy influence in Washington rather than Madrid and let the United States handle Spain." (op. cit., p. 15.) But Cuban historians insist that the purpose was not to secure American intervention against Spain but United States recognition of the independence, and that the Cubans would take care of getting the Spanish troops out of Cuba. In any event, the second contract was never important, and the syndicate put all its emphasis on the plan to purchase Cuba from Spain for the insurgents, with compensation to the mother country for the loss of the island.

† Evidently McKinley did not know at this time of McCook's connection with the Cuban Junta, for as late as March 8, 1898, Whitelaw Reid wrote to the President: "You asked me if Colonel McCook had official relations to the Junta. I had that impression but was not sure of it. On my return I learned it authoritatively." (McKinley Papers, Library of Congress.)

stop fighting except on gaining absolute independence."* He urged Day to persuade McKinley to let Spain know, in his annual message to Congress, that the United States stood squarely behind the Cuban demand for independence, and that it would be wise for her to sell the island to the insurgents.[81]

Despite McCook's warning and despite adverse criticisms in many newspapers, Dupuy de Lôme reported that McKinley was favorably disposed to the autonomous form of government. He informed Madrid on December 2 that the "political situation has never been better nor my mission easier."[32] Four days later, McKinley sent his annual message to the second session of the 55th Congress. In it the President emphasized that the American government had tried all but three measures to end the Cuban crisis: recognition of the insurgents, intervention, and annexation. A discussion of these measures occupied the major part of the section of the message devoted to Cuba. Annexation was dismissed as "criminal aggression." Naturally, the President did not reveal that his ambassador to Spain was maneuvering to consummate such "criminal aggression." Recognition of Cuban belligerency was dismissed as a doubtful measure in international law and contrary to American traditional policy. McKinley quoted at length Grant's message of December 7, 1875 which rejected recognition of Cuban belligerency during the Ten Years' War, but he did not mention his earlier unpublished memorandum in which he referred approvingly to the tradition of American recognition of the belligerency of the insurgents in South and Central America during their struggles for independence from Spain. The President gave most prominence to intervention on humanitarian grounds, conceding that it had received his "most anxious and earnest consideration." But such intervention was unnecessary since the new Spanish ministry was committed to reform, clemency and autonomy. The Spanish government had recalled Weyler and released all American prisoners on the island. The President, therefore, urged that Spain "be given a reasonable chance to realize her expectations and to prove the efficacy of the new order of things to

---

* Edwin Atkins, on the other hand, assured Day that autonomy had widespread support in Cuba, and he urged the U.S. "to have patience a little longer," confident that "all will end well." (Atkins to William R. Day, Nov. 26, 1897, Day Papers, Library of Congress.)

which she stands irrevocably committed. . . ." The message ended with a warning that American action might be taken later:

> The near future will demonstrate whether the indispensable condition of a righteous peace, just alike to the Cubans and to Spain, as well as equitable to all our interests so intimately involved in the welfare of Cuba, is likely to be attained. If not, the exigency of further and other action by the United States will remain to be taken. . . . If it shall hereafter appear to be a duty imposed by our obligations to ourselves, it shall be without fault on our part and only because the necessity for such action will be so clear as to command the support and approval of the civilized world.[33]

Sagasta, the Spanish Prime Minister, ignored the President's warning, approved the message, and predicted that it "must affect the insurrection considerably and in an adverse way; while our reforms will receive a powerful stimulant." [34]* But McCook reminded Day that the President had ignored the fact that the rebels had unalterably rejected autonomy, and that it had absolutely no support among Cubans. He added politely: "I assume, of course, that you and the President are not deceived by the statements made by Spanish officials about the acceptance of autonomy in Cuba by anyone other than Spaniards who are absolutely under the control and domination of the Governor General. So far as I can learn there is no reliable evidence that any one Cuban of importance or any military or civil official connected with the Republic of Cuba has even considered the proposal of autonomy." [35] It was clear that the Spanish program, enthusiastically endorsed by McKinley, was doomed to failure.

In Congress, Republican control of both houses prevented action to repudiate the President's refusal to grant belligerent rights to the Cubans. But the Democrats did pass a caucus resolution which read: "Resolved . . . that we favor the early consideration and passage of the Senate resolutions, recognizing that a condition of war exists between the government of Spain and the Cuban people." In the Senate, too, the Democrats blasted McKinley's message. But only two resolutions

---

* Woodford wrote Sherman that Sagasta was "greatly gratified with the generous tenor of the President's message, and today authorizes me to express this gratification to my Government." (Woodford to Sherman, Dec. 7, 1897, Spain: Dispatches, National Archives.)

on Cuban belligerency were sent to Congressional committees, and December passed without any action taken on the issue.³⁶

Even before McKinley's message went to Congress, the Administration received consular reports from Cuba that Spanish reforms were ineffective. Not only was starvation unabated among the *reconcentrados*, but autonomy was off to a shaky start with little prospect of success. Besides the steady resistance the *insurrectos* made to autonomy, Spanish army officers and jealous government bureaucrats were voicing their dislike of governmental change.³⁷ Signs pointing to a coming crisis prompted Consul Lee on December 1 to request the dispatch of an American ship to Havana harbor, ostensibly to protect citizens of the United States from an anti-American plot being hatched in Matanzas.³⁸* (Somewhat later, Lee predicted that the United States, by sending troops to Cuba to preserve order, could annex the island without firing a shot.³⁹) On December 15, the 24-gun battleship *Maine* was moved to Key West, and its commanding officer, Captain Charles D. Sigsbee, contacted Lee and established the code words, "Two Dollars," as a signal Lee should send if he wanted the *Maine* immediately dispatched to Havana.⁴⁰

In Washington, Secretary of the Navy John D. Long, Assistant Secretary Theodore Roosevelt, and Arent S. Crowinshield, chief of the Bureau of Navigation, held discussions and decided that, in addition to the *Maine,* a cruiser, preferably the *Marblehead*, should be sent to Havana. Long's diary reveals that he favored sending a ship to Havana in early 1897, but realized that such a move would involve "a great deal of friction and risk." Roosevelt, a blatant militarist and expansionist, had no such worries. He had presented McKinley with a document in September, 1897 "showing exactly where all our ships are, and I also sketched an outline what I thought ought to be done if things looked menacing about Spain, urging the necessity of taking an immediate and prompt initiative. . . ."⁴¹

---

* As early as July, 1896, Lee had made several requests for such action. (Cleveland to Olney, July 16, 1896, Olney Papers, Library of Congress.) In June, 1897, he had urged that the government station a warship in Havana harbor to protect endangered American lives and property. The McKinley Administration had refused the request, but replied that if Spain failed to protect endangered American interests, Lee should cable this information and a ship would be sent if necessary. (Day to Lee, June 9, 1897, Instructions to Consuls, CLVI, National Archives.)

Although the cruiser was not sent, the *Maine* was by no means the only American naval vessel ready to sail toward Cuba. In December, the North Atlantic squadron, for the first time in two years, began a voyage to the Gulf of Mexico and the Caribbean Sea for winter maneuvers. The Navy Department had clearly prepared this major naval move with Cuba in mind even before the failure of Spanish political reform in the island.[42]

From Spain, meanwhile, Woodford informed McKinley that "the Spanish government wants me to say things [to you] that cannot be written," and suggested that he might come home with a confidential message from the Queen Regent for the President. When McKinley turned down the suggestion that Woodford leave Madrid, the American minister agreed that this was a correct decision. "The result must be wrought out in Cuba and by facts, rather than at Washington or Madrid and by negotiations."[43]*

The facts coming from Cuba made it clear that independence, not autonomy, was what was needed to end the Cuban crisis. On January 1, 1898, as we have seen, the Autonomist government went into effect, and within less than two weeks, opposition to it was openly displayed in Havana and other parts of the island. Most of it came from Cubans who were determined to accept no compromise in their struggle for independence, but some was promoted by Spanish army officers, especially those trained under Weyler, who were opposed to the new regime and its policies.

The obvious failure of autonomy did not lead the Administration to conclude that recognition of Cuban belligerency or independence was the only logical solution of the crisis. Rather, its effect was to intensify

---

* Just what Spain wished to convey to McKinley through a private message is not clear. Portell Vilá believes that it related to the syndicate headed by McCook which was seeking to purchase Cuba. (*op. cit.*, p. 99.) On the other hand, it may have had to do with the activities of the Cuban *Junta* in the United States, for on January 17, Woodford sent a confidential report of an interview the same day with the Queen Regent in which she declared that after Spain had removed Weyler, tried to alleviate the sufferings of the *reconcentrados* "which are horrible and make my heart sick," and had instituted autonomy, it was up to McKinley to do two things for Spain. One was to issue a proclamation to the American people asking them "to stop giving money and munitions to the insurrections," and the other was for the President "to destroy the Junta of New York." (Woodford to McKinley, Jan. 7, 1898, Reports to the President, Spain: Dispatches, CXXXIA, National Archives.)

the drive for direct American military intervention. Theodore Roosevelt wrote to a friend that though the top executives in the Administration would not "admit even to themselves" that they were preparing for war, yet he surely recognized "such to be the case." The Navy Department gave backing to Roosevelt's analysis when on January 11, it charged the commanders of the several squadrons to retain all men whose enlistments were about to expire.[44]

The day after the Navy Department issued its enlistment order, an anti-Autonomy riot occurred in Havana, during which three Autonomist newspapers were attacked by a mob, led by Spanish army officers, which ran through the streets shouting "Death to Blanco" and "Viva Weyler." The riot was finally brought under control, but Spanish rioters and the guards of the palace were heard to shout for Weyler.[45] Lee's reports to the State Department emphasized that an American warship might be needed in Havana to protect American interests, but he cautiously added that the time for sending the ship had not arrived.* He suggested that the last week of January was a good time to send an American naval vessel, for it would not be so conspicuous—two German ships were to visit Havana in that week. He suggested, too, that some plausible ruse, such as an exhausted coal supply, might serve as a justifiable excuse for bringing an American warship into Havana harbor.[46]

In Congress the riot brought a push for action to recognize the existence of war between Cuba and Spain and with it immediate recognition of Cuban belligerency. On January 19, 1898, in the House of Representatives, Ferdinand Brucker of Michigan proposed a resolution supporting recognition of Cuban belligerency. Although the Administration's supporters blocked a vote on the resolution,† it was becoming clear that as Spanish sovereignty in Cuba continued to collapse, there

---

* Lee kept changing his mind about the necessity of having an American warship in Havana harbor. On January 15, he decided that a ship was not necessary, for the riot showed not an anti-American spirit but only that Spanish factions were fighting one another. He speculated that as time passed, Spain would become weaker and eventually the influential Cubans and Spaniards would ask the United States to intervene in the island's affairs to bring peace. (Lee to Day, Jan. 15, 1898, Consular Letters, Havana, CXXXI, National Archives.)

† William M. Bell, general secretary of the United Brethren Missionary Society, warned McKinley: "There can be no doubt but the throttling of the vote of the Congress of our country on this question [of immediately recognizing Cuban belligerent rights], month after month, is paving the way for the su-

would soon be sufficient Republican votes to pass it regardless of Administration opposition.[47] Indeed, at a private interview with McKinley, Congressman William Alden Smith of Michigan informed the President that the Republicans in Congress were insisting that the pledge of the party platform with respect to Cuban independence be honored. Only a dramatic move by the President could hold back passage of a resolution recognizing Cuban belligerency or independence.[48]

On January 24, 1898, less than a week after the House debate on Cuba ended, McKinley decided to send the *Maine* to Havana harbor. On the surface, the Administration maintained that it was sending the ship as a gesture of friendship for Spain in recognition of her success in Cuba. In mid-morning of January 24, Day met with Dupuy de Lôme and told him that since Spain was pacifying Cuba successfully— an obvious distortion of the facts as the Administration well knew— McKinley believed friendly naval visits which had been discontinued for over two years, should be resumed. When de Lôme replied that the United States should never have discontinued naval visits and that "it would have been better had the usual custom in that respect been maintained since the troubles in Cuba," Day quickly conveyed this information to the President. McKinley, after conference with Day, Long, Joseph McKenna, Justice of the Supreme Court, and Nelson A. Miles, commanding general of the army, decided to send the *Maine*. Lee was quickly notified, and in the afternoon, Lee told de Lôme that the President was sending the *Maine* to Havana on a friendly visit.[49]

But nobody was fooled by this pretense. As the *Maine* steamed toward Havana, it was clear that a concrete step had been taken that was to lead to war in less than three and a half months. Ricardo Díaz Albertini, secretary of the Cuban Legation in Washington, reported to Estrada Palma: "*Yo creo que el fin se acerca.*" ("I believe the end is approaching." [50])*

This was written on January 24, 1898. A month before, Theodore

---

premacy of the Democratic party in 1900." (Bell to McKinley, Jan. 21, 1898, in William R. Day Paper, Library of Congress.)

* This seems to be the only communication between the Cuban revolutionary forces in Washington and New York during this entire critical period. Gonzalo de Quesada did not communicate with Cuban revolutionary headquarters in New York from July 21, 1897 to January 16, 1898, and Estrada Palma had few contacts with the Cubans in Washington. (*See Correspondencia diplomatica,* vol. V, p. 120 and True, *op. cit.,* p. 309.)

Roosevelt wrote to William Astor Chanle, "I do not believe that Cuba can be pacified by autonomy and I earnestly hope that events will so shape themselves that we must interfere some time in the not distant future." Meanwhile, the Assistant Secretary of the Navy was sending out letters on organizing an army unit, and was reminding Secretary Long that the navy would need a month's warning before the war broke out.[51] It has been customary for historians, writing of this period, to dismiss Roosevelt's preaching and actions as the expression of the most rabid expansionists and not reflective of the thinking in the McKinley Administration which, it is argued, still thought only in terms of peace. Yet on January 12, 1898, Alvee A. Adee, the pro-Spanish State Department expert on Cuban affairs—he had served as secretary of the Legation in Spain during the Ten Years' War—sent a "confidential" memorandum to Day, the real Secretary of State because of Sherman's age and ill health:

> The telegram to Lee which Colonel Mitchell will show you, indicates the beginning of the end in Cuba. I fear that the uprising of the volunteers and the general counter-revolution, will not only overthrow the supposed autonomous government, but also the few vestiges of Peninsular authority which remain in Cuba in the same way that they rose up and expelled Captain General Dulce at the beginning of the Ten Years' War.* I think it would be well for our squadrons in the Gulf of Mexico to be ready to enter into action immediately since the emergency could arise at any moment. . . .[52]

It is clear, therefore, that even before the *Maine* left for Havana, there was a growing feeling in the McKinley Administration that autonomy had failed and that Spanish sovereignty in Cuba was collapsing. It was clear, too, that if the United States waited too long, the Cuban revolutionary forces would emerge victorious, replacing the collapsing Spanish regime. The moment was arriving for the United States to step in.[53]

---

* *See* Foner, *op. cit.*, vol. II, pp. 125-26, 149, 152, 162, 169, 178, 179, 180, 181.

CHAPTER XII
The Road to War

IN THE LATE MORNING of January 25, 1898, the *Maine* sailed into Havana harbor. Although Captain General Blanco had protested to Lee over the ship's proposed visit, and accused the United States of ulterior motives, he and other Spanish officials accorded it a proper though cool reception.[1] Since the Cuba harbor was infamous for its filth and disease, especially yellow fever, there was some feeling in Washington that for sanitary reasons, the *Maine* should leave Havana in the first or second week of February. But Lee and Sigsbee protested against sending it away unless another ship relieved it. Lee argued that to remove the ship was to lose control of the Cuban situation: "We are the masters of the situation and I would not like to disturb or alter it. . . ." Sigsbee agreed, and added, in his report to Secretary Long,* that he thought the ship should be moved only after a larger vessel replaced it, and that if the Navy Department would then send a third large ship, the United States would have sufficient naval power to control the situation in Cuba. Obviously both Lee and Sigsbee were seeking to impress Spain with America's overwhelming naval superiority in case of war.[2]†

---

* Sigsbee's report included a four-page study of every large gun in Havana harbor and its field of fire. (Sigsbee to Long Feb. 1, 1898, Miscellaneous Letters, Department of State, National Archives.)

† As far as demonstrating American superiority over Spain, the *Maine* alone had demonstrated this. Both Segismundo Bermejo, Minister of Marine, and Pascual Cervera, Admiral of the Spanish fleet, conceded it. Indeed, the latter warned his superior against involving Spain in a war with the United States because of America's great naval supremacy. (Bermejo to Cervera, Feb. 6, 1898, in Office of Naval Intelligence, compiler, *Notes on the Spanish-American War*, Washington, 1900, pp. 16-18; Pascual Cervera, *The Spanish-American War*, pp. 22-24.)

The Spaniards would have been happy to see the *Maine* leave; most officials in Cuba regarded the ship's visit as unfriendly, believing it encouraged the rebels. Moreover, there was genuine fear in Spanish official circles that the continued stay of the *Maine* could give rise "by means of an accident or some other mishap to a conflict...."[3]

Not only did the *Maine* stay, but the U.S. Navy concentrated its warships into fighting groups at Key West, ninety miles from Havana, instead of dispersing them.[4] Spain, interpreting this as evidence that the United States was preparing for war, announced that it was sending a fleet of torpedo boats and torpedo destroyers to Cuban waters. Segismundo Bermejo, Minister of Marine, notified Pascual Cervera, Admiral of the Spanish fleet, that war with the United States was probable, and that Spain was preparing to buy all the ships it could so as to be ready for military action by April.[5]

On February, 9, 1898, a group of prominent American businessmen delivered in person to McKinley a petition forcibly reminding the President of the United States' financial and commercial stake in Cuba. The memorialists represented the principal American interests in Cuba, merchants who owned sugar estates in the island, bankers who were heavily involved in the industry through advances of capital, and businessmen who had made huge profits from the lucrative Cuban-American commerce.* The memorial claimed an average annual loss of one hundred million dollars in commerce over the three years of conflict. "To this may fairly be added heavy sums irretrievably lost by the destruction of American properties, or properties supported by American capital in the island itself, such as sugar factories, railways, tobacco plantations, mines and other industrial enterprises; the loss of the United States in trade and capital by reason of this war being probably far greater and more serious than that of all the other parties concerned, not excepting Spain herself." The memorialists, one hundred and seventy-four in all, urged the President to give the "most earnest consideration in bringing

---

* There were 70 New York signatures, 40 from Philadelphia, and 64 from Mobile. Included among the memoralialists were Laurence Turnure, Mosle Bros., B. H. Howell Sons & Co. (sugar brokers), National Sugar Refining Co., Hugh Kelly, Osgood Walsh, Czarnikos MacDougall & Co. (sugar brokers), Bartram Bros., Mollenhauer Sugar Refining Co., Munson Steamship Co., Arbuckle Bros. (sugar refiners), and A. W. Corwell (sugar machinery). The National Sugar Refining Co. was part of the American Sugar Refining Co., the Sugar Trust, headed by Henry O. Havemeyer.

about actual peace, and with it restoring to us a most valuable commercial field."⁶ Again, as in the previous May, the petition (which contained many of the same signatures as the earlier memorial) did not state just how peace should be restored in Cuba. But the commercial interests were letting the President know that they wanted action, and this time even more vigorously than on the previous occasion.

The very same day this interview took place, the New York *Journal* printed the fateful de Lôme letter under the headline: "*The worst Insult to the United States in Its History.*"

Sometime between December 15, 1897 and January 1, 1898, the Spanish Minister in Washington sent a letter to a friend in Havana, Don José Canalejas, editor of the Madrid *Heraldo*. Canalejas had just completed a mission as an unofficial Spanish agent in the United States where he discussed commercial relations between the two countries and lobbied against recognition of belligerency of the Cuban Republic. The letter, written shortly after McKinley's message to Congress on December 6, 1897, opened, "The situation here remains the same. Everything depends on the political outcome in Cuba. . . ." Dupuy de Lôme then went on to express the opinion that it was "a waste of time and progress, by a wrong road, to be sending emissaries to the rebel camp, or to negotiate with the autonomists who have as yet no legal standing, or to try to ascertain the intentions of this Government." Referring to McKinley's message, de Lôme remarked:

> The message has undeceived the insurgents, who expected something else, and has paralyzed the action of Congress, but I consider it bad.
> Besides the natural and inevitable coarseness [*grosería*] with which he repeats all that the press and public opinion of Spain have said of Weyler, it shows once more that McKinley is weak and catering to the rabble [*débil y populachero*] and, besides, a low politician [*politicastro*] who desires to leave a door open to himself and to stand well with the jingos of his party. Nevertheless, as a matter of fact, it will depend on ourselves whether he will prove bad and adverse to us. I agree entirely with you, without a military success nothing will be accomplished there, and without a military and political success there is always danger that the insurgents will be encouraged, if not by the Government, at least by part of the public opinion. . . .

The letter closed with advice on how to deal with trade treaties between the United States and Spain: "It would be most important that you should agitate the question of commercial relations even though it should be only for effect [aunque no fuera más que para efecto] and that you should send here a man of importance that I may use him to create propaganda [para hacer propaganda] among the Senators and others in opposition to the Junta and to win over exiles. . . ." [7]*

Since the facsimile of the letter in Spanish with de Lôme's signature appeared in the *Journal*, there was no question of its accuracy. Charges were made that Hearst had stolen the letters from the mails. Although he denied the accusations formally, Hearst made no explanation of the means by which he obtained the letter. Not until the appearance, in 1932, of Horatio S. Rubens', *Liberty, the Story of Cuba*, was a complete explanation available.†

This is what happened: Gustavo Escoto, a friend of the secretary to Canalejas and a Cuban secretly active in the struggle for independence, was pressed into service to help Canalejas pack his belongings in preparation for his return to Spain. While in the office alone, Escoto saw an opened letter from the Spanish legation. He removed it, and on discovering the nature of its contents, placed a blank sheet in the envelope. After showing the letter to a group of Havana revolutionists, Escoto left for the United States with the original, departing in such haste that he arrived in New York's winter climate with only his Cuban

---

* There are several translations of the letter. The one used here is from the New York *Journal* of February 9, 1898, furnished by Horatio S. Rubens. The translation published in newspapers differed somewhat from the official translation of the State Department which is published in *Papers Relating to the Foreign Relations of the United States* 1898 (Washington, 1898), pp. 1007-08. Cuban historians view the official translation as an attempt to whitewash de Lôme. Regardless of which translation is more accurate—and I have included the Spanish for crucial phrases so that the reader may judge the translation used here for himself—the one which appeared in the press was the one which created the nationwide sensation.

† Rubens' book throws important light on the Cuban struggle, especially the work of the *Junta* in the United States. But it must be used with caution. See, for example, the discussion of a spurious document in the book by Thomas M. Spaulding. (*American Historical Review*, vol. XXXIX, April, 1934, pp. 485-88.) This document consists of a memorandum purportedly written by J. C. Breckenridge of the War Department which recommended that United States' policy should be "to support the weaker against the stronger [in Cuba], until we have obtained the extermination of them both, in order to annex the Pearl of the Antilles."

tropical clothing. Shown the letter, Tomás Estrada Palma immediately recognized its significance for the Cuban cause. Nevertheless, the Delegate did not personally like to take charge of disclosing the letter to the press and the U.S. government, and it was decided that he should leave to visit the *juntas* in Tampa and Key West, while Horatio S. Rubens, counsel for the *Junta* in New York, handled the affair.*

Rubens called in reporters from all New York papers. The reporter for the *Herald* asked for the exclusive right to use the facsimile, provided his editors would approve. When Rubens did not hear from him, he gave the rights to Hearst's *Journal*. Meanwhile, the *Herald* had telegraphed its Washington correspondent to ascertain the authenticity of the letter. Apprised in this manner of the impending crisis, de Lôme cabled his government on the night of February 8 that the letter was of such nature that he could no longer stay on as minister.

On the morning of the 9th, the *Journal* published the photographic reproduction of the letter and many other papers printed the translation.[8]† Accompanied by John J. McCook, Rubens went to the State Department on the same morning with the original document in his pocket. On seeing it, Day called in Alvee A. Adee for an opinion. Adee at first labelled the letter a forgery, but Rubens insisted that it was genuine. After comparing de Lôme's signature with the one in documents addressed to the State Department, Adee declared the letter to be authentic.[9]

Confronted with the letter, de Lôme informed Day that he had already cabled his resignation. Thus it was not necessary for the United States to ask for his recall. However, McKinley did ask for an official apology from the Spanish government.‡ It took over a week for Spain

---

* Some newspapers criticized the Cuban revolutionists for lack of sportsmanship in the theft and publication of the letter, but the British *Review of Reviews* answered: "All is fair in love and war, and the insurgents who are fighting for their lives cannot be blamed for striking below the belt." (vol. XVII, March 1, 1898, p. 213.)

† McCook wrote to a friend that he had "had the satisfaction of placing the original of de Lôme's letter in the hands of the President and Assistant Secretary Day and pressing for its acceptance as genuine. . . ." He did so, he explained, because he thought the letter would "be beneficial to the Cubans. . . ." (McCook to James H. Wilson, Feb. 10, 14, 1898, Wilson Papers, Library of Congress.)

‡ McKinley sketched for Day what the apology should contain: "Expressions of pained surprise and regret at the Minister's reprehensible allusions to the

to apologize,* and when she did so, she insisted that de Lôme's letter was, after all, only a private document in which he had expressed his private sentiments to a friend.[10] The McKinley Administration speedily accepted Spain's apology and announced to the American nation that the incident was closed satisfactorily. Luis Polo de Bernabé was accredited as Spanish Minister.[11]

The American people, however, were not so easily satisfied. Granted that the press had its own purpose in stirring up public resentment against Spain over the incident, and that it had said worse things about McKinley and his Cuban policy than de Lôme had said in his letter,† the fact remains that the document exposed Spain's reform policy in Cuba. It was not so much the unflattering reference to McKinley, much as it was played up in the press and in all textbooks and standard works on this period, that made the de Lôme letter significant, as it was that it offered tangible proof that Spain was insincere in her promises to establish reforms in Cuba, and was using autonomy as a mere ruse to placate public opinion, gain time and deceive the American government while the Spanish forcibly suppressed the Cuban insurrection.‡ As H.

President and the American people, and which it is needless to say the Govt. of His Majesty does not share, and promptly disavows." ((Undated memorandum in McKinley's handwriting in William R. Day Papers, Library of Congress.)

* Woodford told Moret that he would resign his position in Madrid if Spain did not apologize. (Woodford to McKinley, Feb. 15, 1898, Reports to the President, Spain: Dispatches, CXXXIA, No. 32, National Archives.) However, not all members of the Administration were so offended by the letter. Indeed, there was some sympathy within the administration for the Spanish Minister. "He is a man of a good deal of ability, and seems to have conducted himself remarkably well," Secretary of the Navy John D. Long wrote in his diary on February 10. (Lawrence S. Mayo, *America of Yesterday as Reflected in the Diary of John Davis Long*, Boston, 1923, p. 163.)

† On February 11, 1898, the Kansas City *Times* stated: "We recognize that Mr. McKinley is a chicken-hearted politician, laboring to play on both sides and breaking his pledge to serve Spain while ostensibly eager to assist Cuba." (Quoted in H. Wayne Morgan, "The De Lôme Letter: A New Appraisal," *The Historian*, vol. XXVI, Nov. 1963, p. 41.)

‡ Another example of Spain's insincerity revealed in the letter was that de Lôme viewed trade negotiations with the United States as a screen behind which Spain could lobby against Cuban independence. Yet on February 3, 1898, Woodford had been led to believe by Spain that she was deeply interested in negotiations for a reciprocity treaty for herself and for Cuba. (Woodford to Sherman, Feb. 3, 1898, Spain: Dispatches, National Archives.)

Wayne Morgan points out: "The vaunted promises of colonial reform which Spain had made in the preceding months were thus shattered." [12]

McKinley, speaking through Secretary of State Sherman in a formal dispatch to Woodford, conceded that the people of the United States were especially disturbed by this disclosure of Spain's policy in de Lôme's letter.[13] But this did not mean that McKinley was any less resolved to back Spain's policy or more inclined to advance the cause of Cuban independence. On the contrary, precisely at the time McKinley was expressing grave doubts about the sincerity of Spain's autonomy policy in Cuba, he called in Horatio Rubens, counsel for the *Junta*, and demanded that the Cuban Revolutionary government accept the armistice profered by the Spanish government and "come together with Spain" under an autonomous form of government. Rubens refused: " 'We can only treat on one basis and one basis only,' I reminded him. 'The absolute independence of Cuba.' " Rubens tried in vain to explain to McKinley that an armistice would mean the disbanding of the Cuban army while the Spanish forces would be kept intact. He also pointed out that nothing would be accomplished and war would again break out. When McKinley asked why the Cubans, as descendants of Spain, could not continue on terms with the mother country, Rubens pointed out that the reasons were the same as those which had made it impossible for the American colonists, descended from the British, to refuse to continue as British subjects.[14]

McKinley could not have been surprised by Rubens' reply since Captain Sigsbee had just reported from Havana, "Autonomy appears to be truly acceptable only by those Spaniards who have established families in Cuba and whose lives and business are involved in the island. The insurrectionists are asking only for independence...."[15]

On February 15, 1898, precisely six days after the publication of de Lôme's letter, at 9:38 in the evening, Fitzhugh Lee sat in Havana writing in a dispatch to Washington: "The letter of Dupuy de Lôme was a great calamity to the Spanish authorities here in every way."[16] At 9:40 P.M., as Lee reached the end of the sentence, a series of explosions was heard from the sea. Rushing to his window, Lee could see the flames leaping from the *Maine* as the heavily armored cruiser sank into the water. He ran towards the fort with thousands of *habaneros*, and soon met Captain Sigsbee and the many officers and a few sailors who had been lucky enough to escape death. The majority of the crew was not so fortunate; the explosion had occurred in the forward part of the *Maine*—directly under the sleeping quarters of the crew—and 264 sailors and two officers had been killed.*

In a telegram to Day, Lee explained the courageous and helpful part Spanish officers and men had played in rescuing Americans from the harbor while ammunition was still exploding, and then caring for the wounded. In a personal letter, Lee informed his government that he believed the cause of the disaster indeterminable. "But I am inclined to think it was accidental." [17]

Apparently a majority of the officials of the Navy Department considered the explosion an accident, and most believed that spontaneous combustion in the coal bunkers, which in some places were separated from ammunition storage rooms by very thick bulkheads, had heated the ammunition to a detonation point. Various naval officers recalled disastrous explosions that had proven fatal in other navies, and mentioned a large number of spontaneous combustion incidents which had occurred recently in the American navy, including seven on the *Indiana*, and one each on the *New York, Oregon, Philadelphia, Boston, Cincinnati,* and *Atlanta*. A few naval officers, however, rejected the accident theory, pointing to the safety precautions followed in modern ships to prevent such accidents, though they did not bother to explain why such accidents had just occurred on other American naval vessels. These officers suggested that a torpedo, mine, or an infernal machine, carried on board by visitors in Havana or placed in the coal bins when the ship was fueled at Key West, might have exploded the ship's magazine.[18]

Immediately after the disaster and before an investigation, Spanish authorities expressed confidence that the explosion had been accidental and had resulted from internal causes. Still with little delay, the Spanish officials ordered an investigation of the causes of the explosion, and within less than an hour, the first witness had been examined. The Spanish court testified on February 20 that it had found nothing

---

* The dead were buried in Havana's cemetery, but even though the majority of the victims were Protestants, the Archbishop of Havana insisted that the services had to be performed in accordance with the Catholic ritual or else the men could not be buried in Cuba. Portell Villá comments: "Thus the regime of privilege established in Cuba four centuries before and maintained in the island in spite of the liberal reforms of autonomy, made no concession even before this horrible catastrophe, revealing itself still indomitable, just as though Weyler himself were governing." (*op. cit.*, p. 73.)

to indicate an external explosion. Seven days later, the court asked for cooperation with the United States in hearing the testimony of the surviving members of the crew of the *Maine* and in examining the bottom of the ship, but the American government preferred not to cooperate, and the Spaniards continued the investigation by themselves.[19]

The United States' Court of Inquiry, headed by Captain William Sampson and made up of officers from the ships of the North Atlantic fleet, left for Havana on February 20. The American court sat for twenty-two days and examined a total of seventy-eight witnesses, including persons on board the ship at the time of the explosion, persons nearby who saw at least part of it, and divers and other experts who had examined the ship. Every witness had been sworn to secrecy, so that until the final report was published on March 28, 1898, no one outside the committee knew what evidence had been taken.[20]

Proposals for a joint Congressional investigation could not rally a majority, although individual members of Congress fulminated against Spain, charging her with responsibility for the disaster, and called for an immediate declaration of war to revenge the victims.[21] But the newspapers, engaged in circulation campaigns, did not wait for the naval court report. In New York City, Hearst's *Journal* devoted, in the first week after the explosion, over eight pages daily to the *Maine,* its circulation soaring from 416,885 copies on January 9th to 1,036,140 on February 18th. Among other things, the *Journal* told its readers that "the *Maine* was destroyed by treachery"; "the *Maine* was split in two by an enemy's secret infernal machine." It publicized "scoops" on how the Spaniards managed to blow up the *Maine,* and fake interviews with authorities who (though far removed from Havana) asserted that a Spanish act of treachery sank the battleship.[22] Joseph Pulitzer's New York *World* was not so certain of Spanish official responsibility, but the editors never doubted that the explosion was external, and caused either by a bomb or a torpedo.[23]

Across the country, some newspapers were willing to wait for the facts, but most aped the "yellow press" of New York. The Kansas City *Star's* headline read: "*We Saw the Torpedo. . . . A Maimed Seaman's Story.*" "Remember the *Maine,* to hell with Spain," became the national slogan as the Hearst press—and its many imitators—declared the guilt of Spain, and demanded that the United States must intervene to avenge the treacherous blow to its national honor.²⁴*

At first, publicly and privately, key Administration officials appeared to be acting to prevent the growth of nationwide hysteria. Captain Sigsbee, in his earliest telegraphic report following the explosion, advised that "public opinion should be suspended until further report." Lee telegraphed a similar request: "Hope our people will repress excitement and calmly await decision." Secretary Long publicly announced his opinion that an explosion in the *Maine's* magazine had caused the accident, and McKinley himself expressed his opinion that the catastrophe had resulted from an internal explosion.²⁵

But the pro-annexationists in the Administration could not let such an opportunity pass without taking as much advantage of it as possible. Lee quickly forgot his earlier conviction that the disaster was an accident, and even though the American Court of Inquiry had barely begun its investigation, assured the State Department that the explosion was an external one, probably caused by a Spanish torpedo or by a few barrels of guncotton which some Spanish officers sank where the *Maine* swung against them. If the Court of Inquiry substantiated this conclusion, as he was now convinced it would, Lee recommended that the United States immediately occupy Cuba as the first step towards annexing the island. He did not doubt that annexation would be the final outcome, for "American capital and enterprising spirit would soon 'Americanize' the island and immigration would be so great that when the matter of annexation came up, the Cuban people would not be a factor in deciding the problem. . . ." ²⁶†

Reports of a Cabinet meeting devoted to the Cuban problem, after Lee's dispatches were received, indicated that McKinley and his advisors

---

* The opposition to the jingo press was often expressed in the most reprehensible chauvinist language, displaying a contempt for Spanish-seaking people. Thus William A. White, the Kansas editor, wrote: "As between Cuba and Spain there is little choice. Both crowds are yellow-legged, garlic-eating, dagger-sticking, treacherous crowds—a mixture of Guinea, Indian and Dago. One crowd is as bad as the other. It is folly to spill good Saxon blood for this kind of vermin. . . . Cuba is like a woman who lets her husband beat her the second time— she should have no sympathy." (Quoted in Walter T. Nugent, *The Tolerant Populists: Kansas Populism and Nativism*, Chicago, 1963, p. 214.)

† For Lee's personal interest in "Americanizing" the island, see below p. 467n.

were moving in the direction the Consul in Havana had outlined. It was decided that if the explosion was external but not traceable to Spanish treachery, Spain should pay a proper indemnity, perhaps $10,000,000 to $25,000,000. If Sagasta refused—and if the explosion could not be attributed to Spanish action it is clear that he would refuse—the United States would use force and seize Havana.[27]

While McKinley and his advisors talked, Theodore Roosevelt, Assistant Secretary of the Navy, acted. "I would give anything if President McKinley would order the fleet to Havana tomorrow," Roosevelt, proudly calling himself "a Jingo," wrote to a friend on February 16.* While he did not do this himself, he came close to it. On February 25, after Lee's report reached Washington, Roosevelt used his authority to warn Commodore Dewey in Hong Kong of impending war, and advised him to keep his ships filled with coal. "In the event of a declaration of war," he cabled, "it will be your duty to see that the Spanish squadron does not leave the Asiatic coast, and then begin defensive operations in the Philippine Islands." In addition, Roosevelt issued a host of other orders to prepare the country for war. Secretary of the Navy Long, who took off an afternoon for a rest even though he had noted in his diary on February 24 that "the slightest spark is liable to result in war," returned to the department to find that Roosevelt had "come very near causing more of an explosion than happened to the *Maine*." The story goes that the Secretary was determined that his assistant should never be left in charge again. But if the story is correct, it is difficult to explain why Secretary Long not only never revoked Roosevelt's order to Dewey but the very next day sent another cable, "Keep full of coal, the very best that can be had." Actually, Long was convinced that Roosevelt had acted "with the best purposes in the world," and he merely ordered his assistant not to take any further steps "which affect the policy of the government without first consulting the President or me." As Herminio Portell Vilá notes, Roosevelt was not dismissed; on the contrary, there "remained in the government, in the very bosom of the Administration, a man whose conduct in such a crisis would

---

* In the same letter, Roosevelt wrote that 'the *Maine* was sunk by an act of dirty treachery on the part of the Spaniards" and that nobody would ever learn the cause of the disaster which would probably be recorded as an accident. (Roosevelt to Diblee, Feb. 16, 1898, Theodore Roosevelt Papers, Library of Congress.)

have, in any other country, brought about his immediate dismissal." Probably, he adds, "Roosevelt had a very clear idea that McKinley was not opposed to war, except for political suitability, more apparent than real, and for this reason proceeded as he did."[28]*

The evidence supports the Cuban historian's conclusion. Less than a week after the *Maine* sank, McKinley suggested to several Senators that the United States purchase Cuba—for herself, not for the Cubans. They flatly refused, arguing first that the cost would be too great, but more important, "that before long Spain will be compelled to relinquish her hold upon the island, and that Cuba will fall into the lap of the United States . . . without the payment of a gigantic sum of money."[29] McKinley did not entirely abandon the idea of purchasing Cuba—Woodford, his minister to Spain, continued to negotiate for the sale—but, believing that war was only a few weeks away, he began to make intensive military preparations. On March 6 he confided to Joe Cannon, chairman of the House Appropriations Committee, that "war was inevitable," and that money was needed immediately to prepare for it. Cannon urged McKinley to send a message to Congress requesting thirty million dollars for defense, and Congress would grant it. (Cannon pointed out that Congress' appropriation for the War Department, made before the *Maine* disaster, had fallen far short of the amount requested and was actually $500,000 less than the appropriation of the preceding year.) But McKinley answered that he could not take such a stand because of pending diplomatic negotiations with Spain. "It would be accepted by Europe as equivalent to a declaration of war and he would be accused of double-dealing." In order that this "double-dealing" be kept secret, the President suggested that Congress make the regular appropriation available ahead of time. Cannon, much as he wanted to oblige McKinley, felt that this was impossible, and the President therefore asked him to introduce from the committee a bill for fifty million dollars. The chairman prepared the bill that very night, and the next morning McKinley presided over a meeting of leading Republicans on the measure.[30]

---

* After a study of the Navy Department's archives, John A. S. Grenville concludes: "The naval campaign against Spain in 1898 was not hastily mounted at the last moment. Preparations for it had extended over a period of at least two years." ("American Naval Preparations for War with Spain, 1896-1898," *Journal of American Studies*, published by Cambridge University Press, for the British Association for American Studies, vol. II, April, 1968, p. 34.)

That same day the Cannon Emergency Bill was introduced in Congress, and on March 9, was passed by the House and Senate unanimously. The major portion of the "defense appropriation" of fifty million dollars was allotted to the navy and the rest to the army and fortifications. The New York *Journal's* headline after passage of the bill read, "*For War 50 Million Dollars.*"[31]

During the seventy-three separate speeches in the House, and the much briefer discussion in the Senate, there were frequent references to the need to recognize the independence of Cuba. McCook urged the Administration to follow this path of action, pointing out that it would guarantee that the Cubans fighting in the island would soon bring peace to Cuba. All that the "thoroughly acclimated force of 40,000 men under experienced commanders now in the Island, under the command of Gómez" needed was sufficient arms and the war would soon be over. But this was of no concern to an Administration busily preparing for war. McKinley discussed with Whitelaw Reid possible American recognition of Cuban independence, but neither man thought it worthy of further consideration.[32]*

Meanwhile, large sections of the press were picturing McKinley as a "peace-at-any-price" President who was seeking only a peaceful solution to the Cuban crisis.[33] McKinley's Papers in the Library of Congress indicate that many Americans believed this analysis of the President's policy, for they expressed approval of his efforts to maintain peace.† The correspondents, of course, knew nothing of the fact that the President had already concluded that "war was inevitable," and, through subterfuge, had obtained the funds to prepare to wage war—and this even before the reports of the committees investigating the *Maine* disaster.

Since McKinley knew in advance or was convinced that the American Court of Inquiry would conclude that the explosion was an external one, he was concerned lest Congress, upon learning of this, complicate

---

* Reid thought that "immediate recognition of Cuban independence" would "certainly be far better than the mischief-breeding recognition of belligerent rights." But he soon abandoned even this suggestion. (Whitelaw Reid to McKinley, March 8, 1898, McKinley Papers, Library of Congress.)

† Approximately nine-tenths of McKinley's incoming mail has been destroyed, but every incoming letter was answered, and the carbon copies on file in the McKinley Papers indicate that most people who wrote the President approved of what they considered to be his peace policy.

his plans for war against Spain by passing a joint resolution recognizing Cuban independence or prematurely declaring war before preparations were completed.[34] To prevent such action, McKinley held a series of conferences with legislative leaders to discuss Congressional action on the *Maine* report. The Congressional leaders agreed with McKinley that "intervention [should] be on broader grounds than the question of responsibility for the disaster of the *Maine*," and that the major issue to justify war should be Spanish misrule and the cause of humanity. McKinley suggested his sending a message for an appropriation of $500,000 to Congress, which would be used for American relief, then "the sword [would be] raised . . . for the purpose of extending succor." He assured the Congressmen that if Spain did not settle the Cuban crisis to American satisfaction by April 20, he would release the consular correspondence to Congress and accompany it with a message asking for American military intervention—for humanitarian reasons, of course. During the discussion, the Congressmen asked McKinley to recognize Cuban independence, but the President, as usual, dismissed the suggestion. Indeed, fearing that if he sent a Cuban relief message to Congress, the debate that would follow might lead to passage of a resolution recognizing Cuban independence, McKinley dropped the plan.[35]

Thus it is plain that even before the reports of the Court of Inquiry on the *Maine* disaster were submitted, the United States government had chosen war against Spain, had even worked out the strategy with which this was to be carried into effect and had decided upon the issue—humanitarianism—which was to justify military intervention. Hence the reports of inquiry themselves are only of academic interest so far as determining the policy which the United States adopted. Nevertheless, it is worth examining them. As might be expected, the Spanish and American reports reached opposite conclusions. From the evidence of witnesses and divers, the Spanish court came to the conclusion that an explosion of the forward magazine of the ship caused its destruction, and that no circumstances pointed to any external cause of the disaster. The refusal of the American government to cooperate had prevented the determination of the exact cause of the internal disaster. The court declared, however, that "unless the bottom of the ship and that of the place in the bay where it is sunk are altered by the work which is being carried on for the total or partial recovery of the vessel," the examination of the *Maine* would show the correctness of the Spanish findings. Nevertheless, the conclusion that it was an external explosion did not require such proof to assure its accuracy.[36]

The findings of the American Court of Inquiry, on the other hand, were simply that the destruction of the vessel was caused by "the explosion of a submarine mine which caused a partial explosion of two or more of the forward magazines." The Court did not attempt to place the responsibility for the destruction, and left that for an imaginative public to decide—a decision already made for it, as we have seen, by the majority of the American newspapers.[37] The printed report of the American Board of Inquiry was made on March 28, and the President submitted it to Congress with a message which held Spain accountable for the *Maine* disaster (even though he did not claim that her agents had set the blast) since her control of the harbor carried with it responsibility for the protection of property and people. The message made no recommendations. Nor did it have to. By the time the report was sent to Congress, the Administration had already gone so far on the road to war that it had little to do with the outcome. A Senate resolution claimed that "so clearly is the destruction of the *Maine* only a single incident in the relations of this government with Spain, that if the calamity had never happened the questions between the United States and that government would press for immediate solution." [38]

After the Spanish-American War was over, the Spanish Commissioners, sitting with the American representatives in Paris, proposed that a joint commission be appointed to investigate the *Maine* disaster, but the Americans stated that they considered the case closed.[39] In 1911, after years of public demand from Americans and Cubans,* the wreck of the *Maine* was finally raised by the United States. Although the *Scientific American* published an account of the findings under the title, "*Maine* Explosion No Longer a Mystery," which concluded that the explosion was an external one,[40] the actual report itself was so vague that no real conclusion could be drawn, and before any impartial

---

* The demands stressed three reasons: (1) to determine whether the battleship was blown up by an explosion from the exterior or by an explosion from within the ship; (2) to remove an obstruction to navigation in the harbor of Havana since a shoal had been formed about the sunken vessel, and (3) to remove the bodies of the sailors and inter them in Arlington National Cemetery. The Cuban government was especially anxious to remove the wreck because of its obstruction to navigation. (Philadelphia *Evening Bulleting* Feb. 15, 1910.)

group could study the hull, it was towed out to sea and "sunk with military honors in water deep enough to render any further study of its evidence impossible." [41]* To this day it is not known what or who blew up the *Maine*.† Walter Millis' conclusion is that "the most probable explanation still seems to be that the U.S.S. *Maine* did in fact destroy herself through the intervention of no outside agency save an act of God." [42]

Those who concluded before, during and after the report of the American Court of Inquiry that the explosion was not an accident, advanced one of four possibilities as to the responsibility for the act.

The first, and the one hinted at in all official American statements at the time, is that the Spanish government set the mine. But to offset this assumption is the fact that Spain knew that an attempt to destroy the *Maine* would lead to war, and there is certainly no evidence that responsible elements in the Spanish government wanted a war which they well knew Spain could not win and which would end in the loss of what she wished to save. As we have seen, Spanish Admiral Cervera was fully aware of the inadequacy of Spain's naval strength, and the purchase of two Brazilian battleships and of two cruisers in London originally intended for Brazil, did not materially affect the overwhelming naval superiority of the United States. The Spanish navy remained in a one to three ratio to the American, for although the Spanish ships were numerous, many were old and useless. Spain's financial condition, moreover, was so bad that the government was unable to buy sufficient ammunition for the guns of her ships.[43]

A second theory is that subordinate Spanish officers perpetrated the crime, and that Weyler was linked to it. Lee was convinced of this; also, François Lainé, a Cuban of French descent, implied that Weyler had something to do with the sinking of the *Maine* before the Senate

---

* Even before the *Maine* was raised, it was predicted that "the memorable hulk will be taken out to sea and given a deep water burial forever." This caused the *Industrial Worker*, organ of the Industrial Workers of the World (I.W.W.) to charge that this was being done so that "there will be no chance of the true facts of the matter being revealed." (Oct. 26, 1910.)

† After a careful study of all the evidence, Donald A. Holman concludes that "there is substance for the belief, which has been held by many, that the essential causative truth of the matter has never been discoverable." ("The Destruction of the *Maine*, February 15, 1898," *Michigan Alumnus Quarterly*, vol. LX, Feb. 27, 1954, p. 160.)

Committee on Foreign Relations on April 18, 1898.[44] But apart from the fact that Weyler is said to have ordered all his correspondence to associates in Cuba destroyed,[45] there is nothing concrete to commend this theory.

A third theory is that the jingos in the United States blew up the *Maine* in order to guarantee war with Spain. This theory was advanced in the radical press both in the United States and abroad shortly after the disaster. An article signed "Il Macai" in the British *Labour Leader* stated that the chances were that the sinking of the *Maine* was an accident. It continued: "If not, it was more likely American than Spanish treachery. The capitalist crew who can prescribe a 'rifle diet' for strikers and plough up a police platoon with a bomb,* will not stick at a few hundred marines. Therefore, when that old Republican, and most human of all the Spanish generals, Blanco, got sent to Cuba with conciliatory powers, some dastard feared success, and tried to force U.S. intervention by an outrage on his own countrymen which would excite suspicion against Spain."[46] Although some Cuban nationalists always believed this theory, it remains only a theory without any substance in fact. To be sure, Ferdinand Lundberg has suggested that Hearst may have had some connection with the explosion, but he bases this supposition only on the fact that the disaster gave the publisher of the *Journal* what he wanted most—war with Spain and more circulation for his newspaper.[47]

We have left for the last the theory most commonly advanced by American journalists and historians who have written of this period. On February 15, 1910, marking the twelfth anniversary of the blowing up of the *Maine*, the Philadelphia *Evening Bulletin* declared that the most "plausible theory . . . is that the battleship was blown up by Cuban insurgents in order to embroil the United States with Spain— a condition which actually followed."† As recently as 1961, W. A.

---

* The reference is undoubtedly to the Haymarket tragedy in Chicago, May, 1886. See Foner, *History of the Labor Movement in the United States*, vol. II, pp. 105-15.)

† This theory was advanced immediately after the disaster by E. A. Atkins, the bitter foe of Cuban independence, who wrote on February 14: "My first idea was that it was the work of the insurgents to provoke the governments of the United States and Spain, but this appears improbable for lack of opportunity, unless when the fuel was taken on in Key West, some dynamite was added by the coal shovelers of the boat. . . ." (Atkins, *op. cit.*, p. 274.)

Swanberg wrote in his biography of Hearst: "If she [the *Maine*] was sunk by plotters, it was most reasonable to suspect those who stood to gain from the crime—the Cuban rebels, whose cause was flagging and would be lost unless the United States would be dragged into the struggle." [48] This theory ignores the fact that Spain was in close control of Havana harbor, which made it almost impossible for any Cuban to have come near the *Maine;* certainly any insurgent would have been detected placing so complicated a machine as a submarine mine. But apart from this, the theory supposes, as do most American historians, that the Cuban rebels wanted U.S. military intervention. As we have seen, the rebel leaders in Cuba definitely did not want anything but U.S. recognition of Cuban belligerency or independence so that the Liberating Army could obtain guns and ammunition to wage the war even more effectively, and they decidedly feared American military intervention. When George Bronson Rea, the anti-Cuban reporter for the New York *Herald,* met Gómez shortly after the *Maine* disaster, the Cuban revolutionary leader angrily observed that the United States was only interested in the money it could get out of Cuba, and that the revolutionary forces in the island had more reason to fear than desire American military intervention. Gómez, Rea reported, placed the United States in the position of an enemy of Cuba.[49]

On March 1 McCook saw McKinley and left him a memorandum outlining a plan whereby the Cubans would purchase the island from Spain. The insurgents were prepared to pay Spain $100,000,000 to be secured by Cuban customs receipts, if Spain and the United States recognized the independence of the Republic of Cuba and all Spanish forces were withdrawn from the island. "Do not misunderstand the Cuban position," McCook wrote to Day following the interview with McKinley. "They feel that they have achieved their independence by force of arms, time, and climatic conditions, but to secure an immediate settlement and to save bloodshed, the destruction and a starving populace, they are ready and glad to pay an indemnity of $100,000,000." Although McKinley stated that the U.S. government was prepared to guarantee Cuba's purchase of bonds by collecting Cuban customs to secure their payment, he was not willing to go along with the demand for recognition of the Cuban Republic.[50]

Late in March, Gómez announced that he favorably considered purchasing Cuba from Spain for $200,000,000, with the aid of financiers from New York City, London, Paris, and Madrid, giving Cuba its independence thereby while the bankers held the bonds. He stated openly that the *insurrectos,* though gaining recruits daily and confident of achieving independence through a military victory, supported the purchase plan only because they did not want American intervention. This position was endorsed by Bartolomé Masó, President of the Cuban Republic.[51] In light of all this, to think that the insurgents would have anything to do with a plot that would hasten American military intervention is to indulge in fantasy.

But what of the Cuban *Junta?* Was it not, as H. Wayne Morgan argues, "awaiting the day when it could announce American intervention to its friends in Cuba?" [52] The truth is that most of the leaders of the *Junta* were now confident of the Liberating Army's ability to defeat the Spanish on the island, and feared rather than desired United States military intervention, for it was now obvious that such intervention might not be accompanied by recognition of Cuban independence. All the *Junta* wanted was recognition of Cuban belligerency. When McKinley, in his interview with Rubens after the *Maine* explosion, accused the *Junta* of desiring the United States "to go to war in behalf of Cuba," the attorney for the *Junta* replied, "We do not ask you to go to war; we only ask for your neutrality, for the recognition of Cuban belligerent rights. . . ." [53] Following the *Maine* disaster, the *Junta* ordered their representatives to abandon propaganda agitation throughout the nation lest it add to the speed with which the United States was travelling on the road to war. As Gonzalo de Quesada explained: "We do not want armed intervention, nor do we ask the United States to take any radical step. The recognition of Cuba will end the war and give us victory. This is all we ask of the United States." [54]

The United States was certainly aware that the *Junta's* confidence in the ability of the Liberating Army to defeat the Spanish was justified. On March 8, Secretary of War Russel Alger informed Day that Spanish military might in Cuba was exceedingly weak. Spanish troops now numbered only 65,000 men capable of fighting; they were of poor morale and poorer training and unable to hold out much longer against the rebels.[55] In his celebrated speech to the Senate on March 17, Vermont's Redfield Proctor, reporting on Cuban conditions which he had observed during a two-week trip in late February and early March, concentrated on starvation in the island and the horrible conditions of the *reconcentrados*. But in describing the military situation, he pointed out that Spain now had only about 60,000 effective troops who were ill-trained and ill-led while the Cuban forces numbered about 30,000. The Cubans were "well-armed, but very poorly supplied with ammunition," a fact which alone, he felt, made them unable to win a large military victory.[56]

Everything but one factor then pointed to a logical conclusion. In the interest of peace, in the interest of humanity which so troubled McKinley, the Administration had but to recognize the belligerency or independence of the Cuban Republic, adopt a true neutrality enabling the Cubans to obtain ammunition and achieve victory and independence with their own forces. But the one factor was decisive. Such a policy would mean that Cuba would be truly independent—independent of the United States as well as of Spain—and this was something the Administration would under no circumstances countenance. On March 17, 1898, Woodford closed a lengthy dispatch to McKinley outlining what he believed was the only course the United States should follow:

> I am thus, reluctantly, slowly, but entirely a convert to the early American ownership and occupation of the Island. If we recognize independence, we may turn the Island over to part of its inhabitants against the judgment of many of its most educated and wealthy residents. If we advise the insurgents to accept autonomy, we may do injustice to the men who fought hard and well for liberty and they may not get justice from the insular government should it obtain control of the Island. We may in either event only foster conditions that will lead to continuous disorder. If we have war we must finally occupy and ultimately own the Island. If today we could purchase at a reasonable price we should avoid the horrors and the expense of war. . . .[57]

When, despite Woodford's ceaseless efforts,* Spain refused to sell Cuba to the United States, war was inevitable. However, McKinley still

---

* Woodford approached Ramón García, a tobacco merchant and a friend of Sagasta and Moret, with the proposal for the United States to purchase Cuba, pointing out to him that if the war continued, Spain would lose Cuba to the rebels anyway with the resulting "race wars and destruction of property" in the island. Was it not preferable for Spain to agree "to the peaceful transfer of the Island to the United States with the resulting cessation of expense and the immediate alleviation of Spanish finances?" García conveyed Woodford's proposal to the Queen Regent and Sagasta. Woodford was confident that the

needed time to complete preparations for war and a period of fruitless negotiations with Spain began. The next two weeks were largely consumed in negotiations involving a program outlined first in a telegram from Day to Woodford, March 25: "For your own guidance the President suggests that if Spain revokes the concentration order and maintains the people until they can support themselves and offers to the Cubans full self-government with reasonable indemnity, the President will gladly assist in its consummation. If Spain should invite the United States to mediate for peace and the insurgents would make like request, the President might undertake such office of friendship." Woodford immediately cabled asking what McKinley meant by "full self-government," and was informed by return cable that the President meant "Cuban independence." [58] The Administration's brief reply to Woodford's question was the first and only time it had raised the question of Cuban independence, and it dropped the demand as quickly as it had raised it. On March 27, the following three-point program was sent to Spain through Woodford and two days later reaffirmed to Polo de Bernabé, the Spanish Minister in Washington, by Day, who informed him that if Spain accepted, 'peace might be secured":

1. A revocation by the Spanish government of its reconcentration order, so as to permit the people to return to their homes and cultivate the fields.

2. The sending of supplies to the needy.

3. An immediate armistice to take effect until October 1st. In the meantime the friendly offices of the President of the United States, if desired, looking to a peaceful adjustment between the Government of Spain and the insurgents. If no agreement should be reached by the first of October, the President to be the final arbitrator between the parties.

---

response would be a favorable one, and that the whole country, "worn out and exhausted," would be grateful to the Queen Regent "if she chose to separate Cuba without war, and would support her, although it might be necessary to change the Ministry to assure this result." But in the end the Queen Regent informed Woodford that "she wanted to pass on her patrimony intact to her son when he becomes of age, and that she would prefer to abdicate her regency and return to the seat of her ancestors in Austria rather than to be the instrument for the renunciation of any part of her colonies belonging to Spain." (Woodford to McKinley, March 17, 19, 1898, Reports to the President, Spain: Dispatches, CXXXI-A, National Archives.)

In a separate dispatch, which was not part of the three-point plan, McKinley sent along the report of the American Court of Inquiry and his own message to Congress which held Spain responsible for the conditions which presumably destroyed the *Maine*.[59]

In what the Administration called its last plan for a peaceful settlement, the demand for "Cuban independence" was not included.* Yet the Administration knew very well that by omitting this demand from the program, it rendered it pointless. For even if Spain would agree, the Cubans would never accept an armistice unless they first gained their independence. On March 22, McCook had sent McKinley a Memorandum which emphasized that "All Plans Must Take Into Consideration the position and wishes of the Cubans, without which they must be abandoned as impracticable theories, and Cuba's unalterable demand is absolute and complete independence."[60] Six days later, Rubens backed this up with the announcement: "The United States may make arrangements with Spain, but the Cubans will never consent to an armistice or any other plan but independence."[61]†

---

* In his study of McKinley's policy, John L. Offner writes that "McKinley had considered Cuban independence as the best solution for months," and that the reply to Woodford's query as to what was meant by "full self-government" was in keeping with this. But he offers no evidence to support this view—indeed, he presents much proof to the contrary—nor does he explain why the demand for independence was not included in the three-point program. Offner, incidentally, believes that McKinley had no real hope of obtaining either Spain's or the Cuban's agreement to his plan, and was advancing it primarily to obtain time to prepare more fully for war. Yet he continues to discuss the plan as an example of "diplomacy to secure a promise of Cuban independence." ("President McKinley and the Origins of the Spanish-American War," unpublished Ph.D. thesis, Pennsylvania State University, 1957, pp. 281, 284-85, 309-09.)

Ernest R. May also cites Day's message to Woodford on "full self-government" for Cuba and his reply that this "would mean Cuban independence," but he, too, does not attempt to explain why this was not included in the three-point plan. (*Imperial Democracy, The Emergence of America as a Great Power,* New York, 1961, pp. 153-54.)

† Without offering any evidence to support his view, H. Wayne Morgan argues that the reason the Cuban rebels would not accept an armistice was because they felt that the United States would declare war against Spain and this would give them all they hoped for. (*William McKinley and His America,* New York, 1963, p. 369.) Since Professor Morgan did not consult a single Cuban source in his work, it is perhaps understandable that he does not know that American intervention was what the rebels did not want. They opposed an armistice because they had no faith in Spain's promises, and because they did not want to give the Spanish government an opportunity to rebuild

Although Cuban independence was no part of McKinley's plan, the President informed Senators and Congressmen who visited the White House that he was negotiating for the independence of Cuba and that he expected a favorable reply by March 31. Indeed, the Congressional visitors told the press afterwards they had been assured McKinley had informed Spain "that he would be satisfied with nothing less than complete and absolute independence for the Cuban people," that this demand was part of the three-point program for peace, and that "the negotiations with Spain were based on the independence of Cuba, and that at all events the independence of Cuba would be included in any solution of the question. . . ."[62] The purpose of this deception was clear. In the Senate and House, resolutions had been introduced calling for a declaration of freedom for the Cuban people, recognition of the belligerency of the Republic of Cuba, and immediate recognition of Cuban independence.[63] Although there was overwhelming sentiment for passage of these resolutions, the Republican leaders in the Senate and House waited to learn the President's views.[64] By assuring the members of Congress that he was negotiating for the independence of Cuba, McKinley blocked passage of the resolutions.

Spain's reply to McKinley's plan reached the White House on March 31. Spain proposed to submit the Spanish and American *Maine* reports to arbitration; to abolish reconcentration in the four western provinces;* to grant 3,000,000 pesos for relief; to accept United States aid for *reconcentrados;* to grant a truce if the insurgents asked for one, and to turn over the question of permanent peace to the autonomous parliament in Cuba which would meet on May 4 and would have full power to negotiate a truce with the rebels. But Spain would not suspend hostilities immediately or accept American mediation. And this, she made it clear, was "the ultimate limit to which [Spain] can go in the way of concessions."[65] Since independence for Cuba was not a

---

its shattered forces in Cuba. "The past three years," Rubens pointed out, "have proved that the Cubans can and will fight during the rainy season when Spain is admittedly powerless to carry on her campaign. All the advantages of the proposed armistice would therefore result to Spain, not only in the money she would save, but in reduced mortality of her troops which would be as much as 40 percent. The Cubans would lose the benefits of the rainy season when they are always stronger in the field. . . ." (Washington *Post*, March 29, 1898.)

* Later Spain agreed to extend this to the entire island.

part of the plan proposed by McKinley, Spain did not even bother to reject it.

After reading the Spanish reply, McKinley decided not to answer. Instead, he stepped up military preparations and discussed with Republican leaders in Congress taxation measures to finance a war. He had promised Congressmen that if Spain refused his proposals, to "put the entire affair in the hands of Congress," and he now concentrated on preparing his message to Congress which would call for the United States to intervene militarily in Cuba.[66]

No one in the Administration, of course, bothered to ask the Cubans who were fighting in the island whether they wanted American military intervention. The United States had decided to settle the Cuban question by war for its own purposes and the wishes of the Cuban people did not enter into the decision.

CHAPTER XIII
Imperial Intervention

ALTHOUGH MCKINLEY had decided on war by April 1, three weeks passed before hostilities began. These weeks were taken up in preparing the presidential message, making final preparations for war, debating in Congress the final form of intervention, and conducting negotiations for peace largely in the European chancellories.

As early as 1896, Spain tried to form a solid front of European powers in opposition to the United States to prevent the latter's intervention in Cuba. In part, she hoped that the European holders of Spain's bonds would put pressure on their governments to act against the United States. (Since Spain's enormous foreign debt was secured by taxes on Cuba's commerce, anything that tended to increase uncertainty of payment would cause concern among the holders of bonds.*) But mainly she hoped that the continental powers, jealous of the United States and its expansion at their expense, would realize that it was to their interest to check the rise of the U.S. to world power status, and come to her support against the American colossus.[1]

Unfortunately for Spain, other factors operated against her efforts to organize a coalition against the United States. In England, where some of Spain's bonds were held, tariff considerations worked against Spain. Owing to prohibitive Spanish tariffs, Britain had little commerce with Cuba or with any other Spanish West Indies. British traders,

---

* Spanish four percent bonds were selling at 75 when the Cuban Revolution broke out in 1895; the price dropped almost immediately to 65, where it remained until the middle of 1897, when it dropped to 54 and remained at this point until March, 1898. Within two weeks after the American declaration of war, Spanish bonds were selling at 29. (London *Economist*, vol. LVII, May 20, 1898, p. 719.)

therefore, had everything to gain from the liberation of Spanish colonial possessions, and the bankers who favored Spain were checked by the merchants who would profit from the overthrow of Spanish rule in Cuba. In the end, the merchant interests were victorious.[2] Moreover, England was growing increasingly concerned over the rising power of Germany, and viewing the United States as a future ally, wished to do nothing to antagonize her. Then too, England's attention was turning toward China, and she hoped for American cooperation "to prevent an extension of Russian and German influence in China" against British imperialist interests.[3]

Although the largest portion of Spain's bonds was held by French bankers; although France favored the *status quo* to protect investors in Spanish securities; and although there was strong anti-American feeling in France, France would do nothing for Spain without England and Russia. England had already made her position clear, and Russia made it known that she believed Cuba belonged to the United States' sphere of influence and that she would not become involved to help Spain.[4] Actually only Germany, which had her own territorial designs on Spanish possessions, hoping to purchase the Philippines and other Spanish colonies in the Pacific, was responsive to Spain's efforts to organize a European coalition against American intervention. Spurred by the Kaiser, Germany, at Spain's request, tried to organize general European action against the United States in Cuba; Woodford reported this to McKinley on February 9, 1898, assuring the President that rumors of Germany's activities were "well founded." These rumors did not include England in the coalition. "The reason for that is possibly the situation in China."[5]

Germany did not get far. The European bloc could only be created if Germany were willing to take the responsibility of leadership herself. This she was unwilling to do, and she would only participate if all other European powers would cooperate, an unlikely possibility in view of Britain's desire to do nothing to antagonize the United States, on whose assistance she counted to preserve British interests in China.[6]*

During the first two weeks of April, 1898, intervention by the Pope

---

* Later, England and Germany engaged in a public dispute over which country was responsible for defeating international intervention against the United States, each claiming the credit. (R. G. Neale, *Great Britain and United States Expansion*: 1898-1900, Michigan State University Press, 1966, pp. 17-31.)

was regarded as holding out hope for peace. Leo XIII was approached on March 26 by Germany to mediate the dispute between Spain and the Cuban rebels, for the Kaiser believed that since the Pope had never condemned Spain's policies in Cuba, not even Weyler's reconcentration program, his mediation offer would be acceptable to Catholic Spain. The Pope felt that it would be impossible to arbitrate on the basis of Spain giving up Cuba; but in order to meet the desires of the European powers, he agreed to make inquiries at Madrid. At the same time, the Cardinal Secretary of State directed Archbishop John Ireland of St. Paul, Minnesota, to visit President McKinley and do all he could to settle the dispute with Spain amicably.[7]

The Pope's offer to mediate was refused by Spain on April 1. On hearing this, Kaiser Wilhelm II noted: "Then there is no helping them! They will lose Cuba all the same!"[8] Von Bulow, the German foreign minister, in an interview with the Spanish Ambassador, said that he would have given the Pope *carte blanche* in order to avoid war with the United States. He told the Ambassador that Spain could not count on active intervention by the European powers in the war because they were then engrossed in the Far East: "You are isolated because everyone wants to be pleasant to the United States, or at any rate, nobody wants to arouse America's anger; the United States is a rich country, against which you simply cannot sustain a war; I admire the courage Spain has shown, but I would admire more a display of practical common sense." The Spanish envoy replied that any further concessions on Spain's part would mean a fall of the dynasty, which would be worse than war. Spain need not fear war, but Europe should fear Spain's defeat and the increase of American power.[9]

On April 3, Spain, realizing that she could not count even on Germany in the event of war, indicated a willingness to allow papal mediation for an armistice, but set as a condition that the United States agree to withdraw the American squadron from Cuban waters and Key West on the proclamation of the armistice. Day promptly replied, "The situation of our squadron is our affair." An effective armistice, Day informed Woodford, would have to be immediate, for the President was completing the final draft of his message to Congress and could not hold it back later than April 5. Woodford urged delay, assuring Day that the armistice would bring "either an autonomy which would be acceptable to the insurgents or recognition of the independence of the Island on the part of Spain, or the cession of Cuba to the United States." [10]

On the evening of April 4, McKinley held a formal cabinet meeting to discuss the final draft of his congressional message. The President and his cabinet decided that the United States should intervene in Cuba on the broad grounds of humanity, neither recognizing Cuban independence nor the Cuban Republic. John Griggs, the Attorney-General, presented a detailed analysis to the cabinet members explaining why, in his judgment, the recognition of the Cuban Republic would violate the principles of international law, but he did not bother to include the views of the authorities who took the position that it would do nothing of the sort. The message would be sent on April 6.[11]

The following day, April 5, McKinley learned from Madrid that the Queen Regent, at the behest of the Pope, might proclaim in the next few hours a six months' armistice which would take effect as soon as the insurgents accepted it. Day informed Woodford that McKinley appreciated the Queen's desire for peace, but he would transmit his message to Congress as scheduled on the 6th. If the President learned of an armistice, he would communicate this information together with the message.[12]*

On April 6, however, the representatives of six European powers called on McKinley and presented a collective note to the President. The action had started on March 26 when the Spanish government, learning that McKinley would send a message to Congress, simultaneously contacted Germany, Austria-Hungary, France, England, Russia, and Italy, and asked the six powers to request the United States to arbitrate Spanish-American differences. The note the powers presented to McKinley, drawn up by Julian Pauncefote, the British ambassador and dean of the diplomatic corps, appealed to the "feelings of humanity and moderation of the President and of the American people," and expressed the hope that their "humanitarian and purely disinterested" representation would help keep the peace and re-establish order in Cuba. McKinley replied that the American government appreciated the good will that prompted the six powers to act, and he shared their hope that peace might be maintained. But only Spain could bring peace. "By

---

* Adee told Day to ignore Spain's proposed actions and to make no changes in the President's message because of them. (Adee to Day, April 5, 1898, Day Papers, Library of Congress.)

affording the necessary guaranties for the re-establishment of order in the island, so terminating the chronic condition of disturbance there, which so deeply injures the interests and menaces the tranquillity of the American nation by the character and consequence of the struggle thus kept at our doors, besides shocking the sentiment of humanity." The Government of the United States was certain that the European powers would appreciate "its own earnest and unselfish endeavors to fulfill a duty to humanity by ending a situation the indefinite prolongation of which has become insufferable." [13]

This ended the European intervention.* McKinley had now cleared all the obstacles which were delaying American intervention. The message to Congress was ready. It was not to be altered even by the bitter and justified opposition of the Cuban *Junta* to the news that McKinley's message calling for intervention would not recognize the Cuban Republic or Cuban independence. *The State* of Columbia, South Carolina wired Gonzalo de Quesada in Washington, inquiring in regard to the Administration's plan of intervention without recognition of Cuban independence. On April 7, *The State* carried the following reply from Quesada:

> Our position should not be misinterpreted. We cannot accept anything which means the perpetuation of Spanish sovereignty in the island. We will oppose any armistice or intervention which does not have for its express and declared object the independence of Cuba. We have our government, and the American people want it recognized. Our motto is independence or death.

Horatio S. Rubens, truthfully expressing the views of the Liberating Army, announced bluntly:

> In the face of the present proposal of intervention without previous recognition of independence, it is necessary for us to go a step farther and say that we must and will regard such intervention as nothing less than a declaration of war by the United States against the Cuban revolutionists. If intervention shall take

---

* In his *Imperial Democracy: The Emergence of America as a Great Power*, Ernest R. May presents a detailed account of the exchanges among the European powers over Spain's appeals for support against American intervention in Cuba. The presentation is based on research in official and unofficial manuscript collections in London, Paris, Madrid, and Vienna.

place on that basis, and the United States shall land an armed force on Cuban soil, we shall treat that force as an enemy to be opposed, and, if possible, expelled, so long as the recognition of a free Cuban republic is withheld. . . .*

Should the United States troops succeed in expelling the Spanish; should the United States then declare a protectorate over the island, however provisional or tentative, and seek to extend its authority over the government of Cuba and the army of liberation, we would resist with force of arms as bitterly and tenaciously as we have fought the armies of Spain." [14]†

A storm of abuse descended upon Rubens for having dared to declare that Cuba was not ready to become the supine victim of American imperialism hiding behind the pious veil of "humanity." "Would Fight American Troops," the Washington *Post* shrieked in its headlines, denouncing Rubens as a "demagogue." But many Americans applauded Republican Congressman William Alden Smith of Michigan when he officially broke with McKinley and supported Rubens, declaring, "I will not be a party to any proposition that falls short of independence. If our action is not intended to help the insurgents, it must merit their opposition; and we are placed in the position of opposing those who have struggled so long and lost so much to secure their liberty." [15]

On April 9, while McKinley waited for Lee to finish evacuating Americans from Cuba so that his message could go to Congress, Spain made its final concession to American demands. The Spanish Minister notified the Pope that, pending a settlement, the Governor General in Cuba would cease hostilities. On the following day, Polo de Bernabé formally acquainted McKinley with the armistice. The Spanish Minister announced that Blanco had ordered an end to hostilities, and would later define the manner of execution and duration. The purpose of the cease fire order, he declared further, was the "pacification of the

---

* Even before Rubens, Estrada Palma had raised the possibility of Cubans fighting American troops. In his "Proclamation to the people of the United States," issued on March 17, opposing autonomy and calling for independence, Estrada Palma had warned that if the United States tried to force the Cubans to accept autonomy, they would fight even American troops sent to support Spain. "In such a case we will be exterminated, but new generations will again take up our flag and our aspirations and Cuba will yet be free." (Detroit *Free Press*, March 18, 1898.)

† This was an accurate description of the policy pursued by the government of the United States after the defeat of Spain.

Great Antilla," and the success of autonomy, although Spain was willing to make changes in its autonomic decrees, "within the bound of reason and of the national sovereignty." Holding the insurgents—"a small minority of the sons of Cuba who have been mainly led and sustained by foreign influences"—responsible for the terrible conditions in the island, the Spanish Minister reminded the American government of Spain's abolition of reconcentration, her designation of 3,000,000 pesos for aiding the *reconcentrados,* and her willingness to arbitrate the conflicting *Maine* reports.[16]

When Day received the armistice plan from Polo de Bernabé on the morning of April 10, he hurried it to McKinley, who was presiding over a cabinet meeting. After studying Spain's final offer, the cabinet was divided over how the government should react. Some members argued that the President should again postpone his Cuban message, but the majority voted to append the new information to the end of the message and to submit it to Congress the next day. McKinley accepted the majority position.[17]

McKinley's decision to send the Cuban message to Congress despite Spain's acceptance of the three-point American plan of March 27 has been pointed to by many American historians as proving the President's weakness and marking his utter and complete surrender to the "yellow press" and the jingoes. After all, they argue, Spain had agreed to everything the United States had demanded and there was therefore no need for anything but to inform Congress of this fact.[18]* Without in the least defending McKinley's decision to go to war which, as we have seen, was not necessary if the purpose of the United States was to

---

* McKinley's action has been explained by many American historians, but no explanation is as weird as that offered by Ray Ginger in his recent book, *Age of Excess: the United States from 1877 to 1914* (New York, 1965, p. 201). Dr. Ginger writes: "One of McKinley's essential conditions (which ironically he dared not state explicitly, fearing that it might leak out and knowing that it would alienate Republicans in the Senate) was independence for Cuba. This Spain would not grant. All chance of an armistice was gone." To depict McKinley as a champion of independence for Cuba is quite a trick, especially since Ginger cites no evidence to support this strange thesis. Actually, as we have seen, McKinley did not make independence "one of the essential conditions" for refraining from military intervention. As for not stating it explicitly for fear of alienating Republicans in the Senate if they learned of it, McKinley did precisely the opposite. He let Congressmen think that he had actually made independence of Cuba an "essential condition" even though this was not the case, and, as we shall see, he was publicly rebuked in Congress for this duplicity.

achieve peace in Cuba, it is nevertheless interesting to note that these historians never bother to consider whether Spain's announcement of an armistice was acceptable to the *insurrectos* who were doing the fighting in Cuba. The fact is that the Cubans refused to accept an armistice unless Spain would at the same time consent to evacuate Cuba. The following letter, written by Máximo Gómez and sent to McKinley by the American Consul in Cuba, gave the insurgent view:

> A year ago we received a proposal to agree to an armistice. We refused then and we must refuse now. The rainy season is at hand, and Spain's troops would like an armistice until it is over. We will not, however, throw away the advantage. I am anxious that hostilities should cease, but it must be for all time. If Spain agrees to evacuate Cuba, taking her flag with her, I am willing to agree to an armistice to last until October 1, when loyal Cubans shall come into their own again.
> Please tell President McKinley this for me. Tell him, too, that I am writing this at the direction of the Cuban provisional government with which he may treat directly if he should so desire.[19]

The Revolutionary Governing Council backed Gómez's declaration with an announcement resolving to continue the war until the triumph of the Republic.[20]

McKinley delivered his long-awaited message to Congress on April 11, 1898 in which, at the very end, he only casually mentioned the Spanish concessions of the previous day. After describing at length how the trade, commerce and capital of citizens of the United States had suffered from the war in Cuba, how Americans had been horrified by the brutal policies of Weyler, and how efforts of the U.S. government to end the war had failed, he declared his opinion that the war would never end except through the weariness of the contending parties or by the extermination of one of them, and this situation the United States could no longer tolerate. McKinley then rejected both recognition of the belligerency or of the independence of the Cuban Republic on the ground that the Cuban government lacked sufficient requisites for being recognized, and that it was not wise "to recognize at this time the independence of the so-called government of Cuba." He declared, however, that "such recognition is not necessary in order to enable the United States to intervene and pacify the Island," and followed this with a statement which gave the true reason for the denial of recognition:

> To commit this country now to the recognition of any particular government in Cuba may subject us to embarrassing conditions of international obligations towards the organization so recognized. In case of intervention our conduct would be subjected to the approval or disapproval of that government. . . . We would be required to submit to its [the Cuban government's] direction and to assume to it the mere relation of a friendly ally.
>
> When it appears that there is within that island a government capable of paying its debts and of carrying out the functions of an independent nation, and has, in reality, the adequate form and attributes of nationality, that government shall be quickly and easily recognized and the relationship and interests of the United States with that nation shall be adjusted.

What McKinley was saying obviously was that if the United States recognized the independence of the Cubans, it would have to treat them as equals with respect to the island and its future—a shocking thought, indeed, in view of the fact that it was the country not of the Americans but of the Cubans. Moreover, as he made it clear, an alliance of this type imposed an international obligation which would have made annexation of Cuba difficult to achieve. In short, the question of Cuban independence was to be subject to the good will of the United States and it alone. Perhaps the clearest indication of what McKinley had in mind was revealed on April 10th by Whitelaw Reid's New York *Tribune* which was generally considered the newspaper closest to the Administration. It pointed out that when the United States drove Spain from the island, it would have to "take care that decent government is provided for in Cuba." And if, as the *Tribune* felt confident, the insurgents were unable to provide such government, then it would be up to the United States to do so. Hence the hands of the U.S. should not be tied in advance by recognizing Cuban belligerency or independence. All this, the *Tribune* said, did not mean "annexation," but it failed to spell out what it really meant—a United States puppet government in Cuba.

Following his rejection of recognition of Cuban belligerency and independence, McKinley presented the case for American intervention. This was justified partly on humanitarian grounds, but principally in order to protect American lives, property and commerce, and "in behalf of endangered American interests which give us the right . . . to act." For this purpose, forcible intervention was necessary with "hostile constraint" on both Spanish and Cubans. He requested Congress "to authorize and empower the President to take measures to secure a full and final termination of hostilities between the Government of Spain and the people of Cuba, and to secure in the island the establishment of a stable government, capable of maintaining order and observing its international obligations, insuring peace and tranquility and security of its citizens as well as our own, and to use the military and naval forces of the United States as may be necessary for these purposes. . . ." [21]

McKinley had put it straight. The United States alone was to determine the future of Cuba, not in the "mere relation of a friendly ally," but with such a degree of control as not to be "subject to the approval or disapproval" of any other government, nor "required to submit to its direction."* As was to be expected, the friends of Cuban freedom were amazed by the President's failure to include recognition of Cuban independence. "The President's Cuban Message Disappointing

---

* Defending McKinley, Margaret Leech writes: "Neutral intervention, without recognition of Cuban independence, was of cardinal importance to McKinley's policy. In terminating the colonial rule of Spain, the United States was necessarily assuming a temporary responsibility for the island's political destiny." (*In the Days of McKinley*, New York, 1959, p. 182.) Miss Leech says nothing of the fact that the Cubans themselves were already "terminating the colonial rule of Spain," nor does she explain what is meant by "neutral intervention." The United States, under McKinley's policy, was hardly neutral; it was predisposed to favor only its own interests.

Miss Leech also defends McKinley's refusal to recognize the Republic of Cuba, arguing: "The self-styled republic of the insurgents could not legally claim to represent the Cuban people. . . ." (*Ibid.*) The question naturally arises whether the government of the United States could "legally claim" to represent the Cuban people. In discussing McKinley's recognition of the government in Hawaii, as the first step in annexing the island, a government established by a few sons of missionaries who deposed Queen Lilioukalani in a bloodless revolution in 1893, "and, with the aid of the minister and the naval forces of the United States . . . had set up a provisional republican government in avowed anticipation of American annexation," Miss Leech writes, "The insular government, if somewhat dubiously established, had proved to be representative and stable." (*Ibid.*, p. 146.) "Representative" of American sugar planters but not of the Hawaiian people! The difference between the Cuban and Hawaiian governments lay in the fact that the Cubans wanted to be independent while the "Hawaiian government" wanted to be annexed to the United States.

to Those Who Want Cuba Freed," ran a *New York Times* headline of April 12. Congress was besieged with telegrams urging immediate recognition of the island's independence. They read: "Public opinion here unanimous for independence of Cuba. It is opposed to intervention without independence." "Our People urge recognition of Cuban Republic. No Recognition; no intervention." "People enraged at President's message. All demand recognition." The Lincoln Post of the Grand Army of the Republic wired: "Give the patriot Cubans our nation's recognition of their independence at the earliest possible moment." [22]

Many Congressmen were also infuriated because in his review of Administration policy, McKinley revealed that at no time had the government asked Spain for Cuban independence. Yet the President had previously led Congress to believe that negotiations had failed over this question. Little wonder that many Congressmen noted that since McKinley had not asked for Cuban independence, Spain had met all of the administration's requests. The Washington *Post* put the issue squarely:

> The foremost ground of criticism and the one which was paramount was the absolute silence of the President [in his message] as to the independence of Cuba. This omission took Congress by surprise and created the utmost feeling of dissatisfaction and disappointment. Whatever else might have been in the President's mind, it was supposed that the ultimate aim of his policy was the freeing of Cuba, but the message gave no corroboration of this fact. On the contrary, independence was not mentioned except for the purpose of arguing that it ought not to be recognized. The semi-official assertions made by persons competent to correctly assert the President's position had previously been to the effect that the President desired to secure to the Cubans fighting for their freedom the logical result of their protracted struggle. The friends of Cuban independence listened in vain for a single word to buoy up their hopes in this regard.
>
> It is true that the public had been in some measure prepared for the unmasking of the President's real policy. All the dispatches from Madrid had persistently stated that at no time has the independence of Cuba been insisted upon by the President, but these statements were pronounced untrue by officials in Washington. It was stated most positively that the President had in view the complete and absolute independence of Cuba, the withdrawal of the Spanish troops, and the abandonment of Spanish sovereignty over the island. These were the points which in the public mind

at least, were prime factors in the settlement of the Cuban question. According to the resume of the situation furnished by the President himself, they have never entered into the consideration of the case.

It is stated on the authority of a Senator who is a member of the Committee of Foreign Relations, and also upon the authority of a cabinet officer, that on the 29th of last month, after the President had informed Spain that self-government must be granted to the Cubans, Minister Woodford asked for an explanation of the term "self-government." The reply was brief and to the point: "Absolute independence" was the answer flashed back to Madrid. This fact was published at the time and until yesterday it was accepted without question. There is nothing in the President's message, however, to indicate that the President ever entertained such an idea.

These facts led yesterday to the query from several Senators as to whether the President had taken Congress fully into his confidence. . . .[23]

Senator Butler expressed a widespread Congressional opinion when he said bluntly: "If I can understand the message it means that the President is opposed to Cuban independence now and forever."[24]

As the House and Senate prepared to discuss and act on McKinley's message, the President stepped up preparations of the armed forces. The army began mobilization by moving its small force of regulars from the West to assembly points at New Orleans, Tampa, and Mobile, and the Navy completed its preparations for war. As Secretary of War Alger noted in a letter to McKinley, it was "a good move not only to get troops ready but to show the country you are getting ready for war."[25]

After receiving McKinley's message, the House Foreign Affairs Committee prepared an intervention resolution. A bitter battle arose over the question of recognizing Cuban independence, with Representative Smith of Michigan vigorously opposing any resolution which did not include this clause. The result, after two stormy meetings, was a compromise. The resolution did not recognize the Cuban Republic, but it did support United States intervention to establish in Cuba, "by the free action of the people thereof, a stable and independent government of their own in the Island."[26] But there were committee members who were not satisfied with the compromise. When the resolution reached the House floor, Democratic committee members introduced a minority resolution which recognized the independence of the Cuban Republic, asking the President to employ force to maintain the Republic's independence, and calling for immediate relief of the starving Cuban people. The resolution reminded Congress that the American people "are practically unanimous in favor of recognizing the independence of the government established by that brave and heroic people by the expenditure of so much treasure and so much blood, and our people will be satisfied with nothing less." In support of its position, the resolution argued that the government which the Cubans had established had "all the forms of a republic, and is a republic in fact, based on manhood suffrage, with legislative and executive departments in full operation, and with a judicial department so far perfect as the exigencies of the situation permit." The army of this Republic, made up of 30,000 men in the field, had defended itself successfully against 225,000 Spanish soldiers, 135,000 of whom were in hospitals or in their graves, and was "now in undisputed possession of three-fourths of the island. Outside her picket lines Spain possesses not one foot of Cuban soil. Within her picket lines three-fourths of the population are insurgents at heart, or will cordially participate in the republican form of government as soon as the Spaniards evacuate the island." Since Spain would never conquer Cuba, the United States would ultimately have to recognize the independence of the Cuban Republic. This being the case, the sooner the United States acted, the better for it as well as for Cuba, since recognition *"will remove from the minds of all men any suspicion that we are preparing to wage a war of conquest and to annex the island from motives of sordid greed, or as the policy of imperial aggrandizement. . . ."* [27]

A great many Representatives wished to speak on the two resolutions, but the Rules Committee, dominated by Administration forces, limited debate to forty minutes. Hence only two speakers were heard, one for the majority and the other for the minority resolution. Hugh A. Dinsmore, Democrat from Arkansas, spoke first in behalf of the minority resolution. He stated that if the United States had recognized the independence of the Cuban Republic a year before, Cuba would now be free. Ridiculing McKinley's argument against recognition, he said that it meant that the United States arrogantly reserved for itself the sole right to "judge the stability of that [the Cuban] government." The President had led Congress to believe that he had demanded of

Spain the independence of Cuba. But now Congress knew it was a hoax. All the President was interested in was a "stable" government in Cuba and he wanted the United States alone to decide what government fitted this description. "We talk about liberty. Then let us give the Cubans liberty. We talk about freedom. Let us give to them the right to establish a government which they think will be a free government, and which does not reserve to us, the Government of the United States, the right to say, after it is established, 'Ah, this is not a "stable" government; we can not turn it over to you yet; we must look after this thing.' " [28]

Adams, a leading Republican, answered Dinsmore by stating the usual arguments, heard since the Ten Years' War, that the Republic of Cuba was not worthy of recognition under international law because it had no capital, civilian government, port, or ships. He urged intervention solely on the grounds McKinley had outlined in his message to Congress.[29]

At the close of the forty minute debate, the House, under the direct control of the Administration, voted down the minority resolution 190 to 154. It then voted overwhelmingly for the majority resolution, 325 to 19.[30] Thus the President was authorized to intervene forcibly in Cuba to stop the war, and to establish there an independent government chosen freely by the people of Cuba. This went further than McKinley wished to go. Still there was to be no recognition of the Cuban Republic already in existence.

In the Senate, too, there were majority and minority resolutions from the Foreign Relations Committee. The majority resolution did not recognize the Cuban Republic, but it did proclaim Cuba already independent—"that the people of Cuba are, and of right ought to be free and independent"—called on Spain to relinquish her authority and withdraw from Cuba, and authorized the President to use the nation's armed forces to insure that this was done.[31] A minority of the committee, while generally agreeing with all the points in the majority resolution, proposed an amendment which called for recognition of the Cuban Republic. Although worded by Senator Joseph B. Foraker of Ohio, it was known as the Turpie Amendment since it was introduced by Senator David Turpie of Indiana. It not only included the declaration of the majority resolution that the people of Cuba "are, and of right ought to be, free and independent," but added the clause "and that the Government of the United States hereby recognizes the Republic of Cuba as the true and lawful government of that island."[32]

It took the Senate four days of heated debate—from the 13th to the 16th of April—to come to a final decision. One speech delivered on April 15 by Senator John W. Daniel, Democrat from Virginia, charged that the Admiinstration had intervened because it feared defeat of the Spanish by the revolutionary forces during the Cuban rainy season (mid-Spring to mid-Autumn):

> ... when the hour has arrived most favorable to revolutionary success and most disparaging to Spain; at a time when she [Spain] wants delay ... on account of the climate ... the Congress of the United States is summoned to turn over the army of the United States to the President to go and enforce an armistice between the two parties, one of which has already stacked its weapons.[33]

The major speech in favor of the Turpie Amendment was delivered by Senator Foraker, one of the foremost constitutional lawyers in the Senate, and it was a powerful indictment of McKinley's attitude toward the Cuban Revolution. He denied that Congress had any right to empower the President or itself "to create and establish a stable government in the Island of Cuba for the benefit of the Cuban people," or, for that matter, any other kind of government for the Cubans. The Cuban people, and they alone, had the power to establish their government. Hence he pointed out the inconsistency in the majority resolution of saying both that the people of Cuba were and ought to be free and independent and that the United States reserved the right and power "to establish for that independent people a government such as in our judgment and opinion may be stable." The reason, in Foraker's judgment, for the refusal to recognize the independence of the Republic of Cuba was because "*this intervention is to be deliberately turned from intervention on the ground of humanity into an aggressive conquest of territory.*" This, he warned Congress, the American people would not tolerate. Challenging the President's argument that the Republic of Cuba was not entitled to recognition, he demonstrated that the so-called "paper government" was "a most excellent actual government as well," holding elections, operating a postal service, collecting taxes, and conducting public schools. True, it had no seaport, but there were a great many countries that had no seaport, and had been recognized by the

United States. It did have a fixed capital located at Cubitas where the government offices operated. But there was another reason, perhaps a selfish one, why the United States should recognize the independence of the Cuban Republic:

> Gomez has now in the field . . . some 35,000 or 40,000 men. He would have many thousands more if he had guns and ammunition for them. The very moment the United States intervenes and recognizes the independence of that Republic, Gomez can swell that army from 35,000 or 40,000 to 50,000, 60,000, 80,000, 100,000 men, and all we have to do is put guns and ammunition in their hands and they will speedily evict the Spanish battalions from the Island of Cuba. If we only with our Navy blockade the harbors so that they can take no more provisions in, the Cubans will speedily put an end to the war, and there will be no necessity for this Government to expose our troops to the ravages of yellow fever and the other difficulties and disadvantages that would attend a campaign in that island in the rainy season.[34]*

Suporting Foraker, Senator William Lindsay of Kentucky asked Administration supporters just what government would eventually assume power in Cuba: "If we are to retain control until a government is formed which meets with our approval, will that government be the act of the people or the act of the United States?" He followed this up later with other questions:

> Who are we to pacify? We refuse to recognize the republican government; we are to break down the Spanish government; we are to leave the people without any government at all; and then we propose to pacify the people who are thus left absolutely in a state of nature.

---

* On April 11, James H. Wilson had written to Foraker: "How a body of reasonable men going to war can deliberately reject the alliance and support of an army of 30,000 seasoned soldiers acclimated and already facing the army which will have to be driven out of Cuba is beyond my understanding. If you deny the legal existence of the Insurgent Government, you must also deny the legal existence of the Insurgent Army, and treat it as carrying on an unlawful war." (James H. Wilson Papers, Library of Congress.) A leading Union Army brigadier-general during the Civil War, Wilson wrote from a long military background.

There are several hundred letters in Foraker's Papers congratulating the Ohio Senator on his speech. See James B. Foraker Papers, Box No. 13, Cincinnati Historical Society.

Pacify them how? Pacify them through our Army, pacify them by military reconstruction, pacify them by setting up an American government which these people shall accept or remain without government?[35]

With Administration supporters refusing to answer these questions, suspicion mounted that Foraker's judgment that a war for humanity was being turned "into an aggressive conquest of territory" was correct. More Senators swung behind the appeal to support the recognition of the Cuban Republic. On April 16, by a vote of 51 to 37, the Senate voted for the Turpie Amendment, agreeing to recognize the Cuban Republic. While most Republicans, loyal to the Administration, lined up against the Amendment, enough Republican members of the Senate rejected McKinley's leadership and broke ranks to swing the decision to recognize the Cuban Republic.[36]

Having adopted the minority amendment, the Senate, on the same day, accepted by voice vote the amendment written by Senator Henry M. Teller of Colorado. This, the historic "self-denying ordinance," was a firm declaration that the United States renounced all power over Cuba once the island was pacified: "That the United States hereby disclaims any disposition or intention to exercise sovereignty, jurisdiction, or control over said island except for the pacification thereof, and asserts its determination when that is accomplished to leave the government and control of the island to its people." [37]

Before sending its resolution to the House, the Senate adopted a motion by voice vote affirming its "recognition of the independence of the people and Republic of Cuba." [38] Thus the Senate had acted to give recognition to the Cuban people and their government, and had committed the United States to forego either annexing Cuba or making a protectorate of it. "According to the Senate version," writes David F. Healy, "the United States, far from becoming the supreme arbiter of Cuba's destinies, was merely to deliver power to the Cuban Republic and withdraw, promising to interfere no more." [39]

Horatio S. Rubens later claimed that it was at his suggestion that Senator Teller wrote his "self-denying" resolution, after the chief legal counsel for the Cuban *Junta* in New York had exposed the plans of the McKinley Administration "to steal the island of Cuba." Rubens asserted further that he had gone to Senator Teller because of the latter's sympathy for Cuba and the special interest he had as Colorado's Senator in opposing annexation of the island.[40]

Although Teller had favored the annexation of Cuba before the second war for independence, he had abandoned this position when the Revolution broke out, and championed United States recognition of Cuban belligerency as the quickest way to help the revolutionists win independence.[41] (On February 26, 1898, the Washington *Post* described Teller as "a man whose pro-Cuban sentiments are so strong that he was one of the five men who voted the other day to place an amendment to the diplomatic appropriation bill recognizing the belligerency of Cuba.") The special interest Rubens referred to was, of course, the fact that Teller represented a state to which, as a producer of beet sugar, the annexation of Cuba would work a great harm.[42] This, plus Teller's natural sympathy for the political aspirations of the Cubans, made him the ideal person to bring forth the historic self-denying amendment and thus temporarily block the imperialistic plans of the McKinley Administration.

But it was not enough to introduce such an amendment in Congress. The amendment also had to be passed, and the lobby for the beet sugar interests was certainly not powerful enough by itself to achieve this goal in the face of Administration opposition. But other forces helped achieve the speedy vote for the Teller Amendment. One was opposition to admitting to the American Union "an alien and insubordinate people, Roman Catholic in faith, with a large admixture of Negro blood."[43]* While the annexationists countered this with the argument that the problem would be solved easily by American immigration to the island after its acquisition, the influence of racism in hastening the adoption of the Teller Amendment cannot be ignored.[44]

Nor can one ignore the role played by those interests who stood to lose if Cuba was annexed—the Janney-McCook syndicate. As we have seen, the second contract between the syndicate and Estrada Palma had provided for payment to the syndicate of Cuban bonds worth

---

* In his famous speech in the Senate, Redfield Proctor opposed annexation as "a not wise policy to take in any people of foreign tongue and training and without any strong guiding American element," and he made it clear that it was the Cuban Negroes he had in mind. In time, he predicted, the Cubans, aided by experience and the "large influx of American and English immigration and money," would prove capable of self-government. (*Congressional Record*, 55th Cong., 2nd Sess., pp. 2916-19.)

$37,5000,000, "if independence is achieved, Spanish troops evacuated from Cuba, the independence of the island recognized by the United States, all of this without paying indemnification to Spain. . . ."

In the weeks before McKinley sent his message to Congress, McCook bombarded the President with memoranda and letters citing historical precedents and the achievements of the revolutionists to justify "the immediate recognition of the independence of the Republic of Cuba. . . ."[45] By the end of March, McCook was convinced that nothing could be achieved through the President who, in his opposition to recognition of Cuban independence, "has developed great force and seems to have hypnotized everybody." The only hope, then, lay with Congress.[46]

Just what the syndicate did while Congress was debating the Joint Resolution is not clear, but only a week before the Senate adopted the Teller Amendment, Charles H. Grosvenor of Ohio arose in the House of Representatives and asked, "Who is John J. McCook?" He answered: "He is the legal representative of the Cuban *Junta* of New York, behind which stands four hundred million dollars, more or less, of bonds that can be validated by the recognition of the independence of Cuba by the United States, and they will be destroyed by a policy that drives Spain out of Cuba in the interest of the American people. . . ."[47]

As one puts together the various pieces of the complicated story, what appears to have happened is that the syndicate promised the delivery of large amounts of Cuban bonds for support of the Teller Amendment in the Senate.* After the passage of the Joint Resolution, with the Teller Amendment included, Samuel Janney, representing the syndicate, came to Estrada Palma and asked for compensation for the partial fulfillment of the second contract. While Estrada Palma objected that the Joint Resolution as finally passed did not recognize the independence of the Cuban Republic, as stipulated in the contract, he felt that the syndicate was entitled to compensation for its work in behalf of the Resolution, especially the Teller Amendment. After the United States had declared war, Estrada Palma informed the Cuban *Junta* that although the contracts with McCook and Janney had not been fulfilled,

---

* Senator Foraker, however, denied publicly that Cuban bonds had influenced any votes since only $75,000 of bonds had been sold. "This he did not consider sufficient to influence the course of events." (Detroit *Free Press*, April 17, 1898.)

"the supreme idea of the Cubans had been achieved in that the Joint Resolution had stated that Cuba was in fact and by right independent," and that

> this result was owed in a large part to the repeated efforts of the forces which Mr. Janney headed, who put to the service of Cuba all their energy, all their influence, all their activity, as may be corroborated by Mr. Quesada who had occasion to observe in Washington the efficiency of the negotiations conducted by the above-mentioned gentlemen in relation to the important elements in that city.*

Estrada Palma stressed especially that it was due in large part to the syndicate "that the American government dropped all annexationist tendency or plan," a clear reference to the Teller Amendment. The Cuban *Junta* then unanimously recommended to the Council of Government "that the services lent to the cause of Cuba by Mr. Janney and his friends . . . have been valuable; that it appeared evident that to their activities is owed in great part the declaration obtained in the resolution of Congress, that the American government is not harboring any plan to annex the island of Cuba, and the information that Cuba, being pacified, the United States will leave the government of the island to the people of Cuba, a declaration which had great importance for the Cubans who placed their hopes in achieving independence for their country." The *Junta* recommended that these services be rewarded "with a compensation in proportion to their services. . . ."

The Council of Government of the Cuban Republic, acting on this recommendation, voted on October 10, 1898 to give the syndicate $2,000,000 in bonds of the Republic of Cuba, bearing six per cent interest, and Estrada Palma delivered them to Janney and McCook. The bonds were gradually redeemed by the Cubans after they received their independence, the final payment occurring on January 11, 1912.[48]

Cuban historians justify the relations between the Cuban *Junta* and the syndicate on the ground that it was made necessary by the "unjustified opposition" of the McKinley Administration to recognition of Cuban independence as part of a plot to annex Cuba, and that since the Teller Amendment frustrated this scheme, the lobbying in its behalf

---

* Gonzalo de Quesada did corroborate Estrada Palma's statement.

was action in a noble cause.⁴⁹* Yet one cannot avoid the conclusion that it was unfortunate for Cuba's future that its struggle for independence became so closely associated with forces which regarded this struggle solely in terms of the profits they could derive from it. The entire syndicate operation cast a dark shadow over the Cuban Revolution, and it was not easy to dispel the feeling among many supporters of Cuban independence that the Revolutionary leaders who had entered into such secret arrangements had strayed a long way from the principles enunciated by José Martí.

On April 18, 1898, the New York *Times* wrote furiously: "We

---

* Although there were rumors of the bond deal during the Spanish-American War, the first real evidence concerning it did not appear until 1904. In the summer of that year, the Cuban Department of Agriculture, Industry and Commerce, published in Spanish and English, in connection with the Louisiana Purchase Exposition in St. Louis, a pamphlet written by Manuel Luciano Díaz. Entitled *The Republic of Cuba: a brief sketch*, the pamphlet dealt mainly with the government of the Republic of Cuba and the economy of the island. Two pages, however, were devoted to the subject, "Cuban Bonds," and they briefly described the contract between the Delegate Plenipotentiary Estrada Palma and "persons of influence and position" in the United States. "As a result of this negotiation," Díaz wrote, "important work was done for the Cuban cause and the Delegate, to cover obligations thus contracted, delivered in May 1898 with the approval of the Cuban Council of Government, bonds to the value of $2,000,000, in payment of said obligations." (pp. 91-92. Copy of pamphlet in Pan-American Union, Columbus Memorial Library.)

This disclosure naturally caused wide repercussions in the American press. The New York *Tribune* accused Estrada Palma of having used bonds "to aid in bringing on war." In a cable to the *Tribune*, Estrada Palma, then President of the Republic of Cuba, declared that the statements made in the pamphlet were published without his "knowledge and authority," and he added "that not a single bond was given by me to any person in the United States except in cases where I received the full value therefor and that not a single one was given to any person in any way connected with any Department of the American Government." Estrada Palma's denial, of course, said very little, but Herbert C. Squiers, U.S. Minister to Cuba, noted in a dispatch to Secretary of State John Hay that Estrada Palma had explained to the Cuban Cabinet that "any other reply" but the one he had sent to the *Tribune* "might have offended Washington." (New York *Tribune*, Aug. 20, 1904; Squiers to Hay, Sept. 9, 1904, Consular Dispatches, Havana, NA.)

In a detailed memorandum to the State Department, Squiers described the whole story of the arrangement with the syndicate up to the time of the decision to pay Janney, McCook and their associates $2,000,000 in bonds which would be delivered "to very influential parties to whom it was due that the United States had pledged themselves never to exercise over Cuba any act of sovereignty or annex the Island." (Squiers to Hay, Consular Dispatches, Havana, Sept. 9, 1904, enclosing memorandum.)

hope the House will stand firm as a rock against that part of the Senate Resolution which recognizes the Republic of Cuba. If it should yield it would be the duty of the President to veto the entire resolution." Actually, McKinley had drafted a message vetoing any joint resolution of Congress that should provide for recognition of the Cuban Republic, meanwhile letting it be known through the press that "the President opposes such recognition."[50] The need for the veto message disappeared as Republican House leaders, headed by Speaker Reed, began to whip the House Republicans into line behind McKinley's position.* On April 18, by a vote of 178 to 156, the House adopted the Senate Resolutions, including the Teller Amendment, but only after striking out the section which gave recognition to "the Republic of Cuba as the true and lawful government of the island." On this vote, thirteen Republicans joined with Democrats to favor recognition, but Speaker Reed's powerful control in the House had prevented others who were wavering in their opposition to recognition from joining their colleagues.[51]

Since the House and the Senate had rejected each other's resolutions, the two bodies selected conference committees. At two o'clock in the morning of April 19, the conferees settled on a compromise resolution which kept the Teller Amendment and the provision for recognition of Cuban independence, but dropped any mention of the Cuban government. In the Senate, Democrats, Populists and a few Republicans continued to fight for recognition of the Cuban Republic, but under mounting pressure from the White House, the upper chamber capitulated and passed the compromise resolution 52 to 35. The House then passed the resolution 311 to 6. President McKinley signed the Joint Resolution on April 20, 1898.[52]

A week passed after McKinley signed the Joint Resolution and before Congress formally declared war. During this time the United States and Spain each maneuvered to make the other appear the aggressor. McKinley tried to use the Joint Resolution as an ultimatum to

---

* On April 19, Asher S. Hinds, chief clerk of the House, wrote in his diary: "Since Sunday we have been living in great parliamentary excitement. The Senate amended the House resolutions on Cuba by a proposition declaring the Gómez republic independent. Mr. Reed and the House leaders generally believed this proposition bad and vicious. . . ." (Asher S. Hinds Diary, Library of Congress.)

Spain, attempting to get Spain to reject it, so that the United States could break diplomatic relations and enter into war. But when the President signed the resolution on April 20, Spain immediately severed diplomatic relations, which prevented Woodford from delivering the resolution to the Spanish ministry. Two days later, McKinley ordered a naval blockade of Cuba, which actually began the war. Although there were demands for peace from labor and Socialist groups in the country,* Spain formally declared war on April 24 after naval action had started, announcing that "the people of North America . . . has [sic] exhausted our patience and has [sic] provoked war by its perfidious intrigues, by its treacherous acts, and by its violations of the law of nations and international conventions." She predicted: "The struggle will be short and decisive. The God of victories will grant us as brilliant and complete a victory as the right and justice of our cause demands. . . ."[53]

On April 25 McKinley asked Congress for a joint resolution recognizing a state of war. Both the House and the Senate passed the resolution by a voice vote the same day, which stated that the "war has existed since the 21st day of April," the day when the Spanish government gave passports to the American minister in Madrid and when the Navy began its blockade of the island of Cuba.

On April 30 Admiral Dewey's squadron of four cruisers and two gunboats steamed into Manila Bay and with a day's bombardment, initiated by the classic order, "You may fire when ready, Gridley," destroyed or put out of action all ten ships of the Spanish squadron as well as the shore batteries. Within four days of Dewey's victory, the leading spokesman for American imperialism, Henry Cabot Lodge,

---

* On April 15, 1898, *El Socialista* of Madrid, organ of the Socialist Labor Party of Spain, issued the following declaration:

"Who in Spain wants peace?

"All, that is the overwhelming majority of her people, her working class.

"The only exceptions are a comparatively small number of individuals, who place their own private interests and the interests of their own set above all other interests. . . .

Let Cuba be free.

"Let those who want war make up their own battalions of volunteers; let them carry on the war at their own risk; let them either go there themselves or send their children. . . .

"We, Socialists, want peace." (Reprinted in *The People*, May 15, 1898.)

wrote, "We must on no account let the islands go. . . . The American flag is up and it must stay."[54]

While the United States entered the war without having recognized the Republic of Cuba, the Cuban *Junta* in New York issued the statement that the resolutions adopted by Congress "as [they] stand are tantamount to the recognition of the Cuban republic," and promised that should force be necessary on the part of the United States to compel Spain to leave Cuba, "there will be the most complete co-operation by the Cuban government and its army, and practical guides will be places immediately at the service of the United States, and in every practicable way the Cubans will co-operate in expelling the common enemy. . . ."[55] Even though Máximo Gómez still believed firmly that American military intervention was not necessary and that the United States should confine its role to supplying the Liberating Army with arms and supplies to drive out the Spaniards, he backed the *Junta's* offer of full cooperation. In the beginning of May, 1898, Captain General Blanco appealed to Gómez that the time had come for Spaniards and Cubans to bury their past differences and unite against the invader from the United States, assuring the chief of the Liberating Army that once the American army was defeated in such a joint effort, and "once the foreign enemy is ousted from the island, Spain, as a loving mother, will open her arms to another new daughter of the nations of the new world which speaks her language." Gómez promptly rejected this appeal. In his reply, never before published in any American historical work dealing with this period, Gómez wrote sharply:

> Your audacity in proposing peace terms to me again dumbfounds me when you know that Cubans and Spaniards can never live in peace on the soil of Cuba. You represent on this continent an old and discredited monarchy, and we are fighting for an American principle, the principle of Bolívar and Washington. You say that we belong to the same race and invite me to fight against a foreign invader, but you are again mistaken because there are no differences of blood or race.
>
> I believe in only one race: humanity, and for me there are only good and evil nations. Spain has been until now an evil one, while the United States at this time is fulfilling for Cuba a duty for humanity and civilization. From the savage dark Indian to the refined blond Englishman, a man for me deserves respect according

to his honesty and feelings whatever may be the country or race to which he belongs or the religion which he practices.

This is what nations are to me, and up to the present I have had only feelings of admiration for the United States. I have written President McKinley and General Miles thanking them for American intervention in Cuba. I do not see the danger of extermination by the United States to which you refer in your letter.* If it does happen, history will condemn it.⁵⁶†

Undoubtedly Gómez, like the Cuban *Junta*, was convinced that the resolutions passed by Congress were "tantamount to the recognition of the Cuban Republic."‡ Orville H. Platt, a bitter foe of Cuban independence, agreed. "I believe," he wrote angrily, "that the legal and practical result of the first resolution consists in recognizing the sovereignty of the would-be government of the insurgents. What else could this resolution signify? The people are free and independent.... It is clear that this phrase is used to designate a free government." ⁵⁷ But there was a wide gulf between what the resolution signified and what the Administration was prepared to do to carry this into practical effect. The truth is that the Cubans had no guarantee that the Republic would be recognized by the United States, and "tantamount to ... recognition" was a far cry from actual recognition. The Cuban revolutionary leaders guaranteed to cooperate fully with the forces of the United States in military action against Spain, but they failed to demand, in

---

* In his letter, Blanco had written that the intentions of the United States, whose "naturally acquisitive nature" was well known, were "not only to deprive Spain of her flag on the Cuban soil, but also to exterminate the Cuban people because of their Spanish blood." (Portell Vilá, *Historia de la Guerra, op. cit.*, pp. 189-90.)

† Gómez's rejection of Blanco's offer was endorsed by the governing body of the Republic of Cuba. On May 10, the governing council, meeting at Sebastopol, Camagüey, rejected a proposal by Spain for an agreement between Spaniards and Cubans to unite in combating the American invading army, with the promise of independence for Cuba following the defeat of the United States. Instead, the council announced that the Cuban Revolution would make common cause with the United States, "a just and strong nation, ready to assist us." (*Ibid.*, p. 192.)

‡ Ramiro Guerra y Sánchez, the distinguished Cuban historian, writes that with the passage of the Joint Resolution, "justice was at last rendered Cuba which for many years had fought to obtain independence and liberation...." (*En el Camino de la Independencia. Estudio histórico sobre la rivalidad de los Estados Unidos y la Gran Bretaña en sus relaciones con la independencia de Cuba*, la Habana, 1930, p. 205.)

return, a concrete guarantee from the Administration in Washington of recognition of the Cuban Republic. This failure almost made inevitable the innumerable difficulties and problems for the Revolution soon after the United States entered the war.

Undoubtedly the revolutionary leaders felt that the Joint Resolution with the Teller Amendment as part of it was sufficient protection of Cuban sovereignty since, as they saw it, it was "a sacred contract in the eyes of the world."[58] Under these circumstances, it is hardly surprising that the revolutionists, forgetting the warnings of Martí and Maceo, enthusiastically greeted the entrance of the United States into the war. In due time many of them were to realize they had made a mistake. For it was becoming clear by the time the United States entered the war that the Joint Resolution was not an insuperable obstacle for American imperialism. To be sure, leading annexationists were embittered by the Teller Amendment. "I deeply regret the fourth paragraph in the resolution as passed," Whitelaw Reid wrote to President McKinley on April 19, 1898. "We are making ourselves morally responsible for decent government in Cuba, and we can't wash our hands of it by turning Spain out, by merely telling them to set up for themselves. I hope they show themselves more orderly and less liable to throw themselves into civil war and banditry than has been believed. But if the result of our efforts is merely to establish a second Haiti near our own coast, it will be so pitiful an outcome from a great opportunity as to make Mr. Gladstone's pledge to 'scuttle out of Egypt' respectable by comparison."[59] The opportunity, of course, was to annex Cuba!

The New York *Herald* which was later to renounce the Teller Amendment, wrote on April 19, 1898, that "it will be accepted and supported loyally by all the people, as an essential and highly important part of the law of the land." But the Chicago *Tribune* urged the disturbed annexationists not to worry excessively. In a prophetic editorial entitled "Our Future Relations to Cuba," it declared on April 23, 1898:

> Such a disclaimer [as the Teller Amendment] is eminently proper. It expresses the present intentions and feelings of the people of the United States. How long their present sentiments will remain unchanged is something which the future alone can determine. . . . It is far from being the intention of the American government or people to drive out the Spanish devil and then allow the devils of disorder, misrule, and anarchy to govern Cuba. The

conditions which have prevailed at different times in Hayti and Santo Domingo will not be permitted to obtain in Cuba. . . . So it may come to pass that the "best interests" of the people of Cuba will call for an indefinite continuance of American guidance and supervision. The American protectorate, once established in Cuba, may not end until the children or grandchildren of those who help to free the island have passed from the stage. . . . The future state of the island must not be allowed to get worse than or as bad as the present state, even although, as the way to avert that calamity, the American flag should float in Cuba forever.

For over a century, Spain has used the bogey of "another Haiti" to justify keeping the Cubans oppressed and crushing their long and frequent struggles for independence. Now, as the United States entered the war against Spain, there were powerful forces in the country who were already preparing to use the same false issue to deprive the Cubans of the independence for which they had fought and were still fighting.

Whether or not it had an inside track to the thinking of the President, the *Tribune,* as recent scholarship has demonstrated, pointed up the direction in which McKinley was moving. In stating his opposition to the "so-called Cuban Republic"—his own phrase—McKinley observed: "In case of intervention our conduct would be subject to the approval or disapproval of such a government. We would be required to submit to its direction and to assume to it the mere relation of a friendly ally." [60] But what was wrong with the role of being a "friendly ally"? Clearly, in that case, the United States would not be able to do with Cuba as it wished. "The United States," notes Jack C. Lane, "would then be forced to seek the approval of such a government for a policy establishing Cuba within America's new empire. If given a choice, the insurgents were not likely to acquiesce quietly to having their country made an appendage of an American empire."

As we shall see in the next volume, the Cubans were not to be given that choice.[61]*

---

* In his defense of McKinley for refusing to recognize the independence of Cuba, Paul S. Holbe writes that after the war, the President "brought about the speedy end of military government in Cuba . . . [and] attempted to protect Cuba from those Americans who sought unwarranted privileges there. . . ." Professor Holbe offers no evidence for this statement and, as will be evident in the next volume, the opposite actually took place. (For Holbe's view, *see* his "Presidential Leadership in Foreign Affairs: William McKinley and the Turpie-Foraker Amendment," *American Historical Review,* vol. LXXII, July, 1967, pp. 1334-35.)

CHAPTER XIV
Why the United States Went to War

IN THE *New York Times Book Review* of January 29, 1961, Frank Friedel, the author of *Splendid Little War,* a pictorial history of the "Spanish-American War,"* wrote: "Today, when Fidel Castro and his claque are screaming epithets at the United States and charging that the Spanish-American War was fought only for imperialistic reasons, it is heartening to be reminded of the fundamentally humanitarian motives that took American into the war." The reminding was done by Ernest R. May's *Imperial Democracy: The Emergence of America as a Great Power* which Friedel was reviewing. But Friedel did not quote from May the following sentences which subvert his thesis: "An imperialist movement had come into being and was not to be demolished. . . . Its leaders had discerned that public opinion could be captured for an imperialist cause, if only that cause could be clothed in the rhetoric of piety. They were stubborn, willful men. . . ."†

As Professor Friedel must know, the thesis that the Spanish-American War was an imperialistic war, fought for imperialistic reasons, did

---

* In his book, published in 1958, Friedel does not refer to a single Cuban source and does not mention the Cubans at all except in contemptuous terms.

† Later, in his book, Professor May forgets this statement and contradicts himself, emphasizing only that mass hysteria, developed over the Cuban situation in 1896 and again in 1897, compelled President McKinley to lead his country "unwillingly toward a war which he did not want for a cause in which he did not believe." (New York, 1961, p. 237.) But he himself pictures McKinley in December, 1897, a period not marked by "mass hysteria," as having concluded that if Spain's reforms should not have brought peace to Cuba by the opening of the rainy season in the Spring, intervention would be necessary. Certainly, then, when McKinley asked Congress for intervention, he was only carrying into effect a program decided upon months before.

281

not originate with Fidel Castro. Long before Castro and the Revolutionary Army ousted the dictator Fulgencio Batista and later set up the first Socialist government in the Western hemisphere, this thesis was already advanced. Keir Hardie, the British labor and Socialist leader, wrote shortly after the Spanish-American war began: "Personally all my sympathies are with the Cubans—that they are entitled to self-government is not to be denied—but I cannot believe in the purity of the American motive. . . . The American man in the street is doubtless honest and sincere in his zeal for Cuban freedom, but he is simply shouting—without knowing it, of course—at the prompting of others." The "others," he made it clear, were the trusts and Wall Street financiers who were intent on extending American economic dominance over Cuba, Latin America and the Far East. Hardie concluded: "Desiring as I do to see Cuba freed, I frankly declare that I have not the slightest sympathy with this American-made war, nor do I believe in the motives which inspire it." [2] His view was endorsed by the London *Justice,* a Socialist paper, which asserted: "Modern wars have within a couple of generations become exclusively wars of commerce. The pretense of humanity, patriotism, religion, etc., is already too played out to deceive any one any more. All who are not willfully blind recognize that the one object of all modern wars is the material gain of the capitalist class. A striking illustration of this is furnished by the present Spanish-American struggle. The pretense of humanitarian sentiment has, of course, once more been trotted out. The interests of civilization and humanity required that America should intervene and rescue Cuba from the Spanish yoke. The real interests that move the humanitarian patriotism of the American nation is a sugar ring with tobacco in the background." [3]

But it was not only the Socialists in England who questioned the humanitarian motives for American intervention. The *Investors' Review* noted that "there is in America a strong financial as well as political interest in the Cuban question." *The Speaker* agreed: "A new order of financial and economic considerations has been substituted for the desire of the slaveholders to find new lands for the employment of their human capital. . . ." Even the *Times* of London argued that "American humanitarian sentiment" was a disguise for economic considerations.[4]

In France, too, the United States' profession of humanitarian motives as a basis for intervention was ridiculed. Socialists and non-

Socialists alike emphasized that humanitarian motives were merely a disguise for commercial desires—the major cause being the desire for commercial conquest of all the Caribbean Islands and Latin America. Paul Louis, the Socialist, declared that the United States, a great capitalist power, was simply following the example of France, England, Germany, and Italy in its desire for expansion. The American promise not to annex Cuba by force was laughed at in France. "Europe, adept and sophisticated at the game of imperialism," writes James Louis Whitehead, "realized that there were other ways than force of achieving one's ends." [5]

In the United States, of course, there were many who questioned that the war was caused by the humanitarian desire to obtain Cuban freedom, and none more effectively than *The People,* official organ of the Socialist Labor Party and edited by Daniel De Leon. *The People* challenged the sincerity of the capitalists' pretended sympathy for the struggling Cubans by pointing to the multitude of oppressions and injustices at home. In America, too, "the 'Reconcentradoes' [sic] are seen all around . . . famishing figures of all ages and all sexes, premature corpses, bearing either the marks of slow and gradual starvation, or the marks of sudden death by bullet and bayonet, or mutilation by factory machine." [6]* Cuban freedom was only a ruse to justify war:

> That Cuban freedom . . . is not the real object of our Government, a cursory review of the situation will demonstrate.
> For three years the Cuban insurgents have been battling against Spain. During this period what was our Government's attitude? It sedulously sought to prevent all aid from reaching the Cuban insurgents. Nor is this all. Having at last come to the opinion that Cuba should be free, what would have been the natural course, if what our Government really was after was the liberation of the island? Would a declaration of war against Spain have been necessary? No.

---

* The *Appeal to Reason,* another Socialist paper, compared the conditions of the laborers in the United States to those of the concentration camps in Cuba. It called the factories of the cities and the coal mines, "*reconcentrados.* . . . In our struggle to pluck the eye of our Spanish brother, let us not overlook the beam in our own." (May 7, 1898.) Keir Hardie made the same point: "When the people of the United States have rid themselves of the Thugs who are throttling American liberty and enslaving the American people, time enough then to spend blood and treasure in removing the woes of others." (British *Labour Leader,* June 4, 1898.)

If the insurrection of Cuba is powerful enough, numerically, to maintain the country free, all that was necessary would have been to recognize her independence, and then open our ports and our markets to both belligerents—Spanish as well as Cubans. The Cubans, suffering from want of arms, could have got here all they wanted; their bonds would have sold readily, and furnished them with an ample treasury to equip themselves. Our Government might have added to that the sending of a Minister Plenipotentiary to reside near Gen. Máximo Gómez. . . . The freedom of Cuba would have been assured. But it would have been assured without war on our part. It is because war was wanted and needed by our Government that the peaceful and natural method was not resorted to.

The *freedom* of Cuba is but a pretext,* the real object was *war* and war is but the means to an end that our ruling capitalist class of the Republican variety has clearly in mind, and promises to pursue athwart the din of "patriotism," and wading knee-deep through the blood of the American as well as the Cuban working class.

War, *The People* argued, was necessary as a result of economic conditions in the United States where "good times" had failed to materialize and external conflict was always a good way of diverting attention from social evils at home. War was necessary "to protect American commercial interests in Cuba." War was necessary because American capitalism was finding it necessary to "spread out and fight for markets," and capitalism had to expand in order to survive. "The capitalist class needs markets. It needs them because it has on hand more goods than the people can buy." Not only would the war provide markets in Cuba for American capitalism, but it would open the vast new markets of the Far East. "To make any attempt to capture part of that new market for the capitalists of this country requires a larger naval force and army than we now have. We will need ships to take territory, and men to hold the territory when taken. To attempt to do that in time of peace has failed; let us therefore raise trouble with some

---

* The Cleveland *Plain Dealer* agreed with *The People*, insisting that the United States should "do away with pretext," hypocrisy and sentimental bosh over intervention for humanity's sake, and admit that its real motive was "the ultimate annexation of Cuba for commercial exploitation." (April 23, 1898, and Auxiery, Jr., "The Cuban Crisis," *op. cit.*, p. 295.)

back-number country—Spain, for instance, and during the excitement get what we want. Presto, it is done." [7]

Algernon Lee, Socialist editor, wrote at the time of McKinley's message to Congress asking for a declaration of war, that the President had spoken truly when he emphasized that "protection of American interests" was sufficient reason for United States intervention:

> This is the real motive of the war. And let us clearly understand what the phrase means. "Protection of American interests" does not mean protection of the Americans who plow and sow and reap, who pick the cotton, who dig the coal and iron, who grind the wheat, who weave the cloth, who build the houses. It means protection of the interests of those who farm the farmers, those who work the workers, the idle capitalist class that lives by the sweat of other men's brows.
>
> If this government wished to establish Cuban independence it had the opportunity more than three years ago of rescognizing the insurgents. And the people would have approved of that act three years ago. But this would not serve "business interest." On the contrary, this government (under Cleveland first, then under McKinley) sent revenue cutters to help the Spaniards by intercepting filibustering parties. And so matters were allowed to go on from bad to worse until a war could be forced upon the country.
>
> And what is to be the end of it all? The United States, say the jingoes, will annex Hawaii, the Philippines and other Pacific islands, Puerto Rico, perhaps even a port in the Canaries, and will gain control of Cuba. . . . To the American capitalists it will mean new fields in which to carry on their operations. . . . We repeat, to establish Cuban independence no war was necessary. Recognition of Cuba was withheld until war became inevitable in order that the Hills, the Rockefellers, the Havemeyers, the Carnegies, the Pierpont Morgans might reapt their harvest. . . .
>
> There are many of the thinking who will call it treason for us to speak as we have. For our part we know of no loyalty higher than loyalty to truth, no treason worse than that of the man who bows to falsehood because it is popular. The history of the past and the conditions of the present justify our words. The events of the future will prove their truth. And many of those who now echo the cry of "Treason" will in two years' time be ready to curse the men who misled and betrayed them.[8]

On October 26, 1907, the Socialist weekly *Appeal to Reason*, published in Girard, Kansas, carried an answer to a question sent in by a reader, inquiring what were the causes "which brought about the war with Spain." The answer read in part:

> Cuba was the prize for which the Spanish-American war was fought. The island was rich in natural resources, the development of which would yield profits to the capital invested as well as supply a market for the growing surplus of American manufacture. . . . The capital of the United States was under the necessity of finding new fields in which to operate. Visions of Havana franchises and fertile sugar plantations rose before the profit-hungry ruling class of this country. . . .

The adherents of the theory that the war was caused solely by humanitarian factors dismissed these Socialist interpretations as reflecting "the Marxist Machiavellian analysis of history." But they could not easily dismiss the analysis presented by Frederick Emory, chief of the bureau of foreign commerce of the Department of Commerce, who wrote in *World's Work* of January, 1902:

> Underlying the popular sentiment, which might have evaporated in time, which forced the United States to take up arms against Spanish rule in Cuba, were our economic relations with the West Indies and the South American republics. So strong was this commercial instinct that had there been no emotional cause, such as the alleged enormities of Spanish rule or the destruction of the *Maine*, we would have doubtless taken steps in the end to abate with a strong hand what seemed to be an economic nuisance. . . . The Spanish-American War was but an incident of a general movement of expansion which had its root in the changed environment of an industrial capacity far beyond our domestic powers of consumption. It was seen to be necessary for us not only to find foreign purchasers for our goods, but to provide the means of making access to foreign markets easy, economical and safe.

Commenting editorially on this analysis by a government official in an important post dealing with trade expansion, the New York *Tribune* concluded: "The war in which we intervened was pre-eminently an economical war, provoked by commercial, financial and industrial forces."[9]

This interpretation of the forces that produced American intervention in Cuba was endorsed in the same year, 1902, by the noted British economist J. A. Hobson in his book, *Imperialism: A Study.*

Hobson stressed the differentiation between colonialism and imperialism. The former had characterized American development until the years immediately before the Spanish-American War which marked the rapid growth of industry, the formation of huge trusts, the lack of outlets for investment of the surplus profits of the trust, and the consequent drive for foreign acquisitions: "It was this sudden demand for foreign markets for manufactures and for investments which was avowedly responsible for the adoption of Imperialism as a political policy and practice by the Republican Party to which the great industrial and financial chiefs belonged, and which belonged to them. . . ." Hobson warned his readers not to be deceived by such slogans as "humanitarianism," "manifest destiny," and "mission of civilization," raised by politicians and propagandists. They were merely the spokesmen for the monopolists. "It was Messrs. Rockefeller, Pierpont Morgan, and their associates who needed Imperialism and who fastened it upon the shoulders of the great Republic of the West. They needed Imperialism because they desired to use the public resources of the country to find profitable employment for their capital which otherwise would be superfluous." Hobson concluded that the Spanish-American War was an imperialist war, and that "American Imperialism was the natural product of the economic pressure of a sudden advance of capitalism which could not find occupation at home and needed foreign markets, for goods and investments."

In his classic work, *Imperialism: The Highest Stage of Capitalism*, written in 1917, V. I. Lenin paid tribute to Hobson's analysis as "an excellent and comprehensive description of the principal economic and political characteristics of imperialism." Although Lenin differed with Hobson on basic issues,* he agreed with the British economist in characterizing the Spanish-American War as an imperialist war, fought by the United States for imperialist reasons.[10]

During the 1920's and early 1930's, several American historians also characterized the Spanish-American War as an imperialist war, although their description of imperialism was closer to Hobson than

---

* While Hobson focused on symptoms of trustified expansionism, Lenin concentrated on the whole system of capitalism in its imperialist stage, showing the inevitable path which imperialism must follow. Again, whereas Hobson found it possible to reform capitalism, Lenin called for its abolition, insisting that imperialism was inevitable in capitalism and could not be reformed.

to Lenin. Harold U. Faulkner stated in 1924 that the cause for the war with Spain was to be found in the fact that by 1898 the United States was "sufficiently advanced for financial imperialism," and that the war was fought for markets and fields for investments.[11] Professor Harry Elmer Barnes wrote in 1930 "that the passing of the frontier in 1890 produced the necessity of discovering a field for expansion and investment elsewhere than within the boundaries of the United States. The dispute with Spain over Cuba provided but a welcome pretext and provided a moral issue which allowed the formal and systematic initiation of a process which had long been in preparation."[12] Likewise, Charles A. Beard, in his study *The Idea of National Interest*, published in 1934, wrote: "Within a few years the movement for territorial expansion, conforming to the commercial type, was renewed in the Caribbean direction, with the Cuban Revolution of 1895 as the occasion for action." Beard acknowledged that American concern about Cuba came under the heading of "the national interest," but that "supplementary interests were plainly economic."[13]

The 1930's also saw the publication of several historical works which challenged the interpretation of the Spanish-American War as having been caused by United States imperialism in need of markets, sources of cheap raw materials, and new fields for investment. Writing in 1930, Louis Hacker suggested that the war resulted from an attempt by the Republican Party "to take men's minds off vexing domestic concerns."[14] Several historians designated the "yellow press" as the primary cause of the war. Marcus M. Wilkinson in 1932 concluded that the press drove McKinley, Congress, and the people into war. He declared that the war marked a triumph of the sensational press which, led by the New York *Journal* and *World*, "left the American public reeling from a bombardment of half-truths, mistatements of facts, rumors, and faked dispatches," and that the McKinley Administration, "sensing the popular tide . . . and egged on by a 'jingo' Congress, proposed war."[15] Two years later, Joseph E. Wisan singled out one sensational newspaper publisher, William Randolph Hearst, and accorded him first place in promoting the war. He concluded that fighting would not have started "had not the appearance of Hearst in New York journalism precipitated a bitter battle for newspaper circulation."[16] This school of interpretation received an additional adherent in 1940, George W. Auxier, Jr., who published a study of the Midwestern press in which he noted that while sensationalism was not particularly well represented in the area, the newspapers caused the war.[17]*

But so far as the vast majority of American historians was concerned, the decisive blow to the interpretation of the Spanish-American War as an imperialist war was delivered by the appearance in 1934 of Julius W. Pratt's "American Business and the Spanish-American War," and in 1936 of his work, *Expansionists of 1898: The Acquisition of Hawaii and the Spanish Islands*. After a study of financial and commercial journals, Pratt stated that the vast majority of business and financial interests of the country until the last moment "strongly opposed action that would lead to war with Spain," and the few who did support it did so solely "on humanitarian grounds." While he does not exonerate the entire American business community of any responsibility for the Spanish crisis, this is clearly implied in his thesis that American business did not favor, but rather actively opposed, the Spanish-American War, and in his statement that "business interests in the United States were generally opposed to expansion or indifferent to it until after May 1, 1898." Not the business community, Pratt argued, but strategically placed intellectuals (with non-economic motives) were responsible for American imperialism.† But once the war

---

* Yet in his unpublished doctoral dissertation, which is a much more careful survey of mid-western opinion, Dr. Auxier notes that "especially from about the middle of March 1, 1898 . . . the economic motive stands out in relief as the administration papers gradually gave way to the war sentiment and the opposition editors more readily admitted the Marxian implications of our purposes." He concludes that editors of a representative cross section of the press, though divided in their attitudes regarding Cuban belligerency, "seemed primarily interested in assisting the President bring back domestic prosperity." (*op. cit.*, pp. 21, 209, 295-99.)

† These influential politicians and intellectuals were Alfred T. Mahan, Theodore Roosevelt, Henry Cabot Lodge, Henry Adams, and his younger brother Brooks. They formed a loose coterie that vigorously sought a policy of expansion. Mahan selected the commercial needs of a great power as the foundation of his theory, and argued that a large navy and foreign bases were necessary to protect markets and a sizeable merchant fleet. Applying his general theory to the United States, he pointed out that basic to American growth were annexation of Hawaii, construction and ownership of an Isthmian Canal and control of Cuba. Lodge and Roosevelt accepted Mahan's ideas as the basis for their "large policy" which called for expansion of national interests. They set out to make their country the leading power in the western hemisphere," possessed of a great navy, owning and controlling an Isthmian canal, holding naval bases in the Caribbean and the Pacific, and contesting on at least even terms with the greatest powers, the naval and commercial supremacy of the Pacific Ocean and

started, and once the expansionists had begun to press for the retention of the Philippines, the attitude of the business community changed. Then the arguments of the expansionists about the commercial possibilities in the new Pacific acquisition brought a significant number of businessmen over to the expansionist side.[18]

> American business had been either opposed or indifferent to the expansionist philosophy which had arisen since 1890. But almost at the moment when the war began, a large section of American business had . . . been converted to the belief that a program of territorial expansion would serve its purposes. Hence business, in the end, welcomed the "large policy" and exerted its share of pressure for the retention of the Spanish islands and such related policies as the annexation of Hawaii and the construction of an isthmian canal.

"The war," Pratt concludes, "was largely the work, not of business men but economists, sociologists, and historians." [19]*

Now American historians, taking their cue from Wilkinson, Wisan, and especially from Pratt, began to construct the thesis that the Spanish-American War was the result of mass hysteria produced by the propaganda of the "yellow press," aided and abetted by the Cuban *Junta;* the "self-assertive egoism and altruistic idealism" of the American people, apart from business leaders, who wanted war and got it after a "popular clamor for war"; the rise of Social Darwinism with its insistence that a struggle for existence "among the nations and peoples would result in the survival of the fittest," e.g., the United States and white Anglo-Saxons; the result of the influence of "a little group of young

---

the Far East." (Julius W. Pratt, "The 'Large Policy' of 1898," *Mississippi Valley Historical Review,* vol. XIX, 1932, p. 223.)

Brooks Adams, related to Lodge through marriage and a friend of Roosevelt, published a volume in 1895, *The Law of Civilization and Decay* in which he observed that an imperialistic nation was healthier than one content with its own borders, and advocated American control of the Western hemisphere and economic dominance of Asia. His brother, Henry, worked actively in Washington in favor of intervention in Cuba.

* Actually, this thesis had been somewhat casually advanced as early as 1928 by Leland H. Jenks: "If ever there was a war which the people of the country, as distinguished from their political and business leaders demanded, it was the war which the United States began on April 21, 1898." (*Our Cuban Colony: A Study in Sugar,* New York, 1928, p. 57.)

Republicans" who sought "national power for its own sake." The latter —the "original imperialists"—were motivated (according to this theory) solely by the "political possibilities of imperialism," and they forced a weak and indecisive President McKinley, who displayed "no interest in international politics" and had "no policy of imperialism on which to stand or fall" to lead the country into war.[20]

In the rush to present the new picture of the causes of the Spanish-American War, economic factors were cast aside. Charles A. Beard joined the group of American historians who emphasized that emotional and psychological factors were largely responsible for the war. In 1939, he advanced the theory that the war was sold to the country by politicians who were frightened by the "specter of Bryanism," and were seeking to divert the attention of the people from the grave problems that lay beneath the revolt of the farmers expressed in the Populist movement. But his earlier emphasis on territorial expansion and economic interests that stood to gain from the war was now abandoned.[21] Twenty-seven years after he had first stressed the prominence of economic causes for the war, Harold U. Faulkner stated in 1951 that "the point of view taken by certain economic historians that the United States went to war with Spain primarily for economic reasons seems not warranted by the evidence." [22] In his own book, *Politics, Reform and Expansion, 1890-1910*, published in 1959, Professor Faulkner found that the business interests in 1898 were worried about the possibility of war, and were definitely on the side of peace.[23] Also influenced by Pratt, Foster R. Dulles rewrote his earlier works on American imperialism to lay added emphasis upon psychological and political factors while virtually eliminating previous allusions to economic causes for the conflict between the United States and Spain.[24]*

The non-economic interpretation of the causes of the war was reflected in nearly all historical works dealing with this period. Matthew Josephson emphasized that opposed to the "war party" was a group strong for peace, the "Big Business faction."[25] Arthur M. Schlesinger wrote that there can be no question that McKinley was for peace and that his desire "was ardently backed by Big Business and Wall

---

* In 1965 Dulles wrote that "economic considerations had little to do with the popular sentiment" that led to war in 1898. (Foster Rhea Dulles, *Prelude to World Power: American Diplomatic History, 1860-1900*, New York, 1965, p. 89.)

Street."²⁶ Thomas A. Bailey stated that during the hectic months before the actual intervention, "perhaps the most single restraint on the jingoistic spirit was big business. Except for a relatively small group . . . the financial and commercial interests of the United States were almost solidly opposed to war."²⁷ Samuel Flagg Bemis called the charge that American business desired intervention "a legend once eagerly accepted in academic circles." But now it was clear that rather than desiring intervention, "business interests in the United States were to the last opposed to any war with Spain."²⁸ Nor, states A. Whitney Griswold, did commercial groups interested in the Far East desire a war, and he goes on to say that "it is safe to say that the handful of Americans engaged in commerce with the Far East at first saw no connection between *Cuba Libre* and the open door in China. Neither did the American people as a whole."²⁹ Howard K. Beale, in his study of Theodore Roosevelt, concluded that Roosevelt was more interested in power than economics. He rejected entirely the influence of economic factors in bringing on the war: "A few men in powerful positions were able to plunge the nation into an imperialist career that it never explicitly decided to follow." But these men were the "political imperialists" like Lodge and Roosevelt, not the business groups.³⁰

If economic forces did appear as a factor in the agitation for the war, they appeared in a strangely inverted way. "The threat to peace came from a new quarter," writes W. E. Leuchtenberg, "from the South and the West, the strongholds of Democracy and Free Silver." The Bryanites had hoped that the war would put a strain on the currency so that the opponents of free silver would collapse. Since they saw that Wall Street opposed the war, they claimed that the Administration's "peace policy" was the product of a bankers' conspiracy to deny free silver to the American people and independence to the people of Cuba. This theory, Leuchtenberg concedes, can be questioned, but there can be no doubt that, in the main, the business interests of the country opposed the war.

> McKinley came to power as the "advance agent of prosperity" and business interests were almost unanimous in opposing any agitation of the Cuban Question that might lead to war. Contrary to the assumption of Leninist historians, it was Wall Street which, first and last, resisted a war which was to bring America its overseas empire.³¹

Richard Hofstadter summed up the position of the dominant school of American historians when he wrote that "since Julius W. Pratt published his *Expansionists of 1898* . . . it has been obvious that any interpretation of America's entry upon the path of imperialism in the nineties in terms of rational economic motives would not fit the facts and that the historian who approaches the event with preconceptions no more supple than those, say, of Lenin's *Imperialism,* would be helpless." While uncritically accepting Pratt's thesis, Hofstadter, in accounting for the Spanish-American War, advances what he calls "The Psychic Thesis." He concedes that a number of factors, in varying degrees of intensity, were responsible for the war, including economic factors. But he argues that war finally came because at the moment these war-producing factors came to a head, the country was undergoing what he calls a "psychic crisis." The depression which followed the Panic of 1893 frustrated the American people, Hofstadter argues, and they responded to their frustrations with aggression in all directions. Imperialism followed naturally from the psychic—not basically economic —necessities of the moment. For their own selfish purposes, the "manufacturers of inevitability," the "yellow press" and the imperialist "junto" around Theodore Roosevelt and Henry Cabot Lodge, were thereby able to pervert the sympathies of the American people for the suffering Cubans into a palatable argument for a war and an empire against the basic interests and traditions of the American people. Pointing to McKinley's war message to Congress, Hoftstadter notes that the Spanish had actually capitulated and that war was unnecessary. "Evidently," he writes, "McKinley had concluded that what was wanted in the United States was not so much freedom of Cuba as a *war* for the freedom of Cuba." [32]

The first critical analysis of the Pratt thesis was made by Arthur Barcan in his unpublished Master's thesis presented to the graduate faculty of Columbia University in 1940, entitled "American Imperialism and the Spanish American War."* Beginning by noting that big

---

* Barcan was also critical of an earlier unpublished Master's thesis submitted to Columbia University in 1937 by Edward N. Saveth entitled, "Economic Background of the Spanish-American War." Saveth, supporting the Pratt thesis, concluded: "Despite the development of a 'large policy' in foreign affairs by certain economic and political leaders and the tendency of American business to advance along such lines, it is doubtful whether American economic interests

business controlled the government of the United States under McKinley, Barcan observed that it was inconceivable "that the administration's decision to enter a war was supposedly unfavorable to big business." He then proceeds to a detailed analysis of business, financial and industrial journals for the period 1895 to 1898, a number of them ignored by Pratt, and concluded that he was convinced from this study that the Spanish-American War was "no more the freak—a nonimperialist venture in an imperialist setting, a war opposed by business men in a country controlled by them—but it now becomes a more plausible account of how the United States was forced into war to satisfy her new imperialist appetites, aided and abetted by business men who were in it to gain directly or indirectly from the war." He found nothing in his research to justify the conclusion of "mass business opposition to war" in commercial, business, and financial journals, or the concept that "the United States did not find its imperialist urge until the war was under way, as if a country can, within the space of one month, develop the necessary resources and needs that produce imperialism." He showed in his study that the rapid economic growth of the United States had developed an increasing need for markets for surplus goods and capital. By 1898, these expanding American capitalists found themselves in discouraging, and even precarious straits. In Cuba, the Revolution had for three years disrupted economic activity, destroyed valuable capital investments, and held back further exploitation of the island's great resources, while Spain had proven herself impotent to restore order, a condition highly necessary for continued imperialist activity in the "Pearl of the Antilles." In Hawaii, Americans had already assumed control, but their desire and need for annexation to the United States was balked by persistent efforts of domestic beet and cane sugar growers, aided by anti-imperialist elements in the country. In China, American capitalists found profitable fields for trade and capital increasingly menaced by the monopolistic encroachments of European imperialisms. American capitalists, Barcan discovered from his research, "now turned covetous glances in the direction of the Philippines, which were sufficiently close to the Asiatic mainland to

---

either favored war with Spain or looked upon it as a means whereby the Spanish colonies might be coveted." Only when the war had started, "was the large policy operative, being hitherto obscured by other factors." (p. 40.)

serve as an excellent base for American navy and ships, thus bolstering the American position in China. It was the need to acquire the Philippines, and the inability to annex Hawaii except under extreme conditions as a 'war measure' that bolstered and gave impetus to the war drive in March and April, 1898, supposedly concerned merely with the desire to free the Cubans from the Spanish 'yoke'. . . . Nor is it mere accident that the first important step in the fight to drive Spain out of Cuba was Admiral Dewey's victory in Manila Bay." Barcan concluded his study with the statement that while the war cannot be explained only in terms of economic factors, "the business imperialist interests were dominant." [33]

Since Barcan wrote his study—in many ways a limited analysis of the whole problem because of a failure to examine many available sources which would have further buttressed his conclusion—the Pratt thesis has come under increasing criticism. In 1935, in an unpublished doctoral dissertation at the University of Pittsburgh, Ralph Dewar Bald, Jr. proved that the journals of the leading industries and businesses in the United States repeatedly emphasized, beginning with 1885, "that the country was faced with the necessity of securing overseas markets for industrial surpluses." These journals published and endorsed the call by Mahan, Roosevelt, Lodge and other imperialist-minded intellectuals and politicians, demanding overseas expansion, and giving special attention to the value of annexing Cuba as a source for trade and investment of capital. Rather than remaining indifferent to imperialism, as Pratt had asserted, the organs of the business community in the early 1890's "contributed importantly to the creation of an atmosphere of opinion favorable to expansion." [34] Since Pratt relied heavily on a few trade journals in reaching his conclusions, Bald's more intensive study of these periodicals showed that the Pratt thesis was in need of revision.

A more direct critical analysis of the Pratt thesis appeared in 1958 in Nancy Lenore O'Connor's article, "The Spanish American War: A Re-evaluation of Its Causes," published in *Science & Society*, a Marxist scholarly journal. Miss O'Connor emphasized that "economic considerations had much more to do with the coming of the [Spanish American] War than has generally been acknowledged by American historians." Challenging Pratt, she notes that his conclusion is based on inadequate evidence, since he relied mainly on "eastern and coastal opinion." Then too, Pratt underestimated the role played by American bankers, merchants, manufacturers, steamship owners and agents engaged in the export and import trade to Cuba who favored intervention. Miss O'Connor finds, moreover, that even in the East there was "a strong split in business opinion" over the question of war with Spain, with a substantial group calling for military intervention. She challenges Pratt's contention that "American business had been either opposed or indifferent to the expansion philosophy which had arisen since 1890," citing specific examples where "industrial and commercial interests demanded new bases of operation." She concludes:

> Thus, on the eve of the conflict with Spain, business interests accepted war as a necessary extension of the American Policy. To assume that the foment of mass ideology, real politik, and lust for power can explain away the operation of economic factors which led the business community to support different forms of expansion in accord with their own best interests is convenient, but misleading. . . . Given the milieu of the expansionist philosophy of the eighteen nineties, the notion that American business opposed the Spanish-American War is subject to considerable revision.[35]

Another challenge to Pratt's thesis was presented by Martin J. Sklar in *Science & Society* a year later in an article entitled, "The N.A.M. and Foreign Markets on the Eve of the Spanish-American War." Analyzing the proceedings of the National Association of Manufacturers, founded in 1895, Sklar points out that "for more than two years, at least, prior to the Spanish-American War, a significant body of U.S. industrialists was convinced of the necessity of expanding their trade into foreign markets. The continued depression following the Panic of 1893 had demonstrated to them that the domestic market had finally passed the stage of indefinite elasticity capable of accommodating the growing productive capacity of the nation's industrial plant;* that

---

* Sklar does not mention it, but in connection with this important point, it is necessary to add that a change occurred in the thinking in the business community on the cause of the Panic of 1893 and the ensuing depression. Originally it was explained as resulting from dangerous or out-moded monetary theories and policies, but by 1895, there was increasing emphasis on overproduction and lack of markets as the basic cause. (*See*, in this connection, Thomas McCormick, "'A Fair Field and no Favor': American China Policy during the McKinley Administration," unpublished Ph.D. thesis, University of Wisconsin, 1960.)

the crisis required for its solution 'the conquest of foreign markets' in order to 'make room for the further expansion of our industries, not to mention the mere restoration of current production to full capacity; that unless something were done in this direction *post haste,* not only economic but social and political disaster for the capitalist way of life as they so fondly knew it might result." Although Sklar does not discuss the attitude of this large and influential body of U.S. businessmen toward the Cuban crisis, he effectively demolishes Pratt's thesis that the American business community was either opposed or indifferent to the expansionist ideology of the 1890's. He proves that, on the contrary, the leading businessmen were among the foremost advocates of this philosophy, and pointed repeatedly to Latin America and Asia as promising "the most glittering market opportunities for U.S. manufactures"—markets needed to "absorb glutted commodities, renew demand, and permit profitable expansion of productive capacity as an investment outlet for accumulated capital." Moreover, it was becoming clear to U.S. industrialists just prior to the Spanish-American War that, in order to obtain "their 'share' of world markets," they had to throw themselves into the struggle for these markets, "and do so without further delay, before the world had been too hopelessly divided by the other industrial nations without U.S. participation. . . ."* Sklar demonstrates that for at least two years prior to the war, the U.S. industrialists embarked upon an aggressive struggle against the business interests of other industrial nations in competition for the markets of the world, and spheres of influence and control. This they did with the full cooperation and support of the business-minded McKinley administration. The implication thus is clear that United States industrial and financial capital viewed war with Spain as part of the aggressive drive to gain a dominant place in the markets of the world.[36]

Over a half century before Sklar presented this thesis, the National Executive Committee of the Socialist Labor Party pointed to the proceedings of the N.A.M. convention in late December, 1897 as throwing "valuable light . . . upon the purpose of the Spanish-Amer-

---

* The New York *Journal* complained in 1896 that "the areas of the world" were being "taken over by naval powers," and that the world's trade routes were falling into the hands of other nations. The United States was in danger, the *Journal* felt, of being entirely excluded from its "rightful share." (Feb. 29, 1896.)

ican War." It described the event as "a Congress of the owners of the United States to decide what their Government should do about expansion." It quoted Warren Miller, chairman of the convention, as telling the delegates: "Wars to-day are for commerce. The killing of a missionary furnishes the excuse for opening up of a market." Charles Emory Smith, Postmaster General in McKinley's cabinet, and a leading Republican spokesman for big business, told the delegates: "The economic problem of the world to-day is the distribution of the surplus. . . . Under this stress the nations of Europe are struggling for empire and trade. . . . We have come to the point in our national development where we must decide. . . . Why should we not obtain our legitimate share of the great stake? . . . The United States must not be counted out in determining the fate even of the coast of Asia." Less than four months later, the Socialist Labor Party pointed out, war was declared against Spain, and the first step taken was to seize its Pacific possessions. The current of events had been started, "under capitalist guidance," by the businessmen and their representatives in Washington. It was "to issue forth like a Gulf Stream, and operate 'way around on the other side of the world on the shores of China. . . ."[37]

Pratt's thesis has also been criticized by Professor William Appleman Williams. He contends that in 1898 many businessmen were convinced that recovery from the recession had been due to overseas economic expansion and thus became advocates of an "active foreign policy." Like Sklar, he cites the president of the N.A.M. as having asserted that "many of our manufactures have outgrown or are outgrowing their home markets, and the expansion of foreign trade is the only promise of relief." And like Miss O'Connor, he criticizes Pratt for underestimating the role of American businessmen whose interests in Cuba were being threatened with destruction by the continued fighting. The Cuban situation had to be stabilized in order to protect these interests, and American investors, looking for new areas for investing capital, did not welcome the prospect of continued strife in Cuba. Moreover, the need to "pacify the island" was supported by businessmen who agreed with McKinley that continued war in Cuba "injuriously affects the normal functions of [American] business, and tends to delay the condition of prosperity to which this country is entitled." Then again, Williams stresses, many businessmen in the United States feared the victory of the radical revolutionaries—"the troublesome adventurers and non-responsible class"—whose attitude toward American interests in Cuba was considered unreliable.* By 1898, many businessmen favored American intervention in order to secure the ascendency of conservative elements (many of them Spaniards) in a Cuba free from Spain. Finally, Williams stresses "the clear and increasing interest in acquiring the Philippines as a base for winning a predominant share in the markets of China," an interest shared by many businessmen and not only by "Theodore Roosevelt and his imperialist cronies. . . ." Williams then concludes that American business, though preferring not to go to war as long as it could attain its objectives peacefully, had no objection to war "as the court of last resort." President McKinley "did not go to war simply because the businessmen ordered him to do so; but neither did he lead the nation to war against their economic wishes, as is so often asserted." [38]

Writing in 1960 and again in 1963, Thomas McCormick demonstrated the tremendous interest on the part of American businessmen and the McKinley administration in "the penetration, and, ultimately, the domination of the fabled China market," and clearly showed the link between the Cuban crisis and expansion in the Far East.[39] During this same period, Walter La Feber's research in materials related to American foreign policy confirmed the findings of other critics of Pratt's

---

* Professor Williams, it seems to me, puts too much emphasis on "the prompt and permanent pacification" of Cuba as basic to American objectives in the crisis over the island. It is true that both Cleveland and McKinley emphasized this theme repeatedly, but Williams does not bother to explain why when it appeared obvious that the Cuban rebels could have defeated Spain if the Republic of Cuba's belligerency or independence had been recognized by the United States, the men who were so anxious to achieve pacification in Cuba continually refused such recognition. Does not part of the answer lie in Williams' point about the fear of radical tendencies in the revolutionary movement?

In his most recent work, *The Roots of the Modern American Empire* (New York, 1969), Professor Williams points out that McKinley's refusal to recognize the Cuban rebels stemmed in part from a fear "that such action would very probably lead to a racist bloodbath *within* that island." (p. 434.) But he appears to accept this as a valid evaluation of the situation in Cuba, and treats the Cuban revolutionists as ineffective in their military campaigns against Spain. Professor Williams cites no evidence to justify these conclusions.

A more favorable view of the Cuban accomplishments in their military campaigns against Spain may be found in John A. S. Grenville and George Berkeley Young, *Politics Strategy and American Diplomacy* (New Haven, 1966, pp. 186-88.) The authors also reject the usual conception of McKinley as a weak president who was forced to go to war against his will.

thesis. He proves in his study, *The New Empire: An Interpretation of American Expansion, 1860-1898*, published in 1963, that the American business community considered foreign markets, especially those of Latin America and Asia, a solution to the domestic depression of 1893 (although he notes that even after 1873 there were signs of excess capacity in major segments of the American economy). Translating this viewpoint into action, businessmen after 1893 not only began systematically opening Latin American markets, but prodded the State Department to assist them in formulating Latin American policies. By 1897-98, they were beginning to move in the same way toward Asian markets and calling upon the McKinley administration to act diplomatically in behalf of their interests in the Far East.

American business, in short, was not a passive onlooker while Roosevelt, Mahan, Lodge and the other "young imperialists" shouted for American expansion abroad, but was the initiator of the expansionist policy, and urged government officials to adopt the necessary strategy to advance the interests of a business community urgently seeking new markets. Many businessmen, La Feber points out, supported intervention against Spain not only because it would open the Cuban market for further U.S. economic penetration, but also because they had their eyes on Spain's possessions in the Far East. "It is possible to suggest," he writes with specific reference to Pratt's thesis, ". . . that by the middle of March important businessmen and spokesmen for the business community were advocating war. It is also possible to suggest that at the same time a shift seems to be occurring in the general business community regarding its over-all views on the desirability of war." In short, businessmen and leading politicians thought alike on the need for foreign markets and acquisition of colonies, and the foreign policy of the U.S. government flowed from this state of affairs.[40]*

---

* Unfortunately, Professor La Feber shows little understanding of the causes and strength of the Cuban Revolution. He attributes the Revolution solely to the fact that the Wilson-Gorman tariff "suddenly removed Cuba's favored position in the American sugar market," assumes that the Spaniards were defeating the rebels in 1898, and falls into the typical assertion of most American historians that the "rebels were reluctant to compromise their objective of complete independence" because they knew that the United States would intervene and wanted such intervention. He also believes that McKinley had only three choices: (1) to leave the Cubans and Spaniards to fight it out; (2) to demand an armistice, and Spanish assurances over the summer would result in some solution which would pacify American feelings, and (3) to intervene mili-

My own research confirms recent conclusions that the thesis advanced by Julius W. Pratt and accepted uncritically by so many historians is not tenable. For one thing, there is ample evidence that businessmen were just as concerned about foreign markets and exports as the only feasible way of overcoming the industrial glut at home as were the imperialist-minded politicians and intellectuals. The Caribbean area and Latin America were frequently mentioned in trade journals and meetings of manufacturers as a field for American investment and trade expansion, but expansion in the Pacific was also increasingly being mentioned and linked with the others. On November 5, 1897, Francis B. Loomis, a leading spokesman for American business, wrote in a "confidential" letter to William R. Day, Assistant Secretary of State:

> *Above all*, let me say in conclusion I would send a commercial attaché to the Orient to operate in China and Japan. It is in that direction the great markets of the immediate future will be found. I happen to know that England sees this with distinctness and is acting promptly on her foresight. This administration can make a powerful and lasting impression upon the imagination and the welfare of the whole business world in the United States, and a richly deserved prestige for originality and progressiveness by taking up and exploiting the idea of trade in the Orient. . . .
>
> If you have not done so, let me suggest to you to read the article by Capt. Mahan in the October number of Harper's Monthly. It is a strategic "Study of the Caribbean sea," and the writer is the foremost of authorities on that subject.[41]

Captain Mahan's article emphasized the need for naval bases, particularly in the strategically important Caribbean area and in Hawaii, as a major step toward expansion of American economic activity in Latin America and Asia. The prophet and apostle of sea power argued that the U.S. must begin to look outward. Deploring the country's self-imposed isolation in the matter of markets and the decline of its shipping, Mahan asserted that the growing production of the country

---

tarily. It never occurs to him that there was a fourth alternative, the one the Cubans were anxious to see adopted: to recognize Cuban belligerency and allow the rebels to purchase arms and munitions as freely as did Spain. (*See* Walter La Feber, *The New Empire: An Interpretation of American Expansion, 1860-1898*, Ithaca, 1963, pp. 286, 397-99.)

would necessitate new markets, and this, in turn, would require facilities for their protection—a powerful navy dominated by an aggressive spirit, a healthy merchant marine, and secure bases and coaling stations from which they could operate. Strategically, the Caribbean area was crucial; Mahan considered control of the Isthmus of Panama by the United States vital. Such control was in turn contingent upon control of its approaches and of the bases that dominated them. Nothing less than American supremacy in the Caribbean would suffice. With the Caribbean and Hawaii, the United States could dominate Latin American commerce and move aggressively into the markets of the Far East. Mahan saw a clear relationship between the Caribbean and the vast market of China—via Cuba and Puerto Rico, the Isthmus, Hawaii, the coaling and cable station system in the Ladrones and Samoa, the Philippines to the Asia mainland. Appraising the value of all the Caribbean islands, Mahan directed American attention to Cuba as offering the best position for the United States in that area.[42]*

As Loomis' letter to Day indicates, Mahan's outlook was shared by leading business interests. On February 3, 1898, the New York State

---

* Although Mahan has received chief credit for the American naval renaissance and the thesis of the influence of sea power in history, he largely popularized the ideas of Stephen B. Luce of the U.S. Naval Academy. See John A. S. Grenville and George Berkeley Young, *Politics, Strategy, and American Diplomacy* (New Haven, 1966), pp. 13-30, and Stephen B. Luce, "Our Future Navy," *North American Review*, vol. CLXIX, 1899, pp. 54-65. Mahan's article and his other writings of this period show how inaccurate is Morris Levy's conclusion that Mahan had no interest in the Philippines or other Asian areas before the war with Spain. (Morris Levy, "Alfred Thayer Mahan and United States Foreign Policy," unpublished Ph.D. thesis, New York University, 1964, pp. 163-64.)

Paul A. Varg argues that the United States had no economic interests in China at this time, and he insists that the whole issue of the China market is based more on myth than reality. (*The Making of a Myth: The United States and China, 1897-1912*, East Lansing, Michigan, 1968.) But, as Thomas J. McCormick points out in his cogent review of this book, Varig does not confront the basic question—"that America's position as 'a pacific power'—its acquisition of the Philippines, for example—was hardly accidental, that it was, instead, the producer of a conscious pragmatic effort to provide an entrepot for the China market and for integrated, protective trade routes across the Pacific." (*American Historical Review*, vol. LXXV, June, 1970, p. 1394.) For further evidence of the importance of the China market, see Helen Dodson Kahn, "The Great Game of Empire: Willard D. Straight and American Far Eastern Policy," unpublished Ph.D. thesis, Cornell University, 1968, and Jerome M. Isreael, "Progressivism and the Open Door: The United States and China, 1901-1921," unpublished Ph.D. thesis, Rutgers University, 1967.)

Chamber of Commerce sent a memorial to President McKinley urging the government to pay careful attention to the opportunities for the expansion of trade with China and the danger that this might be affected by "the changes now going on in the relation of the European powers with the Empire of China." In other words, the American businessmen faced the threat of being cut out of that potentially great market. The memorial was referred to Secretary of State John Sherman, who replied as follows to A. E. Orr, President of the Chamber of Commerce:

> This Government having been the first to bring about the opening of the ports of China to foreign commerce, and the commercial relations of the United States with the Chinese Empire having been of large and growing importance during the forty years since its treaties with that Empire went into effect, this Department necessarily feels a deep interest in conserving and expanding the volume of trade with that country. I have pleasure, therefore, in assuring the Chamber of Commerce of the State of New York that this subject is being given the most careful consideration.[43]

The letters and memorials quoted above are only a few examples of many that could be cited to demonstrate that the important business interests were deeply concerned with the need for foreign markets before the outbreak of the Spanish-American War, and were concerned, too, at the danger of pre-emption of these markets by European interests. In this connection, John J. McCook's report of a meeting with the heads of the Standard Oil Company, America's leading trust, in the fall of 1896, is significant. McCook wrote that the Standard Oil people were extremely interested in "Manifest Destiny in Asia," and added: "Mr. [Henry M.] Flagler thought that the increase of Russian influence in China after the railway [being constructed by Russia] was completed would be hurtful to them as Russia would of course use all its power to have their petroleum, which has become a large article of commerce with them, used in China and in all countries coming under their influence."[44]*

---

*,Henry M. Flagler was, with John D. Rockefeller, the founder of the Standard Oil Company. "It is generally agreed that, next to Rockefeller himself, Flagler was the strongest man in the organization." (*Dictionary of American Biography*, New York, 1946, vol. VI, 451.)

Not long after the start of the Spanish-American War, Henry Cabot Lodge, in a letter to Theodore Roosevelt, expressed the conviction that the McKinley administration had committed itself to the "large policy we both desire." [45] By this Lodge meant using intervention in Cuba as the stepping stone for expansion in the Far East through the acquisition of Spain's Pacific possessions. Many American businessmen were fully committed to the "large policy" long before May 1, 1898. They prodded the government and the government responded. On October 14, 1900, the *Daily People* reminded the American people that "in 1895, the American capitalists organized the American Manufacturers Association, later the American Asiatic Association, etc., to reach into foreign trade." Later, with the cooperation of the McKinley administration, "they proceeded with the further formation of Trusts at a terrific rate, in order better to encounter the world's markets.* By 1898 they were ready, and determined to aid in forcing open the Chinese market, the last considerable unexploited market in the world. Hence occupation of the Philippines as a base at the doorway of China." It continued:

> Hence the Spanish-American War, whereby while fighting Spain in the Antilles, the color of plausibility could be given to the seizure of the Philippines as belonging to the same power. Observe that Manila, so absolutely disconnected from the Cuban question that it lies almost directly straight through the earth from us and Cuba, 8000 miles beneath our feet, was where the first battle was fought! Cuba was simply the fulcrum of the lever used by the capitalists in prying the "Open Door" of China.

The *Daily People* ignored the fact that there were American businessmen who had direct economic interests in Cuba, and, as we have seen, had for three years prior to the war been repeatedly calling attention to the losses they were sustaining because of the government's refusal to intervene.† Most of them were elated by the steps taken by

---

* During 1898, gigantic mergers took place in copper refining, lead, sugar, salt, tobacco, cans, whiskey, baking, street railways, cigarmaking, steel and other industries.

† There were, of course, those who saw in Cuba a rich opportunity for American capitalists once the island became free of Spanish domination. In February, 1897, Fitzhugh Lee, American consul general in Havana, wrote to Secretary of War Daniel S. Lamont (who with William C. Whitney, the New

McKinley for intervention, and they urged prompt and efficient measures to restore peace in the island, which would mean the restoration of a most valuable field for investment and trade.* To what degree were they joined by other business interests? My own research demonstrates that while much business sentiment, especially in the East, opposed war with Spain in the early months of 1898, primarily because "it would endanger our currency stability, interrupt our trade and

---

York financier, was involved in street railways): "Some one told me—it matters not when or where—that you were interested in street railways. So it has occurred to me to say to you—that here in Habana is a gold mine. Picture in your mind a city as large as Washington—with no modern traveling facilities. The car lines are limited to three in number. . . . I have an excellent well posted man looking over the field now, with a view of getting options—buying out old lines and acquiring ocean property outside—so that when peace is declared the business can be proceeded with. Not all can be purchased low. When the war is over everything will be high. In case of a change of flags no one can estimate the possibilities." Lee urged Lamont and Whitney to act swiftly "to look over the bonanza here." He was confident Spain could never defeat the insurgents whose number and enthusiasm was "greater and more intense than when I first came to the island eight months ago." (Fitzhugh Lee to Daniel S. Lamont, February 3, 1897, Daniel S. Lamont Papers, Library of Congress.) Since Lee was a staunch annexationist, it is clear that he regarded American intervention as crucial for realizing the great opportunities Cuba offered for investors.

* In his study, "The Sugar Interests and Ameircan Diplomacy in Hawaii and Cuba, 1893-1903," Richard D. Weigle denies that American intervention in Cuba was affected by "the influence of the American sugar investments in the island. . . . (Unpublished Ph.D. thesis, Yale University, 1939, p. 242.) But Weigle's own study contains significant evidence to the contrary, although he fails to recognize it as such.

In March, 1898, John Adam Kasson, especially appointed by McKinley to negotiate reciprocity treaties according to the provisions of the Dingley tariff bill, tried to work out a reciprocity treaty for the United States in Cuba. On March 24, Kasson informed McKinley that prospects for such an arrangement were dim. Furthermore, he sent the President a memorandum entitled "Why the United States Are Specially Interested in the Restoration of Order in Cuba." Noting that the United States had had "about 70% of the total annual trade of Cuba," he pointed out that the trade between it and Cuba had fallen from $96,803,000 in 1894 to $26,660,000 in 1897. Nor was this the only loss sustained by the United States. It had spent "large sums of money" in "policing our entire continental coast against possible expeditions to Cuba," doing Spain's work for her. And, of course, the war had caused the "destruction of many millions of property of U.S. citizens on the Island. . . ." How long could the United States allow such a situation to continue at a time when the Administration was growing increasingly concerned about economic expansion into foreign markets? (See Tom Edward Terrill, "An Economic Aspect of the Spanish-American War," Ohio History, Winter and Spring, 1967, pp. 73-74, 100.)

threaten our coasts and commerce,"* numerous business spokesmen began to emphasize that uncertainty, generated by the Cuban Revolution, was holding back business recovery. By mid-March many began to feel that even war was better than continued suspense, and that war would not seriously affect American business, for after the first shock, "things would whirl as usual." [46] Senator Proctor's speech had a marked effect upon the business community. The *Wall Street Journal* declared: "Senator Proctor's speech converted a great many people in Wall Street who had heretofore taken the ground that the United States had no business to interfere in a revolution on Spanish soil." For one thing, the men in Wall Street and other business areas had been skeptical of sensational reports in the "yellow press" about terrible conditions in Cuba, and Proctor, who had a reputation for being a moderate, convinced them that these reports were not exaggerated. Then again, Proctor did much to allay conservative fears that if Spanish domination was removed, "the people of Cuba would be revolutionary." The fact that the white population of Cuba was growing more rapidly than the decreasing Negro population, that many educated and intelligent people lived in the island, and "the large influx of American immigration and money," Proctor assured conservatives, "would all be strong factors for stable institutions." [47]

With the stock market moving from one level to another, there was an increasing cry from the business community for an immediate solution. Such business giants as John Jacob Astor, William Rockefeller, Stuyvesant Fish, Thomas Fortune Ryan, and John Gates declared them-

---

* The New York *Financial Record*, however, argued that war with Spain would not depress securities nor injure business but would rather vastly increase the net earning power of every security sold on the market. (Nov. 4, 1897.) The Chicago *Economist* called it fallacious that war would seriously hurt business. (vol. XIX, Feb. 26, 1898.) The Chattanooga *Tradesman* stated that a small prospect of war already stimulated the iron trade in certain lines. (March 1, 1898.) The *Manufacturers' Record*, organ of Southern industrialists, declared in late March, 1898 that war would open vast new markets for American industry and would have no serious effect on the securities market. (Reprinted in *The State*, March 26, 1898.) An April 23, 1898, *Bradstreet's* declared: "For nearly two months the New York banks, and the money market of the country generally, have been preparing for the events of the present week." (p. 257.) On that same day, the New York *Journal of Commerce* observed: "Naturally, the business sentiment of the country has not protested with any unqualified earnestness against the influences under which we have drifted into war."

selves for a more belligerent policy toward Spain, and J. Pierrepont Morgan joined the group in late March, 1898, when he declared that nothing more could be obtained by arbitration.[48]* At the same time, a leading New York journalist sent a telegram to a friend of McKinley which was passed on to the President: "Big corporations here now believe we will have war. Believe all would welcome it as relief to suspense. . . ."[49] On the declaration of war, the *American Banker* noted that "call loan rates which had averaged about 2 per cent in February rose sharply during March and touched 5 per cent at the opening of hostilities."[50] The approach of war, in other words, had had a highly stimulating effect on American capital!

With the support of a substantial section of, if not the entire, business community, McKinley moved to war. Thus it is clear that Pratt's conclusion that most big businessmen opposed the declaration of war in 1898 requires a thorough re-evaluation. Likewise in need of re-evaluation is the concept in many historical works that the President moved hesitantly and fearfully under the impact of a popular clamor too great for him to withstand.[51] As Ernest R. May puts this thesis, "mass hysteria" compelled President McKinley to lead his country "unwillingly toward a war that he did not want for a cause in which he did not believe."[52] A corollary to this thesis is that McKinley moved to war without being aware of, to say nothing of being influenced by, the requirements of expansion to meet the needs of American business for foreign markets. McKinley, like most American leaders, May argues, was "at most only incidentally concerned about real or imagined interests abroad."[53]

As we have seen, McKinley moved resolutely to war, following a course mapped out months before,† and in doing so, contemptuously ignored the overwhelming popular and Congressional demand for

---

* Thomas Beer in his biography of Mark Hanna writes that "his (Beer's) father heard in Washington that Wall Street was solidly lined up against a war with Spain. He retired to New York and men grabbed his arm . . . asking what this insane Hanna meant by trying to head off the war? He noted that John Jacob Astor, John Gates, Thomas Fortune Ryan, William Rockefeller, Stuyvesant Fish, John Pierpont Morgan, and many others in Wall Street were avidly for war." (Thomas Beer, *Hanna*, New York, 1929, p. 200.)

† In his massive volume, *Cuba: The Pursuit of Freedom* (New York, 1971), Hugh Thomas follows the interpretation of earlier works by such Americans as Millis, Friedel, Leech, and Morgan, and pictures McKinley as having surrendered to the "men of war." (*See* p. 379.)

recognition of the independence of the Cuban Republic. In fact, he was so indifferent to popular clamor that he steadfastly refused to yield to the almost universal popular demand to recognize Cuban belligerency, much less Cuban independence.

A study of what McKinley did and said reveals that the demands of the business community and of the political and intellectual expansionists met a very favorable response from the President.[54] McKinley delivered the keynote address at the organizational meeting of the National Association of Monufacturers in 1895, and he pointed out to these leading industrialists, organized to push trade overseas, that industry as a whole "cannot be kept in motion without markets." Foreign markets were essential "for our surplus products." As President, McKinley gave the featured address at the 1897 meeting of the Philadelphia Commercial Museum, also organized to push overseas economic expansion. "No worthier cause [than] the expansion of trade," he declared, ". . . can engage our energies at this hour."[55]

McKinley's "greatest ambition," H. H. Kohlsaat, the Chicago publisher has pointed out in his memoirs, "was to create new markets for American producers and manufacturers." Myron T. Herrick, a close personal friend and political associate of McKinley, agreed with this estimate, and told a 1902 meeting of the New York Board of Trade and Transportation: "When history comes to define and name the leading most prominent feature of the Republican party since the first inauguration of McKinley, it will declare it to be a reaching out for larger markets."[56]

Like all advocates of the "large policy," McKinley called for a big navy and an increase in the American merchant marine. Like them, too, he advocated the immediate annexation of the Hawaiian Islands, recommending it as soon as he assumed office on the grounds of inevitable destiny. When the treaty was first submitted to the Senate, he referred to annexation as the "inevitable consequence" of history and the following year, he observed that annexation was "manifest destiny." McKinley worked to implement other parts of the expansionist program. Upon becoming President, he moved toward the ownership and construction of an Isthmian canal. He also tried to purchase Cuba, and he would have annexed the island or placed it under a protectorate if the Spanish had been willing to sell. As John D. Offner writes in his study of McKinley's foreign policy: "McKinley's naval ideas and his interest in acquiring Hawaii, Cuba, and an American canal appear to form a well-rounded plan of expansion and development of American power . . . [and] his acts indicate that he was aware of the currents of expansionism behind a more comprehensive foreign policy." [56]

These "currents of expansionism" played a crucial part in the decision to go to war. McKinley was aware of the relationship between military action against Spain over Cuba and the establishment of an American base of operation in the Philippines from which to venture into the lucrative Far Eastern markets. He talked about this connection with Theodore Roosevelt and others as early as September, 1897, and he was involved in the plans which readied the entire Pacific campaign for immediate action even before the war was officially declared. Timothy G. McDonald puts it well in his article, "McKinley and the War with Spain":

> McKinley had his eyes on the Philippines as well as Cuba and wished to wage war on both fronts if war came. . . . Exactly when McKinley began to take an interest in the Philippines is uncertain. We do know, however, that strategic discussions involving those islands were underway not later than September 21, 1897. Quite possibly, Spain's Far Eastern possessions occupied the thoughts of Washington strategists from the moment McKinley's diplomatic offensive commenced. . . . In September of 1897, McKinley and his advisors were discussing both operations, but only the attack on the Philippines was carried out. Further, virtually everyone concerned knew the importance of the Philippines and there was general knowledge within and without the government that Americans had better hasten the coming of their Asian base, given the development of China.
>
> American business leaders, increasingly concerned with world markets, heard disquieting reports in the fall of 1897. European nations, it appeared were plotting to restrict the potentially vast Far Eastern markets for American staples. Washington shared this concern—on December 24, 1897, European efforts to dismember the Chinese Empire provided the principal topic at a Cabinet meeting in the White House. One of the participants told reporters that the President intended to keep a watchful eye upon the situation in order that full protection be given to the interests of the United States in China. Again, toward the end of January in 1898, McKinley assured American businessmen, in a speech before the National Association of Manufacturers in New York City, that America must reoccupy the fields temporarily lost to her and

go on to peaceful conquests of new and greater fields of trade and commerce. American naval power, based in the Philippines, would be able to protect present and future American interests in East Asia. Keeping these factors in mind, it would appear that the decision to attack the Philippines was crucial. As a matter of fact, McKinley planned the American conquest of the Philippines almost before the echoes of gunfire at Manila Bay had ceased. . . .

To put the matter briefly, eliminating Spain from both Cuba and the Philippines were equal objectives. . . . [57]

The McKinley Administration was aware that Spain's hold over Cuba was weakening by the day and the rebellion, in contrast, was growing in strength. If the United States did not act soon, it would be faced with an independent Cuba, and the opportunity to use the "pacification of Cuba" as the springboard for expansion overseas would be lost. The war to liberate Cuba was thus a war to prevent its independence, eliminate Spain from Cuba and the Philippines, and open the door for the economic and political domination of both islands by the United States.

To put it again briefly: the Cuban policy of the United States culminating in the use of force against Spain had its root in the rise of monopoly capitalism and its drive for markets. There were political, social and psychological roots, too, and no analysis of the road to war can ignore humanitarian sentiments, the role of the press, the sinking of the *Maine*, the influence of the ideologists of expansionism. But these reenforced economic factors. The predominance of economic factors in the sequence of events which led to the outbreak of conflict between the United States and Spain has been sufficiently demonstrated in recent historiography to warrant the conclusion that the "Spanish-American War" was indeed an imperialist war.

Reference Notes

INTRODUCTION

The discussion is essentially a summary of material in my *History of Cuba and Its Relations with the United States*, Volume I, New York, 1962, and Volume II, New York, 1963.
For the expansionist views of James G. Blaine, see Richard Carlyle Winchester, "James G. Blaine and the Ideology of American Expansionism," unpublished Ph.D. thesis, University of Rochester, 1966; James G. Blaine to James Comly, Dec. 1, 1881, *Foreign Relations of the United States*, 1881, p. 637; James G. Blaine to James Comly, Nov. 19, 1881, in James G. Blaine, *Political Discussions Legislative, Diplomatic and Popular 1856-1886*, Norwich, Conn., 1887, p. 395; John Bassett Moore, *Four Phases of American Development, Federalism, Democracy, Imperialism, Expansionism* (Baltimore, 1912, pp. 187-88.) For José Martí's views on emerging American imperialism in the 1880's and 1890's, see also Emilio Roig de Leuchsenring, *Martí Anti-Imperialist*, translated by Maria Juana Cazabón, Havana, 1961.

CHAPTER I

THE SECOND WAR FOR INDEPENDENCE BEGINS

1. Horatio S. Rubens, *Liberty, the Story of Cuba*, New York, 1922, p. 40; Jorge Meñach, *Martí: Apostle of Freedom*, translated by Coley Taylor, New York, 1950, p. 322.
2. Juan Gualberto Gómez, *Los Preliminares de la revolución de 1895*, Habana, 1913, p. 278.
3. Gonzalo Cabrales, *Epistolario de héroes*, Habana, 1922, pp. 128-29.
4. *Ibid.*, pp. 57-58; José L. Franco, *Antonio Maceo; Apuntes para una historia de su vida*, La Habana, 1954, vol. II, pp. 51-53.
5. Rubens, *op. cit.*, p. 74.
6. Máximo Gómez to Antonio Maceo, Feb. 27, 1895; Antonio Maceo to José Martí, Feb. 1895, Archivo Nacional, Havana, Cuba. Hereinafter referred to as Archivo Nacional.
7. Mañach, *op. cit.*, p. 344.

8. Academia de la Historia de Cuba, *Fassimil del Original del Manifesto de Montectisti, Firmado por Máximo Gómez y José Martí, el 25 de Marzo de 1895*, La Habana, 1961.
9. Cabrera, *Epistolario*, pp. 67-69, 73-74; Franco, *op. cit.*, vol. II, pp. 199-200.
10. Franco, *op. cit.*, vol. II, pp. 106-11; Manuel J. Granda, *Memoria Revolucionarias*, Habana, 1936, pp. 88-92.
11. Maceo to the Forces of Oriente, April 20, 1895; to the Army of Oriente, April 21, 1895, Archivo Nacional.
12. Franco, *op. cit.*, vol. II, p. 125; Cabrera, *Epistolario*, pp. 75-76.
13. José Martí, *Obras Completas*, La Habana, 1946, vol. II, pp. 247-49.
14. *The America of José Martí: Selected Writings*, translated by Juan de Onis, New York, 1953, pp. 317-18.
15. Félix Lizaso, *José Martí: Martyr of Cuban Independence*. Translated by Esther E. Shuler, Albuquerque, New Mexico, 1953, pp. 247-48; Mañach, *op. cit.*, p. 350.
16. Martí, *Obras Completas*, vol. I, pp. 271, 285-93.
17. *New York Sun*, May 23, 1895; Emilio Roig de Leuchsenring, *Máximo Gómez, el Libertador de Cuba y el primer ciudano de la Republica*, La Habana, 1959.
18. Franco, *op. cit.*, vol. II, p. 253n.
19. Juan Marinello, "José Martí and the U.S.A.," *Masses & Mainstream*, vol. VI, Oct. 1953, p. 41; Juan Marinello, "El Pensamiento de Martí y nuestra Revolucion Socialista," *Cuba Socialista*, Jan. 1962, pp. 16-37.
20. Letter to Manuel Mercado, May 18, 1895, *Obras Completas*, vol. I, pp. 271-73.

CHAPTER II

Cuban Revolutionary Strategy

1. See *Diario de la Marina*, Havana, February-March, 1895.
2. *Ibid.*, April 10, 1895.
3. *Ibid.*, March 31, 1895.
4. *New York World*, April 12, 1895.
5. N. Bashkina, "A Page from the Cuban People's Heroic History," 12 documents reprinted from the Russian Foreign Policy Archives, in *International Affairs*, Moscow, March, 1964, p. 18. *My emphasis. P.S.F.*
6. Gonzalo de Quesada, *The War in Cuba: The Struggle for Freedom*, Washington, 1896, p. 61.
7. Enrique José Varona, *De la colonia a la república*, Habana, 1919, p. 167; Jose Miró y Argenter, *Cuba, Crónicas de la guerra: las campañas de Invasión de Occidente, 1895-1896*, Habana, 1945, vol. I, pp. 266-68; Miguel Angel Varona Guerrero, *La Guerra de Independencia de Cuba, 1895-1898*, Habana, 1946, vol. II, p. 1409.
8. Máximo Gómez, *Diario de Campaña*, La Habana, 1941, pp. 421, 424; Laurence R. Nicholas, "Domestic History of Cuba During the War of Insurrectos, 1895-1898," unpublished M.A. thesis, Duke University, 1951, p. 57.

9. Richard Vernon Rickenbach, "A History of Filibustering from Florida to Cuba, 1895-1898," unpublished M.A. thesis, University of Florida, 1948, p. 80.
10. Calixto García to Estrada Palma, Dec. 6, 1896, Archivo Nacional, Havana, Cuba.
11. José L. French, "With Gomez in the Cuban Skirmishes," *National Magazine*, vol. XIV, 1898, pp. 38-40.
12. Reprinted in *Algunos Documentos Políticos de Máximo Gómez*, edited by Amalia Rodríguez Rodríguez, La Habana, 1962, p. 10.
13. *Ibid.*, p. 11.
14. Nichols, *op. cit.*, p. 57.
15. Murat Halstead, *The Story of Cuba*, Chicago, 1896-1898, p. 122; George C. Musgrave, *Under Three Flags in Cuba*, Boston, 1899, p. 61-62.
16. *International Affairs*, Moscow, March, 1964, p. 118.
17. Calixto García to Tomás Estrada Palma, Dec. 6, 1896, Archivo Nacional; Frederick Funston, *Memories of Two Wars*, New York, 1914, p. 143; Quesada, *op. cit.*, p. 143; Emilio Roig de Leuchsenring, *Cuba no debe su Independencia a Los Estados Unidos*, La Habana, 1950, p. 24.
18. Máximo Gómez to Tomás Estrada Palma, Aug. 11, 1896; Máximo Gómez to Campos de Cuba, July, 1897, both in Archivo Nacional; Albert G. Robinson, *Intervention in Cuba*, New York, 1905, p. 44.
19. Máximo Gómez to Campos de Cuba, July, 1897, Archivo Nacional.
20. Máximo Gómez to Tomás Estrada Palma, Aug. 11, 1896, Archivo Nacional.
21. *Documentos históricos*, Habana, 1912, p. 249; French E. Chadwick, *The Relations of the United States and Spain: Diplomacy*, New York, 1909, p. 408.
22. *Algunos Documentos Políticos de Máximo Gómez, op. cit.*, pp. 15-16.
23. Máximo Gómez to Tomás Estrada Palma, Aug. 11, 1896, Archivo Nacional.
24. Chadwick, *op. cit.*, p. 409; Varona Guerrero, *op. cit.*, vol. II, pp. 788-89.
25. Máximo Gómez to Andrés Moreno, Feb. 6, 1897, in Emilio Roig de Leuchsenring, editor, *Ideario Cubano; Máximo Gómez*, La Habana, 1936, pp. 68-72.
26. *Ordenanzas municipales del Ejército Libertador Cubano*, Key West, 1896, pp. 18-19.
27. Emilio Roig de Leuchsenring, *Máximo Gómez, el Libertador de Cuba y el Primer Ciudadano de la República*, La Habana, 1959, p. 31.
28. Gómez, *Diario de Campaña*, p. 133.
29. Antonio Maceo to Carlos Roloff, Nov. 23, 1895, Archivo Nacional.
30. Antonio Maceo to Estrada Palma, Sept. 22, 1895, Archivo Nacional; Estrada Palma to Antonio Maceo, Sept. 25, 1895, in *Antonio Maceo; documentos para su vida*, La Habana, 1945, p. 146.
31. Máximo Gómez to Estrada Palma, Aug. 22, 1895, Archivo Nacional.
32. Miró, *op. cit.*, vol. I, pp. 126-28.
33. Máximo Gómez to Estrada Palma, Oct. 25, 1895, Archivo Nacional.
34. *International Affairs*, Moscow, March, 1964, p. 119.
35. Miguel Angel Varona Guerrero, "Operaciones Militares," *Revista bimestre cubana*, vol. LV, mayo-junio, 1945, p. 249.
36. Varona Guerrero, *op. cit.*, vol. I, pp. 702-03; Grover Flint, *Marching with Gómez. A War Correspondent's Field Note-Book kept during four months*

with the Cuban army, introduction by John Fiske, Boston and New York, 1898, p. 20.
37. Varona Guerrero, op. cit., vol. II, pp. 885-86.
38. Flint, op. cit., p. 276.
39. Ibid., p. 277.
40. Varona Guerrero, op. cit., vol. II, p. 886.
41. Charles M. Pepper, Tomorrow in Cuba, New York, 1899, pp. 78-79.
42. Máximo Gómez to Estrada Palma, Nov. 22, 1896, Archivo Nacional.
43. Benigno Souza, Máximo Gómez, el generalísimo, La Habana, 1936, p. 185.
44. New York Tribune, June 11, 1895.
45. Flint, op. cit., pp. 41-42, 45.
46. Quoted in Halstead, op. cit., pp. 139-40.
47. Thomas W. Steep, "A Cuban Insurgent Newspaper," National Magazine, vol. VIII, May, 1898, pp. 147-49.
48. A. D. Hall, Cuba, Its Past, Present, and Future, New York, 1898, p. 83.
49. Richard Harding Davis, Cuba in War Time, New York, 1897, pp. 91-94.

CHAPTER III

The War in Oriente and Preparations for the Western Invasion

1. Funston, op. cit., p. 143.
2. José L. Franco, Antonio Maceos Apuntes Para una Historia de su Vida, vol. III, La. Habana, 1957, p. 36.
3. New York Herald, June 7, 1895.
4. Miró, op. cit., vol. I, p. 65; Gonzalo Cabrales, Epistolario de héroes, La Habana, 1922, pp. 78-79.
5. José L. Franco, Antonio Maceos Apuntes para una Historia de su Vida, vol. II, La Habana, 1954, p. 141.
6. Miró, op. cit., vol. I, pp. 67-82; Franco, op. cit., vol. II, pp. 147-55; Laurence Richard Nichols, "'The Bronze Titan': The Mulatto Hero of Cuban Independence, Antonio Maceo," unpublished Ph.D. thesis, Duke University, 1954, pp. 369-71; Juan Jerez Villarreal, Oriente: Biografia de una provincia, La Habana, 1960, pp. 270-73.
7. Halstead, op. cit., p. 276.
8. Máximo Gómez to Tomás Estrada Palma, Camagüey, Aug. 22, 1895, Archivo Nacional.
9. Antonio Maceo to María Cabrales, Sept. 3, 1895, Cabrales, op. cit., pp. 83-84.
10. René E. Reyna Cossio, Estudio Histórico-Militares sobre la Guerra de Independencia de Cuba, La Habana, 1954, p. 16.
11. Máximo Gómez to Antonio Maceo, June 30, 1895; Antonio Maceo to Máximo Gómez, July 3, 1895; Antonio Maceo to Bartolomé Masó, July 14, 1895; Archivo Nacional.
12. Nichols, "The Bronze Titan," op. cit., p. 360.
13. Antonio Maceo to Máximo Gómez, July 3, 1895, Archivo Nacional.
14. Salvador Cisneros Betancourt to Antonio Maceo, Sept. 6, 1895; Antonio Maceo to Salvador Cisneros Betancourt, Sept. 12, 1895, Archivo Nacional.

15. "Affairs in Cuba," 35th Congress, 2nd Session, *Senate Report* 885, pp. 30-32; Varona Guerrero, *op. cit.*, vol. I, pp. 637-49.
16. Eduardo Rosell y Malpica, quoted in Franco, *op. cit.*, vol. II, p. 185.
17. Antonio Maceo to Estrada Palma, Sept. 22, 1895, Archivo Nacional.
18. Antonio Maceo to Estrada Palma, Oct. 30, 1895, Archivo Nacional.
19. Antonio Maceo to Salvador Cisneros Betancourt, Sept. 8, 1895, in José Antonio Portuondo, *El Pensamiento vivo de Maceo*, La Habana,, 1962, pp. 76-77.
20. Antonio Maceo to the Chiefs of the First Corps, Sept. 24, 1895, Archivo Nacional.
21. Bernabé Boza, *Mi diario de la guerra, desde Baire hasta la intervención americana*, La Habana, 1900-1904, vol. I, p. 75.
22. Miró, *op. cit.*, vol. 1, p. 117.
23. *Ibid.*, pp. 118-19.
24. Juan Gualberto Gómez, *Los preliminares de la revolución de 1895*, La Habana, 1913, pp. 13-17.
25. Miró, *op. cit.*, vol. I, p. 121.
26. *Ibid.*, vol. I, p. 98.
27. *Ibid.*, vol. I, pp. 98-99.
28. *Ibid.*, vol. I, p. 102.
29. *Ibid.*, vol. I, pp. 126-28; Antonio Maceo to Carlos Roloff, Secretary of War, Nov. 23, 1895, Archivo Nacional.
30. Antonio Maceo to Manuel Sanguily, Camagüey, Nov. 21, 1895, original in Archivo Nacional; reprinted in Portuondo, *op. cit.*, pp. 83-84.
31. Antonio Maceo to Estrada Palma, Oct. 30, 1895, Archivo Nacional.
32. Reyna, *op. cit.*, pp. 16-17.
33. Miró, *op. cit.*, vol. I, pp. 99-100.
34. Antonio Maceo to Estrada Palma, Nov. 21, 1895, Archivo Nacional.
35. *Ibid.*
36. Miró, *op. cit.*, vol. I, p.. 117.
37. Antonio Maceo to María Cabrales, Nov. 20, 1895, Cabrales, *op. cit.*, pp. 84-85.
38. Miró, *op. cit.*, vol. I, pp. 127-28.
39. Quoted in Emilio Roig de Leuchsenring, *Máximo Gómez, El Libertador de Cuba, y el Primer Ciudadano de la República*, p. 18.
40. Miró, *op. cit.*, vol. I, pp. 129-34; Franco, *op. cit.*, vol. II, pp. 251-52.
41. Max Tosquella, "Baragua-Mantua," *Bohemia*, La Habana, Deciembre 4, 1964, pp. 8-9.
42. Miró, *op. cit.*, vol. I, pp.. 139, 144-55; Antonio Maceo to Estrada Palma, Nov. 29, 1895, Archivo Nacional.
43. Franco, *op. cit.*, vol. II, p. 253 and *n*.
44. Miró, *op. cit.*, vol. I, p. 139; Franco, op. cit., vol. II, p. 258.

CHAPTER IV

The Invasion of the West

1. Gómez, *op. cit.*, p. 348.
2. Antonio Maceo to the People of Las Villas, Remedios, Dec. 5, 1895, Archivo Nacional.

3. Colonel Camps y Feliú, *Españoles y insurectos*, Madrid, 1900, p. 122.
4. Gómez, *op. cit.*, pp. 347-48. See also Máximo Gómez to Estrada Palma, Aug. 11, 1896, Archivo Nacional.
5. Miró, *op. cit.*, vol. I, p. 151.
6. *Ibid.*, pp. 161-67; Gómez, *op. cit.*, pp. 348-50.
7. José Luciano Franco, *La Vida Heroica y Ejemplar de Antonio Maceo*, La Habana, 1963, p. 100.
8. Miró, *op. cit.*, vol. I, p. 170.
9. Varona Guerrero, *op. cit.*, vol. I, p. 596.
10. Miró, *op. cit.*, vol. I, p. 170; Reyna, *op. cit.*, p. 21; Franco, *op. cit.*, vol. II, p. 275.
11. Miró, *op. cit.*, vol. I, pp. 168-80; Reyna, *op. cit.*, pp. 25-26; Franco, *op. cit.*, vol. II, p. 277-78.
12. Flint, *o. cit.*, pp. 41-42, 45, 151-56.
13. Miró, *op. cit.*, vol. I, pp. 224-25.
14. *Ibid.*, pp. 226-31.
15. Camps y Feliú, *op. cit.*, p. 141.
16. Gómez, *op. cit.*, p. 351.
17. Miró, *op. cit.*, vol. I, pp. 258-63.
18. *Ibid.*, p. 257.
19. Franco, *op. cit.*, vol. III, pp. 20-21.
20. Miró, *op. cit.*, vol. I, pp. 282-89; Gómez, *op. cit.*, p. 253.
21. Quoted in Franco, *op. cit.*, vol. III, p. 19.
22. José Rivero Muñiz, *Vereda Nueva*, La Habana, 1964, pp. 84-94.
23. Miró, *op. cit.*, vol. I, pp. 288-90; Gómez, *op. cit.*, p. 254.
24. Quoted in Franco, *op. cit.*, vol. III, p. 19.
25. Halstead, *op. cit.*, pp. 192-214.
26. *La Discusión*, Havana, Jan.. 1-7, 1896; Miró, *op. cit.*, vol. I, pp. 301-03.
27. *Diario de la Marina*, Havana, Jan. 4, 6, 8, 1896; Franco, *op. cit.*, vol. III, p. 27.
28. W. Rodney Long, *Railroads of Central America and the West Indies*, Washington, 1925, pp. 157-75; Laurence R. Nichols, "Domestic History," *op. cit.*, p. 121.
29. De Truffin to the Russian Envoy in Madrid, Jan. 8, 1896, *International Affairs*, Moscow, March, 1964, pp. 119-20.
30. Quoted in Franco, *op. cit.*, vol. III, pp. 22-23.
31. Miró, *op. cit.*, vol. I, pp. 314-20; Gómez, *op. cit.*, p. 353.
32. Portuondo, *op. cit.*, pp. 85-86.
33. Miró, *op. cit.*, vol. I, pp. 318-19.
34. Antonio Maceo to María Cabrales, Provincia de la Habana, Feb. 14, 1896, Cabrales, *op. cit.*, pp. 85-86.
35. Miró, *op. cit.*, vol. I, pp. 315-16; Franco, *op. cit.*, vol. III, pp. 41-42.
36. Miró, *op. cit.*, vol. I, p. 320; Laurence R. Nichols, " 'The Bronze Titan,' " p. 332.
37. Miró, *op. cit.*, vol. I, p. 321.
38. *Cf. Diario de la Marina*, Havana, Jan. 15, 1896.
39. *Cf. Ibid.*, Jan. 28, 1896. See also Diego Vicente Tejera, *Blancos y Negros*, Conferencia dada en Cayo Hueso en 7 de Noviembre de 1897, Habana, 1900, pp. 18-19. Copy in Harvard College Library.
40. Franco, *op. cit.*, vol. III, p. 54.

41. Antonio Maceo to the Director of the Washington *Star*, Pinar del Río, Jan. 27, 1896, in Pertuondo, *op. cit.*, pp. 86-87.
42. Miró, *op. cit.*, vol. I, pp. 344-45.
43. *Ibid.*, pp. 342-43.
44. Franco, *op. cit.*, vol. III, p. 55.
45. Miró, *op. cit.*, vol. I, p. 345.
46. *Ibid.*, p. 346.
47. Franco, *op. cit.*, vol. III, p. 56.
48. Miró, *op. cit.*, vol. I, pp. 345-46.
49. *Ibid.*, p. 346; Franco, *op. cit.*, vol. III, pp. 57-58.
50. Antonio Maceo to María Cabrales, Feb. 14, 1896, Cabrales, *op. cit.*, 85-86.
51. Miró, *op. cit.*, vol. I, pp. 344-45; Franco, *op. cit.*, vol. III, p. 56; Nicolás Heredia, *Crónicas de la guerra de Cuba*, 1895-1896. Introducción por el doctor Enrique Gay-Calbó, La Habana, 1951, p. XV. This is a reproduction of the original edition published in *El Fígaro* in 1895 and 1896.
52. *International Affairs*, Moscow, March, 1964, p. 120.
53. Reyna, *op. cit.*, pp. 126,27.
54. Quoted in Franco, *op. cit.*, vol. III, p. 56.
55. Quoted in Franco, *op. cit.*, vol. III, p. 170.
56. Portuondo, *op. cit.*, pp. 87-88.

CHAPTER V

Weyler Versus Maceo

1. Miró, *op. cit.*, vol. II, p. 18.
2. Antonio Maceo to María Cabrales, Provincia de la Habana, Feb. 14, 1896, Cabrales, *op. cit.*, pp. 85-86.
3. Miró, *op. cit.*, vol. II, p. 25.
4. *Ibid.*, pp. 36-42; Franco, *op. cit.*, vol. III, pp. 67-76.
5. Miró, *op. cit.*, vol. II, pp. 42-55.
6. *Ibid.*, pp. 56-57.
7. Valeriano Weyler y Nicolau, *Mi Mando en Cuba*, Madrid, 1910, vol. I, p. 101.
8. Hall, *op. cit.*, p. 123; Miró, *op. cit.*, vol. III, pp. 178-79.
9. Weyler, *op. cit.*, vol. II, pp. 538-40.
10. Antonio Maceo to María Cabrales, Provincia de la Habana, Feb. 14, 1896, Cabrales, *op. cit.*, pp. 85-86.
11. Miró, *op. cit.*, vol. II, 60-66.
12. *Ibid.*, pp. 74-84; Franco, *op. cit.*, vol. III, pp. 87-97.
13. Miró, *op. cit.*, vol. III, pp. 94-95; Franco, *op. cit.*, vol. III, pp. 98-99.
14. Portuondo, *op. cit.*, pp. 88-89.
15. *Diario de la Marina*, Havana, Feb. 28, 1896.
16. Antonio Maceo to Estrada Palma, Cabañas, San Francisco, March 21, 1896, Archivo Nacional.
17. Miró, *op. cit.*, vol. II, pp. 128-30; Franco, *op. cit.*, vol. III, pp. 107-12.
18. Antonio Maceo to Estrada Palma, El Rubí, Pinar del Río, April 4, 1896, Archivo Nacional.

19. Antonio Maceo, Proclamation, Pinar del Río, March 16, 1896, Archivo Nacional.
20. Miró, *op. cit.*, vol. II, pp. 160-63; Franco, *op. cit.*, vol. II, pp. 128-30.
21. Miró, *op. cit.*, vol. II, pp. 117-78; Franco, *op. cit.*, vol. III, pp. 139-40.
22. Antonio Maceo to Estrada Palma, El Rubí, Pinar del Río, April 14, 1896, Archivo Nacional.
23. Weyler, *op. cit.*, vol. III, pp. 113-15.
24. Antonio Maceo to Máximo Gómez, April 14, 1896, Archivo Nacional.
25. See Philip S. Foner, *History of Cuba and Its Relations with the United States*, vol. II, 1845-1895, New York, 1963, pp. 277-79, 281, 289.
26. Laurence R. Nichols, "'The Bronze Titan,'" p. 435.
27. *Diario de la Havana*, Havana, April 15, 1896.
28. Antonio Maceo to Estrada Palma, April 14, 1896, Archivo Nacional; Antonio Maceo to María Cabrales, April 17, 1896, Cabrales, *op. cit.*, p. 87.
29. Miró, *op. cit.*, vol. II, pp. 196-204; Franco, *op. cit.*, vol. III, pp. 163-64.
30. Miró, *op. cit.*, vol. II, pp. 224-28; Franco, *op. cit.*, vol. III, pp. 164-65.
31. Miró, *op. cit.*, vol. II, p. 232; De Truffin to the Russian Ambassador to Madrid, May 1, 1896, *International Affairs*, Moscow, March, 1964, p. 121.
32. Miró, *op. cit.*, vol. II, p. 240-51: Franco, *op. cit.*, vol. III, pp. 183-84.
33. London *Times*, June 6, 1896.
34. Miró, *op. cit.*, vol. II, pp. 256-65; Franco, *op. cit.*, vol. III, pp. 233-34.
35. Antonio Maceo to Estrada Palma, June 27, 1896, Archivo Nacional; Miró, *op. cit.*, vol. III, pp. 12-13; Franco, *op. cit.*, vol. III, pp. 255-56.
36. Miró, *op. cit.*, vol. III, pp. 12-13; Franco, *op. cit.*, vol. III, p. 176.
37. De Truffin to the Russian Ambassador to Madrid, Oct. 14, 1896, *International Affairs*, Moscow, March, 1964, p. 122.
38. Miró, *op. cit.*, vol. III, pp. 82, 89-126; Franco, *op. cit.*, vol. III, pp. 316-30.
39. Miró, *op. cit.*, vol. III, p. 172; Franco, *op. cit.*, vol. III, p. 347.
40. Miró, *op. cit.*, vol. III, pp. 195-98; Varona Guerrero, *op. cit.*, vol. I, p. 596.
41. Varona Guerrero, *op. cit.*, vol. I, pp. 598-602; Capitán Aníbal Escalante Beatón, *Calixto García. Su Campaña en el 1895*, La Habana, 1896, pp. 40-47.
42. Franco, *op. cit.*, vol. III, p. 175.
43. Máximo Gómez to Antonio Maceo, May 20, June 27, 1896; Salvador Cisneros Betancourt to Estrada Palma, June 1, 1896, Archivo Nacional.
44. Franco, *op. cit.*, vol. III, p. 176.
45. Miró, *op. cit.*, vol. III, pp. 173-74.
46. Máximo Gómez to Estrada Palma, Camagüey, November, 1896, Archivo Nacional.
47. José L. Franco, *La Vida Heroica*, *op. cit.*, p. 114.
48. Miró, *op. cit.*, vol. III, pp. 173-74.
49. A. D. Hall, *Cuba, Its Past, Present, and Future*, New York, 1898, pp. 83, 123.
50. Antonio Maceo to Baldomero Acosta, Nov. 6, Archivo Nacional; Franco, *op. cit.*, vol. III, pp. 370-71.
51. Miró, *op. cit.*, vol. III, pp. 184-87; Franco, *op. cit.*, vol. III, pp. 372-74.
52. Antonio Maceo to Baldomero Acosta, Nov. 13, 1896, Archivo Nacional.
53. Portuondo, *op. cit.*, pp. 99-102. For the other letters, see Antonio Maceo to General Emilio Núñez, Nov. 22, 1896; Antonio Maceo to Pérez Carbó,

Nov. 22, 1896; Antonio Maceo to Manuel Sanguily, Nov. 24, 1896, all in Archivo Nacional.
54. Franco, *op. cit.*, vol. III, pp. 389-95.
55. *Ibid.*, pp. 394-96; Miró, *op. cit.*, vol. III, pp. 212-14.
56. Franco, op. cit., vol. III, pp. 404-05.
57. Miró, *op. cit.*, vol. III, pp. 218-55; Franco, *op. cit.*, vol. III, pp. 408-10.
58. *International Affairs*, Moscow, March, 1964, p. 123.
59. *Detroit Journal*, Dec. 13, 1896.
60. S.E.F.C.C. Hamedoe, "Major-General Antonio Maceo: The Idol of Cuba and the Cuban Insurgents," *Colored American Magazine*, Nov. 1900, p. 54; *The Voice of the Negro* (Atlanta), Nov. 1904; Arthur A. Schomburg, "General Antonio Maceo," *The Crisis*, vol. XXXVIII, May, 1931, pp. 155-56, 174.
61. Franco, *op. cit.*, vol. III, p. 419.

CHAPTER VI

The People, the Economy, and the Revolution

1. Foner, *op. cit.*, vol. II, pp. 318-30.
2. Flint, *op. cit.*, pp. 25, 274; *Daily People*, April 16, 1901.
3. Leland H. Jenks, *Our Cuban Colony*, New York, 1928, pp. 36-38.
4. Williams to Uhl, Havana, March 10, 1895, Consular Dispatches, Department of State, National Archives.
5. The full provisions of the new reform legislation were printed in *El País*, Havana, March 29, 1895. See also Nichols, "Domestic History," *op. cit.*,
6. *El País*, April 4, 1895.
7. Enclosure No. 1, in Fitzhugh Lee to Richard B. Olney, June 24, 1896, Richard B. Olney Papers, Vol. 56, pp. 9914-15, Library of Congress.
8. Quesada, *op. cit.*, pp. 74, 94; *International Affairs*, Moscow, March, 1964, pp. 121, 122.
9. Joaquín Ordoqui, *Elementos Para La Historia del Movimiento Obrero en Cuba*, La Habana, 1961, p. 14; José Rivero Muñiz, *El Movimiento Obrero Durante La Primera Intervencion: Apuntes para la historia del proletariado en Cuba*, Las Villas, 1961, pp. 33-34.
10. Santiago Iglesias Pantín, *Luchas Emancipadores*, San Juan, Puerto Rico, 1958, Segunda edición, pp. 31-33.
11. Williams to Uhl, Havana, Oct. 31, 1895, Consular Dispatches, Department of State, National Archives.
12. Williams to Uhl, Jan. 11, 16, 31, 1896, Consular Dispatches, Department of State, National Archives; *Sugar Cane*, vol. XXVIII, Jan. 1, 1896, p. 15; April, 1896, p. 172.
13. Weyler, *op. cit.*, vol. II, pp. 200-06; vol. III, p. 193; Edwin F. Atkins, *Sixty Years in Cuba: Reminiscences*, Cambridge, Mass., 1926, p. 201.
14. *El Boletin Commercial*, Havana, March 7, 10, 1896; Williams to Rockhill, Havana, March 28, 1896, Consular Dispatches, Department of State, National Archives; *Sugar Cane*, vol. XXVIII, Oct. 1, 1896; Jenks, *op. cit.*, p. 31.

15. Jenks, *op. cit.*, p. 40.
16. *Ibid.*
17. Willet and Gray's *Statistical Sugar Trade Journal*, Feb. 20, March 12, April 16, 1896.
18. Williams to Rockhill, Havana, May 20, 1896, Consular Dispatches, Department of State, National Archives.
19. Williams to Olney, Havana, May 19, 1896, Consular Dispatches, and Instruction No. 650, Olney to Taylor, Department of State, Spain, Feb. 12, 1897, National Archives.
20. Varona Guerrero, *op. cit.*, vol. I, pp. 452-53.
21. Marta Abreu de Estévez to Tomás Estrada Palma, Paris, July 10, 1896, Archivo Nacional.
22. Varona Guerrero, *op. cit.*, vol. I, p. 449.
23. Horatio S. Rubens, "The Insurgent Government in Cuba," *North American Review*, vol. CLVI, p. 563.
24. Gasper Jorge, "Influencia de los Tabaqueros en las revolutiones de Cuba," *Revista Bimestre Cubana*, vol. XXIX, 1937, pp. 109-10.
25. Nichols, "Domestic History," *op. cit.*, pp. 59-60.
26. Emilio Roig de Leuchsenring, "Cuba victoriosa contra Espana en la guerra de 1895-1898; raices y justificación," unpublished manuscript in the office of city historian of Havana, p. 258.
27. *La Lucha*, Havana, Aug. 22, 1895; *El País*, Havana, Aug. 22, 1895.
28. Williams to Uhl, Havana, Oct. 31, 1895, Consular Dispatches, Department of State, National Archives.
29. Flint, *op. cit.*, p. 21.
30. Weyler, *op. cit.*, vol. II, pp. 427-28.
31. *Ibid.*
32. Williams to Rockhill, Havana, April 11, 1896, Consular Dispatches, Department of State, National Archives.
33. Varona Guerrero, *op. cit.*, vol. II, p. 780.
34. *El País*, Havana, April 11, 1896.
35. Lee to Rockhill, Havana, June 25, 1896, Consular Dispatches, Department of State, National Archives.
36. Lee to Rockhill, Havana, Dec. 12, 1897, Consular Dispatches, Department of State, National Archives.
37. William J. Calhoun, Report on Cuba, June 22, 1897, Special Agents, XLVIII, Department of State, National Archives.
38. John F. Craig to John Sherman, Nov. 8, 1897, in William R. Day Papers, Library of Congress.
39. Lee to Rockhill, Havana, Dec. 12, 1897, Consular Dispatches, Department of State, National Archives; Nestor Arangueren to Alberto Arangueren, Camagüey, August 4, 1897, Archivo Nacional.
40. Stephen Bonsal, *The Real Condition of Cuba Today*, New York, 1898, p. 121.
41. Madan to Williams, March 13, 1896, Consular Dispatches, Department of State, National Archives.
42. Bonsal, *op. cit.*, p. 99.
43. Flint, *op. cit.*, p. 285; Varona Guerrero, *op. cit.*, vol. II, p. 780.
44. Carlos M. Trelles y Govín, *Bibliografía Cubana del siglo XIX*, Matanzas, 1915, vol. VIII, p. 202 and the prólogo.

45. Hudson Strode, *The Pageant of Cuba*, New York, 1936, p. 123.
46. *Foreign Relations*, 1897, p. 509; 55th Congress, 2nd Session, *Senate Report* 885, pp. 557-58; *New York Tribune*, Jan. 8, 1898.
47. Varona Guerrero, *op. cit.*, vol. II, p. 781.
48. Bonsal, *op. cit.*, p. 124.
49. Carreras y González, *op. cit.*, pp. 11-12.
50. Varona Guerrero, *op. cit.*, vol. II, p. 797.
51. Aurelio Collazo to Enrique L. Collazo, Havana, Sept. 25, 1897, Archivo Nacional.
52. William J. Calhoun, Report on Cuba, *op. cit.*
53. Lee to Rockhill, Havana, Dec. 12, 1897, Consular Dispatches, Department of State, National Archives.
54. Máximo Gómez to Estrada Palma, Camagüey, November, 1896, Archivo Nacional.
55. De Truffin to the Russian Ambassador to Madrid, September 15, 1896, *International Affairs*, Moscow, 1894, p. 122. See also Flint, *op. cit.*, pp. 25, 274.

CHAPTER VII

THE MILITARY AND POLITICAL SCENE IN 1897 AND EARLY 1898

1. *Diario de la Marina*, Havana, Dec., 19, 1896, Jan. 12, 1897.
2. *Ibid.*, Jan. 26, 1897. See also Máximo Gómez to Tomás Estrada Palma, Dec. 15, 1896, Archivo Nacional.
3. *International Affairs*, March, 1964, p. 124.
4. De Truffin to the Russian Ambassador to Madrid, July 15, 1897, *ibid.*, p. 124.
5. Benigno Souza, *Máximo Gómez*, La Havana, 1936, p. 269.
6. Calixto García to Estrada Palma, Baire, March 16, 1897, Archivo Nacional; Escalante, *op. cit.*, pp. 354-79, 383-84.
7. Escalante, *op. cit.*, p. 229.
8. For a detailed account of the Cuban victory, see *ibid.*, pp. 219-62.
9. Calixto García to Máximo Gómez, Tunas de Bayamo, Sept. 3, 1897, Archivo Nacional; Escalante, *op. cit.*, p. 258.
10. Calixto García to Estrada Palma, Tunas de Bayamo, Aug. 31, 1897, Archivo Nacional; Escalante, *op. cit.*, p. 258.
11. Calixto García to Estrada Palma, Las Paras (Holguín), June 26, 1897, Archivo Nacional.
12. *Ibid.*
13. Manuel Sastion, *La Insurrección en las Filipinas*, Madrid, 1897, pp. 460-75; Rafael Guerrero, *Crónica de la Guerra de Cuba*, Barcelona, 1895-97, vol. IV, p. 5; Marcial P. Lichauco, *The Conquest of the Philippines by the United States*, New York, 1926, pp. 26-31; John Foreman, *The Philippine Islands*, Hong Kong, 1890, pp. 370-75; *Senate Document No. 62*, 55th Congress, 3rd Session, pp. 319-20.
14. *El Correo*, Madrid, June 24, 1897, copy in William McKinley Papers, Library of Congress.

15. *Ibid.*; New York *Tribune*, May 20, 1897; Taylor to Sherman, June 3, 7, 1897, Dispatches from Spain, CXXXI, Department of State, National Archives.
16. New York *World*, Oct. 4, 1897.
17. New York *Herald*, Oct. 27, 1897.
18. Madrid *Heraldo*, Nov. 17, 1897, attached to John J. McCook to William R. Day, Nov. 30, 1897, William R. Day Papers, Library of Congress.
19. New York *World*, Oct. 18, 1897.
20. *Ibid.*, Oct. 4, 1897; Estrada Palma to John Sherman, May 12, 1897, Archives of the Secretary of State, Cuba-Notes, National Archives.
21. "God, Country and Liberty . . ." issued September 20, 1897, in Lee to the Department of State, Consular Dispatches, Havana, October 27, 1897, National Archives.
22. *Senate Document* No. 230, 55th Congress, 2nd Session; New York *World*, Nov. 24, 1897.
23. *La Discusion*, Havana, Jan. 9, 1898.
24. *Senate Document* 230, 55th Congress, 2nd Session, pp. 552-53, 557.
25. Stephen E. Barton, "The Red Cross in Cuba," *The Independent*, April 14, 1898; Clara Barton to Judge Wm. R. Day, Dec. 18, 1897, William R. Day Papers, Library of Congress; William E. Warton, *The Life of Clara Barton: Founder of the American Red Cross*, Boston and New York, pp. 205-08, 284; Blanche Colton Williams, Clara Barton, *Daughter of Destiny*, Philadelphia, 1941, p. 351; Ishbel Ross, *Angel of the Battlefield: The Life of Clara Barton*, New York, 1956, p. 222.
26. Report of Central Cuban Committee, New York, June 15, 1898, Clara Barton Papers, Box 42, Library of Congress.
27. J. K. Elwell to S. E. Barton, Habana, Feb. 23, 1898, Clara Barton Papers, Box 51, Library of Congress.
28. P. F. Hyatt to S. E. Barton, Santiago de Cuba, March 19, 1898, Clara Barton Papers, Box 52, Library of Congress.
29. Clara Barton to Stephen E. Barton, March 1, 1898, Clara Barton Papers, Box 6, Library of Congress; Stephen E. Barton to William R. Day, March 15, 1898, William R. Day Papers, *ibid.*
30. Report quoted in John D. Long to William R. Day, Feb. 7, 1898, William R. Day Papers, Library of Congress.
31. *Congressional Record*, 55th Congress, 2nd Session, pp. 5916-19.
32. *United States Foreign Relations Reports*, 1898, pp. 616-44.
33. Emilio Roig de Leuchsenring, *Máximo Gómez, El Libertador, op. cit.*, p. 42.
34. Portell Vila, *op. cit.*, p. 63.
35. Emilio Roig de Leuchsenring, *Máximo Gómez, El Libertador, op. cit.*, p. 41.
36. Lee to Assistant Secretary Day, Consular Dispatches, Department of State, Havana, Jan. 8, 1898, National Archives.
37. Lee to Day, Jan. 18, 1898, in *Senate Document* 230, 55th Congress, 2nd Session, p. 20.
38. *Foreign Relations*, 1898, p. 1025; Lee to Day, Jan. 13, 1898, telegram, Consular Dispatches, Department of State, Havana, National Archives.
39. New York *Sun*, Oct. 11, 1897.
40. *Ibid.*, Nov. 22, 1897.
41. Escalante, *op. cit.*, pp. 288-90.

42. Máximo Gómez to Colonel Ernesto Font Sterling, March 1, 1898, Rodríguez, *Algunos Documentos Políticos de Máximo Gómez, op. cit.*, pp. 19-20.
43. Day to Woodford, March 1, 1898, State Department Dispatches, National Archives.
44. *Congressional Record*, 55th Congress, 2nd Session, p. 3779; 55th Congress, 2nd Session, Senate Report 885, p. 534.
45. Walter B. Barker to William R. Day, March 25, 1898, William R. Day Papers, Library of Congress.
46. *El Socialista*, Madrid, reprinted in *The People*, New York City, May 15, 1898.
47. Laurence R. Nichols, "Domestic History," *op. cit.*, pp. 126-27.
48. S. L. Woodford to McKinley, Madrid, March 31, 1898, U.S. Department of State, *Papers Relating to the Foreign Relations of the United States*, Washington, D. C., 1889, vol. I, p. 727.
49. *Cuadernos de Historia Habanera*, No. 48, and reprinted in Duvon C. Corbitt, "Cuban Revisionist Interpretation of Cuba's Struggle for Independence," *Hispanic American Historical Review*, vol. XIII, Aug. 1963, p. 401.
50. Letter of Sergio Aguirre, Mariano, Cuba, marzo 6 de 1966, in possession of author.
51. Letter of Anibal Escalante, La Habana, marzo 16 de 1966, in possession of author.
52. Letter of Blas Roca, La Habana, abril 26 de 1966, in possession of author.
53. Undated letter of Julio Le Riverend, Havana, Cuba, in possession of author.
54. Foner, *op. cit.*, vol. II, pp. 346, 358-59.
55. Henry A. Himley to Richard B. Olney, April 29, 1896, Olney Papers, Library of Congress.
56. Emilio Roig de Leuchsenring, *Revolución y República en Maceo*, La Habana, 1945, pp. 52-54, 62.
57. Portuondo, *op. cit.*, pp. 90-91.
58. José Luciano Franco, *La Vida heroica y ejemplar de Maceo*, p. 111.
59. *Ibid.*
60. *Ibid.*
61. Franco, *op. cit.*, vol. III, p. 175.
62. Máximo Gómez to Grover Cleveland, Feb. 9, 1897, 55th Congress, *Senate Document 75*, Washington, D. C., 1897.
63. Calixto García to Tomás Estrada Palma, Potosi, Tunas, March 22, 1898, *Boletín del Archivo Nacional*, Havana, vol. 34, 1936, pp. 102-03.
64. Máximo Gómez to Estrada Palma, March 19, 1896, Archivo Nacional; Bernabé Boza, *Mi diario de la guerra*, vol. I, pp. 270-71; Emilio Roig de Leuchsenring, *Máximo Gómez, El Libertador*, pp. 42-44.
65. Emilio Roig de Leuchsenring, *los Estados Unidos contra Cuba libre*, La Habana, 1959, Vol. V, p. 23.
66. Colección Facticia, *Gobierno de Don Tomas Estrada Palma, 1902-1906*, Oficina del Historiador de la Cuidad.
67. Emeterio S. Santovenia, *Los presidentes de Cuba libre*, Habana, 1930, pp. 49-56; Charles E. Magoon, *Report of Provisional Administration: From October 13th, 1906 to December 1st, 1907*, Havana, 1908, p. 15; Panfilo D. Camacho, *Estrada Palma el Gobernante Honrado*, La Habana, 1938, pp. 176-77.

CHAPTER VIII

Latin America and the Cuban Revolution

1. *Patria*, Aug. 1, 1895.
2. Manuel Sanguily, *Brega de Libertad*, Havana, 1949, pp. 203-08.
3. Estrada Palma to Aristides Agüero, New York, Aug. 22, 1895, *Correspondencia diplomatica*, vol. I, p. 16.
4. New York, 1895.
5. The letters of Antonio Maceo, dated October 30, 1895, are in the Archivo Nacional, Havana, Cuba.
6. Franco, *op. cit.*, vol. II, p. 239.
7. Quoted in Emilio Roig de Leuchsenring, *Revolución y Republica en Maceo*, p. 51.
8. J. Fred Rippy, "Pan-Hispanic Propaganda in Hispanic America," *Political Scinece Quarterly*, vol. XXXVII, September, 1922, pp. 394-95.
9. Walter La Feber, "The Background of Cleveland's Venezuelan Policy: A Reinterpretation," *American Historical Review*, vol. LXVI, July, 1961, p. 953.
10. *The People*, New York, Oct. 25, Nov. 1, 1891.
11. Walter La Feber, "American Depression Diplomacy and the Brazilian Revolution, 1893-1894," *Hispanic American Historical Review*, vol. XL, Feb. 1960, pp. 126-48; Lawrence F. Hill, *Diplomatic Relations between the United States and Brazil*, New York, 1932, pp. 206-09.
12. *Papers Relating to the Foreign Relations of the United States*, Washington, D. C., 1896, vol. I, pp. 545-62. Hereinafter cited as *Foreign Relations*.
13. James D. Richardson, editor, *A Compilation of the Messages and Papers of the Presidents, 1789-1897*, Washington, D. C., 1900, vol. IX, pp. 656-58.
14. Walter La Feber, "The Background of Cleveland's Venezuelan Policy . . ." *op. cit.*, p. 948.
15. Varona Guerrero, *op. cit.*, vol. I, pp. 452-53.
16. Marshall M. True, "Revolutionaries in Exile: The Cuban Revolutionary Party, 1891-1898," unpublished Ph.D. thesis, University of Virginia, 1965, p. 192.
17. José Antonio Frias to Estrada Palma, Sept. 7, 1897, *Correspondencia diplomatica*, vol. IV, pp. 94-97.
18. Historia Portell Vilá, *Historia de la Guerra de Cuba y Los Estados Unidos Contra España*, La Habana, 1949, p. 132.
19. Jorge Basadre, *Historia de la Republic del Perú*, Tomo VII, Lima, 1963, pp. 3224-25.
20. Franco, *op. cit.*, vol. III, pp. 57-58.
21. *La Revolución del 95 segun correspondencia de la Delegación Cubana en Neuva York*, editada por Leon Primelles, La Habana, 1932, vol. I, p. 298.
22. Portell Vilá, *op. cit.*, p. 136.
23. *La Revolución del 95 segun la correspondencia de la Delegación Cubana en Neuva York*, *op. cit.*, vol. I, p. 353.
24. *Ibid.*, p. 356.
25. *Ibid.*, p. 358.
26. *Ibid.*, vol. III, p. 95.

27. *Ibid.*, vol. IV, p. 14.
28. Charmion C. Shelby, "Mexico and the Spanish-American War: Some Contemporary Expressions of Opinion," in Thomas E. Cotner, editor, Carlos E. Castaneda, co-editor, *Essays in Mexican History*, Austin, Texas, 1958, pp. 227-29.
29. Aristides Agüero to Estrada Palma, Santiago, Oct. 16, 23, *Correspondencia diplomatica*, vol. II, pp. 27-29, 31-33.
30. Aristides Agüero to Estrada Palma, Rio de Janeiro, Aug. 17, 1897, *ibid.*, vol. II, pp. 6-7.
31. Aristides Agüero to Eduardo Yero, Sucre, Bolivia, Sept. 24, 1896, *ibid.*, vol. II, pp. 60-61.
32. L. G. del Portiello, *Cuba y America*, New York, 1897, p. 21.
33. Indianapolis *Journal*, May 13, 1896.
34. Quoted in Norman Penlington, *Canada and Imperialism, 1896-1899*, Toronto, 1965, p. 103.

CHAPTER IX

The American People and Cuban Independence

1. Foner, *op. cit.*, vol. II, p. 331; Horatio S. Rubens, *Liberty, The Story of Cuba*, New York, 1932, pp. 101-02; *Encyclopedia Americana*, New York, 1898, vol. XVI, p. 252.
2. George W. Auxier, Jr., "The Propaganda Activities of the Cuban Junta in Precipitating the Spanish-American War," *Hispanic American Historical Review*, vol. XIX, Aug. 1939, p. 287.
3. Santovenia, *op. cit.*, pp. 49-56.
4. Estrada Palma to Antonio Maceo, New York, Aug. 20, 1895, Publicaciones del Archivo Nacional de Cuba, *Antonio Maceo; documentos para su vida*, Habana, 1945, p. 143.
5. Auxier, *op. cit.*, pp. 289-93; Raymond A. Detter, "The Cuban Junta in Michigan, 1895-1898," *Michigan History*, vol. LXVIII, March, 1964, pp. 36-37. Melville E. Stone, "The Associated Press," *Century Magazine*, vol. LXVIII, June, 1905, pp. 306-07; Joseph E. Wisan, *The Cuban Crisis as Reflected in the New York Press, 1895-1898*, New York, 1934, p. 34; Marcus M. Wilkerson, *Public Opinion and the Spanish-American War*, Baton Rouge, La., 1932, pp. 5-7.
6. Columbus *Dispatch*, March 3, 1896 and Cincinnati *Times-Star*, Dec. 11, 1896, both quoted in Auxier, "The Cuban Question . . ." *op. cit.*, pp. 41-42. See also Frederick Lawrence Knowles, *Poems of American Patriotism*, Boston, 1918, pp. 228, 234, 245, 246.
7. Omaha *Daily Bee*, Feb. 28, 1895 and Detroit *Journal*, Nov. 5, 1895, both quoted in Auxier, "The Cuban Question . . ." *op. cit.*, pp. 4-5.
8. Daniel E. Sickles to Richard B. Olney, Nov. 26, 1895, Olney Papers, Library of Congress.
9. Columbus *Evening Dispatch*, Jan. 26, 1897, quoted in Auxier, *op. cit.*, p. 103; Walter T. Nugent, *The Tolerant Populists: Kansas Populism and Nativism*, Chicago, 1963, pp. 211-12.

10. Herbert Aptheker, editor, *A Documentary History of the Negro People in the United States*, New York, 1951, vol. II, p. 791.
11. Philip S. Foner, *History of the Labor Movement in the United States*, New York, 1955, vol. II, p. 405. See also John C. Appel, "The Relation of American Labor to United States Imperialism, 1895-1905," unpublished Ph.D. thesis, University of Wisconsin, 1950, pp. 23, 31.
12. Howard H. Quint, "American Socialists and the Spanish-American War," *American Quarterly*, vol. X, Summer, 1958, p. 132. "Shall Cuba Be Free?" *The People*, Oct. 6, 1895.
13. *Journal of the Knights of Labor*, July 11, 18, 1895.
14. *Ibid.*, Oct. 3, Nov. 28, 1895.
15. *Ibid.*, May 20, June 17, July 1, Sept. 23, Aug. 5, 1897, April 1, 1898.
16. *Proceedings, A.F. of L. Convention*, 1895, pp. 63, 102; *Proceedings, A.F. of L. Convention*, 1896, pp. 50-51; *New York World*, Dec. 17, 1896.
17. *Atlanta Constitution*, Dec. 19, 1896.
18. *Proceedings, A.F. of L. Convention*, 1897, pp. 75, 89-90.
19. Foner, *History of the Labor Movement*, vol. II, p. 408.
20. Samuel Gompers, *Seventy Years of Life and Labor*, New York, 1924, vol. II, pp. 64-65.
21. John C. Appel, "The Unionization of Florida Cigarmakers and the Coming of the War with Spain," *Hispanic American Historical Review*, vol. XXXVI, Feb. 1956, p. 42.

CHAPTER X

Cleveland Stands Against the Cuban Revolution

1. "Congresos Nacionales de Historia," VI, en 1947, y IX, en 1957, in Antonio Núñez Jiménez, *La Liberación de las Islas*, La Habana, 1959, pp. 469-70.
2. James D. Richardson, editor, *A Compilation of the Messages and Papers of the Presidents of the United States*, New York, 1900, vol. XIII, pp. 6023-24.
3. "Preventing Conveyance of Articles to Cubans," 55th Congress, 2nd Session, *House Document 264*, Serial No. 3679, pp. 4-5.
4. Marugua to Greshan, Jan. 22, 1895; Dupuy de Lôme to Alvey A. Adee, Sept. 9, 1896, *Foreign Relations*, 1896, pp. 1187, 1199.
5. Horace E. Flack, "Spanish-American Diplomatic Relations Preceding the War of 1898," *Johns Hopkins University Studies in Historical and Political Science*, Series XXIV, Baltimore, 1906, pp. 22-30.
6. See, for example, Allan Nevins, *Grover Cleveland: A Study in Courage*, New York, 1933, pp. 71-215; H. Wayne Morgan, *America's Road to Empire: The War with Spain and Overseas Expansion*, New York, 1965; Ernest R. May, *Imperial Democracy: The Emergence of America as a Great Power*, New York, 1961, pp. 124-28.
7. Olney to Cleveland, Sept. 25, 1895, Grover Cleveland Papers, Library of Congress. See also Allan Nevins, editor, *Letters of Grover Cleveland, 1850-1908*, Boston, 1933, p. 410.

8. Cleveland to Olney, Sept. 29, 1895, Richard B. Olney Papers, Library of Congress.
9. Himley to Olney, unsigned, "Island of Cuba," Nov. 18, 1895, ibid.
10. Richardson, op. cit., vol. IX, pp. 636-37.
11. Published in "Affairs in Cuba," 55th Congress, 2nd Session, Senate Report 885, pp. 1-3.
12. Edwin Atkins, Sixty Years in Cuba: Reminiscences, Cambridge, Mass., 1926, p. 157.
13. Ibid., pp. 210-12; E. Atkins to Uhl, Dec. 9, 1895, Foreign Relations, 1895, p. 1217; Richard D. Weigle, "The Sugar Interests and American Diplomacy in Hawaii and Cuba, 1893-1903," unpublished Ph.D. thesis, Yale University, 1939, pp. 208-10.
14. Charles F. Rand to Olney, April 8, 1896, Olney Papers, Library of Congress.
15. Atkins to Olney, Nov. 20, 1895, Olney Papers, Library of Congress.
16. Atkins, op. cit., pp. 213-14.
17. Senate Report 885, op. cit., pp. 1-3.
18. Weigle, op. cit., pp. 211-12; Atkins, op. cit., pp. 199.
19. Congressional Record, 54th Cong., 1st Sess., pp. 24, 25, 105, 219, 272, 403, 482, 514, 577-78, 607, 725, 810, 815, 1020, 1086, 1376, 1552, 2148-49, 2294.
20. Ibid., pp. 105, 482, 2763.
21. Ibid., pp. 1065-66, 2281.
22. Ibid., pp. 1065-66, 1066-68. See also Eleanor E. Dennison, The Senate Foreign Relations Committee, Stanford University, California, 1942, pp. 77-79.
23. Congressional Record, 54th Cong., 1st Sess., pp. 1927-78, 2054-67, 2105-18.
24. Ibid., pp. 1967-70, 1978, 2163-69, 2246-48.
25. John Bassett Moore, "The Question of Cuban Belligerency," Forum, vol. XXI, May, 1896, pp. 288-300; Joseph H. Beale, Jr., "The Recognition of Cuban Belligerency," Harvard Law Review, vol. IX, Jan. 1896, pp. 406-09; Thomas S. Woolsey, "The Consequences of Cuban Belligerency," Yale Law Journal, vol. V, March, 1896, pp. 182-86; Amos S. Hershey, "The Recognition of Cuban Belligerency," Annals of the American Academy of Political and Social Sciences, vol. VII, May, 1896, pp. 450-61.
26. Congressional Record, 54th Cong., 1st Sess., p. 2257.
27. Ibid., p. 2342.
28. Ibid., p. 2347.
29. Ibid., pp. 2350, 2351, 2352, 2353 2359.
30. Ibid., pp. 2679-85; New York Herald, April 7, 1896; Washington Post, April 7-8, 1896.
31. Congressional Record, 54th Cong., 1st Sess., pp. 2351, 2353.
32. Wisan, op. cit., p. 102.
33. Entries in William L. Wilson's Ms Diary, cited in Nevins, Grover Cleveland, p. 715; Dennison, op. cit., pp. 79-80.
34. American Federationist, vol. III, June, 1896, p. 70.
35. Quoted from Spanish Archives in Orestes Ferrara, The Last Spanish War, New York, 1937, p. 16. Emphasis mine. P.S.F.
36. Cleveland to Olney, April 7, 1896, Olney Papers, Library of Congress.
37. Foreign Relations, 1897, pp. 452-58.

38. Dupuy de Lôme to Olney, Jan. 10, 1896, Olney Papers, Library of Congress.
39. Rayford W. Logan, *The Negro in American Life and Thought: The Nadir, 1877-1901*, New York, 1954, pp. 82-83.
40. *Foreign Relations*, 1897, pp. 452-58.
41. Dupuy de Lôme to the Duke de Tetuán, April 10, 1896, *Spanish Diplomatic Correspondence and Documents, 1896-1900: Presented to the Cortes by the Minister of State*, Washington, D.C., 1905, p. 3.
42. Atkins to Olney, May 5, 1896, Olney Papers, Library of Congress.
43. Olney to Atkins, May 7, 1896, Olney Papers, Library of Congress.
44. Olney to Cleveland, May 11, 1896, Cleveland Papers, Library of Congress; Weigle, *op. cit.*, pp. 218-19.
45. *República Cubana*, May 14, 1896.
46. Duke de Tetuán to Dupuy de Lôme, May 22, 1896; Dupuy de Lôme to Olney, June 14, 1896, *Spanish Diplomatic Correspondence, op. cit.*, pp. 9-13; *Foreign Relations*, 1897, pp. 544-48.
47. Lee to Olney, June 24, 1896; Cleveland to Olney, July 16, 1896, Olney Papers, Library of Congress.
48. Frederick W. Lawrence to Richard B. Olney, May 18, 1896, Olney Papers, Library of Congress.
49. Thomas H. McKee, *The National Conventions and Platforms of All Political Parties, 1789-1900*, Baltimore, 1900, pp. 297, 301-03; *New York Journal*, June 6, 1896; *New York Sun*, June 15, 1896.
50. Richardson, *op. cit.*, vol. XIV, pp. 6148-54. Emphasis mine, P.S.F.
51. *Ibid.*; *New York World*, Dec. 8, 1896.
52. *New York Herald*, Dec. 9, 1896.
53. *Spanish Diplomatic Correspondence, op. cit.*, p. 14.
54. *El Heraldo* and *Correspondencia Militar* of Madrid reprinted in *New York Sun* and *New York Journal*, Dec. 10, 1896.
55. Núñez Jiménez, *op. cit.*, p. 471.
56. Emilio Roig de Leuchsenring, *Cuba no debe su independencia a los Estados Unidos*, La Habana, 1950, p. 69.
57. *Congressional Record*, 54th Cong., 2nd Sess., p. 326. For other resolutions, see pp. 14, 39, 60, 131, 133, 157, 189.
58. "Can Congress Recognize the Independence of Cuba?" *Literary Digest*, vol. XIV, 1896, p. 225; Nevins, *Grover Cleveland*, pp. 717-18.
59. Atkins, *op. cit.*, pp. 212-13.
60. Henry Cabot Lodge, *The War with Spain*, Boston, 1899, p. 20.
61. *New York Evening Post*, Feb. 16, 1897.
62. Atkins to Olney, Dec. 16, 1896; Lee to Olney, Jan. 9, 1897, enclosing Sproton to Stillman, Jan. 4, 1897, Olney Papers, Library of Congress.
63. Lee to Olney, Jan. 23, 1897, Olney Papers, Library of Congress.
64. Olney to Lee, Jan. 18, 21, 1897; De Lôme to Olney, Jan. 19, 1897; Stillman to Olney, Jan. 31, 1897, Olney Papers, Library of Congress.
65. Lee to Olney, Feb. 18, 1897, enclosing Stillman to Lee, Feb. 15, 1897 and Atkins to Lee, Feb. 16, 1897, *ibid.*; Duke de Tetuán to Dupuy de Lôme, Feb. 5, 1897, *Spanish Diplomatic Correspondence, op. cit.*, pp. 19-24.

NOTES 329

CHAPTER XI

McKinley Prepares to Crush the Cuban Revolution

1. Letter from general superintendent of the Juraguá Iron Company to Josiah Monroe, Jan. 20, 1897, enclosed in Monroe to Olney, Jan. 30, 1897, Miscellaneous Letters to the Department of State, National Archives; Willett and Gray's *Statistical Sugar Trade Journal*, Jan. 14, 1897; New York *Sun*, Feb. 9, 1897.
2. Schriftgiesser, *op. cit.*, pp. 164-65; Whitelaw Reid to William McKinley, Phoenix, Arizona, Dec. 5, 1896, McKinley Papers, Library of Congress and Whitelaw Reid Letterbook, *ibid*.
3. New York *Journal*, Jan. 17, 1897.
4. John Sherman to McKinley, Feb. 1897, McKinley Papers, Library of Congress. Emphasis mine. P.S.F.
5. Richardson, *op. cit.*, vol. XIV, pp. 640-42.
6. Undated notes for a speech, McKinley Papers, Library of Congress, Volume IV.
7. Olney to De Lôme, April 1, 1897, Olney Papers, Library of Congress.
8. New York *World*, April 6, 1897.
9. Washington *Evening Star*, May 19, 1897.
10. *Congressional Record*, 55th Cong., 1st Sess., pp. 1186, 1193-94, 1196-1202.
11. Memorial to the Secretary of State, enclosed in George R. Mosle, New York, to Sherman, May 17, 1897, Miscellaneous Letters to Department of State, National Archives.
12. New York *Times*, May 15, 1897.
13. Washington *Post*, April 23, 1897.
14. *Ibid.*, April 29, 1897.
15. William J. Calhoun, Report on Cuba, June 22, 1897, Special Agents, Department of State, XLVIII, National Archives.
16. Sherman to Dupuy de Lôme, June 26, 1897, *Foreign Relations*, 1897, pp. 507-08.
17. Washington *Post*, Sept. 13, 1897.
18. *Foreign Relations*, 1898, pp. 558-61.
19. Woodford to McKinley, Aug. 10, 1897, Reports to the President, Spain: Dispatches, CXXXIA, nos. 1, 2, National Archives.
20. Woodford to McKinley, Aug. 10, 19, 1897, *ibid*.
21. Woodford to Sherman, Oct. 23, 1897, *Foreign Relations*, 1898, pp. 582-83, 594-95.
22. Estrada Palma to John Sherman, May 12, 1897, State Department files, Cuban Notes, vol. I, National Archives.
23. New York *Tribune*, Oct. 3, 8, 29, 1897.
24. Woodford to Sherman, Oct. 16, 1897, Spain: Dispatches, CXXXII, No. 47; Woodford to McKinley, Oct. 17, 1897, Reports to the President, Spain: Dispatches, CXXXIA, No. 11, National Archives.
25. Woodford to McKinley, Nov. 7, 14, 1897, Reports to the President, Spain: Dispatches, CXXXIA, nos. 14, 15, 1897, National Archives.
26. Woodford to McKinley, Nov. 14, 1897, *ibid*. Emphasis mine. P.S.F.
27. Woodford to McKinley, Oct. 20, 1897, Reports to the President, Spain: Dispatches, CXXXIA, No. 11, National Archives.

28. Washington Post, May 23, 1897; New York World, May 24, 1897; New York Tribune, May 25, June 8, 1897. John J. McCook to J. B. Foraker, Jan. 3, 1896, J. B. Foraker Papers, Cincinnati Historical Society.
29. Margaret Leech, In the Days of McKinley, New York, 1959, p. 107.
30. The above account of the two contracts is based on Herminio Portell Vilá, Historia de Cuba en sus relaciones con los Estados Unidos y España, La Habana, 1939, vol. III, pp. 348-61; Herminio Portell Vilá, Historio de la Guerra de Cuba y los Estados Unidos contra España, pp. 140-52; Report of National Congress of Cuban Historians, in Antonio Núñez Jiménez, op. cit., pp. 475-77; Emilio Roig de Leuchsenring, Cuba no debe su independencia a los Estados Unidos, pp. 74-77.
31. John J. McCook to William R. Day, Sept. 11, 14, 16, 17, 23, Oct. 7, Nov. 17, 30, 1897, Day Papers, Library of Congress.
32. Dupuy de Lôme to Gullón, Dec. 2, 1897, Spanish Correspondence, op. cit., p. 43.
33. Richardson, op. cit., vol. XIV, pp. 654-63.
34. New York Sun, Dec. 12, 1897.
35. McCook to Day, Dec. 17, 1897, Day Papers, Library of Congress.
36. Congressional Record, 55th Cong., 2nd Sess., pp. 35, 39-40; Washington Post, Dec. 7, 15, 1897.
37. Lee to Day, Nov. 27, Dec. 27, Dec. 1, 7, 1897, Consular Letters, Havana, CXXXI, National Archives.
38. Lee to Day, Dec. 1, 1897, ibid.
39. Lee to Day, Dec. 31, 1897, ibid.
40. Lee to Day, Dec. 1, 15, 1897, ibid.; Charles D. Sigsbee, The Maine, An Account of Her Destruction in Havana Harbor; Personal Narrative, New York, 1900, pp. 1-3, 5, 9-10.
41. E. E. Morison, editor, The Letters of Theodore Roosevelt, vol. I, Cambridge, Mass, 1951, pp. 750-51; Laurence S. Mayo, America of Yesterday as Reflected in the Journal of John Davis Long, Boston, 1923, pp. 154-55; Millis, op. cit., p. 81.
42. Dupuy de Lôme to Gullón, Dec. 16, 1897, Spanish Correspondence, op. cit., p. 52; Roosevelt to William A. Chanle, Dec. 23, 1897, Theodore Roosevelt Papers, Library of Congress.
43. Woodford to McKinley, Dec. 26, 1897, Jan. 8, 1898, Reports to the President, Spain: Dispatches, CXXXIA, National Archives.
44. Roosevelt to William A. Chanle, Dec. 23, 1897, Theodore Roosevelt Papers, Library of Congress; Secretary of the Navy, Annual Reports of the Navy Department for the Year 1898, Washington, 1898, p. 3.
45. Lee to Day, Jan. 13, 1898, Consular Letters, Havana, CXXXI, National Archives.
46. Lee to Day, Jan. 12, 13, ibid.
47. Congressional Record, 55th Cong., 2nd Sess., pp. 760-61, 767-69; Washington Post, Jan. 20, 1898.
48. Gonzalo de Quesada to Tomá Estrada Palma, Jan. 21, 1898, Correspondencia diplomática de la delegación cubana, . . . op. cit., vol. V, p. 122.
49. Memorandum of an interview with Dupuy de Lôme, Jan. 24, 1898, Day Papers, Library of Congress; Dupuy de Lôme to Gullón, Jan. 24, 1898, Spanish Diplomatic Correspondence, op. cit., p. 68.

NOTES 331

50. Letter of Albertini to Estrada Palma, Jan. 24, 1898, *Correspondencia diplomática, op. cit.,* vol. V, p. 123.
51. Roosevelt to C. Whitney Tillighast, Jan. 13, 1898; Roosevelt to Long, Jan. 14, 1898; Roosevelt to William Astor Chanle, Dec. 14, 1897, Morison, *op. cit.,* vol. I, pp. 358-59, 746-47.
52. Alvee A. Adee to William R. Day, Jan. 12, 1898, marked "confidential," Reports of Bureau Officers, Department of State, National Archives.
53. Portell Vilá, *op. cit.,* p. 77.

CHAPTER XII

THE ROAD TO WAR

1. Sigsbee, *op. cit.,* pp. 24-30; Lee to Day, Jan. 26, 1898, Consular Letters, Havana, CXXXI, National Archives.
2. Day to Lee, Feb. 4, 1898, *Foreign Relations,* 1898, pp. 1027-28; Lee to Day, Feb. 5, 1898, Consular Letters, Havana, CXXXI; Sigsbee to Long, Feb. 1, 1898, Miscellaneous Letters, State Department, National Archives.
3. *Washington Post,* Jan. 26, 1898; *Foreign Relations,* 1898, pp. 672, 1026; Portell Vilá, *op. cit.,* p. 71.
4. Secretary of the Navy, *Annual Reports,* 1898, p. 325; De Lôme to Gullón, Feb. 7, 1898, *Spanish Diplomatic Correspondence, op. cit.,* vol. I, p. 117.
5. *Washington Post,* Feb. 5, 1898; Pascual Cervera, *The Spanish-American War,* New York, 1903, pp. 22-24.
6. George R. Mosle, William Moore Carson, and George Turnure to Day, Feb. 9, 1898, enclosing memorial, Miscellaneous Letters, Department of State, National Archives.
7. *New York Journal,* Feb. 9, 1898.
8. Rubens, *op. cit.,* pp. 287-90. *See also* Portell Vilá, *op. cit.,* pp. 89-90.
9. Rubens, *op. cit.,* pp. 290-91; Sherman to Woodford, Feb. 23, 1898, *Foreign Relations,* 1898, pp. 1018-20.
10. Woodford to Sherman, Feb. 17, 1898, Spain: Dispatches, State Department, CXXXIII, National Archives.
11. *Washington Post,* Feb. 15, 1898.
12. H. Wayne Morgan, "The De Lôme Letter: A New Appraisal," *The Historian,* vol. XXVI, Nov. 1963, p. 47.
13. Sherman to Woodford, Feb. 23, 1898, *Foreign Relations,* 1898, p. 1019.
14. Rubens, *op. cit.,* pp. 326-29.
15. *Foreign Relations,* 1898, p. 672.
16. Lee to Day, Feb. 15, 1898, Consular Letters, Havana, CXXXI, National Archives.
17. Lee to Day, Feb. 16, 1898, *Foreign Relations,* 1898, p. 1029; Lee to Day, Feb. 16, 1898, personal, Consular Letters, LXXXII, National Archives.
18. *Washington Post,* Feb. 17, 18, 1898; *Washington Evening Star,* Feb. 17, 1898; *New York Tribune,* Feb. 17, 1898.
19. "Report of the Spanish Board of Inquiry," 55th Cong., 2nd Sess., *Senate Report* 885, pp. 595-98.

20. "Destruction of the Battleship Maine," 55th Cong., 2nd Sess., Senate Document 207, pp. 279-80.
21. Washington *Evening Star*, Feb. 16, 1898; Washington *Post*, Feb. 17, 1898.
22. Wisan, *op. cit.*, p. 391.
23. *Ibid.*, pp. 391-92.
24. "The Disaster to the 'Maine,'" *Literary Digest*, vol. XVI, 1898, pp. 242-44.
25. Sigsbee, *op. cit.*, pp. 75-79; New York *Herald*, Feb. 17, 1898; New York *World*, Feb. 18, 1898.
26. Lee to Day, March 1, 1898, Consular Letters, CXXXII, National Archives.
27. Washington *Evening Star*, Feb. 25, 1898; Washington *Post*, Feb. 25-27, March 1, 1898.
28. Roosevelt to Diblee, Feb. 16, 1898, Roosevelt Papers, Library of Congress; Adelbert Dewey, *Life and Letters of Admiral Dewey*, New York, 1899, p. 204; Mayo, *op. cit.*, pp. 169-70; Millis, *op. cit.*, p. 112; Portell Vilá, *op. cit.*, p. 82.
29. Washington *Post*, Feb. 20, 1898; John L. Offner, "President McKinley and the Origins of the Spanish-American War," unpublished Ph.D. thesis, Pennsylvania State University, 1957, p. 236.
30. L. W. Busbey, *Uncle Joe Cannon*, New York, 1927, pp. 186-90; Washington *Evening Star*, March 7-8, 1898; Washington *Post*, March 8, 1898.
31. New York *Herald*, March 10, 1898; New York *Journal*, March 8, 1898.
32. Washington *Post*, March 11, 13, 1898; McCook to James H. Wilson, March 5, 1898, Wilson Papers, Library of Congress; Royal Cortissoz, *The Life of Whitelaw Reid*, New York, 1921, vol. II, pp. 220-21.
33. *Cf.* New York *World*, March 16, 1898.
34. Oscar S. Straus to James B. Angell, March 22, 1898, Oscar S. Straus Papers, Library of Congress.
35. Washington *Evening Star*, March 21, 23, 24, 28-29, 1898; Washington *Post*, March 22, 23, 24, 28-29, 1898; New York *Tribune*, March 24, 29, 1898; Allen, *op. cit.*, p. 77.
36. Report of the Spanish Board of Inquiry," *op. cit.*, pp. 595-98.
37. "Destruction of the Battleship Maine," *op. cit.*, pp. 279-95.
38. "Affairs in Cuba," 55th Cong., 2nd Sess., *Senate Report* 885, p.v.
39. "Treaty of Peace Between the United States and Spain," 55th Cong., 3rd Sess., *Senate Document* 62, p. 642.
40. *Scientific American*, vol. CVI, Jan. 27, 1912, p. 85.
41. Millis, *op. cit.*, p. 129.
42. *Ibid.*
43. Cervera, *op. cit.*, p. 25.
44. Lee to Day, March 30, 1898, Consular Letters, Havana, CXXXII, National Archives; "Affairs in Cuba," *op. cit.*, pp. 508-10.
45. New York *Journal*, March 17, 1898.
46. *Labor Leader*, April 23, 1898, p. 133. See also John H. McMinn, "The Attitude of the English Press toward the United States during the Spanish-American War," unpublished Ph.D. thesis, Ohio State University, 1939, p. 31.
47. Ferdinand Lundberg, *Imperial Hearst*, New York, 1936, p. 81.
48. W. A. Swanberg, *Citizen Hearst: A Biography of William Randolph Hearst*, New York, 1961, p. 137.

49. George Bronson Rea, *Facts and Fakes About Cuba, op. cit.*, p. 249; "Affairs in Cuba," *op. cit.*, p. 395.
50. John J. McCook, "Memorandum on a Cuban Settlement, March 1, 1898," and McCook to Day, Friday 2 P.M., Day Papers, Library of Congress; Whitelaw Reid to Max G. Seckendorff, March 9, 1898, Reid Papers and Whitelaw Reid to McKinley, March 9, 1898, McKinley Papers, Library of Congress.
51. *Washington Post*, March 27, 29, 30, 1898; *New York Journal*, March 18, 1898.
52. H. Wayne Morgan, *William McKinley and His America*, Syracuse, New York, 1963, p. 331.
53. Rubens, *op. cit.*, pp. 326-29.
54. *Washington Post*, March 30, 1898; *Detroit Free Press*, Feb. 23, 1898; Detter, *op. cit.*, p. 43.
55. Alger to Day, March 8, 1898, Day Papers, Library of Congress.
56. *Congressional Record*, 55th Cong., 2nd Sess., pp. 5916-19.
57. Woodford to McKinley, March 17, 28, 1898, Reports to the President, Spain: Dispatches, CXXXI-A, No. 143, National Archives.
58. Day to Woodford, March 25, 1898, Day Papers, Library of Congress; Day to Woodford, March 26, 1898; Woodford to Day, March 27, 1898; Day to Woodford, March 28, 1898, *Foreign Relations*, 1898, pp. 704, 712-13.
59. Day to Woodford, March 27, 1898, *Foreign Relations*, 1898, pp. 711-12, 1936-37; "Memorandum of interview with Mr. Polo, March 29, 1898," Day Papers, Library of Congress.
60. McCook to McKinley, enclosing Memorandum, March 12, 1898, McKinley Papers, Library of Congress; *Washington Post*, March 29, 1898.
61. Woodford to McKinley, March 26, 1898, Reports to the President, Spain: Dispatches, CXXXI-A, National Archives. Hereinafter cited as NA.
62. *Washington Evening Star*, March 30, 31, 1898; *Washington Post*, March 30, 31, 1898.
63. *Congressional Record*, 55th Congress, 2nd Sess., pp. 3293, 3294, 3341, 3401 3414.
64. *Washington Post*, March 30, 1898; *Washington Evening Star*, March 30, 1898.
65. Woodford to Day, March 31, 1898, *Foreign Relations*, 1898, pp. 726-27; *Spanish Diplomatic Correspondence, op. cit.*, pp. 107-08; *New York Tribune*, April 1, 1898.
66. *Washington Post*, April 2, 1898; *New York Tribune*, April 1, 3, 1898.

CHAPTER XIII

Imperial Intervention

1. Orestes Ferrara, *Tentativas de Intervención Europea en América, 1896-1898*, Habana, 1933, pp. 12-15.
2. London *Economist*, vol. LVI, March 12, 1898, p. 383; vol. LVII, May 20, 1898, p. 719.

3. R. G. Neale, *Great Britain and United States Expansion*: 1898-1900, Michigan State University Press, 1966, pp. 5, 118, 122.
4. J. Fred Rippy, *The European Powers and the Spanish-American War*, Chapel Hill, N. C., 1927, pp. 12-16.
5. Woodford to McKinley, Feb. 9, 1898, Reports to the President, National Archives.
6. Lester B. Shippee, "Germany and the Spanish-American War," *American Historical Review*, vol. XXX, July, 1925, pp. 754-56; Rippy, *op. cit.*, p. 24; Neale, *op. cit.*, pp. 13-14.
7. Otto von Bulow to German Foreign Office, March 20, 1898; Otto von Bulow to Radowitz, March 31, 1898, *Die Grosse Politik der Europeischen Kabinete*, 1871-1914, Deutsche verlagsgellschaft für Politik und Geschichte, Berlin, 1924, vol. XV, pp. 16, 18, Nos. 4132, 4138; John T. Farrell, "Archbishop Ireland and Manifest Destiny," *Catholic Historical Review*, vol. XXXIII, 1947, pp. 289-99.
8. *Die Grosse Politik*, *op. cit.*, p. 19, No. 4134.
9. *Ibid.*, p. 20, No. 4136; Ferrara, *The Last Spanish American War*, p. 128.
10. Woodford to McKinley, April 3, 1898, Reports to the President, NA; Day to Woodford, April 3, 1898; Woodford to Day, April 5, 1898, *Foreign Relations*, 1898, pp. 732-33, 736.
11. Washington *Post*, April 4, 5, 1898; Washington *Star*, April 4, 5, 1898; New York *Tribune*, April 5, 1898.
12. Woodford to McKinley, April 5, 1898; Day to Woodford, April 5, 1898, *Foreign Relations*, 1898, pp. 734-35.
13. *Foreign Relations*, 1898, pp. 740-41.
14. Washington *Evening Star*, April 6, 1898; Washington *Post*, April 6, 8, 1898; Detroit *Journal*, April 7, 1898; Rubens, *op. cit.*, pp. 339-41.
15. Washington *Post*, April 8, 1898; Detroit *Free Press*, April 7, 1898; Detter *op. cit.*, p. 44.
16. Polo de Bernabé to Sherman,. April 10, 1898, *Foreign Relations*, 1898, pp. 747-49.
17. Memorandum, April 10, 1898, Day Papers, Library of Congress; Offner *op. cit.*, p. 335; Washington *Evening Star*, April 9, 11, 1898; Washington *Post*, April 11, 1898.
18. Millis, *op. cit.*, p. 140.
19. Washington *Evening Star*, April 11, 1898; London *Times*, April 12, 1898.
20. Portell Vilá, *op. cit.*, p. 119.
21. Richards, *op. cit.*, vol. X, pp. 139-47.
22. *Congressional Record*, 55th Cong., 2nd Sess., pp. 3765- 3380.
23. Washington *Post*, April 12, 1898.
24. Washington *Evening Star*, April 11, 1898; New York *Tribune*, April 12, 1898; *Congressional Record*, 55th Cong., 2nd Sess., p. 3732.
25. Alger to McKinley, April 15, 1898, McKinley Papers, Library of Congress; Secretary of the Navy, *Annual Reports*, 1898, p. 326.
26. *Congressional Record*, 55th Cong., 2nd Sess., pp. 3810, 3847; Detter, *op. cit.*, p. 45; Detroit *Free Press*, April 12-13, 1898.
27. *Congressional Record*, 55th Cong., 2nd Sess., pp. 3815-16. Emphasis mine. P.S.F.
28. *Ibid.*, pp. 3815-16; Washington *Post*, April 14, 1898.
29. *Congressional Record*, 55th Cong., 2nd Sess., pp. 3817-18.

30. *Ibid.*, pp. 3819-21.
31. *Ibid.*, p. 3773.
32. *Ibid.*, pp. 3293, 3776.
33. *Ibid.*, p. 885.
34. *Ibid.*, pp. 3777-80.
35. *Ibid.*, pp. 3842, 4031.
36. *Ibid.*, p. 3988.
37. *Ibid.*
38. *Ibid.*, pp. 3992-93.
39. David F. Healy, *The United States in Cuba, 1898-1902*, Madison, Wisconsin, 1963, p. 27.
40. Rubens, *op. cit.*, pp. 341-42.
41. Elmer Moore Ellis, *Henry Moore Teller, Defender of the West*, Caldwell, Idaho, 1941, pp. 300-09.
42. Herminio Portell Vilá, *Hostoria de Cuba en sus relaciones con los Estados Unidos y España*, La Habana, 1939, vol. III, pp. 446-48.
43. Margaret Leech, *In the Days of McKinley*, New York, 1959, p. 188.
44. Auxier, Jr., "The Cuban Question," *op. cit.*, p. 16; James P. Shenton, "Imperialism and Racism," in Donald Sheehan and Harold C. Syrett, editors, *Essays in American Historiography in Honor of Allan Nevins*, New York, 1960, pp. 234-35; Philip Wayne Kennedy, "The Concept of Racial Superiority and United States Imperialism, 1890-1910," unpublished Ph.D. thesis, St. Louis University, 1962, pp. 28-29, 154-64; Oscar S. Straus to McKinley, March 12, 1898, Oscar S. Straus Papers, Library of Congress.
45. Memorandum, March 22, 1898, attached to John J. McCook to McKinley, March 22, 1898, McKinley Papers, Library of Congress.
46. John J. McCook to James H. Wilson, March 26, 1898, Wilson Papers, Library of Congress.
47. *Congressional Record*, 55th Cong., 2nd Sess., pp. 3684-85.
48. This account is based on the following sources: Report of Congress of National Cuban Historians, 1947, in Jiménez, *op. cit.*, pp. 477-80; Portell Vilá, *Historia de la Guerra de Cuba y los Estados Unidos Contra España*, pp. 147-57, 170-71; Portell Vilá, *Historia de Cuba, op. cit.*, pp. 355-61; Herbert C. Squires to John Hay, Sept. 9, 1904, enclosing memorandum, Consular Dispatches, Havana, NA.
49. Jiménez, *op. cit.*, pp. 479-80; Portell Vilá, *Historia de la Guerra, op. cit.*, pp. 170-71; Emilio Roig de Leuchsenring, *op. cit.*, pp. 74-75.
50. Leech, *op. cit.*, p. 188; Charlies G. Dawes, *A Journal of the McKinley Years*, Chicago, 1950, p. 154; *New York Times*, April 19, 1898.
51. *New York Tribune*, April 18, 1898; *Congressional Record*, 55th Cong., 2nd Sess., pp. 4041-43.
52. *Congressional Record*, 55th Cong., 2nd Sess., pp. 4040-41, 4062-63.
53. Williams to Sherman, April 24, 1898, Department of State, Manila, Consular Letters, NA.
54. *Congressional Record*, 55th Cong., 2nd Sess., pp. 4228-29, 4244, 4252.
55. *Detroit Free Press*, April 20, 1898.
56. Portell Vilá, *Historia de la Guerra, op. cit.*, pp. 190-92.
57. Louis A. Coolidge, *An Old-Fashioned Senator: Orville H. Platt*, New York, 1919, pp. 281-82.

58. Letter of Sergio Aguirre, Mariano, Cuba, marzo de 1966, in possession of author.
59. Reid to McKinley, April 19, 1898, McKinley Papers, Library of Congress. See also Cortissoz, op. cit., vol. II, pp. 222-23.
60. James D. Richardson, *A Compilation of the Messages and Papers of the President*, vol. XIII, p. 6289.
61. Jack C. Lane, "Instrument for Empire: The American Military Government in Cuba, 1899-1902," unpublished paper presented to sessions of Southern Historical Association, Houston, Texas, November, 1971, p. 3.

CHAPTER XIV

Why the United States Went to War

1. New York, 1961, pp. 23-24.
2. *Labour Leader*, June 4, 1898; McMinn, op. cit., pp. 92-95.
3. Reprinted in *The People*, May 22, 1898.
4. McMinn, op. cit., pp. 79-81, 84; London *Times*, April 14, 1898.
5. James Louis Whitehead, "French Reaction to American Imperialism, 1895-1908," unpublished Ph.D. thesis, University of Pennsylvania, 1943, pp. 77-79.
6. *The People*, April 24, 1898.
7. *Ibid.*, April 17, 24, May 1, 8, 15, 22, 29, 1898.
8. Undated newspaper clipping, Algernon Lee Papers, Tamiment Institute Library of New York University.
9. *World's Work*, January, 1902, p. 224; New York *Tribune*, March 23, 1902.
10. J. A. Hobson, *Imperialism, A Study*, London, 1938, pp. 77-78. V. I. Lenin, *Imperialism: The Highest Stage of Capitalism*, New York, 1939, p. 15.
11. Harold U. Faulkner, *American Economic History*, New York, 1924, pp. 624-25.
12. Harry Elmer Barnes, *World Politics in Modern Civilization*, New York, 1930, p. 233.
13. Charles A. Beard, *The Idea of National Interest*, New York, 1934, pp. 65-70, 78-83.
14. Louis M. Hacker, "The Holy War of 1898," *American Mercury*, vol. XXI, Nov. 1930, p. 326.
15. Marcus M. Wilkinson, *Public Opinion and the Spanish-American War: A Study in War Propaganda*, Baton Rouge, La., 1932, p. 132.
16. Joseph E. Wisan, *The Cuban Crisis as Reflected in the New York Press, 1895-1898*, New York, 1934, p. 458.
17. George W. Auxier, Jr., "Middle Western Newspapers and the Spanish-American War, 1895-1898," *Mississippi Valley Historical Review*, vol. XXVI, 1940, pp. 528-29.
18. Julius W. Pratt, "American Business and the Spanish-American War," *Hispanic American Historical Review*, vol. XIX, May, 1934, pp. 163-201.
19. Julius W. Pratt, *Expansionists of 1898: The Acquisition of Hawaii and the Spanish Islands*, Baltimore, 1936, pp. 22, 230-316.

20. *Cf.* Oscar Handlin, *Chance of Destiny: Turning-points in American History*, Boston, 1945, pp. 121-42; John D. Hicks, *The American Nation*, Boston, 1949, p. 113; Sidney Hook, *The Hero in History*, Boston, 1955, pp. 53-54.
21. Charles A. Beard, *Giddy Minds and Foreign Quarrels: An Estimate of American Foreign Policy*, New York, 1939, p. 236.
22. Quoted in Foster R. Dulles, *America's Rise to World Power*, New York, 1955, p. 41.
23. New York, 1959, p. 223.
24. Compare Dulles, *America in the Pacific*, New York, 1932, pp. 22735, with *China and America*, Princeton, N. J., pp. 101-04; *The Imperial Years*, New York, 1956, pp. 165-83; and *America's Rise to World Power*, pp. 40-41, especially note 1, p. 41.
25. *The President Makers*, New York, 1940, p. 79.
26. *The Rise of Modern America, 1865-1951*, New York, 1951, p. 185.
27. *A Diplomatic History of the American People*, New York, 1950, p. 504.
28. *A Diplomatic History of the United States*, revised edition, New York, 1936, p. 437.
29. *The Far Eastern Policy of the United States*, New York, 1938, pp. 8-9.
30. *Theodore Roosevelt and the Rise of America to World Power*, Baltimore, 1956, pp. 55, 449.
31. "The Needless War with Spain," in *Times of Trial*, edited by Allan Nevins, New York, 1958, pp. 179-86.
32. "Manifest Destiny and the Philippines," in *America in Crisis*, edited by Daniel Aaron, New York, 1952, pp. 188-89.
33. Arthur Barcan, "American Imperialism and the Spanish American War," unpublished M.A. thesis, Columbia University, 1940, pp. 5, 11, 21, 100-01, 108-10.
34. Ralph Dewar Bald., Jr., "The Development of Expansionist Sentiment in the United States, 1885-195, as Reflected in Periodical Literature," unpublished Ph.D. thesis, University of Pittsburgh, 1953, pp. 121-25, 216-16.
35. *Science & Society*, Spring, 1958, pp. 129-43.
36. *Science & Society*, Spring, 1959, pp. 133-62.
37. *Daily People*, Oct. 14, 1900.
38. William Appleman Williams, *The Tragedy of American Diplomacy, 1750-1955*, New York, 1959, pp. 31, 32-33, 34; *The Contours of American History*, Cleveland & New York, 1961, pp. 349, 363-68; *The United States, Cuba and Castro*, New York, 1962, pp. 5-6. See also Williams' review of Ernest R. May's *Imperial Democracy: The Emergence of America as a Great Power*, in *Studies on the Left*, vol. III, 1963, pp. 94-99.
39. Thomas McCormick, "'A Fair Field and no Favor': American China Policy during the McKinley Administration 1897-1901," unpublished Ph.D. thesis, University of Wisconsin, 1960, pp. 145-46, 153-54; "Insular Imperialism and the Open Door: The China Market and the Spanish American War," *Pacific Historical Review*, vol. XXXII, May, 1963, pp. 155-69.
40. Ithaca, New York, 1963, pp. 385-406.
41. Francis B. Loomis to William R. Day, Nov. 5, 1897, Day Papers, Library of Congress.
42. Alfred T. Mahan, "Strategic Features of the Caribbean Sea and the Gulf of Mexico," *Harper's New Monthly Magazine*, vol. XCV, Oct. 1897, pp. 680-91.

43. A. E. Orr, President of the New York State Chamber of Commerce, to William McKinley, enclosing memorial, Feb. 3, 1898, McKinley Papers, Library of Congress; John Sherman to A. E. Orr, Feb. 11, 1898, John Sherman Papers, Library of Congress.
44. John J. McCook to James H. Wilson, Nov. 17, 1896, Wilson Papers, Library of Congress.
45. Henry Cabot Lodge to Theodore Roosevelt, May 24, 1898, *Selections from the Correspondence of Theodore Roosevelt and Henry Cabot Lodge, 1884-1918*, New York, 1925, vol. I, p. 278.
46. *Commercial and Financial Chronicle*, vol. LXVI, Feb. 12, 1898, p. 308; *Bankers' Magazine*, vol. LVI, March, 1898, p. 358; John C. Spooner to Frank Bigelow, March 8, 1898, John C. Spooner Papers, Library of Congress.
47. *Wall Street Journal*, March 19, 1898; *Congressional Record*, 55th Cong., 2nd Sess., pp. 5916-19; Russell Hastings to McKinley, March 27, 1898, McKinley Papers, Library of Congress. See also Michelle Bray Davis and Robin W. Quimby, "Senator Proctor's Cuban Speech: Speculations on a Cause of the Spanish-American War," *Quarterly Journal of Speech*, April, 1969, pp. 131-41.
48. Washington *Post*, March 27, 1898; Washington *Evening Star*, April 6, 1898; Offner, *op. cit.*, p. 304.
49. William C. Reick to Joan Russell Young, March 25, 1898, telegram, in McKinley Papers, Library of Congress.
50. *American Banker*, vol. LXIV, p. 9.
51. Leech, *op. cit.*, p. 180.
52. May, *op. cit.*, p. 269.
53. *Ibid.*, p. 270. See also Pratt, *Expansionists of 1898*, pp. 326-27.
54. Williams, *The Contours of American History*, p. 363.
55. Roosevelt to Lodge, June 17, 18, Sept. 15, 1897, Morrison, *Letters of Theodore Roosevelt*, vol. I, pp. 627-28, 676-77; *American Naval Policy as Outlined in Messages of the Presidents of the United States from 1790*, Washington, 1922, p. 22; Pratt, *Expansionists of 1898*, pp. 326-27; Olcott, *William McKinley*, vol. I, p. 379; *Senate Report* 681, 55th Cong., 2nd Sess., pp. 65-67.
56. H. H. Kohlsatt, *From McKinley to Harding* (New York, 1923), p. 72; Myron T. Herrick, "The Middle West," manuscript of speech in Myron T. Herrick Papers, Western Reserve Historical Society.
57. Offner, *op. cit.*, p. 81.
58. Timothy McDonald, "McKinley and the Coming of the War with Spain," *The Midwest Quarterly*, vol. VII, April, 1966, pp. 233-35.

www.ingramcontent.com/pod-product-compliance
Lightning Source LLC
Chambersburg PA
CBHW022026290426
44109CB00014B/773